Global Conflict and Security since 1945

Series Editors: Professor Saki R. Dockrill, King's College London, and Dr. William Rosenau, RAND

Palgrave Macmillan's new book series *Global Conflict and Security since 1945* seeks fresh historical perspectives to promote the empirical understanding of global conflict and security issues arising from international law, leadership, politics, multilateral operations, weapons systems and technology, intelligence, civil–military relations and societies. The series welcomes original and innovative approaches to the subject by new and established scholars. Possible topics include terrorism, nationalism, civil wars, the Cold War, military and humanitarian interventions, nation-building, pre-emptive attacks, the role of the United Nations and other non-governmental organisations (NGOs), and the national security and defence policies of major states. Events in the world since September 11, 2001, remind us that differences in ideology, religion, and values and beliefs held by a group of societies or people affect the security of ordinary peoples and different societies often without warning. The series is designed to deepen our understanding of the recent past and seeks to make a significant contribution to the debates on conflict and security in the major world capitals.

Advisory Board Members:

Professor Mats Berdal, Chair of Security and Development, King's College London

Ambassador James Dobbins, Director International Security and Defence Policy Center, RAND

Professor Sir Lawrence Freedman, Vice Principal (Research), King's College London

Professor Bruce Hoffman, Georgetown University and former Director of RAND's Washington Office

Titles in the series include:

Niklas H. Rossbach
HEATH, NIXON AND THE REBIRTH OF THE SPECIAL RELATIONSHIP
Britain, the US and the EC, 1969–74

Lowell H. Schwartz
POLITICAL WARFARE AGAINST THE KREMLIN
US and British Propaganda Policy and the Beginning of the Cold War

T.O. Smith
BRITAIN AND THE ORIGINS OF THE VIETNAM WAR
UK Policy in Indo-China, 1943–50

Forthcoming titles:

Ken Young
WEAPONS SYSTEMS AND THE POLITICS OF INTERDEPENDENCE

Global Conflict and Security since 1945
Series Standing Order ISBN 978–0–230–52123–0 hardcover
(*outside North America only*)

You can receive future titles in this series as they are published by placing a standing order. Please contact your bookseller or, in case of difficulty, write to us at the address below with your name and address, the title of the series and one of the ISBNs quoted above.

Customer Services Department, Macmillan Distribution Ltd, Houndmills, Basingstoke, Hampshire RG21 6XS, England

Heath, Nixon and the Rebirth of the Special Relationship

Britain, the US and the EC, 1969–74

Niklas H. Rossbach

palgrave
macmillan

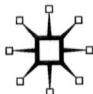

First published 2009 by
PALGRAVE MACMILLAN

Palgrave Macmillan in the UK is an imprint of Macmillan Publishers Limited, registered in England, company number 785998, of Houndmills, Basingstoke, Hampshire RG21 6XS.

Palgrave Macmillan in the US is a division of St Martin's Press LLC, 175 Fifth Avenue, New York, NY 10010.

Palgrave Macmillan is the global academic imprint of the above companies and has companies and representatives throughout the world.

Palgrave® and Macmillan® are registered trademarks in the United States, the United Kingdom, Europe and other countries.

ISBN-13: 978–0–230–57725–1 hardback

This book is printed on paper suitable for recycling and made from fully managed and sustained forest sources. Logging, pulping and manufacturing processes are expected to conform to the environmental regulations of the country of origin.

A catalogue record for this book is available from the British Library.

A catalog record for this book is available from the Library of Congress.

10   9   8   7   6   5   4   3   2   1
18   17   16   15   14   13   12   11   10   09

Printed and bound in Great Britain by
CPI Antony Rowe, Chippenham and Eastbourne

For Anna

Contents

List of Tables

List of Abbreviations

ABM	Anti Ballistic Missile Defences
BAOR	British Army on the Rhine
CAP	Common Agricultural Policy
CIA	Central Intelligence Agency, US
CSCE	Conference on Security and Cooperation in Europe, CSCE
EC	the European Communities
EFTA	European Free Trade Association
EPC	The European Political Cooperation
EURATOM	European Atomic Energy Community
FCO	Foreign and Commonwealth Office, UK
GATT	General Agreement on Tarriffs and Trade
MBFR	Mutual and Balanced Force Reductions
MLF	Multilateral Force
MoD	Ministry of Defence, UK
MIRV	Multiple Independently-targeted Re-entry Vehicle
NAFTA	North Atlantic Free Trade Area
NATO	North Atlantic Treaty Organisation
NPT	Non-Proliferation Treaty
NSC	National Security Council, US
SALT	Strategic Arms Limitation Talks
UK	United Kingdom
US	United States
USSR	Union of Soviet Socialist Republics
WEU	Western European Union

In the notes

BOAPAH	British Oral Archive of Political and Administrative History
CAB	Cabinet Papers
CF	Country or Chronological File
DEFE	Ministry of Defence File
DoS	Department of State
FCO	Foreign and Commonwealth Office

FRUS	Foreign Relations of the United States
Hetherington	Alastair Hetherington papers
LSE	Archives, the London School of Economics. From the British Library of Political and Economic Science (BLPES), London.
Memcon	Memorandum of Conversation
NARA	National Archives, US. Including the Nixon Presidential Materials Project.
NSC	National Security Council
NSSM	National Security Study Memorandum
NSDM	National Security Decision Memorandum
PREM	Prime Minister's Office File
RG	Record Group, National Archives, US
Seventies	The Seventies Archive
SF	Subject File
TNA	The National Archives, the UK
u/a	Unauthored document
u/d	Undated document

Acknowledgements

This book is possible thanks to the generosity of the European University Institute and the Swedish Research Council. I owe these institutions a debt of gratitude. I would also like to give special thanks to the EUI Department of History and Civilization and the London School of Economics, which generously allowed an exchange at a crucial stage of my research. I would like to thank Piers Ludlow and Pascaline Winand, for support and enthusiasm, and also Beatrice Heuser and Arfon Rees for stimulating and insightful comments.

Many thanks are due to the archives and libraries where I conducted research, and especially their respective staffs. I would like to thank: The National Archives in Kew, the UK; the National Archives, including the Nixon Presidential Materials Project in College Park, Maryland, the US; the European University Institute Library, and especially Serge Noiret; the Historical Archives of the European Union, Florence; and the Archives at the London School of Economics, the British Library of Political and Economic Science. I would also like to thank the Nixon Presidential Library and Museum and the National Security Archive at the George Washington University for their assistance.

Thanks also to *The Daily Telegraph, The Financial Times, The New York Times, The Times* and *The Sunday Times* for allowing me to quote from articles. Thanks also to *Foreign Affairs/Council on Foreign Relations* for allowing me to quote from Edward Heath's 'Realism in British Foreign Policy', in *Foreign Affairs/Council on Foreign Relations*, Volume 48, Nos 1–4, October 1969–July 1970.

I am also very grateful to Harvard University Press for allowing me to quote from the Godkin Lectures at Harvard University 1967, permitting the following: Reprinted by permission of the publisher from OLD WORLD, NEW HORIZONS: BRITAIN, EUROPE, AND THE ATLANTIC ALLIANCE, by Edward Heath, pp. 2, 6, 9–12, 18–19, 26, 29–30, 49, 53, 66–68, 72–76, Cambridge, Mass.: Harvard University Press, Copyright © 1970 by the President and Fellows of Harvard College. I would also like to thank HarperCollins Publishers for allowing me to quote from Alec Douglas-Home, *The Way the Wind Blows: An Autobiography by Lord Home*, London: Collins, 1976.

I would like to thank the following for being able to use tables: the Office for Official Publications of the European Communities for allowing me to use a table from *External and Intra-European Union Trade – Statistical Yearbook, Data 1958–2005,* 2006; Eurostat; and the Cambridge University Press for allowing me to use a table from B. W. E. Alford's *British Economic Performance 1945–1975* (Cambridge, 1995) Original source: A. Cairncross, 'The Postwar Years 1945–77' in R. Floud and D. McCloskey (eds), *The Economic History of Britain since 1700.* Vol. 2 (Cambridge, 1981), p. 376 (Jones, 1976, 80).

Many thanks to Saki Dockrill who made this book possible, and to my editors at Palgrave Macmillan, Michael Strang, and especially Ruth Ireland, who gave her support at important stages.

I would like to thank a number of professionals, who inspired my turn to research: Pierre Hassner, Paris; Adrian Lyttelton, Florence; Thomas Row, Bologna and Vienna. And those who helped it along the way in Florence and London: Martin van Gelderen (the EUI), Harold James (Princeton), Dr Kristina Spohr Readman (the LSE), Antonio Varsori (Florence University), and Pascal Vennesson (the EUI). I would also like to thank Roderick Abbott, Lord Carrington, and Andrew J. Pierre, for taking the time for interviews and to discuss events past.

I would also like several colleagues both at the EUI and else-where, especially in the Richie and HEIRS associations. A great thank to colleagues at the EUI who became supportive friends, especially: Eleni Braat, Richard Carney, Evelyn Huebscher, Alexis Rappas, Kristina Stoeckl, Gunvor Simonsen, and above all Lucy Turner Vokes, and at the LSE, Takeshi Yamamoto, and in Sweden Mikael Eriksson, Stefan Borg and Per Hedman.

Finally, thanks to my parents, Klaus and Alfhild Rossbach. I have incurred many debts but none more to than to Anna, who has been a patient and encouraging partner, and who has also reminded me that of all important things in life research is only one. I dedicate this book to her.

Introduction

President Richard M. Nixon and Prime Minister Edward Heath unintentionally gave new life to the Anglo-American special relationship between 1969 and 1974. This unintended rebirth of the special relationship was in part the result of the Heath government's attempt to arrest and reverse Britain's decline as a great power. It was also a consequence of the Nixon White House's efforts to recoup the position of the US in the international system. This book demonstrates why, until now, this period was a crucial juncture for Anglo-American relations, and how a reshaped relationship emerged during these years. Both Nixon and Heath left office with lasting foreign policy legacies. The Nixon administration's foreign policy initiatives influence world politics to the present day. The Heath government made a reluctant Britain take part in European integration, with political consequences that reverberate to this day. This book demonstrates that these foreign policies also had a substantial impact on the Anglo-American special relationship.

It is often the case that special relationship is seen as a continuous special relationship between Britain and the US from the Second World War onwards. Then the era of Nixon and Heath represents a short anomaly or rupture. A conventional interpretation of the Nixon–Heath years is that the Heath government pursued a European objective for Britain while being indifferent with regard to the special relationship. Instead, the Nixon–Heath years should be seen as a period that defined and eventually sustained the Anglo-American special relationship. Hence, the aim of this book is to contribute and continue the emerging reassessment of Britain, the US and transatlantic relations from the sixties onwards.[1]

By the end of the sixties Britain together with its Empire had declined, from a position of near equality to the US during the Second World War to a junior role within the special relationship.[2] Divested of its Empire, and without a cohesive Commonwealth, Britain had re-emerged as a nation-state similar to other Western European states. Edward Heath meant to rectify Britain's position in the international system by making Britain an EC member and by replacing the Anglo-American special relationship with a US–EC special relationship of equals within the Atlantic Alliance.[3] Anglo-American relations remained a key factor for the foreign policy of the Heath government, as it sought to maintain Britain's great power status. In the process it assumed that with the help of an enlarged and increasingly integrated EC, Britain could once more provide the US with an equal partner. The Heath government's plans were not intended to be a challenge to the US nor were they an attempt to avoid international obligations.

Heath's ideas centred on Europe, but not at the expense of Britain's traditional global role. This may appear as a paradox but, in fact, his ideas reflected a desire to end the kind of relationship where Britain had become a junior partner to the US. Heath's plans for a Britain integrated in Europe were a remedy against British decline both in the economic and the international sphere. Heath's analysis was that the other Western European nation-states had avoided decline and evolved beyond their nation-state status by participating in European integration through membership of the EC.

Integration was a project that Heath thought best corresponded to the requirements of the late twentieth century.[4] Britain had done the reverse to its continental neighbours. It had shed ties to a global grouping by dismantling the Empire; reducing Britain to nation-state status without the compensation of belonging to a grouping, regional or otherwise, similar in strength of purpose to either the Empire or the EC. Heath's intentions and the scale of his ambitions for Britain resembled de Gaulle's approach, if not his ideas: on the one hand Heath embraced modernisation by arguing for membership in the, potentially supranational, EC, on the other hand his outlook was a throwback to the nineteenth-century idea of a powerful and zealous statesman leading his country towards a single goal.

By the time Heath came into office the process of a renewed British application to join the EC was in place. But it was the Heath government, which eventually saw to it that Britain attained membership. Unlike his predecessors, Harold Macmillan and Harold Wilson, Heath was an enthusiastic supporter of European integration and aspired to become a European statesman. Nonetheless, he wanted to preserve the domestic British post-war consensus. For Heath joining Europe was not merely an instrumental act to safeguard the British economy, nor was it just another step towards ever closer union. Heath saw the Community as an evolving political project and he wanted Britain to prepare for nuclear and monetary cooperation. The reason for this was that Heath, like Nixon, saw a future where regional actors dominated the international system.

Heath sought to give Britain a leading position within one of the coming poles of a multipolar system. Macmillan and, to a lesser extent, Wilson had operated within the remnants of the Churchillian foreign policy idea of Britain as a great power, alongside the superpowers, at the centre of three circles: the Empire-Commonwealth, including both colonies and dominions; the US; and a united Europe.[5] Since this concept eventually failed to support Britain's claims Heath was prepared to break with the circles, including the Commonwealth. He was also prepared to gradually ease out of the special relationship, provided that the EC simultaneously established a new special relationship with the US. Heath agreed with Macmillan's view that British membership would make the EC more outward looking. However, he did not share Macmillan's belief that Britain could be a force alongside Europe and the US. Nor did Heath believe that a single country, like Britain, could maintain a special relationship with the US indefinitely.

Nevertheless, Heath could not ignore the fact that any British decision in regard to the EC would be circumscribed by Britain's dependence on the US. Britain had tried to join the EEC, twice: in 1961–63 and in 1967. Each attempt underlined the significance of the Anglo-American special relationship. It was either a support or an obstacle; unimportant it was not. The US was a support in the sense that it could help to shore up Britain's position but if Britain proved too dependent on the US, the relationship could also become an obstacle preventing Britain from qualifying for membership.

Unlike his predecessors Heath engaged with an American administration in the process of fundamental changes to its foreign policy.[6] Heath's crucial ideas in regard to special relations reflected the American ideas of the last part of the Kennedy presidency of a twin-pillar Atlantic alliance, where Europe would become an equal to the US.[7] This should be contrasted with the view that it was a combination of US interests and European desires that in the first case led the Europeans to invite the Americans to establish US hegemony in Western Europe after the Second World War.[8] The ideas of the Kennedy era, however, fitted Heath's and also initially Nixon's respective plans. Hence, as this book shows the idea allowed Heath and Nixon to come to an understanding on transatlantic relations. Britain's accession to the EC was both expected and welcomed by the Nixon administration. The implementation of the Nixon administration's new foreign would, nevertheless, eventually come into conflict with the understanding that Nixon and Heath had reached on the future of the special relationship and relations between the US and Europe.

From the beginning the success of Heath's plans would depend on whether it was helpful to Nixon's efforts of remaking of American foreign policy. By the late sixties the unsuccessful US involvement in the Vietnam War alerted both friend and foe to the limits of American power and the possibility of general decline of the West. This underlined the Nixon administration's interest in how its closest ally dealt with its diminishing global influence. Britain's reduced international standing was an important reason why the US had supported previous British applications to take part in European integration.[9] The American position had been that EC membership would help post-imperial Britain by simultaneously providing its foreign policy with a purpose and by strengthening the British economy. This was supposed to enable Britain to remain a viable US partner for the future. Coming to power the Nixon administration decided to uphold American support for the British EC membership application. Since Britain was moving towards new negotiations with the EC the Nixon administration had to consider the consequences of Britain possibly attaining EC membership. It also had to weigh the outcome of the agreement among the six existing EC members at the Hague in 1969 to deepen European integration. Nixon, in fact, represented the traditional post-war American support for European integration; a view he confirmed as President in a speech in 1970.[10]

This book offers an explanation of the impact of Heath's vision of Europe and the Nixon administration's policies on the Anglo-American special relationship and, to a lesser extent, on transatlantic relations. It addresses the question: how did the Heath government try to disentangle Britain from its traditional post-Second World War special relationship with the US in order to pursue a viable European Union, by the end of the seventies? This involves analysing how the US reacted to the progression of Heath's plans, and how Britain dealt with the evolution of American foreign policy, and what the consequences were for the special relationship in the seventies. The aim is not to speculate as to whether Britain would have been able to join the EC under another prime minister and with another US president. What is of concern here is Heath's, and the American, interpretation of the relationship. The aim of this book is to further our understanding of the consequences for the Anglo-American special relationship and transatlantic relations from the failure of Heath's vision and the simultaneous changes in American foreign policy.

The importance of the relatively short time period that Nixon and Heath were simultaneously in office is augmented by the fact that the Western world as a whole faced a series of suddenly changed conditions and severe challenges during these years. It has been argued that the difficulties in the relationship during Nixon–Heath years can be explained, at least in part, by unfortunate exogenous factors.[11] These alone are not enough to explain the Nixon–Heath years. Accordingly, this book demonstrates a clash both between ideas, and between a vision and an international system that was suddenly and unexpectedly transformed.

A new explanation about the Nixon–Heath years' impact on the special relationship requires previous explanations and associated assumptions to be contrasted with a re-evaluation of both Heath's plans and the special relationship. Accordingly, the following chapters deal with more than one single aspect of the special relationship, such as, for example, the economic special relationship. While useful, solitary topics are not enough to capture the complexity of Anglo-American relations in regard to Europe in the years 1969–74. The multiple analyses of several parts of the special relationship allow a reassessment of the Nixon–Heath years. The book does not, however, cover all aspects of American foreign policy, nor the Heath government's domestic policies. These matters are only brought to bear on the analyses when they pertain to the explanation. Consequently, the book does not delve into all the Anglo-American reactions to contemporary important events in the manner of many historical studies that cover earlier decades of the special relationship.

New arguments have a tendency to become enmeshed with old observations. Hence, an effort has been made not only to argue against previous conclusions but also to shift the perspective. This book relates to two major strands of historiography, which are often dealt with separately: the special relationship and Britain's relations with Europe. Arguably Heath's plans cannot be fully understood without relating them to their consequences for the special relationship. Here Anglo-American relations are related to Britain's third attempt to join the EC, in order to provide a new perspective.

At the time of the EC's first enlargement European integration was gathering pace. Inter-community disputes about where power rested in the Community had already occurred but were not yet a recurrent feature. When the Heath government took office Britain seemed to have

one last chance to join before the EC changed dramatically; from something likened to a customs union to a new regional entity. It appeared
to be a race against time. Later, during the seventies, European integration would stagnate. However, it did not seem to be stagnating to
Heath nor to Nixon. On the contrary the EC seemed to move rapidly
forwards, a process that the Heath government dearly wanted Britain to
participate in.

Actually, approaching the themes of European integration and special
relations simultaneously becomes easier if they are related to the view
that Britain was in decline. In 1962 the former US Secretary of State,
Dean Acheson, coined a phrase that has remained with the historiography of post-war Britain. He stated that Britain was trying to find a place
for itself in a post-imperial world.[12] Such views were unpopular with the
British establishment.[13] The phrase acknowledged that the special relationship was not one between equals, because Britain's importance was
diminishing. In 1970, the year Heath became Prime Minister, Acheson
said that developments had confirmed his opinion.[14]

Concerns about decline provided the necessary impetus for Heath's
ideas.[15] Heath and his contemporaries in politics recognised the idea
that Britain was falling behind.[16] In the sixties many discussions on
decline were about the end of the Empire and whether Britain should
continue to remain a great power.[17] Any remedy for decline had to deal
with both relative economic decline and Britain's diminished influence.
Attaining EC membership for Britain has been regarded as the major
achievement of the Heath government.[18] However, Heath's vision was
not an off-the-shelf solution where EC membership meant that decline
would be averted.[19]

Heath's plans were a personal interpretation of further European integration as a means of reversing decline. The historiography of the Heath
government has allowed for several interpretations of the government's
aims.[20] This plethora of views obscures rather than elucidates how Heath
tried to countermand decline with the help of his ideas for Britain in
Europe. In fact, many of the domestic reforms that the Heath government pursued were linked to his vision of Britain in Europe.[21] The
Heath government pursued its economic policies based on a traditional
pragmatic approach in order to rejuvenate the domestic economy and
prepare it for membership to further the overarching goal of success as
an EC member. The Heath government consistently pursued European
integration and other promises were second to that aim.

Previous attempts at grasping the Heath government's intentions shy
away from the full implication of Heath's vision, choosing instead

to regard Heath taking Britain into the EC as primarily a pragmatic necessity.[22] Membership, however, was only the first stage of Heath's plans, where the second stage was a deepening of European integration towards unity. The EC Summit at the Hague in 1969, which paved the way for enlargement, also aspired for increased integration.[23] A lot of the seemingly erratic behaviour of the Heath government is easier to understand in view of the fact that the government pursued Heath's vision, despite radically altered circumstances, up to the General Election of February 1974. Because the Heath government aimed at positioning Britain in Europe it also had implications for nearly everything that the special relationship was concerned with, such as economic relations, nuclear relations, transatlantic relations and Cold War diplomacy.

The same is true with regard to the policies of the Nixon administration, which also had consequences for all three areas. Yet, the view that neither Britain nor Europe was a major concern for the Nixon administration is still reflected in works on Nixon's foreign policy. Most works on Nixon's foreign policy are about other foreign policy issues than Europe. When they deal with Europe it is usually in relation to the Cold War détente.[24] Unlike the Heath government's foreign policy on Europe the American foreign policy towards Europe changed during these years. Previously, it has often been assumed that there was a unified Nixon White House view on all important foreign policy issues. This has contributed to the confusion about the state of the Anglo-American relations. President Nixon and his foreign policy adviser, and later Secretary of State Henry A. Kissinger, did not share a unified Nixon–Kissinger view of Europe or for that matter, on the plans of the Heath government. These differences of opinion eventually had considerable influence on the implementation of the plans of the Heath government and on the special relationship. These reassessments are best understood if the nature of the special relationship is reconsidered.

The special relationship was not a constant entity with a set of defined, tangible parts, even if one considers the emergence and endurance of the nuclear special relationship.[25] Nor did the Anglo-American relationship have mythical properties.[26] By the late sixties, the term the 'special relationship' was, in fact, better known than its meaning. Actually, the meaning and the content of the special relationship altered over the decades after the Second World War.[27]

In long-term narratives of the special relationship the Nixon–Heath years are often seen as a period when the Anglo-American relations seemed to loose its *raison d'etre*.[28] However, reconsidering the Nixon–Heath years on their own it becomes clear that Heath intended to reconstruct the special elements of the Anglo-American relationship on a different level. Some earlier studies have touched upon this possibility.[29] Heath's wish to change Anglo-American relations was no mere play with words where the relationship would be changed from a special to a cultural one. Heath, actually, sought to preserve cultural or natural Anglo-American relations. Special post-war cooperation, such as nuclear relations, and cultural and historical aspects of the Anglo-American relationship somehow became entangled whenever convenient for either partner. References to cultural heritage and common bonds, however, gave rise to myths that strengthened the concept of an enduring special relationship. This played into the hands of decision-makers, like Kissinger, who claimed that the unequal special relationship, between the US superpower and the weakened great power Britain, was a normal state of affairs. Accordingly, the blend of special functions and myth could be used against those who wished to alter real constituent parts of the relationship, such as agreements.

The Heath government came to experience how it could run into problems of terminology, explanation and credibility when it sought to change the relationship. This makes it all the more important to look at key elements of the Anglo-American special relationship. It is also important to understand how the various decision-makers envisaged Anglo-American relations in order to acquire a better account of the special relationship during the Nixon–Heath years and after.

An international history reassessment requires multi-archival research from both sides of the Atlantic.[30] Many of the sources have not been available or used for this purpose previously. Hitherto many texts on this period have relied on secondary sources, although now both books and articles based on primary sources have begun to appear. However, it is necessary to stress the following caveat: it is impossible to escape the present, and yet it is not the case that we all see either the present or the past in the same way. The reflections on the historiography have allowed for some considerations of the methods of international history and political science.[31] Suffice to say that these ruminations are imbedded in the subsequent chapters.

In order to benefit from a re-evaluation of previous assessments the book is organised into five chapters. Chapters 2–5 each deal with an aspect of Anglo-American relations based on the implications of British and American policies for their separate foreign policy goals, with regard to Europe and their mutual relationship. The first chapter introduces the general and immediate background to the Nixon–Heath years and deals in particular with Heath's vision and Nixon's foreign policy approach to Europe. The second chapter sheds new light on the consequences of the economic special relationship of Heath's vision and of the Nixon administration's new monetary policies. It shows that the fate of the economic special relationship was intimately linked to the goals of the Heath government. In fact, Britain's part in what became the beginning of the end of the Bretton Woods system was different from what has hitherto been assumed.

The third chapter examines the Heath government's attempt to bring about nuclear interdependence with France at the same time as Britain maintained nuclear ties with the US. It reveals that nuclear affairs in this period have often been misunderstood and that the result of the Heath government's attempts had far reaching consequences both for Britain and for nuclear relations more generally. There are very good studies of the special Anglo-American defence relationship, but some are indicative of the search for a repetitive pattern.[32] The expected constancy of British intentions is also reflected in broader studies of transatlantic nuclear relations, which otherwise come very close to appreciating the audacity of the Heath government's efforts.[33]

The fourth chapter deals with Anglo-American approaches to European integration and the consequences of the White House's reappraisal of its foreign policy towards Europe. It demonstrates the growing importance of Nixon's key foreign policy adviser, Kissinger, and his reappraisal of American foreign policy towards Europe. Kissinger's memoirs had for a long time been taken as a key account of what became known as the Nixon–Kissinger foreign policy, this chapter contributes to a more nuanced view of Nixon and American foreign policy. Additionally, it explains the result of the clash between Heath's vision and Kissinger's views on transatlantic relations, especially as these views were juxtaposed during the US diplomatic initiative called 'the Year of Europe'.

The fifth chapter looks at Anglo-American relations in relation to East–West détente and how the Cold War Anglo-American relationship was coordinated during the Nixon–Heath years. One argument has been that Britain chose a low profile in regard to the Soviet Union in order to secure a smooth path to EC membership and to avoid the risk that other diplomatic efforts would disrupt the EC negotiations.[34] In contrast, the chapter demonstrates how the Heath's vision led to British détente scepticism for the first time during the Cold War. It also analyses the extent of Anglo-American cooperation in this early era and the effects of diplomatic efforts overseas, with regard to China and Vietnam.

Finally, the conclusion provides an explanation on the basis of a comprehensive analysis of the analyses in the chapters. This shows how the special relationship evolved as it has been recognised since, with Britain uneasily wedged between the US and Europe.

1
Heath's European Ideas as a Response to British Decline and Nixon's New American Foreign Policy

The accession

When the triumphant British Prime Minister Edward Heath arrived at the d'Egmont Palace in Brussels on 22 January 1972, where he was to sign the document that would allow Britain membership of the European Community (EC),[1] he walked towards the staircase of the entrance hall, flashed a smile to the assembled media, and was then greeted by the contents of a small bucket of ink. The press reported that this was thrown by a young English woman who was protesting against Britain's entry into the EC.[2] Since coming to power in 1970 the Heath government had worked steadily, to attain EC membership. Although humiliated at what should have been his moment of triumph Heath could be content to note that he had achieved what his predecessors Harold Wilson and Harold Macmillan had attempted, but had failed to achieve. It was Heath who signed the treaty of accession.

Only a month before the Brussels episode, at another summit, Heath had looked slightly embarrassed when Nixon referred publicly to the relationship between Britain and the US as being special.[3] At the time, Heath claimed that the world was in a 'fantastic period of readjustments, in which all relationships have been thrown into the melting pot'.[4] Consequently, he found the reference to the Anglo-American special relationship counter-productive vis-à-vis the changes he wanted to bring about.[5] Despite Heath's awkwardness about the use of famous phrase, the 'special relationship', Anglo-American relations were in a good shape in early 1972. It may seem a contradiction but it was not. Heath simply meant that relations between the US and Britain could be good, without a special relationship. The interpretation of deteriorating

Anglo-American relations due to an intransigent Heath has been given credence by Henry A. Kissinger, Nixon's national security adviser and later secretary of state. He likened Heath to Charles de Gaulle, who as president of France caused the transatlantic alliance a lot of problems.[6] Such comments have contributed to the impression that the Heath government's enthusiastic turn to Europe meant that Britain turned away from the US. If this was correct, it would make for a straightforward narrative of disengagement. This chapter belies common assumptions about Heath's ideas for Britain in Europe and also shows the difference in the attitude of the Nixon administration towards Heath and his predecessor, Wilson.

British decline and the United States

According to Alan Milward, Britain pursued a distinct political course until 1963 where domestic welfare was given priority over the continued exercise of world power.[7] That the post-war approach of British politics had become unstuck was becoming evident by the mid-sixties making decline a political concern.[8] Debates about British decline and the future of Europe stimulated varying remedies, such as Heath's ideas that Britain should join the EEC and work for deepened European integration.[9] However, the British attempts to make Britain partake in the process of European integration in 1961–63 and 1967 were not necessarily associated with keeping Britain's traditional great power role. Nevertheless, by the end of the sixties when Heath was the Leader of the Conservative Party neither he nor his political opponent, Prime Minister Wilson, was prepared to abandon Britain's great power status. In contrast to a possible membership in the EEC Britain's ties to the US were regarded as necessary for the traditional ambition to maintain Britain as a great power.

The post-war special relationship had became increasingly important for Britain as its international role was reduced, but despite the increasing importance of the relationship to Britain, it did not offer a remedy to reverse Britain's diminished status. Instead of being a near equal, as during the war, Britain, by the mid-sixties, had in effect become the junior partner in the special relationship. For example, Beatrice Heuser has shown that the American assistance on nuclear armament was initially seen as temporary support for Britain until it again had become as strong as it was before the war.[10] By the sixties the question was how Britain's great power status, in a whole host of areas, should be maintained.

The Kennedy administration had favoured Britain becoming a member of the EEC member. This would ensure that Europe became outward looking, or at least that was how the British Prime Minister Macmillan saw it in the early sixties. He regarded Britain as one of the three great powers of the West, alongside the US and Europe. He suggested that Britain should maintain the special relationship while inserting itself as the leader of Western Europe. However, American efforts at dealing with Atlantic affairs in the early sixties always took second place after more pressing Cold War concerns.[11] Occasionally, Cold War crises confirmed Britain in the role of a junior partner offering its counsel on global events.

The preservation of the special relationship, 1964–1970

On becoming Prime Minister in 1964, Wilson laid out his plan of regeneration of Britain by seeking a state-guided industrial revolution.[12] Helen Parr believes that the foreign policy that accompanied Wilson's domestic efforts was very pragmatic.[13] In contrast Chris Wrigley argues that it is difficult to separate the rhetorical elements from Wilson's real foreign policy intentions.[14] In either case, Wilson only aimed to alter the means by which to support Britain's traditional role. Parr has shown that it was only after Wilson's initial economic programme failed in 1966 that he turned to Europe, to make it serve the same purpose. Consequently, the economic argument for European integration, meaning support for growth and the need for a market, dominated the Labour Party's considerations.[15] Wilson saw membership as a means to serve British economic needs and its international standing, which would have been, to paraphrase Milward, a late rescue of the nation-state.

Economic strength is often the prerequisite for a political plan but economic demands can at the same time be the driving force behind new schemes. Despite a golden age of domestic economic prosperity, the two main British political parties fretted about decline. British economic growth was, in fact, lower than that of other Western European states. Hence, the parties tried to find ways to break out of so-called economic 'stop-go' cycles in order to sustain economic growth. Britain's lesser economic success also influenced the standing of its currency, sterling, and Britain's international role. According to Alan P. Dobson it had initially been Britain's economic weakness that brought Britain and the US closer in an economic special relationship towards the end of the forties. As a consequence, two decades later, the weakness of sterling haunted the relationship and pulled them apart. Britain's monetary weakness had consequences for many policy areas, including defence policies, and her chances of EEC entry, during the so-called second attempt in 1967. Dobson argues that the US tired of supporting Britain and that the special economic relationship effectively came to an end in the late sixties.[16] In contrast Jonathan Coleman points to Britain's economic problems as being central to the special relationship during the Johnson–Wilson years.[17]

Recently a more favourable interpretation of the Johnson administration's foreign policy has been espoused by, amongst others, Rajarshi Roy and Thomas Alan Schwartz. In Schwartz's view the Wilson–Johnson relationship was one between two deft and unsentimental politicians who agreed when they could. According to him, Britain was of vital help to the US administration's efforts at reforming the international monetary system. They managed to sustain the value of sterling, thus prolonging British overseas commitments. This, in turn, gave the US enough time to deal with the consequences for the dollar stemming from both sterling's devaluation in 1967 and of British troop withdrawals from East of Suez.[18] Roy concurs with Schwartz that previous judgements of the American economy in the sixties, like Dobson's, have been too quick in seeing the era as the beginning of the end of American economic hegemony.[19] During the late sixties economic issues were, evidently, very important for the US, but how important were economic concerns for the special relationship?

Roy points to the curious but real compartmentalisation of the different policy areas that constituted the Anglo-American relationship during the latter part of the sixties. He argues that the economic special relationship functioned independently of Britain's overseas commitments and that the concern that Britain's monetary problems could lead to a break-up of the Bretton Woods system was crucial enough for the US to help Britain. Furthermore, he emphasises that American influence over British economic policy was considerable during these years.[20] Roy and Schwartz both believe, albeit for different reasons, that the economic special relationship remained close. In fact, the economic special relationship continued and the monetary links were still intact when Heath became Prime Minister in 1970. As a close but weakening ally Britain continued to have a hold on the US as long as the Bretton Woods system continued. However, the very closeness of the US was uncomfortable for those who wanted Britain to develop along European lines rather than as a version of American capitalism.

By 1966 Britain's economic problems were severe.[21] There had been some speculation in government about a possible free trade area with the US, called the North Atlantic Free Trade Area, NAFTA, but it had foundered on the basis of a lack of US interest.[22] Such an entity could further have strained relations between allies at a sensitive time, given France's partial withdrawal from NATO in 1966.[23] When EEC membership finally became the primary objective the Wilson government thought that official enquiries about the possibility of a NAFTA were counterproductive in the dealings with Europe.[24] Besides, Britain would forever have been the junior partner in such a constellation.[25] This was not thought desirable since Britain would lose its great power status, and Wilson was a traditionalist who wanted to keep as much as possible of Britain's status. However, even without a NAFTA Britain was still dependent on the US.[26] In fact, in the long run the special relationship could suffer if Britain was not effectively part of Europe.

Parr makes the case that in regard to Britain's second attempt, in 1967, to join the EEC, the Wilson government was primarily reactive and more focused on conditions of entry than what they actually would enter.[27] Nevertheless, Wilson did not define what he meant by European unity nor did he envisage an idea about Europe.[28] The Labour government was more focused on exiting ties.

According to Parr a crucial element motivating the second attempt to join the EEC was the Foreign Office's (FO) concern with France's withdrawal from NATO. Taken together with the institutional EEC crisis of 1965, known as the 'Empty Chair crisis', the FO feared the break up of the containment of Germany if the Atlantic system dissolved. Hence, it argued that Britain should join, not to replace France in the EEC, but instead to strengthen the EEC and the continuation of a European integration within the framework of the Atlantic alliance.[29]

As long as Britain's traditional international role continued it underlined the global partnership with the US. According to James Ellison, Wilson was always an atlanticist. The NATO crisis following France's withdrawal from the organisation allowed the British to be of significant help to the Johnson administration in its effort to reform NATO. It was as part of the joint Anglo-American efforts to shore up the Atlantic partnership and stave off de Gaulle's plans for French leadership of Europe and his independent détente that Britain applied to the EEC.[30] This was a sign of active Anglo-American cooperation on an issue that emphasised the Atlantic perspective and the importance of European security over other overseas affairs. Dealing with NATO and de Gaulle was perhaps where the Wilson government worked best with the US.

According to James Ellison, despite a second French refusal to allow British EC membership, the application had some desired effects which the US understood and appreciated.[31] The US accordingly continued to support Britain's efforts to join the EEC.

In fact, de Gaulle's veto of 1967 was something of a last stand on the part of the French according to Piers Ludlow.[32] Similarly, Melissa Pine has shown that British European diplomacy after the veto actually continued with some success by taking some cursory steps towards cooperation on foreign policy in the organisation of the Western European Union, the WEU.[33]

Apart from helping to shore up NATO the Wilson government had actually managed to retain a core element of the special relationship. Wilson managed to avoid the creation of a nuclear Multilateral Force, MLF, or any other versions of it. Especially what the FO dreaded, a Western European nuclear force without Britain, which was expected to have thwarted British sway in Washington.[34] Although the nuclear relationship was not as intimate as between 1958 and 1963, John Baylis claims that talk of change to the relationship was mostly cosmetic.[35] Faced with the risk of relinquishing effective control the Wilson government had a near allergic reaction to losing nuclear independence, meaning the British right to decide when to use the weapons.[36]

The Wilson government continued a close nuclear relationship with the US.[37] Nevertheless, Christopher Bluth argues that there was a distinct turn to Europe in defence matters in the Wilson era.[38] This stemmed from Britain's decreased economic resources. In the mid-sixties it became clear that Europe was the main concern in all Whitehall debates about how to manage reductions in defence spending.[39] The Wilson government, of course, failed to re-engage the French, who left the integrated command structure of NATO in 1966. In effect, defence issues would remain important in Britain's relations with the continent.

When Johnson took over as President, Britain was the most significant among Cold War allies. Yet, the actual interpretation of 'the special relationship' remained unclear. The Cold War conditions that had originally fostered the post-war special relationship still applied in the sixties, but the relationship had evolved into something less than what Winston Churchill, amongst others, had intended.

The American involvement in Vietnam demonstrated the limits of the relationship to Washington. It could not make the British participate in that conflict.[40] Nonetheless, Britain did fight the jungle-war of Confrontation, in the defence of Malaysia against Indonesia for two years until 1966.[41] It could be said this final security obligation of the Empire in the Far East helped to save Britain from involvement in the US South Asian imbroglio.

There has been discussion about a deal between Wilson and John-son involving American economic support in return for British political support over Vietnam. Johnson realised that such an agreement would have dire consequences for the future of the relationship. Wilson, how-ever, understood that American financial support for the role of sterling depended on Britain sustaining its great power status and its defence commitments like the East of Suez policy.[42] The British commitment to the Far East was tied to the East of Suez policy of keeping bases in the Indian Ocean, which in turn was tied to the British Army on the Rhine, all of which were of concern to the British Treasury and thus to sterling, which in turn was tied to the dollar. This was the situation that both Heath and Nixon stood to inherit at the end of the sixties.

During the sixties Britain retained a high profile in international affairs, British diplomacy was successful in helping to bring about a Non-Proliferation Treaty, the NPT. Britain was instrumental in reach-ing an important compromise about the role of EURATOM. This was, of course, potentially important for Britain given its wish to join the EEC.[43] The NTP of 1968 was also an important step towards a détente between the superpowers.

As the sixties drew to a close the personal Anglo-American ties that officials had built up after the Second World War were decreasing in importance and actual achievements became more important in keep-ing up the special relationship. In contrast to the forties and fifties and despite the importance of institutional bonds and existing net-works between officials the special relationship seemed more, not less, dependent on the individual statesmen in the seventies. According to Coleman the two states were still much interconnected at the end of the sixties and, as Saki Dockrill have asserted, an important relation-ship does not have to be one between equals. However, Coleman finds that after the Wilson government's decision to devalue sterling and to withdraw British commitments from East of Suez in 1967 both the US State Department and the Johnson White House felt that Britain was in decline.[44] Nevertheless, on coming to power in 1970 Heath inherited a functioning special relationship, something which has hitherto not been fully appreciated. Unlike Wilson, however, Heath had a distinct vision of Europe.

Heath's remedy for decline and his vision of Europe

Before Heath became an enthusiast for European integration he became a conservative. The ambitious Edward Heath, born in 1916, was propelled upwards in society through a grammar school all the way to Oxford University in the thirties. Robert Rhodes James argues that it was during that ideological decade that Heath became a conservative, through reasoning and by conviction.[45] However, as Andrew Roth observed Heath did not have the kind of ideology grounded in political theory.[46] At university Heath invoked Disraeli's One Nation conservatism, which embraces all classes working towards a common goal.[47] Yet, later in his career there were those in the Tory Party who doubted that he was a conservative at heart.[48] He clearly was not ideological in the sense that he held a collection of abstract goals neatly fitting under a suitable sobriquet with an '-ism' attached.

Robert Armstrong, a civil servant close to Heath during his years at Number 10, could not make out the set of principles behind Heath's ideas, yet he claims there was one.[49] In fact, Heath's approach to politics was issue-oriented. While at Oxford he visited civil-war ridden Spain in 1938 from which he came back aware of the risk that a greater conflict threatened to engulf Europe.[50] Consequently, he took a stand against appeasement in Oxford University politics. He showed himself an organiser and a doer rather than a philosopher in politics.[51] Despite the lack on an '-ism' his interest in politics was strong enough to survive the war.

Heath managed to become a full-time politician when he was elected to Parliament in 1950.[52] During the fifties Heath kept a silent and efficient regime in the Whips' Office.[53] Keeping the Parliamentary Party members in check was an inauspicious task for anyone interested in serving in the cabinet.[54] Eventually, Macmillan, whose path to the leadership Heath had helped to smooth, appointed him as Minister of Labour.[55] Shortly afterwards he was made Lord Privy Seal with the specific task of taking Britain into Europe.[56] After the attempt to join the EEC failed he served a brief stint as Secretary for Industry, Trade and Regional Development and as President of the Board of Trade in Sir Alec Douglas-Home's (hence after Home) short-lived government.[57] After the Tory Party lost the 1964 General Election Heath was appointed Shadow Chancellor.[58] During the rest of the sixties his fortunes marched in the opposite direction of his party.

In 1965 Heath became leader of the Tory Party. Politically he was at the political centre of his party; a non-ideological issue-oriented politician mostly identified with the question he felt most strongly about, namely membership of the EEC. The pro-European paper *The Economist* depicted Heath as a man from a humbler background, a modern figure, who saw Britain's future in Europe.[59] In his 1950 Parliamentary maiden speech he had argued that Britain should not only support the Schuman Plan but also participate in the integration of coal and steel industries. Part of his rationale was to have Britain as balancer between France and Germany and he came to lament that Britain had lost an opportunity.[60] It would, however, be an underestimation of the nature politics, which is subject to contingency, and an overestimation of Heath – the politician – to say that his speech was a prescient statement of his role as British negotiator for EEC membership a decade later, 1961–63.

It is actually likely that it was precisely that he was not fanatical about Europe that he was later thought of as suitable as a leader for the negotiations for EEC entry in 1961.[61] Later, after the negotiations were short-circuited by de Gaulle in 1963, Heath declared that Britain was still turned towards Europe.[62] His view was that the right course had been frustrated and that future chances should not be lost due to bitterness. Overcoming the failure became a challenge for Heath.[63]

Membership of the EEC seemed also to be the only remaining option open to Prime Minister Macmillan if Britain was to remain a great power. He did not think that the Commonwealth would develop into an alternative market for Britain.[64] In 1965 under the auspices of the conservative politician Lord Carrington a study was undertaken that suggested that a break should be made with the past and that Britain instead should participate in European integration as a means to create a new grouping of near equal standing to the superpowers. Heath agreed with this analysis.[65]

A dominant characteristic of Heath was his way of deciding on a goal and then with dogged determination setting about achieving it. Such willpower often borders on stubbornness. He was generally not thought of as an intellectual amongst politicians.[66] His mindset was more like that of an athlete. However, sportsmen might fail to take account of when the rules of the game may change. Achieving the goal may, for dedicated individuals, remain the priority even if the circumstances change, perhaps in the hope that success will redeem the lack of a renewed analysis of the situation.

Heath did not break with the domestic policies of his predecessors. Churchill, Eden, Macmillan and Home had all adhered to the domestic post-war consensus. By inheriting their pragmatic conservatism, he appeared vague in his overall views in the more ideologically tainted sixties. His political ideals were so full of goodwill towards his fellow men that it was a diluted brew acceptable to most, but without the necessary political sting of the concoction that his Labour opponent, Wilson, provided.[67] Heath's patriotic appeal was not well packaged for political consumption with its combination of One Nation Toryism and pro-European stance, which meant that a modern society would look to the future while keeping the best of the past.[68] Society was changing and it was becoming increasingly difficult for traditional Tory pragmatism finding the firm foothold for doing the right thing at the right time.

Heath set out his vision for Britain's future in the Godkin Lectures given in 1967 at Harvard. These mainly focused on Britain's future role and foreign policy. He intended to change and adapt British society to the continent; consequently, the Heath government's domestic policies were a result of his foreign policy vision of Britain in Europe. In face of Britain's changing situation, often thought of as decline, he saw himself as a leader of rejuvenation, on the scale of Franklin Roosevelt or de Gaulle.[69] Like them, however, he kept his own council on foreign affairs, and unlike President Nixon he would have no intimate confidant on foreign affairs. Heath's most important ideas were primarily about international politics. This fact has often obscured the need for the Heath government to deal with an increasingly difficult domestic economic situation and industrial strife. He relied on the existing domestic machinery to make British society ready for entry. Nevertheless, he was a radical who wanted to break down the national frontiers and to attach Britain to Europe in political union. He believed that '[w]hilst the European countries concerned were moving on from the nation state because in their view it was inadequate to meet modern requirements, the British were still thinking in terms of the power which they had previously exercised and which they believed still belonged to them'.[70] His approach to politics made Heath construct his vision of a better future around a concrete goal – Britain in a united Europe.

However, Heath advanced carefully: in 1965 at the time of the EEC's institutional crisis, known as the Empty Chair crisis, he was not prepared to say that he was convinced that a close knit European political union was necessarily the way European integration would go.[71] In the mid-sixties it was clear that a political response to British decline was needed. The Conservative party claimed that its pragmatism was better than the ideological approach of its opponents.[72] At this stage, he thus appeared as a traditionalist. Nevertheless, the One Nation approach required a goal in order to appear credible. He did not find it by theoretical reasoning about economic freedom or alternative monetary approaches as people on the fringes of his party would have. Instead he found it in a concrete cause – British participation in European integration, which to him also meant that he went beyond traditionalist searches for a cure for decline towards a goal that would transform society.

To Heath joining Europe was primarily a political choice, and not merely an economic one, something that Home acknowledged.[73] Speaking in 1967 about Britain's first attempt to join the EEC, in 1961–63, he disparaged the popular

> myth...that we were concerned only with economic affairs and obsessed with minor details. Nothing could be further from the truth. The main purpose of the negotiations was political. This was made plain at the level of Heads of governments. It was fully recognized by the members of both the Community and EFTA. In my opening statement in Paris on 10 October 1961 I said: "In saying that we wish to join the EEC, we mean that we desire to become full, wholehearted and active members of the European Community in its widest sense and to go forward with you in building of a new Europe."[74]

Heath's ideas on Britain, Europe and the future had matured by 1967 and changed remarkably little after that. He originally presented his vision in the Harvard lectures in 1967 and to him the lectures remained valid when he came into power three years later.[75] They were not only applicable, in fact they were the core of his whole political programme and the means by which he would reinvigorate Britain and turn himself into a European statesman.

Heath believed that the European Coal and Steel Community had peace as a clearly defined political goal because crucial military necessities were embedded in a joint organisation.[76] He emphasised the necessity of European harmony by using the short hand, the Community, over the phrase better known in Britain – the Common Market – that he found misleading since it stressed market mechanisms that were not yet fully developed. Heath's view was that European integration was primarily a political project, nevertheless the latter expression remained in currency reflecting both how the EEC was perceived and how difficult it was for Heath to get his message across. Heath hoped that the debates on integration in the late sixties would move from discussions on issues like the agricultural policy and instead recapture the drive of integration towards economic union and the harmonisation of foreign and defence policy.[77] His ideas for European integration was after all mostly about the future of Europe rather than actual entry.

A dilemma in 1967 was that 'a stagnant Community...proved increasingly unattractive to British opinion'.[78] To Heath that meant an opportunity for a new member to inspire moves forwards. He was impatient with the Treaty of Rome and he wanted to transcend it and look at the possibilities of cooperation in defence and monetary affairs.[79] This and the fact that his ideas were concerned about Britain's decline illustrate that his ideas were a result of his own reflections and not a standard promotion of EEC integration. According to Heath, European collaboration would make the Community stronger and hence more able to look outwards to the benefit of other regions of the world: 'in the long run Europe will either be outward looking or it will be nothing'.[80] The same thing could of course be argued by a traditionalist about Britain.

He warned that '[t]he countries of Europe have been inclined to take it for granted that the United States, and in particular areas Britain and France, will provide the essential framework of stability within which their affairs can prosper'.[81] According to him, a Europe working in unison would create a 'better balance' within Atlantic alliance based on equality between the US and its European partners.[82] He believed that he could work with the French. He even suggested that the Europeans should hold regular meetings on foreign policy in a manner akin to the French suggestions in the Fouchet plan of 1962, which had been supported by de Gaulle.[83] He argued that the '[p]eople in the West have a feeling that the clear sense of direction which they once possessed – whether it was in support of the Atlantic Alliance when confronted with the obvious threat from the Warsaw Pact, or whether it was in the strong and sturdy movement towards closer European unity – has been lost'.[84] He aspired to arrest this trend and reverse it. This conveys the sense that he believed that Western Europe like Britain risked decline, but that this could be solved by bringing Britain into the EEC.

According to Heath's logic, Britain the nation-state could not stand on its own in the world and he dismissed the Commonwealth as an alternative pointing out that it had never had a 'genuine pooling of sovereignty'[85] although he could see it becoming a basis for networks of 'human activity'.[86] He also thought EFTA inadequate in the long run and at worst a hindrance during new negotiations with the EC, much as the Commonwealth had been during the first membership negotiations.[87]

Heath's ideas primarily answered the needs of Britain. After all he was a British politician so this was essential. For him, steeped in traditions of university and the experience of army service during the Second World War the British identity was not territorial. He, however, thought that Britain would best show its qualities in friendly competition with others within Europe. Europe was not only a remedy for British ailments, but also a way to avoid Britain slipping back into hibernation as a mere nation-state amongst others. His interpretation of Britain and European integration was very personal: both in his choice of what earlier ideas of future integration to highlight, and how to combine them. He also brought the ideas with him into office in 1970. In the years after 1967 when he first presented his ideas the hey-days of early European integration had passed. Therefore, it became increasingly important that the US agreed with his vision.

Heath's ambitions for Anglo-American relations were as low as for the Commonwealth ties; they could 'be expected to flourish as a means of helping forward the innumerable contacts between groups and individuals'.[88] In others words the links were cultural, based on language, history and tradition and family relations, or as Heath would put it 'natural'. This would mean a natural relationship, rather than a special relationship. Listening to some, he argued, it appeared as if 'the world is in fact run by the British Prime Minister and the President of the United States meeting daily in conclave in a command post on some island in the middle of the Atlantic'.[89] He ascribed it to a mind-set among British officials conditioned by the wartime alliance in such a way that they had to instinctively ask for the American view on foreign affairs, especially on defence matters. This cordial deference was becoming one-sided according to Heath. Instead, '[a]s Britain becomes more closely involved in Europe the instincts of officials will no doubt turn more to Paris, Bonn, or Rome'.[90] He believed that greater European unity would make the US improve consultation procedures with its Western European allies instead 'of taking decisions on matters of interest to America's allies ... [through] a process of semi-public debate between different government agencies culminating in a compromise'.[91] However, he did not argue for a confrontational attitude towards the US but for a modernisation of the relations in the Atlantic alliance.

Heath did not want to see a continued European dependence on the US and therefore defence was a key issue for European integration.[92] He professed that it was an astonishing change that European defence was thought anti-American in the late sixties when Washington had wished for greater European defence efforts in the fifties.[93] His preferred solution was a new basis for British interdependence based on French and British capabilities, eventually in a form of trusteeship for Europe. Naturally, this was a topic on which he would have been ill-advised to have expounded on. He stated his desire, however, that Europe should be allowed to complete its new form of a union, both political and economic, with a defence arrangement if that was thought needed.[94] He professed that a responsible Europe should continue as a group, not in order to keep up appearances of its past status, but for the sake of the security of the world in the form of a political pole on which global peace could rely.[95]

It was by committing Britain to Europe that he believed Britain could keep a say in world politics as well as commitments to international security overseas as a part of an evermore united and powerful Europe. This, rather than his One Nation and his Tory pragmatism, or any other '-ism' was his guiding vision during his years in office, but first Heath had to become Prime Minister and convince Whitehall about the desirability of his ideas.

The General Election of 1970 and Heath, the FCO and 'the dwindling asset'

On 11 May 1970 the EC decided that negotiations with Britain and other applicants should formally open in Luxembourg on 30 June. Seven days later Harold Wilson announced that there would be a General Election on 18 June. It appeared as if Labour had a good chance of winning. The negotiations were not a decisive factor in the decision about when to hold the election. However, since there seemed to be another opportunity to enter the EC it effectively foreclosed debates about Labour's previous failure to take Britain into the EC in 1967. Earlier in 1970 a laborious White Paper on the Common Market was critical about the possibility of quick economic gains from joining.[96] This helped the Labour government to defuse the issue as non-acute and mostly an economic concern.

When the White Paper was debated in late February 1970 Heath brushed aside alternatives to EEC membership such as EFTA, the Commonwealth, greater Anglo-Soviet trade or versions of a NAFTA and pointed to the failure to understand what the Community was about.[97] Unfortunately for Heath there was little electoral mileage to be had out of clearing up these misconceptions. According to Anne Deighton public support for entry in 1966 to 1967 was tangled up with support of Wilson, and that there was little understanding of the greater issues of integration.[98] It is also likely that the public became disillusioned after the second veto, in 1967. The issue of membership, so dear to Heath, was certainly not a way to secure votes in the General Election of 1970. Since 1966 the number of those in favour had slipped considerably, and those against had risen remarkably.[99] Heath was prudent and, in May 1970, cajoled popular opinion by portraying himself as cool on the issue of membership. Just before the election he said that the Community had to show acceptable terms that were clearly advantageous to Britain in the long run.[100] Eventually, since the British public was unenthusiastic about Europe the Conservatives let other issues, rather than Heath's plans for European integration, come to the foreground.

When, in early 1970, the shadow cabinet met at the Selsdon Park Hotel near Croydon to plan for the General Election, Europe was not a key subject.[101] To many Conservative supporters the Selsdon meeting and the promises of the 1970 election seemed to promise a turn to the right.[102] This would be a radical break from the tinkering of previous conservative governments to changes on the basis of ideas of economic liberalism. Heath went along with this image. It was immensely helpful in the short run but it was a poisoned chalice.[103] The promises of regeneration of Britain by liberal economic means came to partially fill the popular imagination when there was no clear issue at stake in the election and when Heath could not campaign on his own European ideas.

By the time of the election in June no decisive set of issues stood in front of the electorate.[104] Wilson adopted a statesmanlike posture of steady-as-she-goes when the election was announced.[105] This risked appearing conceited in view of negative economic signals which became evident in June. Lord Cromer, former Governor of the Bank of England and bête noir of the Labour Party, warned on television on 1 June that the financial situation for the next government would be much worse than the one Labour had faced in 1964.[106] This seemed to be confirmed by the publication on 15 June of trade figures that showed an unexpected deficit. It cracked Wilson's pose. On the same day Heath appeared on television. In an appeal to the people, he exploited the British fear of decline, including a promise to end the second rate status that Labour had let the British sink to. Heath was increasingly buoyant as the polling day approached as if carried victory by his own enthusiasm.[107] The day after the election a stunned political elite woke up to the greatest move to a party since 1945.[108]

The election was clearly a repudiation of Wilson, nonetheless it was unclear as to what it actually favoured. Heath had been handed an impressive majority of 30 seats but he had no mandate on any single issue. On the whole the victory was very much a personal achievement for Heath. His colleagues in the cabinet who had been less convinced of victory were tied to his political fortunes and would remain remarkably loyal.

The new Cabinet met for the first time on Tuesday 23 June, but soon underwent crucial changes.[109] Seven days after the initial meeting Sir Alec Douglas-Home (Home), now the Foreign and Commonwealth Secretary, and the Chancellor of the Duchy of Lancaster Anthony Barber, a favourite of Heath's, travelled to Brussels to discuss the set up of the negotiations for EC entry.[110] The Foreign Office had already despatched Sir Con O'Neill in the middle of April to lead the British team for Europe.[111] In July the government was deprived of an efficient communicator, when the Chancellor of the Exchequer Iain Macleod died.[112] Barber was moved to fill Macleod's shoes and Barber in turn was replaced by Geoffrey Rippon. Both Barber and Rippon, like Heath, came from non-privileged backgrounds.[113] Unlike Heath and Barber, Rippon came from the right-end spectrum of the party, but Heath trusted Rippon's judgement more than that of neo-liberals such as Keith Joseph.[114] Home likewise found Rippon to be a very competent negotiator.[115] There would eventually be future changes, but rather than managing the cabinet by switching around ministers, Heath held sway by a method of firmly summing up the result of the discussion of each relevant issue when the cabinet met.[116]

Home was one of only two political heavy weights in the Heath government. Home was the Party leader Heath replaced in 1965.[117] Home remained loyal to his successor and when invited to continue with foreign affairs he did 'so for it was there that my prime interest lay'.[118] Loyal service by the Foreign Secretary was what Heath wanted in order to ensure that the Foreign and Commonwealth Office (FCO) would help him implement his plans for Britain in Europe.

The FCOs had recently been merged into one and Home, who at various times had headed both, was given the task of managing the new constellation. Heath intended the division of labour to be similar to when they worked together in 1961–63, with the EEC-negotiations as Heath's fiefdom and Home shouldering the rest of the world.[119] Only now Heath was not the negotiator but was instead Prime Minister. Nevertheless, it could not be a simple return to old habitats. However, Home's chief characteristic was loyalty.[120] Although Heath admired Home's self-deprecating charm their relationship was businesslike.[121] Mutual trust in some way made up for the lack of amity between the two and, of course, Home could never again emerge as a threat to the top post. Yet, he was a senior politician with potentially divergent views on the crucial issue of European-American affairs, but Heath counted on Home's loyalty to surpass any doubts.

Home understood Heath's ideas about Europe as a political entity, which supported NATO, but which was not primarily driven by an economic rationale, even though this aspect was important. In Home's opinion Heath had 'instant politician' behaviour and a visionary method of setting goals to be achieved by certain dates.[122] Hence, it probably suited Home that European integration was Heath's domain.

To Home new institutional arrangements, like joining the EC, were less important than the overall necessity to keep the peace between East and West in the Cold War – a peace the US and Europe were required to work together to maintain.[123] Therefore, he thought the closer they were to the Americans the better. On this he disagreed with Heath, whom Home described as not 'anti-American . . . [but believing that] you had to hold the Americans off'.[124] There was no direct or implicit contradiction between EC membership and working to keep the peace; rather the opposite was the case. Nonetheless, Home and the FCO, dealing with the issues of the Cold War, had to consider the special relationship from a global and more traditional perspective.

In 1970 the FCO's view was that the famed Anglo-American relationship was severely run down because of: Britain's 'relative economic decline' and competition for a special standing from other allies; President Johnson personally and his conduct of the Vietnam War; the British decision to withdraw from East of Suez; but also due to a 'marked loss of national self-confidence in the United States'; and a more disorderly state of international affairs in general.[125] The FCO found little new in the statements of the Nixon administration but it regarded the Nixon Doctrine of 1970 as important for Western allies, and 'welcome[d] the re-affirmation of the importance which the . . . Administration attach[ed] to the relationship with Europe'.[126]

The FCO did not believe that there had to be a contradiction between good Anglo-American relations and increased European integration if Britain became an EC member – an assumption based on its recollection of the Kennedy administration's support for a 'Grand Design' of US-European partnership. This ' "two-pillar" arrangement' of the West would ensure that Western Europe did not fall behind the US and fall prey to Soviet influence. According to the FCO Britain should try and retain as much influence as possible in Washington both out of 'self-interest' but also to ensure continued American support for European integration. The FCO was aware that it was necessary to ensure continued American support for the British application and that this was by no means guaranteed. It believed a careful approach that involved the Americans, instead of confronting them, to be the best strategy.[127]

In fact, the position of the FCO was very compatible with Heath's plans. The Kennedy idea of a twin pillar approach to Atlantic affairs was very close to Heath's own idea of forging a special relationship between Europe and the US. In his Harvard lectures he had quoted Kennedy when he claimed that a union in Europe was 'still the first order of business' for the Europeans.[128] Heath and the FCO agreed that EC entry was of vital importance for Britain and that American support was necessary. The difference between the FCO and Heath was that while the FCO focused mainly on how to achieve entry Heath was also preparing for Britain's role inside the EC.

The FCO was more moored to the traditional interpretation of the special relationship than Heath. It assumed that the British were the first Washington looked to when it felt isolated in foreign affairs. And after all Anglo-American partnership was still valuable to Britain: since '[o]n balance, we still get more than we give, in some fields a great deal more'.[129] However, it found it difficult to assess how efficiently the Nixon administration could conduct American foreign policy. The American foreign policy-making process appeared untidy and the FCO did not know whether President Nixon's National Security Adviser Henry Kissinger could do something about it. Furthermore, the US was obviously riddled with domestic difficulties.[130] The British were convinced that Nixon could control the domestic scene but believed that he was 'probably more a prisoner of circumstance than any of his post-war predecessors'.[131] Nevertheless, the FCO, actually, believed that the Nixon administration wished that the EC would evolve in the political and defence spheres, so that Europe would incur less of a cost for the US. Accordingly, the FCO found no reason to think that Nixon would discontinue the tradition of American support for European integration as long as the EC did not end up as a mere trading block.[132]

Since the first time when Home was Foreign Secretary the world and Britain's role within it had changed and Home wanted to make sure that Britain had an adequate analysis of its international position, so in 1970 the FCO undertook a complete 'modern' and secret analysis.[133] Britain was shown to be slightly more important to the US than France and roughly equal to West Germany.[134] Home was impressed with the result which he recommended to Heath.[135]

The results were helpful to 10 Downing Street, and appeared to give statistical confirmation of Britain's decline. The analysis confirmed that a new strategy was needed. It also helped to tie the FCO to the Heath government's ambitions to remake foreign policy.

The analytic efforts would also support Heath's case that new commitments would have to wait until there was an established 'general and coherent strategy'. Already in June 1970, Heath warned the Chancellor, and the Foreign Secretary and Lord Carrington, the Defence Secretary that he was worried about Britain's limited resources, lest there be more overseas commitments. Hence overseas and defence policy had to be reined in by what was economically feasible.[136] The new Cabinet agreed to go ahead with Europe, but there were also other long-term problems that the Heath government had to tackle 'East of Suez, Rhodesia Africa, Industrial Relations, Government Expenditure'.[137] But the issue of EC membership was the one that presented an opportunity not a problem.

The FCO was, of course, already receptive to the need for the changes that its own study implied. Denis Greenhill, the Permanent Under-Secretary at the FCO, was concerned about how long Britain could 'walk the tightrope' between European integration and at the same time keep 'special links' with the US on both nuclear and intelligence matters. The US was expected to become increasingly wary of sharing knowledge with Britain as it moved closer to Europe, but a British failure to enter Europe was even worse since it was expected to marginalise Britain in world affairs.[138] Evidently, the FCO's reasoning interlocked with Heath's vision; accordingly, all other foreign policy commitments were directly or indirectly linked to Britain's European future, since it appeared to be the key to continue to matter in the world.

Heath seemed fortunate in that his government faced what appeared, at least superficially, to be an unlikely rerun of the state of affairs at the beginning of the first application. This time with the chance of getting it right; the Hague EC Summit in 1969 had revived the integration process and preparations for negotiations with Britain had already been made. Appearances, however, can be deceiving.

Sir William Nield, responsible for coordinating between Rippon at Whitehall and Number 10, told Heath in the summer of 1970 that they were in fact not facing a repetition of history; they were going for make or break with the negotiations. According to Nield more depended on the negotiations than had been the case in the sixties, for two reasons. The first reason was that American support for European integration was not guaranteed. There could eventually be sweeping changes to American diplomacy, due to the US 'external misadventures, external deficit and internal tensions' which were thought to have weakened the will of the US to carry the same burden as before. However, Nield believed that this had not so far dawned on the Nixon administration, but it might before the EC negotiations were over.[139]

The second reason was rather ironic. The change in French policy at the EC Summit at the Hague away from rigid Gaullism towards increased integration and enlargement meant that the Six were prepared to deepen integration and move ahead on 'monetary, political, economic, and industrial harmonisation'. However, since 1963 British bargaining powers had eroded.[140] Although the aim of enlargement was an integral part of 'the spirit of the Hague' this alone could not guarantee that Britain would get a favourable deal. Due to both reasons the crucial decisions about negotiations would 'more than ever' need to be taken on at the level of the Prime Minister, the Foreign Secretary and the Chancellor of the Exchequer.[141] The now-or-never approach was fuelled by the pervasive fear of decline, a decline that seemed very real in comparison with the EC member states. If the EC was again on an upward trajectory Britain needed to attach itself to European integration before the discrepancies between Britain and the Six became insurmountable.

Compared to the sixties the Heath government did have a better understanding of how the Community functioned and it preferred a quick agreement, which meant that they would have to 'break the back of the negotiations' by the summer of 1971.[142] The Heath government was fully behind the aims the Six had expressed at the Hague Summit in December 1969, with Europe moving towards 'ever closer union among the European peoples'.[143] Heath was supported by a united Cabinet, and was able to blend his enthusiasm with the language of applications past.

The pressures of decline and the fervour with which Heath was committed to his ideas could easily lead to the conclusion that his was a hands-on approach. That was not the case, but Rippon did brief a committee, consisting of the colleagues, including Home, and also separately Heath.[144] However, to Rippon's Private Secretary the diplomat Crispin Tickell Heath appeared emotionally involved to a considerable degree. He appeared jealous when Rippon scored successes in the negotiations and Tickell thought that he would 'have preferred to do the job virtually single handed' and 'rescue the negotiations from disaster' and 'avenge the events of 1963'.[145]

Heath took a keen interest in the EC study, the Werner Report, which considered the possibility of a monetary union within ten years and in the Davignon Report that was seen as the first attempt since 1962 to move the EC forwards on political cooperation. What mainly interested the FCO in the Davignon Report were suggestions on how to synchronise foreign policy. It found the report was lacking in substance, since it did not foresee any new institutions and because it did not include defence, which it saw as the necessary support for diplomacy. Nevertheless, the FCO thought that the Davignon Report would be welcomed by those friendly to Europe in the American administration.[146]

Despite his interest, Heath did not involve himself in these issues. He preferred working pragmatically towards specific goals. His approach to politics did not readily include action by rhetorical means. He was afraid that speeches on the future of Europe would disturb the chances of British EC entry. After all he had already said nearly everything he wanted in his Harvard lectures. He employed oratory only when the negotiations were going slowly in February 1970 when he spoke to a group of European parliamentarians visiting London.[147] On that occasion he referred to 'new institutions'. This intrigued the new President of the European Commission Malfatti who asked Heath, when they met in March 1971, what he had meant. Heath then explained that he thought the academic debates about 'federation or confederation...sterile' and that they should instead come up with entirely 'new concepts'.[148] This illustrates that Heath was not a theoretician or an ideologue. When necessary Home played down Heath's bursts of creative enthusiasm, suggesting that these displays were merely the consequence of Heath's pragmatic approach, and similar to that of French President Pompidou, meaning that new institutions should only come about if there was a real need, as in the monetary field.[149]

Heath took note of many of the details of Britain's relations with Europe after he entered 10 Downing Street. This included giving instructions on semantics and urged civil servant to refrain from identification by using 'we', meaning the British and 'they', for the Europeans. He also expected the diplomat Michael Palliser to be able 'muscle in' on the EC Commission and convince it to make the same change from its perspective.[150] It was a sign on how he thought Europe should be run – by its governments. In November 1970 Heath also urged Jean Monnet to focus his influential pressure group the Action Committee for the United States of Europe on enlargement when it met during the spring of 1971.[151] The group had had considerable influence on leading US opinion.[152] Monnet had also inspired Heath and they shared the idea that Europe should be a partner of the US. Nevertheless, while Monnet had influenced British politicians since the early sixties, Monnet neither then nor later decided as to what the British policies should be.[153]

For all his determination Heath knew that the attempt at entry could fail and that the responsible course was to study the options.[154] This secret and sensitive FCO analysis was completed in March 1971 at the same time as the negotiations were entering their final phase. It echoed the belief that there was no other single entity to which Britain could attach itself, which could do as much as the Community to fulfil British requirements. It also assumed that Britain's ability to achieve its interests internationally in the '1970s and 1980s [was] likely to decline' without 'an alternative means to widen [the] political and economic base'.[155] Hence the conclusion confirmed to Home and Rippon that the pursuit of EC membership was the right one.[156]

The FCO's analysis regarded '[t]he choice – Europe or America – [as] a false one' because it saw European integration as the only way for Britain and Europe as a whole to have more influence with the US.[157] To ensure that the US stayed committed to European integration the FCO suggested that the government ensured support 'at the highest level' by convincing the American administration that Britain was genuine in its commitment to 'political as well as the economic integration of Western Europe'.[158] The FCO was not under any illusion that British influence with the US was a 'fixed sum'. In view of Britain's reduced fortunes and the US's own problems British influence on the other side of the Atlantic was 'a dwindling asset'. It also held that if the EC did not enlarge it could not increase its leverage with the US.[159] Only through Europe could Britain continue to matter, to the US and the world.

According to the FCO the benefit to the US would be 'an outward-looking Europe in partnership with an outward-looking United States'. The alternative could be a disunited Europe with a number of weak allies that would cost the US a lot to defend. At worst there could be 'a political vacuum' in Europe. The development of a Europe as a superpower might then be seen as preferable.[160] The FCO, like Heath, assumed that it was in the US own interest to support a greater integrated Europe.

Number 10, the Cabinet and the FCO shared the view that EC entry was necessary if Britain was to remain one of the top European powers. It was also clear that Britain had nowhere else to turn than the EC. Nevertheless, membership was not a choice between Europe and the US. In fact, US consent was central for Heath's plans to succeed. Actually, all means were used to ensure success in the negotiations and to make sure that the US was committed. For Britain to remain of importance Heath and his government had to convince the White House that it was in the interest of the US to have a strong Britain, and that this necessitated British membership in the EC.

Nixon, Europe and the control of US foreign policy

Few were more aware of the post-war ascent of the US than Richard Nixon, who in 1968 was elected the 37th President of the US. After the Second World War the US had eclipsed the British Empire as a world power and had completed its rise to supremacy as one of only two super powers. By 1970, after two decades of Cold War the US, had to re-assert its position as the Western hegemon. As President Nixon had to ensure that the US remained powerful, although it was not altogether clear as to what role that would leave for Britain.

From the beginning of his political career Nixon was a member of important committees, such as the Congressman Christian Herter's Committee, with which he travelled to Europe in 1947 to report on the proposed Marshall Plan for economic aid to Europe. He supported the Marshall Plan despite the isolationism still prevalent among Republicans. It was a formative experience, which made him place issues before ideology.[161] A trait he shared with Heath. They also had similar backgrounds. Born in 1913, into a humble Californian Quaker family, Nixon served in the US Navy during the war and became a politician in the late 1940s.[162]

It was not Nixon's commitment to make the US engage in the world that made him a household name but instead his work on the House Un-American Activities Committee where he exposed the US diplomat Alger Hiss for perjury in relation to charges of being a soviet spy. In 1950 Nixon was catapulted into the senate and in 1953 he became Vice-President under President Eisenhower. As Vice-President he travelled widely and actively and reported to the meetings of the National Security Council, the NSC. These experiences gave him an unusually high degree of foreign policy experience for a US politician.[163] Unlike Edward Heath, Nixon did not require the manners or elocution of the elite and instead he based his appeal on being a typical American.[164] It was only after the American political order that had been built on the New Deal was disintegrating, largely due to the domestic upheaval following the expanded war in Vietnam, that Nixon was elected President.[165] At a time of domestic turmoil he was recognisable as a figure from the more stable era of the fifties and in 1968 Nixon was chosen as the Republican Presidential Candidate who was most acceptable to all factions of the Republican Party.[166]

Nixon knew that when his ambitions met with success he would inherit the Vietnam War.[167] In fact, foreign policy was an unusually big issue in the 1968 Presidential Election, something for which Nixon was well prepared. In 1967, the same year Heath gave lectures at Harvard on Europe, Nixon devoted considerable time to Europe when speaking about foreign affairs. He argued that a whole new framework for Atlantic cooperation was necessary: 'Today Western Europe is strong economically and economic independence has inevitably led to more political independence. The winds of détente have blown so strongly from East to West that except for Germany most Europeans no longer fear the threat from the East.' Quoting the British Prime Minister Harold Macmillan he warned that 'Alliances are kept together by fear, not by love'.[168] To Nixon's mind the original Cold War conditions that had created and shaped the post-war special relationship were altering. Nixon may have included Britain among the European powers that were complacent about the East–West détente but as his quote indicated he had some sentiment for the closest ally of the US.

Overall, Nixon found the allies in Europe ungrateful for what the US had done for them. Nevertheless, the very strength of Western Europe both militarily and economically had forced the Soviet Union to seek a peaceful accommodation in Europe. Accordingly, he did not want to risk the success of Western cohesion, especially considering that NATO had so recently been dealt a blow by France's partial withdrawal in 1966. Therefore he claimed that '[t]he highest priority American foreign policy objective must be to set up a new alliance, multilateral, if possible bilateral, if necessary, which will keep [West] Germany solidly on the Western side'.[169] Nixon's interest in a viable and stable Atlantic alliance that would give the US freedom in other areas fitted well with the ideas that Heath articulated the same year.

Nixon, however, did not conduct his campaign for the presidency on the finer points of the American alliance system but instead on the American involvement in Vietnam. He was a realist.[170] Not surprisingly, he defended the so-called domino theory. To him the Vietnam War was only the front line behind which was the prize of Asia–Indonesia and to him the fight against a regional communist threat should not be limited by the niceties of national sovereignty: 'Viet Nam's neighbours know that the war there is not internal, but our own allies in Europe have difficulty grasping the fact.'[171] Incidentally, his limited regard for sovereignty may have had the benefit of him being able to see Western Europe as a regional entity and not merely as a collection of sovereign states.

He did not see the US as the first among equals, or as a nation-state amongst others. To him American interest was conflated with the interests of the West as a whole. Although he had been a supporter of American involvement in Vietnam he came to believe that US foreign policy had been kidnapped by Johnson's policy in Vietnam. To rectify the problem of dealing with one issue at the time, such as the Vietnam War, he intended to first deal with Europe when he became President in 1969; thereby ensuring the reliability of the Western alliance and giving the new administration a firm basis for dealing with the East.[172]

In order to pursue his agenda he wanted to take control of the US foreign policy-making process so that he could fashion foreign policy from the White House. For this he needed a reliable adviser who could assist him in the restructuring of the foreign policy-making process. The choice eventually fell on Henry A. Kissinger, a refugee from Europe and a Harvard academic.

It was not an obvious choice. The ideas about why Kissinger was singled out have varied: such as Kissinger being one of the few bright foreign policy analysts associated with the Republicans, to conspiratorial theories about Kissinger giving secret information to Nixon enabling him to make an underhanded deal with South Vietnam's leaders to ensure his election.[173] Actually, the most important reason was fairly straightforward. Yet, Nixon could not spell them out because he did not want to antagonise the State Department.

During Kissinger's first in-depth meeting with Nixon, in November 1968, Nixon spelled out his wish to appoint someone capable of reviving the NSC, which had worked well during Eisenhower's time when he had actively participated as Vice-President. Kissinger suggested to Nixon that the NSC could synchronise options for policy decision on international affairs.[174] Furthermore, Kissinger agreed with Nixon's analysis that the executive should by-pass the State Department to assume control over foreign policy.[175] In a manner typical of Nixon, he himself stated to the press the exact opposite of what he intended, claiming that the new National Security Adviser would not isolate the State Department from the White House.[176] In fact, Kissinger was taken on board because he understood Nixon's wish to see the White House running foreign policy, and not because of any great meeting of minds between two realists.

However, Kissinger and Nixon shared an unfortunate number of personality traits that reflected insecurity and budding ego.[177] Rather than complementing each other their views, their temperaments overlapped. Yet it would be difficult to imagine them with their roles reversed, with Kissinger the outgoing intellectual as President choosing Nixon the loner and conservative Californian as his adviser.

In order for the President to accrue power over foreign policy Nixon and Kissinger had to circumvent the State Department. Nixon's choice of a pliant Secretary of State was his friend the Manhattan lawyer William P. Rogers. He had no foreign policy experience and approached foreign policy as a lawyer, case by case, without an overall approach. Rogers would eventually be subjected to Nixon's and Kissinger's technique of secretive dealing that also became a vital part of Nixon's and Kissinger's methods of diplomacy.[178]

Unlike Rogers, Kissinger had been an ardent researcher of diplomacy.[179] His PhD thesis was about the peace settlement after the Napoleonic wars and was laden with assertive Hegelian-style judgements. The image of the European Concert system was a potent historical analogy implying an international system that allowed limited wars for decades instead of a final (nuclear) Armageddon. However, he never claimed that his study of nineteenth-century European diplomacy could be applied as a design for solving the problems facing the US in the seventies.[180] Nonetheless, his basic ideas were based on elements lifted from his analysis: it was necessary to establish order by the mutual consent of the great powers, by creating a legitimate but not necessarily just order capable of staving off revolutionary changes in the international system.

According to Kissinger the consequences of a nuclear war threw doubt on whether it was worthwhile to fulfil obligations and come to the aid of the European allies. He saw the Partial Test Ban Treaty and the Nuclear Non-proliferation Treaty as steps in the right direction. He believed that future strategic arms talks needed to involve the European allies. Otherwise they were all but forced to accept what the superpowers dictated to them, in turn gradually wearing down European trust in the US. However, he also wanted the Europeans to take on a greater share of the responsibilities within the NATO framework and therefore argued for the development of a common outlook on international affairs.[181] Like Nixon, Kissinger believed that the US had to reassure the Europeans and bring them back into line so that the US would have the necessary freedom to pursue foreign policy in the interest of the US, and accordingly the rest of the West. Like Nixon he also recognised that a multipolar world was emerging.[182] Kissinger's first task was to serve Nixon's views and wishes. However, Kissinger and Nixon saw the emergence of multipolar world differently. In one way Heath's plans followed naturally from the development of a multipolar world, but such a world also allowed the possibility that a united Europe could present an undesirable change to the international system for the US.

Yet, Kissinger was not a Sancho Panza figure doting on a menacing Don Quixote. He was both Nixon's intellectual equal and prepared to work as his handyman, re-modelling the way American foreign policy was made. Nixon had ambitious ideas for his foreign policy and required maximum flexibility. Concentrating power to the White House was only one step to ensure this. Another was to assert that the Atlantic alliance was a stable factor in a changing world. Nixon wanted the US to lead and set the agenda but he was not against greater European cohesion, believing that in the long run it made the West stronger as a whole. Against this background of broad changes to US foreign policy making – and under a President eager to delve into foreign policy – Heath had to develop his British foreign policy programme; his vision for Britain in Europe.

Nixon's new diplomacy and the American attitude to British EC membership

In a speech in February 1970 Nixon explained his Nixon Doctrine to the US Congress. Because the US had lost its dominant post-war economic role among the Western powers he argued that it was time that the US made a reasonable reassessment of its interests, which would then be the foundation for commitments rather than the other way around. His suggestion was a foreign policy that aided and supported allies, without undertaking to take over their security obligations.[183] It was an advocacy for the greater self-reliance of allies.[184]

Nixon's view was that the situation within Europe was changing and that it faced the most fundamental of challenges in 20 years. It was, according to him, time to reaffirm the European-American partnership after the fledging relationship of the sixties. Nevertheless, he heralded NATO as an on-going triumph, and acknowledged the growing strength of Europe. Accordingly, he claimed that he wanted to talk with the Western European allies instead of talking at them. The present European institutional arrangements were less than clear and consequently he promised continued US support for the development of the European Community. However, he stated that it was up to the Europeans to unite not the US. In the meantime the administration stood firm in its level of military support for NATO, which he saw as underwriting European economic collaboration.[185]

Nixon had reaffirmed his intention to put Europe back in focus with a tour of Western Europe a year earlier in 1969. At that visit Wilson had been keen to develop good relations with the new President but his reputation had preceded him and his overtures were met with scepticism.[186] Kissinger, nevertheless, came to believe that Wilson was sincere in his commitment to continued Anglo-American cooperation in international affairs.[187] When Wilson and Nixon met in January 1970 it was their third meeting, and the frequency seemed, at least superficially, to emphasise the special relationship with Britain, which the White House thought would please Wilson.[188] Yet, the press questioned whether the frequent meetings between the President and the Prime Minister were really worthwhile.[189] Given that Wilson lent support to Nixon's foreign policies, including Vietnam the administration wanted to reassure him about Britain's special status.

In regard to the other European allies the Americans believed that the British still distrusted the French. Hence, the Americans initially believed that the British government for that reason tried to circumvent the French by strong support for the West German Federal Chancellor Brandt and his new policy towards Eastern Europe, known as *Ostpolitik*.[190] Wilson, however, told Nixon the new French President Pompidou was different from de Gaulle and although Pompidou lacked the latter's panache he had the more desirable characteristic of being reliable.[191] At the January meeting Nixon restated his support for British entry into the EC but asked if mute support was preferable, to which Wilson agreed. Wilson also claimed that an enlarged community had to compensate the US by assuming greater responsibilities, though he emphatically ruled out a separate European defence community since 'you can't have an alliance within an alliance'.[192] However, that was exactly the kind of ideas that his successor – Heath – was open to.

Nixon revived the use of the 'special relationship' 'to the embarrassment of his hosts' when visiting London in 1969.[193] At this time Nixon's view was that the term had originated with Churchill's speech in 1946 and that its meaning had subsequently come to mean a 'combination of tradition, commitments and common purpose'.[194] Nixon was prone to accept the special relationship as a combination of the Second World War mythology and actual functions. In explaining Nixon's use of the phrase Kissinger said that it had been deliberately used to confront a new attitude of thought in America, which claimed that the best way to get Britain into Europe was to cut off the special relationship with Britain. Nixon had only wanted to show that the special relationship was something organic and not a question of organisation. While the White House wanted Britain to become an EC member it did not want to do it by trying to 'thrust the British away'. In an attempt to further underline the value of having a special relationship the Americans stated that Nixon's aim was to bring other nations up to the level of the relationship that the Americans enjoyed with the British.[195]

This was not a development that Heath wanted but exactly what the FCO's studies showed was happening. He wanted the Europeans to be united as an equal to the US and not a herd of multiple special partners. Worse for Heath, Kissinger's description of the American view of the Anglo-American relationship was exactly the kind where the myth of special relations was confused with its parts, like actual agreement.

In fact, the 1970 White House's assessment of Britain was surprisingly optimistic compared to the British self image. The NSC still regarded

Britain as 'a major power although it has given up its Empire'.[196] The full impact of the decision to withdraw from East of Suez had not yet been reached. Accordingly, the NSC could state that Britain had so far kept its economic and political interests in 'all quarters of the world'.[197] Despite the fact that the run down on commitments and Britain's economic problems had resulted in the search for a European role the White House expected Britain to 'place a high premium on its close relationship with the United States'.[198] After all, Britain had continuously supported the main objectives of the American foreign policy, and the NSC saw it as 'one of the United States most valued allies'.[199] The White House was clearly prepared to have better relations with Britain than the FCO believed US interests warranted.

Likewise the Nixon administration's ambition was to ascribe Europe with a high degree of importance in its diplomacy.[200] Usually, European issues always risked being given a lesser priority if the White House concentrated on issues pertaining to the Cold War. However, the EC's decision to go ahead with political and economic union as decided at the Hague Summit in December 1969, which also opened the way for enlargement and British membership, gave an added push to efforts at US-European diplomacy.[201] Actually, Nixon had asked the NSC to make a study of British membership even before the European summit.[202]

After his tour of Europe in 1969 Nixon thought EC enlargement likely. It was not only de Gaulle's resignation in April 1969 that made the Nixon administration expect that the way to EC enlargement lay open. They believed that the de Gaulle era had taken the wind out of 'supra-nationalism' and geared the member states to a more pragmatic approach making enlargement possible.[203] Even before the Hague Summit the NSC considered it likely that all the community members were open to negotiations for membership with the British.

It was well known that Nixon had been an outspoken supporter for European integration.[204] The State Department, which was well acquainted with Nixon's traditional stance, easily rehashed it for a report on the consequences to the US of EC enlargement. This annoyed Kissinger's staff, who alleged that the State Department was prepared to 'put the position of the past 15 years further into concrete'.[205] Since Europe, at least in theory, was high on the foreign policy agenda and because Europe seemed to be moving towards enlargement and deepened integration, the NSC wanted to make sure that Nixon had freedom to manoeuvre, and if need be to by-pass the State Department. This the White House would later do on all other aspects of foreign policy. The

NSC critique seemed more to defend this principle than suggesting a radical departure for US foreign policy.

Actually, it was the State Department that raised question marks about the benefits to the US of Britain joining the EC, although these were few and not the basis for a recommendation of a change in policy. What it did do was to underline the importance of British membership for continued integration.[206] It suspected that de Gaulle had wanted Britain to join the EC after West Germany had performed well during the monetary crisis of November 1968. His successor Pompidou appeared to have reasoned along similar lines and concluded that the best way of dealing with West Germany was to let the British in and allow deepened integration to 'contain' West Germany. Without Britain the EC would become dominated by the Germans, which would dissuade the French from further integration according to a State Department analysis.[207]

The State Department understood that the EC, though it aimed to become a union, was a different animal from the US. Its analogy for the EC was the German nineteenth-century Zollverein, which had preceded German unification. In the same way the EC could eventually lead to European unification driven by economic processes that masked a political course. However, the State Department rejected economic determinism. The progress of the EC was not certain and Washington was more acquainted with the American path of development, where defence and foreign policy came first and preceded economic and social affairs. Nonetheless, Britain's membership was seen as 'the final creation of a European Community' and the necessary step which would begin the process towards European unification.[208] In other words Britain was regarded as far more important than any other candidate country, because it was crucial for European unity.

The NSC shared many of the State Department's assumptions. Enlargement was thought to make the EC more liberal on trade and a potential European monetary union was at the time seen as more of a solution than a problem.[209] The Nixon administration intended to safeguard its trade interests through negotiations within the General Agreement on Tariffs and Trade, GATT.[210] Accordingly, trade issues did not necessarily have to become a major issue for transatlantic relations.

Furthermore the State Department judged the Treaty of Rome as insufficient for political cooperation. This meant that it would take a long time before Europe could make effective decisions in foreign policy and assist the US globally. However, it was assumed that a European foreign policy would have difficulty in emerging as the 'thought of ceding a portion of British sovereignty in the foreign field [was] politically sensitive in the UK'. According to the State Department the EC was thought more likely to be run by inter-governmental cooperation rather than supranational cooperation. Like the NSC it thought it to be in the long-run interests of the US to have 'an emerging Western European entity' that would be able to help with the costs and efforts of securing the peace.[211]

The NSC expected British membership to alleviate the tense relationship of the US with West Germany that had stemmed from Brandt's new *Ostpolitik* towards the East. With Britain as member the NSC believed that West Germany would be unable to dominate the EC. The success of the EC could then be translated into greater political, that is economic responsibility for NATO, while British traditions guaranteed that the EC developed towards a 'democratic, liberal and outward looking character'.[212] This kind of vague belief was partially based on mythological reminiscences about the special relationship. Evidently, in 1970, there clearly was little discrepancy between the views of the State Department and the NSC about costs and benefits to British membership in the EC.

The Hague Summit had convinced the State Department that European integration would not evolve into merely a larger free trade area but that it would evolve towards political unity and that the question of British membership depended upon if this development was in congruence with US foreign policy aims.[213] This was of course based on the assumptions of a Britain where Wilson was still in power and not a Britain led by a man with ideas about European integration. Wilson did not expound European visions about Europe. Instead he reminded the White House of the British economic problems and the NSC did not recommend that the US should be 'saddled with the UK and the pound in a permanent client status'.[214]

The NSC was not convinced that EC membership would be profitable for Britain. In fact it believed that the economic consequences to Britain were 'uncertain at best'. It believed that 'Britain's desire to enter the Community [was] basically politically motivated', which was taken as welcome realisation that a 'merger with Europe' would end 'the drift in British policy'. It would achieve a new sense of purpose and mission, and stimulate its economy.[215]

Both the State Department and the NSC had based their respective analyses on a Britain that chose to join the EC because it had to. When the Heath government took office the White House had settled on a policy of support for EC enlargement as long as the costs to the US were acceptable, although as will be shown it was difficult to discern just exactly what were acceptable costs. However, neither Nixon nor his two foreign policy machineries, the State Department and the NSC, had counted on Heath's enthusiasm for Europe or analysed its consequences for Anglo-American relations or US-European relations.

Nixon was eager to establish good personal relations with Heath after his unexpected victory in the 1970 General Election.[216] The Nixon administration continued the traditional American support for further integration. However, John Freeman, the British Ambassador to Washington when Heath came to power, warned him that after Nixon had re-emphasised his support for a stronger and broader EC in his foreign policy statement to the US Congress critics had emerged. These critics were among special economic interests groups, representatives in Congress but also members of the administration such as the Secretaries of Commerce and Agriculture. Nevertheless, Freeman believed that Nixon would continue to favour membership. He would accept economic losses in some sectors, because political and security elements were more important in Nixon's reasoning.[217]

The increased importance of individuals for the special relationship

The British initially believed that the Secretary of State William Rogers had considerable weight with the White House both because of the office he held and since he was a personal friend of Nixon. The FCO knew, however, that he was excluded from discussion on Vietnam, and that 'Dr Kissinger [had] emerged as the President's principal adviser on foreign and defence policy'. Nonetheless, Kissinger's influence was seen as limited to certain issues. Initially, in October 1970, it did not seem to the FCO that Rogers and Kissinger held differing opinions in regard to Europe. In any case the British assumed that the State Department was handling European matters.[218] But soon there were worrying signs about the unity of support for British entry in Washington.

In October 1970 the FCO and Number 10 learnt that the US Ambassador to the EC, the pro-European Robert Schaetzel, believed that there was a difference between Kissinger and Nixon over European affairs.[219] He believed that Kissinger did not favour the idea of the US assisting in the emergence of a new global actor in Europe, and that he was quite content with the US holding sway over a number of states in Europe.[220] However, Schaetzel was exactly the kind of State Department officials whose interference the White House did not want when forging new policy. Experienced in European affairs Schaetzel was perhaps also too associated with the European network around President Kennedy.[221] The White House took little notice of Schaetzel, but the British listened. He informed them that, in the White House, it was only Nixon who favoured European integration and supported Britain's European policy. The British also learnt that the decision-making machinery in Washington was unusual in its concentration to the White House.[222] Given Nixon's support for British EC membership this was assumed to be a good thing. However, because the normal foreign relations with the US were in flux due to Nixon's reinforcement of the NSC Heath would have to work through Nixon to achieve his aims.

Schaetzel's information came against the background of what the FCO regarded as disarray in the US foreign policy machinery. It was annoying since this made it harder to continue the personal touch so important to Britain's traditional Anglo-American relations. Home soon found it difficult and confusing to find out who was responsible for what in the US foreign policy, whether it was the State Department or the White House. The FCO found it hard to believe that White House would try and 'conduct all serious business' and besides Home found it 'improper and unwise' to go behind the back of Rogers.[223] While the FCO and Home became conscious of Nixon's efforts to appropriate the conduct of foreign policy for the White House, neither it nor Home had realised how far the post-war network of personal contacts had faded since the early sixties. Although annoyed by the new White House regime it did not strike Home or the FCO as the harbinger of a shift in US policy towards Britain.

The British were right in assuming that there was little difference in attitude between the State Department and the NSC, including the White House, initially. Neither reflected a radical departure in Anglo-American relations. British EC membership was still seen as a means to underwrite Britain's world role, about which the White House was positive.

When there is a transition from one party and person to another in a democratic state it does not follow that it, or the individual, will pick up foreign policy where the predecessor left of in a smooth transition. When it happens it is because, as in the case of Nixon, the successor wants to continue the policy; as when Nixon sought to continue the Anglo-American special relationship. Despite his deftness at analysing international affairs he was a man who had cut his teeth in the environment of the fifties and his view of the relationship was influenced by what the relationship had been till then. To some extent, meeting

Wilson probably countermanded these sentiments. On the other hand, they also confirmed that there was a continuation of the traditional outlook in Britain. Hence, when he was in the process of safeguarding the stability of the Western alliance in 1969 there was no need to reconsider the US attitude towards Britain.

Kissinger has claimed that Heath did not care much for the British ties to the US or individual Americans.[224] As seen above this was patently untrue, in fact Heath clearly understood the centrality of President Nixon for continued American support for British EC entry and Britain's role in an enlarged and united Europe. He therefore wanted good relations with Nixon.

In a sense both Heath and Nixon represented a throwback to the ideas prevalent in the early sixties. When they replaced Wilson and Johnson respectively there was not a small degree of erase and rewind.[225] Of course, in politics, events intervene making it more or less difficult to pursue the goals originally set. For example, the Vietnam conflict altered American politics and the conditions for how a realist like Nixon could go about his business, including altering American foreign policy. Nixon, nevertheless, realised that he needed stability within the Western alliance as he set out to strengthen the position of the US in the world. Hence, he needed Britain to continue to play a stabilising role in the alliance. Initially, Britain and the renewed efforts at European integration seemed to contribute to that. Both Heath and Nixon looked favourably on European integration and old ideas like Kennedy's grand design of an Atlantic partnership between equals, but the question remained: in how far the plans of the Heath government were compatible with the aims of the Nixon White House? Both Heath and Nixon were set on ambitious foreign policy changes, which meant that different aspects of the Anglo-American special relationship would be tested simultaneously in more ways than it had perhaps ever been challenged before.

2
Monetary Catharsis: Anglo-American Economic and Monetary Affairs

Reversing economic decline

Strange as it may seem in hindsight the Heath government seemed to sit down at a table with everything laid out. The economy appeared healthier and steady after the ups and downs of the sixties and the devaluation of 1967.[1] The new chancellor of the exchequer, Iain Macleod, intellectual, political heavy-weight and a good communicator was extremely well prepared for his assignment. Unfortunately, he died after only five weeks in office.[2] Upon hearing that he was to replace Macleod Anthony Barber commented 'this is going to be some assignment'.[3]

Barber was originally supposed to conduct Britain's negotiations with the EC. He understood what Heath's main political aims were. All the Heath government's major policies were aimed at attaining membership from an advantageous position. Britain had to be prepared so that the economy would eventually be able to reap the benefits of membership as European integration deepened. One of the potentially greatest challenges in adaptation was how to manage, the British currency, sterling's role as a reserve currency. Catherine Schenk argues that sterling's function as a reserve currency had been a major complication for the first two applications to the EEC. Yet, monetary affairs were conspicuously little talked about.[4]

When the Heath government took power the Bretton Woods system was intact so was the economic special relationship despite the 1967 devaluation. This chapter asks what implications Heath's vision had for the Anglo-American economic special relationship where monetary affairs took centre stage.[5]

Sterling was a reserve currency, with the benefit for Britain that it could make cheaper purchases. Sterling's post-war role originated with the so-called sterling area. It had been formalised during the war. Member states loaned Britain money during the war by accepting sterling as payment for imports and re-investing them in London; these debts were the so-called sterling balances. The Bretton Woods system, the post-war global monetary system, gave the sterling area a chance of survival vital to the British economy. Hence, sterling could continue to function as a reserve currency within the whole system. This required sterling to have a stable value. This was threatened by inflation, which would make sterling less valuable in relation to the dollar, which had a fixed price in gold. Since the currencies were pegged against the dollar, devaluation was an indirect threat to the dollar as well as the Bretton Woods system. Likewise the position of the City of London as a financial centre depended on the attractiveness of sterling. As long as Britain was doing well and its balance of payments did not go into deficit this was under control.[6]

The Bretton Woods system was not a classical gold standard system. It was also a currency system where the US dollar and sterling were the reserve currencies. However, the system came to require US deficits. The problem was that the US balance of payments could not be regarded in the same manner as that of any other state because of the dollar special status. At the same time as the dollar provided the system with liquidity it was expected to keep its value vis-à-vis gold. Worries about the US balance of payments grew throughout the sixties. The sterling crisis and eventual devaluation in 1967 showed what could happen to a reserve currency if there was a crisis in confidence.[7] The devaluation in 1967 had begun the disintegration of the sterling area and the role of the sterling as a reserve currency.[8] After the devaluation an agreement was reached in Basle in 1968, to the effect that certain central banks agreed to support the parity of sterling. In return sterling balances were guaranteed their value in dollar. This had had the undesired effect of actually increasing the sterling balances.[9] Accordingly sterling, and indirectly the Bretton Woods system, was propped up by the so-called Basle agreement that would finance Britain if there were unexpected and quick withdrawals of sterling balances.[10] Sterling's international role and its dependency on the US during the first two applications set it apart from the EC countries and contributed to de Gaulle's second veto.[11]

The Basle agreement went some way towards assuaging the Europeans about sterling at the end of the sixties but they remained apprehensive about importing a problem into Europe that required an international solution. However, while sterling was far less of a reserve currency than at the beginning of the sixties it still presented a potential problem.[12] Its lingering role as a reserve currency easily made it seem overvalued especially if there were balance of payments problems. In the sixties Britain had been plagued by 'stop-go' policies. As growth policies were pursued imports increased. This caused a balance of payments deficit. This had to be met by policies that curbed growth, hence 'go' and then 'stop' policies.[13] Heath wanted to come to terms with these two problems which were intractably linked.

In his 1967 Harvard lectures Heath argued that the difficulties with sterling depended on its role as reserve currency. He believed that an international solution was required to correct the limits to liquidity in the international system. He recognised that it was a problem that could not be solved 'in a European context' but did believe that as far as Britain was concerned steps had to be taken 'at an early stage' of negotiations to prepare its economy for EC membership.[14] By 1969 he was more precise about his views. He believed that British debts and the US deficit contributed to the world's monetary problems. The US had allowed dollars to leave the country thus contributing to a Eurodollar market and uncertainty about the dollar's value. This, according to him, had two consequences. First, 'the gold-exchange system envisaged at Bretton Woods has effectively been put into suspense and replaced by a dollar system'; and second, 'under the de facto dollar system the world is forced to march in step with the United States'. He wondered whether the Europeans should not create an alternative 'to American domination'. He believed that the EC had run up to the limits of the Treaty of Rome and that it therefore had to go beyond it and forge ahead with integration of monetary and fiscal matters or some other internal way of relegating the EC currencies to achieve economic union.[15] Unsentimental about sterling, and consequently also about the Anglo-American economic special relationship, Heath's plan was to prepare Britain for membership, then join, and once inside help to create a European response to monetary problems. This required relinquishing sterling's reserve role.

To make certain that the Treasury pursued his vision Heath wanted firm control. Heath was distrustful of the Treasury mainly because of its longstanding scepticism of the economic benefits of joining the EC.[16] Heath had been President of the Board of Trade, which was a position that often bred envy of the Treasury's strength. Despite his belief in managing the country by turning knobs and pulling levers, without a strong politician like Macleod, he decided to exercise control through a loyal confidant. Though experienced Barber was less prepared than Macleod.[17] The Treasury recognised that Macleod had been his own man.[18] Instead, Barber was uneasily wedged between Heath and the Treasury and expected to follow Number 10's marching orders.

The government advocated a policy of less intervention in the economy.[19] Uncompetitive industries would be made ready for the greater competitiveness of EC membership. New legislation on industrial relations would be introduced to manage the unions. According to Robert Carr, Secretary of State for Employment and responsible for the Industrial Relations Act, the only key fixture of the government's overall strategy was EC membership. He later said that although the main commitment of the Heath Cabinet was economic growth – the European Community 'that was the first priority, [and] always ... given the first priority'.[20] Clearly, the domestic programme of economic rejuvenation was tied to the overall goal of making Britain a powerful player in the EC.

At the Tory Party convention in Blackpool on 10 October 1970 Heath encouraged the party. He argued for what amounted to a 'quiet revolution' calling for a change of attitudes and measures to restore the post-war settlement.[21] It was intended to have wide-ranging consequences and affect the country into the next decade.[22] He meant to prepare the country for a European destiny. Many, however, regarded it only as an ideological step to the right to set market powers free in accordance with the Selsdon promises. His European plans were already suffering from having been obscured in the electoral campaign and his rhetoric could not convey his odd match of domestic traditionalism and radical foreign policy. However, alternative approaches, based on free markets and monetarism, held no allure for Heath. In October 1970 he met the then infamous American economist Milton Friedman. Heath explained that the state should act against the 'barnacles on the economy' in the form of uncompetitive firms and some of the trade unions practices. Friedman claimed that as long as the British balance of payments, which was eagerly observed by the markets to find if the value of the sterling could be sustained, was the 'primary consideration and constraint' there could be no reasonable growth in its economy. He accordingly recommended that the dollar/sterling rate should float.[23] While Heath wanted to rework the system Friedman argued that it should be transcended. Heath was not ready for such radical measures. He remained unconvinced by new methods. Upon hearing from his economic adviser, Brian Reading, that inflation and unemployment did not follow a well-known model, which was a cornerstone for post-war Keynesian economics, Heath requested a policy mix to reverse the trend and change the structure back to fit the model.[24] Heath wanted greater efforts to break through stop-go cycles but no experiments with new theories.

Sir Eric Roll of the Bank of England confirmed Heath in his conviction that '[i]t would not be possible to rely solely on monetary policy to check inflation'. Roll also thought that the 'Common Market would need to develop monetary cooperation'. However, Roll thought 'this would be a slow process, and should not be allowed to stand in the way of world-wide cooperation on international monetary questions'.[25] However, the traditional attraction of European integration was not monetary cooperation but economic growth.

The British growth pace was not impressive when compared to that of the Six (see Table 2.1).[26] Britain wanted part of the European growth pattern – a pattern that they assumed would continue. It was not only the success in Europe that was impressive but the fact that the EC was trumping Britain on transatlantic trade. US-Community trade had 'trebled since 1958' (see Table 2.2). Most years the US exported more to the EEC in the sixties than it imported. Nevertheless, this trade grew more than that between the US and the EFTA countries, of which Britain was a member.[27] Despite trade disputes the Americans favoured the growth of an important trading partner, which was reflected in the US investment abroad; the EEC received a continuously increasing amount of investment in the sixties while investment in Britain stagnated.[28] Accordingly, it was not only the market within Europe that was appealing to Britain but also the growth in transatlantic trade.[29] The EC, unlike Britain and

Table 2.1   Comparative economic performance 1950–73

	Average % growth in GDP per annum				
	1950–55	**1955–60**	**1960–64**	**1964–69**	**1969–73**
UK	2.9	2.5	3.1	2.5	3.0
France	4.4	4.8	6.0	5.9	6.1
West Germany	9.1	6.4	5.1	4.6	4.5
Italy	6.3	5.4	5.5	5.6	4.1
Japan	7.1	9.0	11.7	10.9	9.3*
US	4.2	2.4	4.4	4.3	4.4

Note: * GNP.

Source: Table 1 on page 5 from B. W. E. Alford, *British Economic Performance 1945–1975* (1995), adapted from the table on page 376 of Roderick Floud, D. N. McCloskey, *The Economic History of Britain since 1700*: Vol. 2: *1860 to the 1970's*, Vol. 2. 1st edition (1981).

Table 2.2 Import to the EU/EC-6 (EEC) from the US

	Import from the US	
	Value (bn ECU/Euro)*	**Share (%)**
1958 – EU 6	2.8	17.9
1960	3.8	19.8
1970	9.0	19.8

Note: * From 1958 to 1970 included, the convention is 1 ECU = 1$.
Source: Table 'From EU 6 to EU-25: External Trade Trends with Main Partner Countries' in *External and intra-European Union Trade – Statistical Yearbook, Data 1958–2005*, p. 30 (Eurostat, Office for Official Publications of the European Communities, 2006).

EFTA, was also a group to reckon with in international trade talks, which was proven by its success in the Kennedy round of the General Agreement on Tariffs and Trade which was concluded in 1967.[30] Membership seemed to be the ticket to success. Without it Britain risked being sidelined in trade and growth.

Heath's experience at the Board of Trade made him aware that industry was unhappy with the previous Conservative policy of slamming on the breaks when the economy got going due to consideration for the balance of payments or the risk of inflation.[31] His focus was to a considerable degree on industry. EC membership was hoped to create greater markets that improved growth and inside the Community British firms would learn to be more competitive. However, it was understood at Number 10 that things were not quite as simple. Membership by itself could not bestow any guarantee of growth or reverse economic decline. Heath's economic adviser Brian Reading gave advice just as harsh as the Treasury, saying that membership in the EC was not 'a crutch for a weak and ailing British economy'; in fact, it was 'a challenge and an opportunity'.[32] Membership was not taken to be an economic cure by itself but the opportunity that could create the necessary economic renewal. In other words, at the core of the Heath government's economic strategy lay the hope that membership in the EC would help Britain break through from the post-war growth pattern of 'stop-go' cycles in the economy.[33]

The Heath government's economic policy assumed that the EC membership would eventually stabilise conditions so that the economy could break through to sustained growth. It wanted the economy to be growing before entry to carve out a strong position for Britain. Economic policies were bent to prepare industry and society for the opportunity that membership seemed to offer. At the same time there was a political necessity to portray the EC as beneficial and, in fact, close to a cure. This easily built up unrealistic expectations. If the process of entry and membership created growth it would then be easier to advocate another leap – to European monetary solutions. That required Britain to be rid of sterling's international obligations for which Britain required US support just as it needed American acquiescence in regard to Britain's EC entry.

Ensuring Nixon's support

The new British government needed to make sure it had the same support for its EC membership application as Nixon had promised the preceding Labour government. Geoffrey Rippon, Barber's replacement as responsible for the EC negotiations, and his diplomacy towards the US during the negotiations for membership is discussed in Chapter 4. Here the focus is on the continuation of the Anglo-American economic special relationship. Shortly after the General Election, in July 1970, Sir Alec Douglas-Home (hence after Home), the Foreign Secretary, and Barber met with the US Secretary of State William P. Rogers to explain the benefits of British membership in the EC. Taking a guarded approach Home said that the possibility of a 'fair' deal was unknown, adding that EC membership was Britain's only and precarious opportunity to find a basis to continue as a great power. Rogers confirmed that that this truly was so, especially since there were no conjectures from the Nixon administration about the old idea of a North Atlantic Free Trade Area.[34] Barber told Rogers that the British hope was that the negotiations would be completed by the summer of 1971. Short negotiations would minimise the adverse impact on the public, which associated membership with price rises. He added that neither the Common Agricultural policy nor the way the EC budget was calculated was beneficial to Britain.[35] The British wanted to demonstrate that the EC was not an economic quick-fix. Accordingly, the US should not count on Britain's fortunes to improve drastically. Rather the opposite was the case. The implication was that for Britain to regain its strength as a US partner it needed American support to ensure that the negotiations went smoothly.

Barber, making virtue out of Heath's desires, explained that since economic unity in the EC would lead to political cooperation Britain had to join. Rogers commented that he found the political arguments for entry 'more important'. Barber sugar-coated his argumentation by claiming that despite the arduous path ahead for Britain there were two things in it for the US. A more unified Europe would make it easier for the Europeans to eventually shoulder a greater share of the defence burden. Furthermore, once inside, Britain would work to the benefit of the US on 'political and commercial' concerns.[36] Continued British support for liberal world trade was, of course, exactly what the US wanted to hear. Little was said about sterling. The British made its case as a weakened, yet loyal, ally that with the help of the US could live up to its full potential. At this stage Nixon confirmed his administration's support and added that he admired the British ability to stay engaged in the world despite economic upheavals.[37] The White House support was completely in accordance with its support for the Wilson government attempt to join and believed that the Heath government shared its predecessor's traditionalist outlook.

It was crucial that Nixon was made aware of Britain's difficulties to prevent the US from creating problems between the US and the EC that could be avoided.[38] Nixon's personal support was pivotal to rein in doubters Washington so that the British would have a fair chance. Sceptics in the US government doubted that membership could be achieved, mainly for two reasons. First, they were not convinced that the British economy was healthy enough for Britain to be let in. Second, they were not confident that Heath's majority of 30 in the British Parliament was enough to pass a negotiated treaty.[39] However, the doubters did not make sterling a major issue.

The EC's common agricultural policy, the CAP, presented much more of a threat. Already in the autumn of 1970 Britain adapted to the EC's agricultural policies. The State Department noted that this made it possible for Britain to adapt to the higher prices in the EC after entry.[40] Number 10 was aware that the US feared that the British would adopt 'EEC-style protectionism'. Therefore, there was some fear that Nixon might change his mind about supporting Britain if he risked losing the electoral support of US agricultural groups.[41] Agriculture eventually had no substantial effect on the White House support for British entry.[42]

The adjustment in agricultural was a part of the early adaptation to the EC system that the 'quiet revolution' actually represented. The Nixon administration was impressed by the quiet revolution and subsequent spending cuts including a complementary shift in defence policy overseen by Lord Carrington, the Defence Secretary.[43] The US Embassy in London interpreted it to mean 'a fundamental redirection' that showed that the British government wanted to 'maintain Britain's place in world affairs and reduce the role of government at home'. However, the embassy calculated that Britain could not in the long run both cut spending and remain a great power.[44] The US Embassy thought that Britain's attempt at remaining a great power could be undermined by the Selsdon policies that were seen as both a means and as an end. The Americans hoped that what was saved in the domestic context would go towards propping up Britain's position in the world. In any case Heath's programme was seen as one with only long-term benefits. Doubts about whether Britain could make it lingered. In late 1970, after the negotiations had begun the Embassy reported, in November, that 'what is probably Britain's last chance to join the European Community is being negotiated now, and the next twelve months will be critical.'[45] The US Embassy in London was convinced that Britain's global position was tenuous, but also that this had not diminished the British government's will to keep Britain a major power.

The British government was of course satisfied with Nixon's 'low profile', to avoid European accusations of Anglo-American collusion.[46] Nonetheless, Heath knew that when he met Nixon for the first time as Prime Minister he had to make clear that Britain could not both negotiate for entry and together with the US fight EC policies on trade.[47] Heath would have to convince Nixon that Britain would merely suspend its advocacy for liberal trade. On Saturday 3 October Nixon and Heath met for a brief lunch meeting at Chequers. Nixon invited Heath to see the 'special relationship' as a personal one, with free communication of ideas and policy suggestions.[48] Like the British hoped it was especially the security situation in the world that warranted close contacts according to Nixon.[49] The meeting dealt with traditional Anglo-American concerns such as security issues globally and in Europe, rather than new entanglements such as the EC.[50] Heath came to the conclusion that US would be a reliable partner provided that American interests did not suffer greatly.[51]

Formal negotiations with the EC began a few weeks after the meeting on 29 October 1970. The Treasury remained stoically sceptical. The senior civil servant F. E. Figgures produced a report for Barber that stated that entry would cause a balance of payments deficit. Figgures added some pertinent advice. The transition to membership made devaluation necessary. If this was within the government's control it was recommended that it ideally should take place in 1975, 'i.e. halfway through the transition period'.[52] But that required the economy to do well in 1973 to 'manage all calls on us, including adequate repayment of debt'.[53] Unfortunately, information would be available for others to conclude that the size of the burden of accession would be such that devaluation would be unavoidable. So instead of devaluation in 1975, Britain might be forced to do it in 1972 or even earlier in the summer of 1971. This had to be avoided according to the Treasury. Instead the government should give the impression both of being in control of the British economy, and especially inflation, thereby creating maximum confidence in sterling and creating the impression that 'entry into the EEC [would] be on balance beneficial'. '[Britain's] negotiating tactics must be directed to secure something which can be represented politically as reasonable and equitable and abjuring any arguments in support which are based on what we can afford. Since we can in any sense not really afford anything', as Figgures put it.[54]

Devaluation might conceivably help exports and the growth that the government wished for. However, it risked undermining confidence in Britain's economic policies and its currency. It made it all the more necessary that Britain's economic situation be stabilised after EC entry to avoid inflation and balance of payment problems. These concerns pushed trade matters to the background. Monetary affairs came to the fore of the Anglo-American relationship just as much because of the US problems as of British ambitions.

As the Britain's new Ambassador to the US Heath had chosen Lord Cromer, a man who could convince the Americans that the new British government remained reliably traditionalist. Heath attached great value to Cromer's opinions.[55] One reason for this was that Cromer, a former Governor of the Bank of England, was keen to find new monetary solutions for Europe, and urged his government to study the European plan for a monetary union, the Werner plan.[56] Cromer understood Heath's wish to give Britain a leading role in European monetary affairs and was also willing to talk about monetary issues with the Americans if necessary. Perhaps the choice of Cromer also to some extent further limited the influence of the Treasury with 10 Downing Street.

There was no Anglo-American scheme to play down the issue of sterling. However, the Americans thought that the pro-market people in Britain knew that monetary union was an integrated part of a future European union and consciously avoided debates on the issue that would cause domestic concerns about 'sovereignty'.[57] After the Hague Summit in 1969 the Community was trying to re-launch integration. The British understood the Werner plan on European monetary union as being dependent on political will, which if it existed could make the monetary union a reality by 1980.[58] This fitted well with Heath's vision and given the opportunity he intended to add to the necessary political will.

There would be no chance to enter the EC if the issue of sterling was not first satisfactorily dealt with. At de Gaulle's funeral in November 1970 it was clear that French apprehensions of the past remained.

The French President Pompidou told the British Ambassador, Christopher Soames, that he did not like the reserve role of sterling. Pompidou claimed that he would 'do everything' to avoid the burden of a European reserve currency, the existence of which he argued could bring Europe into conflict with the US. According to him the dollar was in reality the only possible reserve currency and since the EC enlargement would damage the US economically he did not want to add to that by creating a European reserve currency.[59] This was on the face of it a startlingly radical reversal from the French policy in the sixties of provoking the US on monetary affairs. More likely Pompidou feared that sterling could work as a Trojan horse, saddling the EC with responsibility for a system the French did not approve of. Actually, in 1970, a European reserve currency was exactly what the Americans wanted.

Already when the US Secretary of the Treasury David Kennedy met Heath in the summer of 1970 he expressed his delight to see 'a strong European reserve currency as an alternative to the dollar'.[60] In early December, the influential US Under-Secretary of the Treasury for international monetary affairs, Paul Volcker, who later was said to be inspired by Friedman, was happy at the prospect of the Europeans underwriting the Basle agreement instead of the US.[61] By this time the British understood that it was mainly the issue of sterling, not trade, which could become an intrinsic economic problem in regard to Anglo-American relations and Britain's entry. If sterling was not allowed to become a normal European currency Britain might get stuck between the wishes of the US and the refusal of the French.

Heath was to meet Nixon on 17–18 December in Washington and knew that this was the time to ensure US support for the EC negotiations. The Chequers meeting had touched on every conceivable topic in some detail except the EC. By now that the British knew that the negotiations with the EC could be successful.

Britain would need the personal support of Nixon to counter other less 'sound' presidential advisers in the US or those, like Henry Kissinger, who they thought simply uninterested. Heath had to do three things. First, bolster Nixon's willingness to quash critics in the administration by convincing him that the parliament would agree to membership and that thus British EC membership would come about. Second, tell Nixon that he should not cave in to protectionist tendencies in the US that could provoke an EC-US trade war.[62] Third, Britain also needed the US understanding for whatever way they dealt with the status of sterling. The British assumed that Nixon's administration would support Britain because it had a vested interest in a stable and economically successful

Europe. So the British felt that Nixon should be told that once inside the British would work towards stability and prosperity in Europe through integration 'in the economic, political and defence field'. This was to follow from a practical rather than 'theoretical' process, a reflection of Heath's distrust of approaches based on ideas rather than concrete goals. The aim with which to tempt the Americans was that eventually the process would ensure that the Europeans would shoulder a greater burden in the defence of the 'free world'.[63] The bait was to appeal to Nixon's security-oriented world view.

During the meeting Heath outlined his plan for EC entry and treated Nixon and Kissinger to a 'highly technical analysis of outstanding economic issues'.[64] Heath said that there were to be no allowances made on behalf of the US before accession, first because Britain did not want to appear as a 'Trojan Horse'.[65] This applied to all fields, but he added that 'We can best defend your interests inside the Common Market and should not pay a price to you before we get in. The best reason though, for our entering the Common Market is political, and this is why you were for it to begin with'.[66] Nixon acknowledged that '[t]he British have the political and diplomatic skills to make Europe into an entity.' Nixon said that '[t]here are some in this country who don't want you to go in because they are afraid of Europe, but Europe is essential for the balance of power'.[67] Nixon was convinced that the Heath government would work for a cohesive Europe that would ease American burdens.

Nevertheless, Nixon reiterated that EC protectionism was a very sensitive issue and took agriculture as an example of an issue that stirred up protectionist feelings in the US.[68] His modest wish was that Heath would take a low profile over agriculture so as not to upset the US Senate which was in a protectionist mood. Heath claimed that the British had to raise the price level for the benefit of British farmers when entry came about and that it should not be seen as British protectionism.[69] It was chiefly an adaptation to price levels in the EC. He reassured Nixon that the chances of the Community going completely protectionist 'were probably nil' and that the EC would not countermand the trend of greater liberalisation of international trade.[70] This was more important than agricultural prices. Heath preferred a matter-of-fact approach and this seemed to resonate with Nixon. He was satisfied by Heath's understanding of the situation and suggested that 'the problem was what price Britain was going to have to pay to get in'. Heath agreed that this was an essential point, but explained that the price 'was very hard to quantify'.[71]

The British were successful. They promised to work for liberalisation of world trade and increased burden sharing. Nixon stuck to his original policy of muted support for British EC entry. However, there was a small proviso the delineation of which was hazy; the US would support enlargement despite some 'but not excessive' economic costs. Only time and events could show if and what 'excessive' really meant.[72]

By and large, Nixon had taken the advice of his National Security Adviser, Henry A. Kissinger, to 'minimize...potential friction over economic issues' when talking to the British.[73] The State Department underlined the view that the British had enough problems because the Six worried about taking in a 'loser' because of Britain's potential domestic economic problems. The State Department believed that if Heath's economic strategy did not work the British government would have to resort to incomes policies.[74] These policies were the official answer to inflationary pressure on wages and earnings when there was full employment.[75] Their implementation would mean going back on the promises of government disengagement from intervention in the domestic economy. The State Department believed that if by the summer of 1971 Britain still suffered from inflation that could not be stopped except by government intervention, Britain would 'once again [move] into serious troubled waters, the enthusiasm on the continent [might then] get lost and the crucial moment could pass'.[76] Evidently, the American administration was convinced that the British government's claim that the British situation was precarious was true. It recognised that EC membership was not just another policy amongst others to reverse decline but the primary policy for the Heath government.

The Washington meeting went well although at a press conference Heath made a face as Nixon called the bilateral relationship between Britain and the US special instead of natural. Nixon was also pleased with Heath's continuing British support for the US efforts in Vietnam.[77] Nixon was firm in his public supportive of the British application and the press noted that he had overridden questions about economic disadvantages to the US and that '[t]he word is now: "Forward to the grand design" of Atlantic union'.[78] At the end of 1970 Heath had exactly the kind of understanding that he had wished and worked for.

Sacrificing sterling

In the spring of 1971 the Nixon administration knew that the British government was under economic pressure domestically. At the same time, it was conducting the all important negotiations for entry.[79]

Heath's tough non-intervention approach suffered a blow with the bankruptcy of Rolls-Royce. The company had to be nationalised in February 1971 to ensure contracts and especially the delivery to the US aeroplane manufacturer Lockheed.[80] The fact that this was a decision based on national interest and defence contracts was obscured by the damage it had on the government's national rhetoric. Trade issues were fading out of focus, but the US realised that monetary concerns would increase.

The same month Paul Volcker, at the US Treasury, was irritated by the lack of British consultations when dealing with important monetary issues, such as the fate of sterling. He wanted to tell the British that the US was leaning towards discontinuing its support for the Basle agreement, leaving it to the EC to 'pick up the ball', that is the support, for the sterling guarantees. It was only the intervention of colleagues who were more in tune with the administration's official low-key line of support that stopped him.[81] However, he did talk it over with the now retired British civil servant Figgures.[82] This was not the kind of close consultations that Volcker had in mind. However, the US Embassy still wondered about how the British would avoid speculation on a falling pound, since many expected them to devalue before entry.[83] Figgures's earlier predictions were becoming a reality.

Before deciding on the value of sterling the British had to convince the French President Pompidou, a former banker, to let them into the EC. Pompidou was also alleged to have said in private that the Brussels negotiations were in fact an Anglo-French affair. Geoffrey Rippon believed that Pompidou wanted to appear strong by preventing the British from keeping a prestigious currency.[84] Yet, the French understood that the British government's need for a reasonable treaty was important. Heath's talks with Pompidou, towards the end of the negotiations on 20–21 May in Paris, were intended by them to sort out the remaining issues.

As politicians, both Heath and Pompidou had an interest in making it seem that their talks were crucial to the outcome of the negotiations.[85] When they met, sterling was one of the major remaining issues to be dealt with. Pompidou commented that sterling's reserve currency status was 'a relic of the British Empire'. He argued that the dollar guarantee in the Basle agreement, of which France was not a member, made sterling dependent on the dollar. This made sterling 'abnormal' as a European currency. Pompidou explained that the French merely desired the same system for all members and that France would not wish to reduce the value of the pound. Heath assured Pompidou that he saw things in the same way and that the dollar underwriting sterling 'was a short-lived phenomenon'.[86] Although, Heath agreed with Pompidou's analysis that sterling should cease to be a reserve currency, he asked him to accept that he was unable to commit Britain to specific figures in regard to the run down of sterling balances, because the Basle agreement that sustained the reserve status was not to be renegotiated until 1973. He could, however, commit Britain in principle, and did.[87] Since an economic and monetary union was the goal of the Community as well as for Heath, he acknowledged that Britain had to make sterling similar to the other member states' currencies and that Britain had to stabilise the size of the sterling balances between 30 June 1971 and the time of entry. This would be done by renegotiating the 'Basle arrangements and associated agreements with sterling area countries' after entry. This would help to make a monetary and economic union feasible.[88]

With the EC negotiations concluded on 23 June, the British government argued for entry, in a government White Paper presented in July. It explained that sterling would be adapted to a European standard, and sterling balances would be brought down. The case for entry echoed Figgures's recommendations and revolved around the government's promise to reverse economic decline with the help of EC entry; which was presented as a great chance to stimulate British industry and to provide it with a larger market at the same time.[89] By sacrificing sterling, Heath at the same time freed Britain from the obligations to support a reserve currency making an eventual devaluation less dramatic. It also opened the possibility, under the right circumstances, for Britain to take the lead in European efforts at a monetary union, achieving a prominent place for Britain in the EC, and allowing for the creation of stable economic conditions to sustain growth. This desire had to be balanced with the promise to the Americans that Britain would work for liberal trading policies once inside the EC.

The end to sterling's reserve status did not worry Washington, but the State Department was concerned that the British government missed an important source of earnings. The US State Department had grasped the importance of 'invisibles', that is the earnings from the finance sector such as transport, banks and insurance. These, not industry, brought crucial earnings to the British economy. Without them Britain's current account – Britain's trade in goods and services – would still have been in deficit in 1969 and barely balanced in 1970, with negative consequences for the overall balance of payments. Sidney Weintraub, Deputy Assistant Secretary of State for International Finance and Development, subscribed these incomes to the key international role of 'The City', the global financial centre in London. According to the

Americans the question of how this financial hub would fare after it was 'de-internationalized' was even more important in terms of earnings than the benefits of having sterling as a reserve currency. However, they had little idea as to what would happen after entry.[90] The British government was not very concerned with the City, although it took account of the City's wishes when in 1971 it presented a reflationary budget.[91] However, it began to worry about rising unemployment.[92] And, its focus came to be on the needs of industry.

The American priority regarding the British economy was the opposite. The City had become the base for the growing Eurodollar market, a position that it had carved out since the sixties and which gave it a new important position even without sterling as a reserve currency. Eurodollars were US dollars that had left the US, due to the US long-standing balance of payments deficit, and thus escaped US regulations. These were then used by others for transactions such as loans.[93] Heath saw them as a source of instability since they undermined the confidence in the dollar. Hence, the City's success indirectly undermined the system that Heath wanted to reform. He believed that the international monetary system, the Bretton Woods system, was malfunctioning. Without reforming it a European economic union was not possible. He wanted the EC members to either take 'a giant stride towards integration of monetary and fiscal policies' or agree to a method of adjustments which was compatible with the EC's development to date.[94] Both options assumed the continuation of a reformed system. In the beginning of 1971 Volcker also expressed the wish to find some measure of control over the Eurodollar markets.[95] However, no Anglo-American collaboration on the issue came about.

As the EC negotiations drew to a close the Americans were becoming restless. Ambassador Cromer reported in June 1971 'that the United States Administration were [sic] feeling very lonely', and regarded many European countries with various degrees of disdain. Heath was surprised that the new tough-talking US Secretary of the Treasury, Texan John B. Connally, could not understand that the enlarged EC would not tolerate the fixed rate of the dollar at the same time as the US was increasing its payments deficit.[96] This was a sign of a new and hardened attitude in the US Treasury, one which indicated that the Nixon administration was considering just how much of a cost for EC enlargement and European integration the US could tolerate. Cromer had also picked up on speculations in the US about a possible new but unknown initiative on monetary affairs.[97] The British had achieved what they wanted with sterling without the US disturbing the negotiations. However, by the summer of 1971 the US low-key approach also masked the mutual lack of consultations on monetary affairs.

Heath wanted the international monetary system to reform and expected the US to want the same. If there was a rift in the transatlantic relationship over monetary affairs, Heath would have to side with the EC in order to ensure Britain a prominent role in the Community. Working for European monetary cooperation under such circumstances and simultaneously arguing for trade reform, in a matter palatable to the US, would be beyond Britain's diplomatic ability. It would become difficult to live up to the promises given to the US. However, Heath appeared to believe that the US promises of support, keeping a low profile and avoiding a US–EC rift, remained valid for the whole of the accession process.

The end of the economic special relationship

By the summer of 1971, the dollar was under pressure. Nixon was obsessed with keeping the domestic US economy humming so that he could win re-election in 1972. Hence, he was less inclined than any predecessor to safeguard the Bretton Woods system. If there was to be a monetary crisis, he wanted it well in advance of his re-election campaign. Already in December 1970 he discussed with Arthur F. Burns, chairman of the Federal Reserve, whether 'the United States should provoke a crisis'.[98] American concerns very quickly had systemic consequences for the whole Bretton Woods system.

In early 1971, at the same time as Nixon pressed for expansionary monetary policies for the sake of the domestic economy the US experienced a balance of trade deficit, which was blamed on an overvalued dollar.[99] In the beginning of 1971 Burns eased monetary conditions leading to a huge outflow of dollars, to the extent that many European central banks stopped dollar operations on 5 May 1971.[100] In the system the dollar had a fixed gold value. More dollars meant that its value seemed unsustainable. Accordingly, huge amounts were taken out of the country and changed into other currencies in anticipation of a devaluation of the dollar.[101]

On 28 May, Connally confronted US allies in a speech to the American Bankers Association in Munich. He said that the US would not make its own economy suffer in order to pay for the US balance of payments deficit. He wanted the US allies to make sacrifices, such as burden sharing and agreeing to more liberal trade practices, as defined by the US.[102] Connally led a charge of economic nationalism that would force a crisis.[103] The Nixon administration had prepared for a dollar crisis for some time and if it came it was to be used to devalue the dollar and to make the US more competitive in comparison with the EC and Japan.

Angry at Connally's speech, Heath commented harshly that 'We need to treat this seriously and work out our position. The United States cannot be allowed to get away with this.'[104] Not only did Connally dump the US problems on its allies but it is also made difficult for Britain to be of effective assistance in the areas where the British had promised to help – burden sharing and trade policies – since Britain would run a higher risk of being branded a Trojan horse. The consequences to sterling if the US decided not to defend the system it underwrote were unclear since the whole basis for propping up sterling under the Basle agreement was the continuation of the Bretton Woods system.

Connally's speech came against the backdrop of the latest stress on the international monetary system, which began after West Germany decided on 10 May to allow the Deutschmark to float, after the central banks opened up dollar operations again. Heath's economic adviser, Reading, suggested that Britain should not follow the German float, because if others in the EC revalued and the pound remained undervalued it would boost the British economy.[105] Indeed, it was the 'real hope for a British economic miracle', according to Reading.[106] His assumption was that the government would be prepared to conduct some economic nationalism of its own before delving into monetary schemes.

Reading was right. Neither Heath nor Barber wanted the negotiations, which were still going on, to be unnecessarily disturbed. The monetary disturbances made Barber pour cold water on schemes put forward by Cromer for Britain to take the lead in European economic and monetary union.[107] Instead, Cromer satisfied himself with advising Connally that if there was a European monetary bloc, the best way to ensure good relations between such a bloc and the US was to have Britain as a member of that bloc.[108] Cromer's claims were not an invitation to Anglo-American collusion where Britain would be a Trojan horse. Heath believed that any future course of action on monetary affairs had to be based on responsible transatlantic compromises. Cromer merely tried to make the case, as Heath had done with trade, that Britain was reliable and that its European endeavour was compatible with future support for an economic world order that was in line with US interests.

While the strain on the dollar increased, the British government remained fairly sanguine about Britain's economic prospects. In July, Heath agreed to Barber's suggestion that Britain pay off its debts to the International Monetary Fund, the IMF. Britain had a good margin and by paying in advance they would not have to have consultation meetings with the IMF.[109] This freed Britain from international dictates and gave it some protection against speculation against sterling. It also gave the British government freedom to prepare the economy for EC membership.

The dollar crisis came sooner than the White House expected. On 6 August the US Congress Joint Economic Committee's Subcommittee on International Exchange and Payments, chaired by Henry Reuss, released a report that claimed that the dollar is over expensive.[110] This meant that an attack on the dollar was unavoidable when the markets opened on 16 August. Nixon held a weekend meeting on 14–15 August at Camp David in an effort to stave off a crisis. Among those present was Nixon and his closest economic advisers, but not Kissinger. The result was the 'New Economic Policy', the NEP, which suspended the convertibility of the dollar to gold and imposed a 10 per cent import surcharge together with a few other drastic measures of varying effect on other countries.[111]

According to an often repeated story, cited in excellent works such as those by Frank Gavin and Diana Kunz, British requests for guarantees of their gold holdings allowed Connally to swing the discussion in favour of the policy eventually chosen. To emphasise the severity of the crisis he mentioned a recent demand from the Bank of England from 13 August asking for a guarantee of its dollar holdings against an American devaluation. It would perhaps have had the fitting symbolism of a dependent Britain contributing to US monetary decline, but as Kunz acknowledges it could have been a ruse.[112] And, it was. Connally's claim was without foundation and in fact Britain's intention was to avoid having to 'rock the boat at a difficult moment'.[113]

The American methods disrupted an orderly change of the system, which was what Heath had wanted. Heath's immediate reaction was anger about the sudden measures and he had to be dissuaded from threatening the US with retaliatory measures.[114] The lack of consultations was a blow to the prestige of the British government and to traditional Anglo-American relations. Cromer was equally strident. In the NEP he saw a sign that 'the Americans no longer consider it necessary to consult with the UK as an imperial or World Power'.[115] Cromer also believed that the 'the old concept that the dollar and Sterling should stand together as the two major world trading currencies' had become 'obsolete'. To Cromer all this showed the necessity of a European monetary bloc.[116] On 17 August, Heath was advised by the Treasury to let the pound float when asking for exchange controls to hinder huge inflows of dollars.[117] On 23 August, sterling was allowed to float up to a fixed ceiling.[118] The same day the exchange rate stabilised and in the evening Heath was calmed by a rather normal banking day.[119]

Britain was hard hit by the NEP.[120] It damaged what the government regarded as Britain's 'most important market', namely the selling of machinery and equipment to the US.[121] This shows that it was not only with regard to Europe that it focused on industry.

The US State Department had the contrary perspective. It did not worry about the fall in British exports but it was concerned that Britain would use its strength in the financial sector against the US.[122] Presumably, the US feared that the British would use the City and, for example, hurt the US by its influence on the Eurodollar. The monetary crisis of the autumn of 1971 was thought to provide the British with an opportunity to show the worth of their financial knowledge to the Community, which could be used against the US.[123] The State Department was afraid that the White House was instigating transatlantic discord.

These State Department concerns were not without foundation. In late August, Barber told his counterparts in the EC that the British desire was to act closely with them in the present monetary situation. While Barber wanted to show 'Community spirit', the EC ministers, however, could not agree to what degree their commonly held 'anti America-ness' should apply.[124] Nevertheless, Barber's critique was not lost on Connally, who believed that Barber took every chance to curry favour with the French.[125] Even Heath voiced his concerns, in the middle of October, at the Tory Party conference in Brighton, where he made a strident call saying that Europe could no longer rely on the US.[126] He spelt out the consequences of an American economic nationalism that was bent on safeguarding the US role in trade and its balance of payments.[127] This made the American administration realise the negative impact which its actions had in Britain and for the Anglo-American relationship.

In the middle of October, Connally was heard to have said that British membership was not 'in the best interest of the United States'. The Community would be stronger while the US was loosing its 'best friend ... but also the most susceptible to American influence'.[128] Cromer had heard of Kissinger voicing similar concerns. However, Kissinger retracted these worries when he realised that his opinion might spread.[129] The Americans realised that as a consequence of the American measures on 15 August the British might not be willing to live up to their promises. Martin J. Hillenbrand, US Assistant Secretary for European Affairs, frankly concluded that because of Britain focusing intensely on EC entry and it being hit hard by the NEP, the ' "special relationship" in economic matters' had all but disappeared.[130] The loss meant that Britain could take sides against the US and this had not been the intention of the Americans.

While the Americans had second thoughts, their actions could be used as an excuse for the British not to act on its promises to the US. After the immediate dangers of the US measures were over, Britain, unbound by traditional Anglo-American consultations, could not be expected to use sterling to prop up a system that the dollar did not support. It could move more easily towards the monetary aspects of Heath's European plans, even if not by the route he had originally intended. The Anglo-American economic special relationship seemed to disintegrate at the same pace as the Bretton Woods system but US policies remained supportive of Britain's European future, which was important given that the British parliament voted and approved the negotiated treaty on 28 October.

In fact, the US administration's leading economic advisers were anxious to avoid further alienation between the US and Britain, hoping instead that Britain would work to mend the transatlantic rift. In November, the otherwise strident Paul Volcker told the British that they 'were not in the firing line', but that the US wanted the EC to make concessions of presentational value to the US domestic scene, such as a freeze on CAP prices. Arthur Burns realised that there was some confusion on the part of the Americans themselves as a whole as to what exactly the US demands were and how they were prioritised and suggested that the British act as a bridge between their new friends in the EC and the US. The British formed the impression that the US strategy was in disarray and hoped that Burns would be successful in his attempts to convince Nixon that Connally's approach was unfruitful.[131] The British government, however, did not take up the invitation act as an intermediary. It believed that any bridge building was secondary to EC membership, and hence it could not be forthcoming.

Heath thought that British monetary policies should focus 'on 1 January 1973, the effective date of British accession to the European Community'. That required that Britain enter from a position of strength, by which Heath meant that it should be competitive in industrial production.[132] In his focus on the needs of industry, over the earnings of finance, Heath was similar to his predecessor Wilson. Such an approach required government control of monetary affairs. Heath and Barber agreed that they should aim to keep the exchange rate of sterling as low as possible in international monetary talks without disclosing to EC states that Britain sought depreciation against all EC currencies.[133] But, the official position was such that Britain could not say no to an early realignment. The benefits of a continued float were not quick in coming either. And, a downward float would not be popular with the EC.[134]

A quick solution was best. Heath wrote to Nixon in November to hurry reform efforts along.[135] He warned Nixon of the consequences to the global economy of a continued situation without fixed parities and complained that the US professed to believe in free trade while making other countries pay for the removal of its trade barriers.[136] Since the traditional channels of consultations had deteriorated Heath had to use the personal element of the traditional special relationship, of which he himself had been a sceptic, to make an appeal.

Nixon and Heath decided to meet on the British territory of Bermuda before Christmas 1971. In early December, the pound continued to be pressed upwards, and Heath 'feared that the United States Government was succeeding in their objective by encouraging the pressures of speculative movements to work'. The complaint was that the higher sterling went 'the more we should be playing their game'.[137] In preparing for the summit, Whitehall felt that 1971 had not been a good year for Anglo-American relations, despite mutual understanding on minor issues such as the nationalisation of Rolls-Royce. However, as seen in Chapter 5 the way the American administration handled its switch in policy over China caused some friction with Britain. On top of that, the monetary shocks and the issue of Britain and EC entry, together with US–EC trade disputes, threw a long shadow over the relationship.[138] To countermand all these issues, the personal report between Nixon and Heath would have to be exceptional.

It was actually Pompidou who came to the rescue and paved a way towards a new agreement on international monetary affairs when he met Nixon in the Azores in the middle of December 1971. It smoothed the way for a major international realignment of exchange rates. This made it possible for the so-called Group of Ten committee, the G-10, which had been formed to support the international monetary system in the early sixties to work out a solution. This became known as the Smithsonian Agreement. It was signed in Washington in the middle of December by the G-10. The US achieved a de facto devaluation and agreed to take away the import surcharge but there was no return to convertibility of dollars to gold.[139]

The British still depended on continued US support. The FCO aimed to reiterate the original British approach to the Nixon administration.[140] According to the FCO, 1972 was 'a crucial year' for Britain, since everything would be concentrated on achieving enlargement.[141] Heath agreed with the FCO. The Americans had to be told that it was necessary for the US to be 'prepared to consult before acting'.[142] Heath was 'determined to work for an enlarged Community capable of coherent political as well as economic dialogue with the US'.[143] The end of the economic special relationship had come quicker than Heath had anticipated and he was now anxious that this would not interfere with his long-term plans of creating a US-European special relationship. Hence, as the immediate crisis was over he wanted to be conciliatory. Meanwhile, Britain's balance of payments had improved and was good at the end of 1971. In fact, the overall balance of the British balance of payments did not show a deficit until 1973. Throughout 1970–74 it was invisibles that consistently showed positive figures.[144] But while the balance of payments was better than in 1970 it also mattered less. The government believed that its domestic policies were working but found that 'the safety margin between success and failure [was] narrow'.[145]

Nixon was informed by the US Embassy that the British government pinned its hopes on a '[c]ompetitive stimulus from above [that] would give [a] much needed shot in [the] arm to business investment plans for export led growth'.[146] The British government was reflating the domestic economy, which could once again bring about inflation and an upward wage-price spiral. This would damage the British ability to compete at the crucial moment of EC entry, which by itself would incur balance of payments costs. This in turn could force devaluation in the near future, according to the NSC.[147] The British Treasury's expectation that others would expect devaluation of sterling held even after the Bretton Woods system began to disintegrate.

At the December summit Heath argued that EC membership would alter the outlook of Britain and the other members. He explained that the members had to get the benefits of scale in industry, since each country could not have its own industry in each individual field.[148] Heath took Concorde as an example of a European project and said that he wished the US had built a supersonic aircraft too, but if 'we had not built Concorde, there would have been no supersonic aircraft built in the free world'. This was, to him, an example that competition between the US and the EC should be constructive and not destructive.[149] This was his attempt to explain what a friendly rivalry should be like between two equals.

Heath had moved back to the position he held before the crisis that had begun with the measures of 15 August. However, he admitted that he had thought in terms of a European solution to trade and monetary problems but realised that it required a global solution, viewed in terms of 'competition rather than confrontation'. He hailed the results of the meeting between Nixon and Pompidou.[150] Heath believed that the 'Western world must work together if it is to survive'.[151] His views were still that a united Europe should be created in the economic, defence and political field, but he had shifted somewhat in how he envisaged the policies of this future entity because Western cohesion was important. Nixon told Heath that he was heartened that Heath favoured continued cooperation within the alliance.[152]

The US had Britain's agreement on many details of monetary affairs, so it was felt that the best thing would be to demonstrate these similarities and to tell Heath that in order to resolve the monetary crisis, trade had to be dealt with as well.[153] A protectionist Europe would have disastrous consequences and Nixon welcomed institutionalised venues of cooperation.[154] However, on the same day Rogers explained to Home that the US desired a 'formal machinery' for US–EC consultations but after earlier talks with both Brandt and Pompidou it was felt that it was better left until after the completion of enlargement.[155] This, of course, suited the British who would then not be required to live up to any promises until accession was completed.

Nixon claimed that while all their differences were important they were after all merely 'tactical'.[156] A joint statement stated their common aim as: 'To maintain their close and continuing consultation at all levels in their approach to world problems.'[157] Both the British and the Americans hoped to repair the damage of the past months that had pulled them apart but there were no exchange rate commitments and thus no return to the traditional economic special relationship.

Barber and Connally also met in Bermuda. Connally said that he and Volcker questioned whether there was any purpose in doing anything about the long-term monetary problems when the EC might upset everything as it moved to a common currency. Barber tried to reassure Connally saying that it would take a long time for a European currency to come about and explained that even to achieve narrow internal margins was hard.[158] Connally did not hesitate to state to the press that he had asked for Britain's help to persuade the EC to lower tariffs.[159] He further upset Heath by trying to upstage one of his press briefings.[160] Neither Connally's lack of personal touch nor nearly brandishing Britain as a Trojan horse ingratiated him to the British or helped to resuscitate Anglo-American relations.

Despite Connally's tactlessness it seemed to some observers that Heath had reached his aim at Bermuda by making Nixon realise that the 'big three' of the Western World were the US, Japan and the EC – adding that Heath could be confident and lean on a substantial surplus, a good balance of payments, strong reserves after most of British debts had been paid.[161] Instead of having sacrificed sterling, it seemed like the Heath government had created a strong sterling.[162] By the end of 1971 it seemed as if the Heath government had salvaged sterling from the faltering Bretton Woods system and the ending of the Anglo-American economic relationship. The Smithsonian Agreement enabled Heath to abandon a confrontational stance and continue his work for a US–EC special relationship.

'The end of a long song'

While the balance of payments improved, and the disagreement with the US was overcome the domestic economic reforms failed to prevail over the domestic economic problems. In February 1972, 18 months after the promise of a 'quiet revolution', Annenberg, the American Ambassador to London, saw few results. He believed that the government was relying on the EC to change the mood sufficiently so that growth could ensue with confidence. Heath expounded 'exuberant Europeanism'. Annenberg thought it important to shore up the remaining and important aspects of the special relationship that were still helpful to Western unity.[163] He did not fully grasp Heath's long-term plans to reshape relations on a different level.

His impressions were formed just before a so-called 'u-turn' of the Heath government's quiet revolution policy. On 28 February the Upper Clyde Shipbuilders were given aid by the government – this represented a humiliation for the government. It was a move which signalled the beginning of the Heath government's espousal of dirigiste methods, to direct the economy, a new, and altogether different, attempt to revamp British industry before entry. Barber's March budget was set to fight unemployment over inflation. The government wanted to attempt, what the Conservatives tried in 1963–64, and break through stop-go policies towards sustained growth. With a swift push towards expansion of the economy, it hoped to take advantage of the good balance of payments, a return to full employment, and to take a growing and competitive British economy into the EC.[164] Barber was worried about inflation, but he agreed to a highly expansionary budget that promised a 5 per cent growth rate. There would be no more turning 'tap on and off' – no return to 'stop-go' policies.[165] This was the beginning of the 'Barber boom', although it really was Heath's.[166] EC entry would take place under the desirable conditions of high growth and low unemployment.

Heath said at the time that the 'Government has not changed its objectives since it came in'.[167] For Heath it was the truth but it did not ring true or coherent to those who primarily had put their faith in the Selsdon objectives rather than EC-membership. Simultaneously as the government expanded the economy Britain took an important step towards Heath's European goals by joining the so-called European currency 'snake in the tunnel' which was established on 24 April. The member currencies were restricted to a narrow band of fluctuation against each other, the 'snake', and floated in broader band, a 'tunnel', vis-à-vis the dollar.[168] Two weeks later Connally told Cromer that he believed that Europe would remain introspective for the next ten years while it was sorting out its monetary and trade affairs. He feared a world of monetary blocs and said that he wanted a 'one world' solution to international payments. Cromer disputed Connally's concerns claiming that all the EC wanted was an internal system comparable to the US system.[169] Unfortunately for the British, Connally actually turned out to have underestimated the Europeans' problems.

There was inflation in 1971 because the government refused to raise interest rates but this time the dash for growth was not going to be slowed down by risk of balance of payments deficits.[170] It was as if the Heath government was copying Nixon's defiance from a year earlier, but for sterling as for the dollar the pressure grew. It was later held that the events that forced sterling to float began on Friday, 16 June 1972. There was nervousness in the market over inflation, industrial unrest and disappointing trade figures.[171] Another factor was the expected rise in food prices after EC entry.[172] The following Monday, 19 June, the situation was aggravated by the Opposition Shadow Chancellor Denis Healy, who spoke against devaluation, that by know was expected by him and others, being put off until after the summer. This made the markets jittery.[173]

Barber acted decisively and followed his natural inclination to trust the markets. He convinced Heath that Britain should let sterling float despite the consequences for its commitments to the European snake.[174] Barber told Heath that even a temporary float was against the Community agreement to have narrower margins. A float could also require action against inflation, according to Barber. He told Heath that a controlled float with a return to a fixed parity before entry into the EC on 1 January might not be possible. If the economy was in good order it might even float too high before entry, but a statutory prices and incomes policy to combat inflation could impress the outside world.[175]

There was to be a temporary float. The Heath government remained optimistic about the chances for growth and its ability to control events.

The option of floating was chosen over having the reserves bled dry. As Heath later told Nixon, '[n]othing could be gained by allowing the haemorrhage to go on'.[176] Britain had more to benefit from growth than from shoring up sterling. It would be easier to work for European monetary cooperation after entry if the economy was strong.

Under the guise of a pre-planned meeting on the situation in Ireland, Heath informed key figures of the Cabinet about the imminent float. Afterwards, Heath signed a statutory instrument, which redefined the sterling areas as the United Kingdom, the Isle of Man, the Channel Islands and the Republic of Ireland: 'in other words, it abolished the rest of the sterling area'. Robert Armstrong, Heath's Principal Private Secretary, 'pointed out that this was the end of a long song'.[177] A long-term float was in the long run incompatible with the EC aims and Heath's vision of leading the EC on a path to union by monetary means, but the government placed its hopes in the boom.

However, the first consequence of the float was that sterling could not participate in the European currency snake of stable exchange rates. Luckily for the British ambitions the scheme was an EC Council Resolution, which meant that it was not formally binding, either for the actual member states or Britain. The scheme of EC margins was in fact seen as experimental, and leaving it was not a major failure.[178] Nevertheless, the French took the sterling float badly, with Michel Jobert, at the Elysée, 'saying we had entered an agreement three months back and this decision had blown it sky high'.[179] Later, however, Pompidou was conciliatory and relied on Heath's promise that the measures were temporary and that Britain would soon return to a fixed parity so that they could go on with the foundation of progress in Europe – monetary cooperation.[180] Unlike the promises made to the Americans, which were made to enable entry, this promise articulated what Heath wanted to achieve after entry.

In Washington there was no surprise at the British float. The Americans were only worried that others would follow.[181] Even if educated opinion now viewed a pound float as almost admirable, it was after all a blow to the Smithsonian accord.[182] Heath and Nixon agreed that 'radical reform' was required and that 'patching up the Bretton Woods system' was not enough.[183] However, Nixon's adviser on International Economic Affairs, Peter M. Flanigan, wrote to the President that '[t]he British action shows the wisdom of the U.S. refusal to consider convertibility until a new and stable monetary system is in place'.[184] Ironically, Britain which had been falsely blamed for exasperating the crisis that led the US take the measures it did on 15 August 1971 now actually contributed to the collapse of the Bretton Woods system. Like the US had done, Britain acted upon its national economic interest.

While the British actions contributed to the end of the Bretton Woods system Heath seemed to think it would be replaced by another system. In June 1972, Cromer wrote to Heath saying that he 'never expected Bretton Woods to be felled by the denizens of Great George Street [the Treasury] who have been spending so much intellectual energy shoring up with progressive esoterics this decaying forest'.[185] Cromer suggested a plan where Britain led in the creation of a 'world currency unit' with the IMF as a world central bank and also a possible European reserve currency, 'the Europa', under the auspices of an EC monetary institute.[186] The Treasury, no fan of Cromer, did all it could to pour cold water on Cromer's schemes.[187]

In July, Nixon let Heath know that the Americans were also looking for a fundamental change to the international payments system.[188] Heath was hopeful and actually thought that what had happened could highlight what was actually needed for a European monetary union to come about.[189] He was certain that there would be no new 15 August and that any 'drastic changes' would instead be dealt with by getting 'people round a table'. He believed that the enlarged EC would be equal to the US in terms of currency resources and that the EC would have 40 per cent of world trade and thus be greater than the US. In an interview he referred to President Kennedy's Grand Design and said that this would be a 'healthier' balance.[190] Now sterling was not only free from the Anglo-American economic relationship, but it was also temporarily free from the restrictions of the snake, with the British economy in a gamble for higher growth.

Dollar drama

In the early summer of 1972 it became clear that the float would not be temporary and Pompidou said that he was 'disappointed with Mr Heath'.[191] Heath merely thought it typical of the 'characteristic French gambit to achieve a result which suits French interests by a combination of insults, bullying and wooing'.[192] Ambassador Soames believed that the French had a less clear idea about monetary affairs and the British found it difficult to make out the French opinion. The French seemed only to know what they did not want and not what they wanted and it seemed that the French view in general was that the world was not ready to give up on a gold-standard–based system like the Bretton Woods system. Nor were the French aware that the European monetary union that they called for appeared inconsistent with their wish for limited supra-nationality. According to Soames, a European monetary union might require greater economic cohesion, forcing more supra-nationality in the long run, which would expose the 'gap in the logic of their thinking'.[193]

In July, Soames believed it urgent to explain to the French that the British would deal with the sterling agreements without talking to their European partners. They hoped that the French would be pleased to know that the British were thinking along the lines of going ahead with European monetary unity, even if there was no progress on the world monetary system.[194] On 12 July, Soames met with Michel Jobert, Jean-René Bernard and M. Raimond, from the Elysée. They were told that Heath was resolute in keeping inflation down – to the point of implementing statutory intervention. The French understood that success in industrial relations was imperative for Britain to be able to return to a fixed exchange rate. The French were told that the British government wanted to go back to a fixed parity as soon as possible.[195] Upon learning that the British now favoured pressing ahead with European monetary plans even if no progress was made on the international scene the French did not respond as enthusiastically as the British had expected. The French were only keen on safeguarding the 'acquis' rather than making progress on European monetary affairs.[196] Evidently, the British were more eager for Europe to lead the development of a new international monetary system but since Britain did not participate in the snake the British enthusiasm was less convincing.

Barber believed they were caught in their promises to the French. He saw that the progress on Community affairs that Britain wished for could be endangered if they could not fulfil the promise of returning to a fixed exchange rate. The French and others would see this as a breach of trust even if Britain reaffirmed its support in principle for a return to fixed exchange rates.[197] In August, the French Foreign Secretary, Schumann, and Heath talked of monetary affairs. Heath underlined that Britain had 'quietly and gradually done a lot to change the sterling area in fulfilment of his agreement with' Pompidou. He promised that it was his earnest desire to return to a fixed parity as soon as possible.[198] He now had to ensure that this would happen. In early October, Number 10 tried to 'smoke out the Treasury on the question of the return to a fixed parity, well before the Summit'.[199]

The recent experience of the Treasury made it unwilling to return to a fixed parity for another year or more.[200] Re-pegging sterling to a fixed exchange rate now depended, to a great extent, on the success of talks between employers and unions. If these met with success it would also be more difficult to keep the sterling un-pegged, if the government would so wish.[201] By late 1972 Heath's hope of European monetary cooperation had become the hostage of a solution to industrial strife. Before that was resolved the Treasury might even be won for a new orthodoxy in favour of a floating exchange rate.

Meanwhile, as employers and unions were engaged in talks, the British economy was expanding feverishly. At the same time the EC Summit Conference took place on 19–20 October in Paris and it was agreed to forge ahead with the economic and monetary union, with plans ensuing in the beginning of 1974.[202] The re-elected Nixon wrote to Heath on 8 November and expressed his pleasure at seeing the Community 'moving with resolve and new elan [sic] toward the high goal of European union'.[203] He believed that Heath had been instrumental in improving US-European relations at the EC Summit over 'economic, monetary, and commercial' matters. He praised Heath's acceptance of the importance of the 'political relationship' between America and Europe.[204] The same day Heath called Nixon to congratulate him on his re-election victory and then Nixon enquired about what happened about the control of wages and prices, since the talks between government, unions and employers had reached an impasse leading to the government introducing statutory incomes policies to quell price rises and fight inflation.[205] Heath acknowledged that they were 'having quite a battle' over it, with the unions 'being rather silly'. Nixon to his pleasure and surprise learned that a poll showed that 70 per cent of the British public was behind the government.[206] That was of little help.

On 13 December, Heath wrote to Pompidou describing how prices and incomes policies and other anti-inflation measures would have to become effective before the pound could be fixed again. Heath promised that this would happen in the foreseeable future.[207] But, in effect it meant that the struggle to re-peg the pound before entry was over. Floating successfully averted the costs of a forced devaluation but it had also shown that Britain had not escaped the grip of the markets. Britain entered the EC with sterling floating on 1 January 1973, and Heath's plans were stuck, halfway to his vision. The government, as originally planned, tried to engineer an economic boom when it entered the EC. The cost of this was that sterling had to float but the domestic problems of industrial relations prevented Britain from returning to a fixed parity.

In the beginning of 1973 Burns visited Britain to study the consequences of entry. He admired Heath's brave stand over 'prices and pay policy' and was convinced that things would turn out well. He told Heath that he was 'despondent' about the international monetary reform and did not feel that there was any dynamic drive in Europe on the issue. Heath agreed with him that Europe and the US had to deal with these issues together and not be pulled apart by the failure to do so.[208] Nixon and Heath were scheduled to meet on 1–2 February in Washington and Burns told Kissinger that he put a lot of fate in Heath's ability to change the EC's stance on trade and monetary affairs, but pointed out that as a new EC member the British would initially have to tread carefully in pursuing such policies.[209] The press speculated that Barber would pursue discussions on 'the outlook for the Common Market's monetary union scheme'.[210] There would, however, be little of this.

Heath's visit to the US came at the same time as the dollar came under renewed pressure.[211] Only now were the British ready for bridge building and set on presenting Britain as an important EC interlocutor. This was important in view of the planned developments within the EC, with a fully integrated EC in partnership with the US 'before the end of the decade'.[212] This was to be the recreation of the 'special relationship' on a transatlantic scale. In an effort to link its past promises to new efforts Home tried to convince Rogers that the appointment of Christopher Soames to the post of Commissioner for External Affairs would improve US–EC relations and would allow the new Commissioner to work for liberal trade, thereby beginning to fulfil the promise made to the US to work for Anglo-American views once inside the EC.[213] Home ignored the uncomfortable fact that Soames would not speak for Britain in his new job, but for the EC. In any case it was hardly an impressive way of living up to the government's earlier promises that Britain would work for increased liberalisation of world trade.

Heath was in a quandary about his own position and was concerned that the Americans would not understand that he could neither speak for Europe nor engage in technical details on economic and financial affairs. Kissinger accepted that the US could not pressure the British for help since they then would reawaken the old charge of the British being a 'Trojan Horse'.[214] Kissinger believed that eventually US–EC disputes on trade and monetary matters would be solved in talks and it was important to have a strong and friendly Heath on the US side.[215] He obviously hoped that Britain would continue to share the same sentiments as the US and live up to its past promises. Rogers held a similar view. He believed that Heath's political future was tied to the success of his economic policy. The planned diplomatic initiative towards Europe, the so-called Year of Europe, was supposed to begin with Heath's visit in February 1973, and Rogers expected that if the US used it well they could win Heath's support and improve the US chances of its diplomacy being understood in the rest of Europe.[216]

During the visit Heath became aware that Nixon was worried that the Smithsonian accord would not hold until there was a long-term solution in place.[217] The NSC thought that Heath was favourably disposed to the US and better US–EC relations. Nixon had been advised to praise Heath's efforts at the EC Summit in October 1972 and to affirm US support for European Union by 1980, thus hoping to speed up monetary reform.[218] Nixon intended to say that the US neither wanted nor needed a 'Trojan horse'. He sought to appeal to Britain's traditional interest thus hoping that the British would make the EC recognise that it and the US had to have a common view of trade and monetary problems.[219] Although Nixon did not want Britain to be a Trojan horse it was typical of Nixon to make a disclaimer of what he desired – Britain voluntarily undertaking to do some bidding along the lines of American interests.

To the press, Heath explained that the EC 'was a new type of union'.[220] The establishment of this union would take place in 'constructive dialogue' with the US. Heath claimed that free trade would ensure that the European market would be of benefit to the US. He also said that he wanted to cement the relationship between the US and the EC and make it 'strong and durable . . . and find common solutions which meet your needs and interests as well as our own'.[221] Heath not only had to assure the Americans about the reliability of the EC so that he could pursue his vision but he also had to reassure them to safeguard US investments in Britain – because he could not afford to alienate American investors who had great interests in Britain.[222]

Shortly after the visit the new Secretary of the Treasury George P. Schultz declared dollar devaluation against the Deutschmark and the French Franc.[223] This was not the ideal international background to begin an Anglo-French understanding on monetary affairs. At the same time, the British Treasury claimed that there was not enough market confidence to re-peg sterling.[224] The new Cabinet Secretary, John Hunt, pointed out that the French government did not appreciate that Britain found it difficult to return to a fixed exchange rate. If Britain was still floating after the month of April, political problems with the EC would grow rapidly. Worse still, Britain would most likely hinder the implementation of the Community process towards economic and monetary union.[225] Ironically, Heath's plans were thwarted not by the actions of any other state but by Britain's failure to live up what he had believed possible.

The British would be able to save their face, if not their plans, because of the new currency crisis this time around the dollar. On 28 February a new dollar crisis began. Kissinger advised consultations with allies to find solutions, instead of unilateral measures.[226] When the crisis deepened in early March, Heath wrote to Nixon explaining that potentially a joint Community float would not necessarily harm the US; instead it would make the EC a more reliable partner by making it more cohesive.[227] On 3 March Nixon protested against Heath's criterion that a new monetary solution being acceptable or not depended upon whether it added to European integration or not. Nixon said that he had always supported European integration for the sake of the Atlantic partnership, but never so that one side could 'proceed unilaterally on a matter of fundamental concern to the other'.[228] Clearly, this was a frank statement about what cost the US would tolerate regarding British ambitions for European integration. It was now Nixon's turn to stress that consultations were essential if there was to be a US-European special relationship.

Nixon understood that American aims were in congruence with a possible joint EC float.[229] His was the last laugh however. During a crisis meeting in Paris, on 9 March, and the following week it became clear that the Bretton Woods system had finally ended. On 19 March all were floating jointly or independently. This ended the 'tunnel' and only the 'snake' remained with Britain still on the outside. The dollar continued to reign supreme since no one replaced the US as the lender of last resort and because the US did not blackmail its allies over its military protection; the US was the de facto leader of the new 'non-system' and there was now no gold standard only a dollar standard.[230] The situation that Heath had complained about and wanted to rectify before taking office had now been formalised.

During these dramatic days, Heath was informed by his civil servants that '[f]ull EMU is an essential element in complete political union in the Community'. It would bring about all the promises kept in store by the economic union and Britain was committed to this 'supra-national economic and monetary policy with pooled reserves and co-ordinated economic and regional policies'. Without them there would only be a 'customs union'. The recent currency crisis, however, had upset the chances of implementation of this in 1974.[231] What Heath desired was just out of reach. As the rapid boom in the British economy continued, the European integration for which it was intended ground to a halt. This also had a negative impact on the expansion of the British economy that Heath had initiated.

In the spring of 1973 the British economy was over-heating.[232] Hence, Barber temporised and recommended that Britain should 'wait and see' before rejoining the snake.[233] At the end of June 1973, there were renewed fears that the US would once again inadvertently hinder British plans. The Nixon administration's attempt to decontrol the US economy led to rapid price rises during the spring of 1973.[234] Cromer was greatly worried about the state of the dollar and he thought that the political crisis over 'Watergate' could push the world into the abyss of a 'first-class financial crisis of major dimensions'.[235] On Thursday 5 July, Heath and Barber met with the Governor of the Bank of England and economic advisers to discuss what Heath referred to as Cromer's Wagnerian style-scenario and other nightmarish possibilities.[236] However, if there was trouble demand had to be dampened to fight inflation. Heath urged the continuous presentation of favourable figures.[237] On 9 July the Governor of the Bank of England informed Heath that the Central Bank Governors at Basle after acrimonious discussions had agreed to intervene to help the dollar, beginning with the US secretly intervening on the following day. Sterling was not dealt with to any great extent.[238] There was no longer an Anglo-American special economic relationship by which sterling could benefit from association with the dollar as the dollar was given assistance. This was indicative of sterling's fall from grace: what mattered now to Britain and others was the rate of the dollar. It did nothing to help Heath's plans for further European integration.

On 25 July, the sterling exchange rate started to slip and Barber wanted to spend reserves to prop it up.[239] The next morning the pound slipped even more against the dollar, although it was temporarily steadied by the fall in the dollar at mid-day caused by Nixon's refusal to be subpoenaed.[240] The British government had not yet learned what was possible, and what was not, in the new world of floating exchange rates. By mid-August, Heath was informed that the Governor foresaw a balance of payments deficit continuing for a year.[241] At the end of August, the prediction was extended to 18 months. Heath still wanted to fulfil his promise to Pompidou and to re-fix the parity and to borrow to support it if need be. It was the only way left to continue to pursue economic and monetary union. Barber explained that such a political choice might be viewed unfavourably.[242] It could actually make the economic situation worse.

Heath's vision with regard to leading Europe towards monetary union had actually failed before the fall of 1973, although he did not appreciate it. The direct cause of this was the attempts to adapt the British economy and the domestic economic scene to EC membership. This was augmented by the adverse effects of the US of restricting the suffering it was prepared to endure for the sake of European integration. There was no great dollar Wagnerian-opera-style collapse after Bretton Woods came to an end, nor did the British government rejoin the snake. Hence, there was no opportunity to see if new monetary gods, like a European currency, could be forged. The new international monetary world remained monotheistic with the almighty dollar as its standard.

The US reaffirms its leadership

In 1973 Heath reached his primary goal. He had managed to steer Britain into the EC without the US revolting but the currency problem remained the Achilles' heel of Heath's European policy. However, Heath still held hopes that the second part of his political vision could be realised, namely European union. Sterling had ended up the prisoner of the markets, with the Treasury as a new custodian. Heath, a stalwart believer in the powers of managerial politics, wanted to press ahead with the European project despite the difficulties. After all, his method of steadfastness had got Britain into the EC. October 1973, however, brought new economic shocks to the Western world and that would test the commitments of the EC members and the partnership with the US that Heath had said he sought in February. The British, like the rest of Europe, were dependent on Middle East and African oil supplies. Between them, Britain and the US owned or controlled all of the major oil companies in the free world. For this reason alone it was worth holding close contacts on matters of oil.[243] The British and the US had been worried about what OPEC was up to since the winter of 1970/71, and touched upon the idea of taking a 'stand' against possible OPEC demands, but they believed that provocation could result in interrupted oil supplies.[244] Energy was actually an area where Heath wanted the EC to start, or re-start, its cooperative efforts.[245]

In view of the deteriorating situation in the Middle East, in June 1973 Heath wrote to Nixon of his concerns about the West's heavy dependence on oil from Arab countries. Heath said that the Arab-Israeli conflict might lead to 'our whole industrial power and progress' coming under threat. He added that a frustrated Arab world would 'look for scapegoats and find them in the west'. This could make them hurt the West by the interruption of oil supplies or by the use of its financial muscles. Heath thought that Israeli intransigence would in the end damage 'vital Western interests'. Accordingly, he wanted Nixon to put pressure on Israel to meet Palestinian demands.[246] Heath was advising Nixon in a fashion that almost amounted to a traditional special relationship manner.

Full scale war broke out between Israel and its neighbours on 6 October when Egypt and Syria invaded Israel as the Jews celebrated Yom Kippur. Nixon decided that Israel had to be supported, which resulted in a Saudi Arabian oil embargo against the US, and on 16 October OPEC put up the oil price without talking to the oil consumers.[247] This was only the beginning of a series of price rises. Only days before Heath still hoped that the OPEC demands could be talked down in negotiations by appeals to reason and common interests, but the OPEC preferred drastic action over talks.[248]

By this time the government had realised that the domestic boom it had created had become difficult to sustain.[249] The oils shocks were an added terrible blow for the British economy. However, matters were made much worse when the talks with coal miners broke down in November, resulting in a three-day working week in December.[250] Inflation rose and Barber had to end the growth spurt by taking drastic and severe deflationary measures on 17 December.[251] Heath was defiant. He wanted the upcoming EC Summit in December, in Copenhagen, to pursue European union by 1980, while improving transatlantic relations so as to show that the unity of the Nine contributed to the greater unity of the West.[252]

The Copenhagen Summit, on 14–15 December, agreed that work should continue towards European union following the original time plan.[253] This was in line with what Heath wanted, but not with what turned out to be feasible. The summit also had to decide on a US initiative, led by Kissinger, to instigate an Energy Action Group. The British wanted the Community to be able to attend discussions without a common energy policy. It feared that if the EC insisted on creating one first then it would seem to that the EC was not a reliable 'partner in a crisis'. Attending without a common agenda would also make it easier for Britain to state its concerns.[254] Acting under the pretence that there was a US-European special relationship of mutual trust the British were prepared to forego a common EC standpoint. This of course made it back-sliding into the Anglo-American special relationship easier.

At the summit Kissinger's proposal to work together for a solution to the energy crisis was welcomed.[255] After this warm welcome of Kissinger's proposals there was silence, which began to cause some distress all around. The British believed that it might be due to the fact that 'Dr Kissinger, as is his wont, does not seem to have consulted the other Departments of the Administration'.[256] Kissinger was dissatisfied with the summit. He did not really find it encouraging, except for its stance on the actual problems in the Middle East. He thought that despite the fine words there was no momentum on joint approaches to energy.[257]

By the end of December oil prices rose again, making for a total fivefold increase of the oil price in 1973 alone.[258] Nixon wrote to Heath that the US now had 'a clear indication of the magnitude of the immediate problem we face'. He was grateful for Heath's endorsement of the Kissinger's proposal at the Copenhagen Summit. Nixon looked forward to discussing, later in the spring, with the British a programme for cooperation that the US was about to suggest to the Energy Action Group on the matter.[259]

It seemed to Home that the states were making deals on oil – something which had previously been done by the major oil corporations. He also believed that the British stance within the EC on energy, oil and its connection to other plans was becoming untenable and he wondered whether they should argue that the expected North Sea oil was a British asset until there actually was a European union.[260] Heath's Cabinet was forced to fall back on economic nationalism. It had to let the EC down on energy policy.

In the beginning of January 1974 the French view was exactly what the Americans feared. They wanted an EC policy before sitting down to Kissinger's Energy Action Group.[261] In this moment of crisis it was the US that took the lead, and not the new Europe. The US wanted the foreign ministers of the major industrial countries to meet in the middle of February, to make headway on the energy issues in Washington.[262] Home recommended that Britain should accept swiftly so as not to appear 'lukewarm'.[263] By 9 February, the atmosphere had already turned sour in Washington as the NSC noted that the Community was trying to have a joint approach of its own.[264]

When Europe made no headway, Heath authorised secret help to the US government to prepare for the talks in February. This amounted to rebuilding traditional consultations from the top. It had been Nixon's personal wish to have the help of a high ranking British civil-servant. Heath assented but he knew that it was contrary to his European plans and made it clear that they would have to keep it a secret from Britain's EC partners.[265] It was a curious way to return to the habit of consultations of the Anglo-American special relationship.

On 7 February, Heath sent a message to Nixon that he had decided on a general election to be held on 28 February. He told Nixon that there was no economically feasible solution to the miners' demands, and that there now was a strike. His government had 'decided that the right course is to ask the country to affirm … its support for the Government's position', to fight inflation by voluntary or if need be by statutory means. Heath was unsure as to what impact the election would have on the exchange rate, but he was glad that sterling was floating.[266] Nixon was understanding of Heath's priorities, and added that the US would respond quickly with help and would make arrangements if sterling was to sink.[267] A startling throwback to the sixties, when the US used to sustain sterling, this was indeed a return of sorts to the traditional economic Anglo-American relationship. Sterling did not sink but Heath's majority did, and with it his government. Despite all the efforts of the Heath government, Britain at the end of his government veered back to the Anglo-American economic special relationship that Heath had wanted to transform.

The French found that the Energy 'Conference had been good for nothing'. It had left the French isolated and had exposed all the disagreement within the EC. It had crystallised conflicting positions needlessly. It was clear to both the French and the British that in energy terms, as in monetary affairs, the US had an advantageous position. But, the French thought this increased the need for a Europe acting on its own while the British saw it the other way around; that Europe would lose in any competition with the Americans, and accordingly had to act with them.[268] This was reminiscent of the instincts of both countries after their debacle over Suez in 1956, when the US had put a stop to their efforts to overrun Egypt and regain control over the Suez Channel. The French then turned away from the US and amongst other things towards European integration, whereas Britain faced up to its limits and decided to cooperate with the US.

Alan P. Dobson argues that the Anglo-American special relationship came to an end before Heath became Prime Minister. According to him, the 1967 devaluation of sterling was also a devaluation of the relations.[269] Rajarshi Roy states that the Anglo-American economic special relationship was in decline when Heath and Nixon came to power.[270] However, as shown above, the decline of sterling as a reserve currency was embraced by Heath, who wanted to move away from the old international monetary system and ensure that Britain had a viable currency with which to contribute to European monetary cooperation.

The economic nationalism of Nixon's administration altered the conditions for change from within the system. Heath's plans of bringing a buoyant economy into the EC came to nothing because of the failure of the state engineered expansion of the economy. Even with a successful boom, it is not certain that the EC members were as ready as Heath's Britain to go further with monetary cooperation. However, by not being able to re-join the snake the British government was not even given the chance of trying to fulfil Heath's ideas about European integration and the goals the EC had set itself. Successful economic growth seemed just out of reach. Another reason for the failure was the emergence of a non-system that the US had begun on 15 August 1971 and that Britain advanced, albeit unintentionally, when it floated in the spring of 1972. The British government had thought that the sterling float would be temporary, but it would continue until there again seemed to be a chance of a European cooperation on monetary affairs 15 years later.

Since sterling could not be re-pegged, this meant that Heath's wish to take the lead in deepened European monetary cooperation had faltered before the oil-shocks of 1973. These, in turn, forced the British government to think in terms of economic nationalism and to look first at what would benefit Britain. The US had been willing to help Britain into the EC but the US was no longer engaged enough in Britain to help Heath's plans for a European monetary union. The US had enough economic problems of its own in 1973. The Heath government and the Nixon administration had virtually ended the Anglo-American economic special relationship by ignoring consultations. The Americans eventually had second thoughts about its behaviour towards Britain. Later, both sides worked to restore consultations. As the following chapter will show, consultations in the other power political link in Anglo-American relations – the special nuclear relationship – remained much more consistent.

By 1974 Heath's vision was in tatters, and so was the British economy that had been forced to support a political goal now incomplete. Heath had also tried to change the British post-war consensus with the focus still on the needs of industry. Heath, through Barber, had a firm grip over the domestic economy. When his initial liberal policies failed his government lost credibility since these were widely regarded as an important aim since Heath could not state clearly that they were merely a means to an end – a competitive Britain at the heart of Europe. Anthony Seldon is probably correct in saying that Britain would have become more similar to the economies of the continental European countries had he succeeded.[271]

The monetary catharsis, partly self-imposed, partially forced upon Britain, shifted received wisdom and made way for new monetary thinking and at the same time altered the conditions for any European plans for monetary union. The British government, in order to protect its own fortunes in world on a de facto dollar standard as in 1969, collapsed back into the Anglo-American special relationship, which proves the old adage that all things have to change so things can remain the same.

3
The Anglo-American Nuclear Special Relationship and New Interdependence

Heath's vision of Europe and the nuclear deterrent

Britain's nuclear deterrent was to have at least one of the four Polaris submarines, Resolution, Repulse, Renown and Revenge, patrolling in the North Atlantic at all times. From there one of the nuclear avengers could reach targets in the Soviet Union.[1] These submarines constituted a vital aspect of Britain's defence. Defence was also a key part of Heath's vision of European integration and this chapter shows how his plans for European defence cooperation affected the core of the Anglo-American special relationship – the nuclear relationship.

Hitherto, it has been assumed that the special nuclear relationship was relatively inactive during the Nixon–Heath years. It has been said by John Dumbrell and John Baylis that Britain focused more on updating its deterrent than on European integration in defence.[2] Beatrice Heuser suggests that the update foreclosed any Anglo-French cooperation.[3] All the three mention Heath's interest in developing an Anglo-French nuclear force to be held for Europe in 'trusteeship'.[4] This chapter argues that there was no contradiction between the update and a drive towards European defence integration through Anglo-French cooperation. In fact, nuclear relations with both the US and the French were highly active. Like so many of Heath's ideas Anglo-French cooperation was originally suggested by someone else. In this case by Harold Macmillan, the Prime Minister during the first attempt at EEC membership.[5] Heath belonged to those who believed that the British deal over Polaris with the US had gotten in the way of the first attempt to join the EEC and that it epitomised the difference between Macmillan's and de Gaulle's view of Europe.[6] Heath wanted to overcome any differences between France and Britain and he thought that an Anglo-French nuclear agreement might be necessary for entrance and suggested that it might help to restore the links between France and the other NATO members.[7] This chapter illustrates the actual depth of and the activity of the Anglo-American nuclear relationship, with needs going both ways, and how Britain and the US tried to involve France in a nuclear interdependence.

Was the proposal of an Anglo-French trusteeship only meant to help pave the way for admission into the EC? Heath first suggested collaboration in 1965, and then in his Harvard lectures in 1967 and again to parliament in 1972.[8] He admitted in his lectures that he could not know what the precise requirements of a future European defence system would be. Anglo-French collaboration was intended to make a European defence credible and to create a basis capable of absorbing the rising costs for research and development of future nuclear deterrents, which were likely to be more than 'any individual medium power' could finance. He wanted European defence to make the future EC an equal in the 'Atlantic partnership' with the US. He argued that creating a European force was not an anti-American policy but exactly what the US had advocated less than a decade earlier. He wanted to avoid the kind of disputes that had surrounded the MLF proposal in the early sixties. Instead, progress was to be made by pursuing practical goals instead of specific military designs.[9] This approach could also, if need be, be conducted in secret.

Heath wanted to use or defuse the nuclear issue during the negotiations for EC entry. Depending on whether the issue arose, he would either promise British cooperation in French or European schemes or merely set his suggestion aside while giving the necessary impression that Britain was a reliable partner for future developments. In either case, it was a strong indication that he was prepared to look beyond the Anglo-American nuclear special relationship. However, two things stand out. First the appeal to rationality: of arguing the case in economic terms. Second that he was as specific as he was as to how much European cooperation he eventually wanted. With transatlantic equality as a goal Heath was prepared to do a lot to adapt to European requirements.

The Anglo-American nuclear relationship was usually based on US support for the independent British nuclear deterrent. In many ways it was the inverse of the monetary affairs analysed in the previous chapter. Unlike exchange rates that eventually fluctuated dramatically for all to see, alterations to nuclear affairs were partly secret and made at a different pace. Lord Carrington, Defence Secretary during most of the Heath government, has pointed out that a time-frame of several decades in terms of nuclear planning is to be expected.[10] Carrington and Sir

Alex Douglas-Home (hereafter Home) were the two with whom Heath discussed the key features of his European plans for defence coopera-tion and the British nuclear deterrent.[11] All the three shared a sense of traditional British patriotism.

Carrington, like Home, was loyal to Heath. Christopher Hill and Christopher Lord have pointed to William Wallace's argument that Carrington was almost a 'second Foreign Secretary'.[12] There is some truth in this, especially in terms of Britain's security. He certainly was very involved in discussions with the French about nuclear cooper-ation. Home and Carrington also worked well together. Vis-à-vis the Americans, Home and Carrington had different effects: Home was an insurance policy of the continuity and reliability of the new British gov-ernment. Carrington was instead obsessed by Britain's security and the keeping of the independent deterrent and not prepared to risk American commitments to Europe for Anglo-French adventures.[13] The benefits of this was that it would be possible for Heath's plan in defence to make progress with Home ensuring smooth dealings with the US, while Car-rington kept a keen eye on Britain's own security requirements. This ensured that any efforts would be responsible and not rash. However, the downside was that any changes to British interdependence and the special Anglo-American nuclear relationship would take a lot of time. This was unavoidable since Heath's sense of patriotism obliged him to avoid risking Britain's deterrent. He also believed that Britain needed a viable nuclear deterrent to spur European developments in the defence field once Britain was an EC member.

European defence and the Anglo-American nuclear relationship

Before Heath came to power his predecessor Harold Wilson had elicited a promise from the Nixon administration to disclose to the British if the French approached them over nuclear affairs. The White House did not regard this as promise given to any one administration, but was instead given to Britain.[14] The continuation of this promise also reflected the American assumption that Heath was essentially a traditionalist. The Heath government naturally wanted the promise of information to continue.[15] There was no attempt at creating a distance to the US in this area. This helped foster the impression that the new British government was traditional in its adherence to the special relationship.

However, the Nixon administration was attentive to the future inten-tions of its closest ally. The State Department picked up on speculation about Anglo-French nuclear collaboration. Before the Conservatives were back in power it learned that the Conservative Party had tried to sound out the French as to whether Anglo-French nuclear cooperation would be a part of the negotiations for entry.[16] It turned out that Anglo-French nuclear collaboration fell outside the framework of the EC-negotiations just as nuclear weapons affairs had not been an integral part of the formal negotiations in 1961–63.

US concerns about the British willingness to remain engaged in the world were alleviated by statements by the Heath government in the late fall of 1970. NATO remained the 'first priority' but there was also an increased need for troops in Northern Ireland.[17] Carrington promised to stop cuts in the defence budget. After six years of reductions and changes he wanted to give the armed forces a more stable time. He was not directed by sentimentality. There would be no full reversal of the withdrawal from East of Suez as the Conservative's had pledged before the General Election. It was one of those contested issues that eventually went with a whimper rather than a bang and it petered out in 1970.[18] The international scene had simply changed too much since the late sixties. Instead, renewed commitment to areas traditionally regarded as East of Suez would be made with the existing capability.[19] Like Barber's economic policies, defence policies were intended to help Britain into the EC and to give it a prominent position once inside. Nuclear forces were very important in this respect. However, the policies also had to demonstrate Britain's reliability to the Americans.

The Americans were not concerned that the new British government was abandoning its traditional outlook. The State Department regarded Carrington's statements as a resolute stand to 'maintain Britain's position in world affairs', and the US welcomed the undertaking to halt cuts in the British military budget. Nevertheless, the State Department questioned as to whether this policy change was compatible with the British aim of cutting public expenditures.[20] The American assessment that Britain remained traditionalist was strengthened by Carrington's reaffirmation of support for NATO.[21] A weakened level of deterrence would only provoke the very aggression successfully staved off for so long.

At this time the US was involved in talks on strategic arms limitation, SALT, with the Soviet Union. These talks paradoxically increased the US need for British support. In July 1970 the US approached the British government and asked for the use of the Phoenix Islands in the Pacific for a Missile Monitoring Facility where the US could try out Multiple Independently-targeted Re-entry Vehicles, MIRVs. MIRV technology was a key issue in the Strategic Arms Limitations talks with the Soviet Union, and for security in the West. The only other places to test the new generations of weapons were the Aleutians, 'which would be provocative to the Russians' since it would mean firing in the direction of the Soviet Union, which the Kreml would find very disagreeable, or for the US to use expensive and inaccurate airborne facilities.[22]

During the Johnson administration MIRV technology emerged as the answer to the Soviet Union's Anti Ballistic Missile defences, ABMs. The idea was that instead of more missiles, each missile would carry many more warheads that would be dispersed upon approaching the target and drown-out the ABMs by allowing enough warheads to get through.[23] Without MIRVs retaliation or attack would become difficult giving the Soviets a tactical and perhaps a strategic advantage. These were classical Cold War concerns for both the US as well as Britain.

The Ministry of Defence (MoD) still regarded the US as 'the main ally; their consultation on SALT [was] proof of this'.[24] Likewise the Foreign and Commonwealth Office, the FCO, did not want to endanger these consultations, and argued that the tests were of 'national and to the broader Western defence interest'.[25] The US was very impatient for a response.[26] At the end of July 1970 Home, the Foreign Secretary, told Heath that Britain had to agree since Britain should not harm the US 'in the nuclear field, on which our own nuclear capability heavily depends'.[27]

This was the kind of closeness that was typical of the traditional special nuclear relationship. It demonstrates that it was very active in 1970, with the US banking on a traditional British outlook in regard to security matters. Nevertheless, if known to others, the new use of the islands could disturb British diplomatic attempts to bring about a European defence, since it would show that Britain was still very close to the US and not so oriented towards Europe as the Heath government had claimed.

Yet, in the autumn of 1970 Heath questioned what Britain really got in return for all the facilities to which they had given the US access.[28] He also worried that it could seem as if Britain was unduly favoured. Home rushed to the defence of the existing order and told Heath that '[o]verall the balance seem[ed] to be right' between the US and Britain.[29] There was, of course, from 1958 an agreement to collaborate on issues both of information and equipment and about nuclear weapon technology, such as the agreement on Polaris.[30] There were also joint ventures. Britain provided island dependencies as 'real estate' while the US contributed technology and facilities.[31] In 1970, Britain and the

US cooperated in the construction of bases in the Indian Ocean to counteract the growing influence of the Soviet Navy.[32] Other bases were used for joint intelligence monitoring of others including the French.[33] Whether Heath liked it or not he had inherited a functioning and active Anglo-American special nuclear relationship.

It was not only the British who were concerned about its alliance partners. While on a visit to New York in October, Heath met a group of distinguished senior US statesmen who told him that the US nuclear advantage over the Soviet Union, which had held the peace for 25 years, was slipping fast.[34] Combined with the issues of American involvement in Vietnam and American domestic problems the British worried about the US ability to live up to its European defence obligations, which pointed to the need to improve the alliance.

Nixon and Heath shared a desire to reform the alliance by cutting costs and modernisation. Heath believed that the alliance would benefit from a more independent Western European element. The US wanted its allies to shoulder more of the costs.[35] In 1970, the US State Department was not worried about European defence efforts or about European armament cooperation. It anticipated that Britain would try to be self-sufficient in terms of arms production. Accordingly, the European arms industries would compete with each other and each bear the burden of research and development. This would benefit American arms exports.[36] In terms of its size and its resources the US had the benefits of scale and could easily compete with any state in Europe. Later, in the autumn of 1971, when the EC negotiations were over, the US Embassy in London warned Washington about complacency. It pointed out that Britain was already a part of the European defence market on European projects, like MRCA, Jaguar, Martel, Exocet and so forth. This partly reflected British wariness of US competition, and partly a desire to have 'economies of scale'.[37] However, since Britain was already involved in European armament production, it was not a reason for the US to reconsider the benefits of Britain becoming an EC member.

The Eurogroup was one arena for discussing burden sharing. The members were the Defence Secretaries of the European NATO members, who aimed to demonstrate increased European unity. It was also a venue for Britain to talk to five of the EC countries. France was not a member of the group, which made it difficult to build on an initiative by Nixon in December 1970 that urged better use of resources and more cooperation between the allies in Western Europe and the US. The efforts of the Eurogroup also symbolised the British and West German commitment to a viable NATO and for the British it constituted a possible means to involve France again. The French instead wanted to revive the Western European Union, the WEU, as the centre for European Defence Efforts.[38] The WEU was with but not of NATO, however, it was also a potential basis for an Anglo-French nuclear 'trusteeship', other than NATO.[39] In December 1970 a Eurogroup meeting was held that led to the creation of a European Defence Improvement Programme, hoping that with investments in European defences it could keep the American commitment, but because its funds were small it did not greatly impress the US.[40]

Once in government, Heath wanted to know how to increase European defence cooperation in the widest sense.[41] Heath wanted more Western European unity in defence and in December he suggested European Defence Community. It met with little continental enthusiasm.[42] After this attempt Heath would concentrate on setting up a new nuclear interdependence for three reasons. First, Britain's considerable capability in the defence industries was supposed to help Britain attain leverage in the EC after entry. Carrington opposed the most commonly suggested solution for increased European defence cooperation – the standardisation of weapons and weapons procurement that would mean 'more defence per £'. Logic suggested that there was no need for each European state to have its own capability in every field.[43] This was the kind of rational argument that Heath was apt to use in other circumstances. However, standardisation could potentially mean dismantling national defence industries. The British government was not prepared to do that.

Second, the FCO indicated a more immediate dilemma. It warned Carrington and Heath that any drive towards closer European defence was likely to accelerate the emergence of problems within the Atlantic alliance, with the result that the Anglo-American ' "special relationship" with the United States in intelligence and nuclear affairs would be more quickly eroded'.[44] At the same time the US wanted Britain to join the EC. Yet, neither the British nor the Americans had any specific plans for European defence. Defence was not part of the EC negotiations and hence not a problem in the membership negotiations. The lack of progress on this issue was, however, a potential problem for Heath's ideas about integration and a future Anglo-American special relationship.

Third, the drawback was that Britain was committed to a multilateral aim – to create an improved cohesive European defence. This became evident when Carrington met his French counterpart Michel Debré on 20 November 1970. He was the most significant French interlocutor in regard to defence and an old school Gaullist; British scepticism about

American reliability paled in comparison with the disdain in which Debré held the other NATO members. He believed that without the Americans the others in Europe, except for France and Britain, would go neutral. He favoured bilateral approaches and dismissed Carrington's query about a common European defence organisation. According to Debré, 'everything pointed to closer Anglo/French co-operation' but he emphasised that it 'was now really up to the UK'. Despite the differences in approach Carrington was cautiously optimistic about future 'areas of co-operation' opening up.[45]

However, the basic outlines of a political dilemma were already evident; forging a European defence without France and nuclear weapons was hardly credible, yet bilateral collaboration with France meant the means hindering the aim, which was a common European effort. To find a way out of this impasse Britain had to consort with the US. Paradoxically, Heath's vision for a future European defence became dependent on more, not less, of a well-functioning Anglo-American special relationship in the security field, including close consultations. Therefore, the Americans would be told of what seemed as an opening of the door to cooperation by Debré's.[46] The Heath government had to develop a strategy to alter British nuclear interdependence that would allow Britain to work towards the aim of a European defence around a European nuclear capability under a NATO roof.

This required working with the Americans and not against them. When Heath brought up Anglo-French collaboration during his Washington visit in December 1970 Nixon told him that as far as he was concerned the British had 'a great deal of running room' in the hope that it would bring the French closer to NATO.[47] Nixon only supported discussions and not wholesale support for new schemes. Kissinger explained the electoral risks that the President was running if his assent even to go this far became known.[48] Nixon was well aware that such talks were not needed for British EC negotiations and that they in fact went further towards a more cohesive Europe.

The US did not have a plan for restructuring the alliance and the White House was prepared to rely on the Heath government for three reasons. First, the Heath government apparently remained a trustworthy partner. Second, Heath's suggestions for alliance reform appeared similar to the US own intentions and could conceivably achieve some of the things the Nixon administration wanted, such as greater burden sharing. Third, the US needed the Anglo-American nuclear special relationship much more than usual.

Just before their December meeting, Heath and Nixon agreed to extend the traditional agreement that the US would consult with the British government before using US nuclear weapons in Britain for anti-submarine warfare nuclear weapons and to ensure that the same applied to certain storages of nuclear weapons.[49] Heath signed up to the smooth continuation of a very active Anglo-American nuclear special relationship. It was the only way to maintain Britain's security while his government developed a policy that could fulfil his plans for European defence cooperation.

A 'three way exchange'

After the December 1970 summit the British government had to use the opportunity that Nixon had given it to discuss nuclear matters with the French. It also had to pursue the needs of its own deterrent. Fortunately, the EC negotiations had not provoked any problems over the independent nuclear deterrent and its needs. There was a small interruption in April 1971 when the NATO Secretary General, Joseph Luns, gave reporters the impression that Geoffrey Rippon had been advised to accommodate the French by some action in the nuclear field. Rippon successfully downplayed the issue later the same day.[50] However, the nuclear question tore at the British nerves and anything that seemed to disrupt Anglo-French understanding or the Anglo-American nuclear special relationship rattled the Heath government.

Despite the success in keeping the issue away from public debate the FCO and the MoD had not been able to agree on an approach.[51] Home believed that in order for new nuclear cooperation to work, the US had to give its 'blessing', which required some kind of credible re-involvement of France in the defence system of Western Europe. In March 1971 he reminded Heath that they had told Nixon that they would try and make France 'more "outward looking"'. The only way to do so, according to Home, was to tempt France with nuclear collaboration and not by conventional defence efforts.[52] Carrington disagreed with Home's view that nuclear defence cooperation was a necessity for European defence initiatives to work. Carrington feared that such initiatives might put Britain's own deterrent at risk, since an approach to the French might jeopardise Britain's own crucial relationship with the US.[53] Heath's vision, however, required Anglo-French nuclear cooperation.

Another who favoured the Anglo-American link was Sir Burke Trend, the Cabinet Secretary, who had little enthusiasm for Heath's European plans.[54] Despite this he offered an argument in favour of Heath's ideas.

On the one hand he did believe that '[i]t would be fatal to sacrifice the substance for the shadow'.[55] They could not take unnecessary risks but there was no risk-free option. Doing nothing was also a risk – since they could not know for how long the US would continue its nuclear relationship with Britain if the British did nothing to begin a nuclear collaboration with the French.[56] British EC membership might make a similar change in Britain's nuclear interdependence seem natural to the US. Accordingly, even Atlanticists were not certain that an adherence to the Anglo-American nuclear interdependence offered more security.

Unlike Trend, Carrington was not an Atlanticist. For Carrington Britain's security came first. As long as Britain's security was safeguarded Carrington was prepared to go along with Heath's ideas. In fact he would prefer that Britain did as much as possible itself, minimising future dependence, but that was the most expensive position. From the start of the government, Carrington had pushed for a study of an improved deterrent. He was opposed by Solly Zuckerman, the government's chief scientific adviser, who would have none of Carrington's costly plans and cautioned Heath against an escalating defence budget. Zuckerman thought that Carrington exaggerated the dangers since the scenario he presented was the unlikely case of a separate British strike against the Soviet Union without the US. According to Zuckerman, Soviet ABMs would easily be overwhelmed if the British and the US fired their missiles together.[57] However, having nuclear weapons that could be used separately and effectively was the real interpretation of what was meant by an independent deterrent. Zuckerman argued that Carrington's ideas might have appeared as an endorsement for British nuclear independence but in fact it was the opposite. According to him Carrington's advice required greater US assistance to improve the deterrent making an agreement with France on nuclear policy less likely.[58] Zuckerman had laid bare the nerve that made the government twitch. The study went ahead but a solution for the strains had to be found, which protected Heath's plans and safeguarded an adequate level of security.

The original intention in the fifties had been to have a deterrent, which was truly independent.[59] This had become impossible due to the costs and problems of research. However, dependence, on the US, did not necessarily create trust. It could also create apprehension about the longevity of the commitment. The US external actions and its pressure on its allies for more burden sharing had not alleviated French or British misgivings. In view of détente and US-Soviet arms talks and political problems in the US, Heath's original view of Anglo-French nuclear cooperation to safeguard Europe seemed remarkably prescient. If American and European security was not always intertwined, Europe had to build up its defences, but rather than having many attempts at nuclear deterrents, which would undermine NATO and the efforts at greater spending on conventional arms, a European nuclear capability was best served by an effort of the existing European nuclear powers in a European framework.

The ongoing EC negotiations made the nuclear issue sensitive not only with the Six but also with the US. In April 1971 the British Ambassador to Washington Lord Cromer advised Heath that were the British to make 'an approach now, whatever our denials, [it] might be seen by the Americans, in the context of the E.E.C. negotiations, as an attempt to bribe the French with United States' secrets'.[60] Such apprehensions had surfaced during the first application.[61] Home understood the fears. It was pivotal that they should not spoil the emergence of a US–EC special relationship with a short-sighted deal that would leave them half-way to the Heath's goal of further European integration, that is only attaining British accession. If they could strike up a relationship with the French then the US would like it to be a 'three way exchange' and in line with what Nixon had said in December according to Home. At that time Kissinger had warned them about the intrinsic difficulties involved in the matter. Hence, Heath in 1971 was not in a position to say more to Pompidou than Carrington had said to Debré the previous year. Both Home and Carrington recommended delaying approaches to Pompidou on defence until after both the EC negotiations and Heath's summit with Pompidou were over.[62] Heath agreed.

Home and Carrington were instrumental in the three-way formula being adopted. There would be no sudden switch of interdependence but only change under the auspices of a coordinated Anglo-American approach. This would not risk the update of the deterrent. The choice to pursue the strategy of a three-way exchange at the same time as the British received assistance for its update was a solution that offered a seamless transfer from the Anglo-American nuclear special relationship to a new nuclear interdependence and European defence cooperation.

The compliance of the Nixon administration in the changed nuclear interdependence had less to do with American use of the Anglo-American nuclear special relationship and more to do with the US not yet having decided on what approach to take on nuclear strategy. When Nixon took office the era of easy American nuclear superiority was coming to a close. This quickly helped to usher in the era of super power détente but the administration had no set plans for how to adapt US nuclear strategy to requirements of the new era.[63] The US Department of Defense recognised that the Heath government's decision to go ahead with a study for an update had given earlier preparations a considerable push.[64] In April, Nixon ordered a study of Anglo-American nuclear relations, not because of Britain's European plans, but to deal with the issue of the capability of Britain's existing deterrent and what that would mean in terms of British requests.[65] However, a response was delayed because the NSC was also preparing an analysis of French nuclear affairs.[66] In both cases it was a matter of American reaction rather than initiating action.

The need to begin Anglo-American cooperation on a study for an update came at the same time as the EC negotiations approached their final weeks at the end of the spring of 1971. The British study to update its existing Polaris system focused on the Super Antelope project, later known as Chevaline, which was designed to break through Soviet ABM systems. The British requested advice from American experts, information from underground American nuclear tests and hoped to be able to use, if the need arose, a US testing facility in New Mexico. However, there were US concerns that the British wish to update its deterrent might conflict with Britain's goal of becoming an EC member. In fact, the US was so keen on this that it hesitated in its traditional support for the Anglo-American relationship, wishing for a smooth development on nuclear affairs. The CIA was worried that if American assistance became known it might endanger both US-French relations as well as Britain's EC entry. Helmut Sonnenfeldt, of the NSC staff, listed the objections to a secret widening of the Anglo-American nuclear relationship. First of all, the administration put not only Britain's EC entry at risk, but also the efforts towards more European defence collaboration, which were hoped to relieve the US of some of the defence burden. It might also at some stage conflict with SALT. However, the US was already involved in the efforts at a British update. He therefore recommended that the US should not commit itself to more than the study of an update so as to retain maximum flexibility at a later stage.[67] The White House obviously did not have an initiative on transatlantic nuclear relations of its own ready. It remained reactive which fitted its commitment to the British of keeping a low profile.

Keeping Anglo-American-French relations free of friction was easier said than done considering the strained nerves of the British government. A new challenge presented itself on 28 April when Kissinger asked Cromer to convey information in strictest secrecy about a new American initiative on French nuclear cooperation to Heath.[68] This opened up two possible nightmare scenarios. Sir Denis Greenhill, the Permanent

Under-Secretary at the FCO, worried that the US and the French would agree to a far reaching bilateral agreement making it difficult for Britain 'to get into the act at a later stage'. It did not bode well that this came just before Heath was to meet Pompidou to wrap up the EC negotiations.[69] Heath was concerned about the other scenario; that it would look as if the British had put the US up to it. Heath worried about reliving the Nassau agreement, which allowed Britain to buy Polaris missiles, and which many believed had destroyed the chances of British EEC entry in 1963.[70] At the time de Gaulle had probably been insulted by the US offer to buy Polaris when it was first offered to the British, seeing it as a snub and put down of France's capabilities.[71] Matters would be made worse if Pompidou rejected an American initiative.

Matters were made worse by Kissinger who, in April, was 'fishing for an invitation' to Britain.[72] The British did not actually know why he wanted to come. Notwithstanding their worries he wanted the British to help find 'a proper cover story'. They knew that his preference was for June, which was initially the month when Heath and Pompidou were expected to meet.[73] Understandably, this made London very anxious. Heath wanted to try and delay the visit until after the meeting with Pompidou so as not to add to suspicions of British-American collusion.[74]

In early May 1971 Home took the precaution of instructing Cromer to make it absolutely clear to the Americans that they could not tell the French that the British had any prior knowledge of a new initiative. He was also instructed to say that Heath would only speak in general on nuclear matters to Pompidou and that there was no 'blueprint for closer defence collaboration with France'.[75] This was presumably to reassure the American administration which the British assumed was as fidgety as they themselves were. The British wanted to stave off possible American attempts at striking a deal with France before the British could develop a three-way strategy.

The nervous tension of the British found its outlet in mistrust of the US. There was no small sense of taking a leap into the dark. After all, Britain was leading the changes towards a new interdependence. This was a risk for Britain. If it went very wrong it could accelerate decline and end Britain's great power status. The British government wanted to get out of decline and not provoke a further reduction of its precarious status as a great power. Its interpretation of the American behaviour made it speculate whether the US was wrecking the EC negotiations by design or by accident.

On 13 March, however, Kissinger got back to them saying that he understood the ' "Trojan horse" significance' if he came to London just before Heath was to see Pompidou. The British could breathe a sigh of relief. It turned out that their fears were unfounded. The US-French nuclear agreement was on a low level and according to Kissinger entirely unconnected to the impending Heath–Pompidou meeting. Kissinger stated that he actually wanted to improve relations with France with a new move but said that it would have to wait until after Nixon was re-elected, which would be close to the time of the now very likely British EC entry.[76] The American administration was actually taking pains to ensure good relations with the French, which could only improve the chances for a three-way exchange. Consequently, Heath could meet Pompidou without fear of being upstaged by the Americans. The Heath–Pompidou Summit itself was something of an anti-climax in regard to defence, which was barely touched upon.[77] The Anglo-American relationship did not stir up any problems nor did Heath cause any by bringing up his own ideas about European defence and collaboration. Since the US had to be won for the three-way format Heath was not yet prepared to take the plunge.

However, Kissinger remained secretive about the purpose of his travels.[78] The State Department had wanted to tread carefully, since it knew that the Heath government had 'adopted a pragmatic, basically self-interested approach to foreign relations'.[79] It did not want Kissinger and the NSC to provoke a reappraisal of the Anglo-American defence relationship. Finally on 1 June, Kissinger let Heath know the real reason for his wanting to come to London. It was because Kissinger was about to begin secret talks in Paris with North Vietnam. He needed the British to help 'connive in a cover plan' so that he could travel clandestinely to France.[80] The British agreed to help.[81]

At the same time, the State Department, the Department of Defense and the Joint Chiefs of Staff all supported the proposal that the US should help with the British study for a nuclear update – an attitude that represented the best special relationship tradition. It was recommended by Kissinger.[82] He, nevertheless, advised Nixon against a deepening of the Anglo-American relationship to the point where an 'Anglo-French or West European defense cooperation after likely British entry into the Community' was put at risk.[83] The White House was not yet prepared to underwrite Heath's schemes. The Nixon administration wanted to keep its long-term policy option open since it did not have a clear nuclear strategy. In any case, it only expected possible Anglo-French nuclear collaboration to ensue when 'European construction' had gone further.[84] Consequently, Nixon approved continued US cooperation on the study of a British update.[85] The British government's apprehensions were clearly exaggerated. In fact, the outlook of the White House indicated that a three-way strategy might be feasible.

The Nixon administration was aware that Anglo-American nuclear collaboration could be a problem for the British with the French until entry. On the other hand, it knew that British requests were ultimately tied to the overall strategy of the Heath government to forge a new Anglo-French interdependence as a basis for European defence. The White House feared that if it curtailed support for the British deterrent too soon, in an attempt to retain US flexibility to work out a strategy, a ' "Skybolt-type" situation' might arise.[86] Skybolt was an air-launched missile which the US regarded as being superseded by new technology. Therefore, the US cancelled the production and selling of Skybolt technology to Britain in 1962, suddenly leaving the British without a credible deterrent. At Nassau, Macmillan had then made a deal with Kennedy, ensuring that Britain received viable Polaris missile technology.[87] The US did not want to confront the British with a drastic cancellation of support and then be forced to solve the situation by a new deal in accordance with the traditional nuclear special relationship, which, if public, could undermine the progress and flexibility of US diplomacy.[88]

Trend used Kissinger's visit to Britain, at the end of July, to 'test the temperature of Anglo-American relations at the top', meaning the White House, as opposed to relations with the State Department and the Pentagon. Trend and Kissinger were fairly close and Kissinger sought to calm British worries about the Anglo-American nuclear relationship.[89] He made a careful and cursory remark to Trend that reflected that the administration had not yet made up its mind about nuclear strategy. To Trend, however, the National Security Adviser's comments appeared as being mutually exclusive remarks. On the one hand, Kissinger said that the US would not be led into a nuclear war with the Soviet Union by a third party. On the other hand, he did not favour a world where the Soviet Union and the US were the only nuclear powers. Trend understood him to mean that the US would only accept a third nuclear entity that was responsible, meaning strong and independent. The British naturally interpreted this as a description of their own future reliable leadership in a Western Europe able to deter the Soviet Union, without involving the US in any nuclear exchange.[90] Keeping the US out of the conflict was a potential benefit to the US of the creation of a European defence with nuclear weapons.

Kissinger's suggestions implied the acceptance of an economically as well as militarily viable Europe. As seen in Chapter 2, the US balance of payments problems were growing during the spring of 1971, which possibly contributed to enhancing the advantages of a more independent Europe that would mean lesser overseas defence costs for the US.[91] While the White House was not exalted in its support for Heath's vision in the nuclear field, this depended on a wish to avoid transatlantic rifts by keeping a low profile. This would ensure both British entry and retain a maximum of flexibility to develop a US policy at a later stage. Nevertheless, without a new long-term US nuclear strategy of its own, which convinced the Europeans, the US followed the Heath government's strategy in pursuit of Heath's ideas for European integration. The day after Trend's meeting with Kissinger, Heath approved a message to Nixon saying amongst other things 'that the longer term aim of closer co-operation with the French may in the end lead us to contemplate some form of collaboration with them in the field of nuclear defence'.[92] This was the real beginning of the pursuit of a three-way strategy.

The economic turmoil caused by Nixon's economic measures on 15 August could have offered an opportunity to approach the French on defence, by arguing for the economic benefits of cooperation. However, an appeal of economic reasons might make Britain look weak. Furthermore, Heath was, clearly, not prepared to jeopardise US help with the update. He criticised US actions, but there were limits to the risks he was prepared to take with Britain's security and hence to his temporary distancing from the US in the autumn of 1971.

The question was also what kind of nuclear weapons to discuss with the French. The Labour government had been close to West German thinking on tactical nuclear weapons.[93] Working with the French on tactical nuclear weapons could cause problems with the West Germans. The French had curtailed the possibility of technological cooperation on tactical nuclear weapons since they had just developed their own tactical missile; the Pluton system.[94] Hence, the French were unlikely to be tempted by cooperation in this field. The following year, France decided to deploy it on its own border, which was not a good sign for the Germans since the range of Pluton was such that '[i]t would be bound to kill millions of Germans after the battle for Europe had been lost'.[95] There was no possibility to involve West Germany in the British plans for Anglo-French cooperation. It was also clear that any Anglo-French cooperation would be about the next generation of strategic deterrents.

On 22 September 1971, Carrington again met Debré. The British did not yet think the time was ripe for discussions about a new defence initiative such as a 'European Defence Organization'. Although the British government knew where it wanted to go, it did not know how to proceed with the French. NATO was a divisive issue but the British hoped to lure the French away from their bilateral attitude by tempting them with membership in the Eurogroup.[96] That, however, also involved West Germany.

Always mindful of Britain's safety, Carrington claimed to share Debré's fears that the US would use future talks with the Soviet Union on Mutual and Balanced Force Reductions, MBFR, 'as a cloak for withdrawal'. Debré agreed and described what he saw as the flaw in the US logic, which was that the Americans were mistaken in their assumption that the ongoing SALT talks with the Russians would allow them to simultaneously convince the Europeans to do more. Instead, most European states would only lose heart and do even less according to Debré. Carrington pointed out that this would make the British and French nuclear arsenals even more important, adding that Britain's ties to the US did not necessarily apply to the longer perspective, which could make Anglo-French collaboration possible. Debré welcomed this but was unsure as to whether they should cooperate on more than equipment.[97]

The French and British positions had not yet crystallised. They did not talk past each other. Their perspectives were not the same; they merely overlapped. The question is just how much they really overlapped. Debré wanted Anglo-French collaboration that excluded other European states and West Germany in particular. The British saw collaboration as the centre piece of a wider European defence effort and were quite clear that American acquiescence and assistance were necessary to make progress possible if a sufficient measure of security was to be retained in the meantime.

The necessary update and 'the only card'

Only Home, Carrington and Greenhill knew what Nixon and Heath had said about the Anglo-French nuclear deterrent when they met at Bermuda at the end of 1971. There, it emerged that the Americans were prepared in principle to extend their nuclear talks with the French to a trilateral collaboration, but that this was not part of present policy. In any case the State Department wanted to go slowly with the French before presenting them with such a challenge.[98] It was a potentially radically new departure for all involved.

Given the sensitive nature of the idea, it was clear that Nixon did not want public discussion about it in 1972 – the year of his re-election campaign. He agreed that the British could talk about it but only with Pompidou, or as Nixon put it, 'just do it and don't tell anybody'. The

British felt that this was difficult since they might feel obliged to inform the Germans as well.[99] However, Nixon had also asked them not to 'let it go any further' than talks.[100] After all it might not have been prudent to tempt fate when they had come this far.

Pompidou's support for the Anglo-French consultations, which Debré and Carrington had talked about, was necessary even if only to find out the facts and concerns about their respective deterrent. The British knew that Pompidou would avoid everything that seemed like an attempt at Anglo-American collusion aimed at re-integrating France back into NATO. The British, unlike the French, saw their own security as an integral part of the security for the whole of Western Europe. Therefore the French had to be made aware that this could mean that the West Germans had to be informed if there were Anglo-French talks. However, requesting consultations with the French was a significant step because the British would 'for the first time be formally telling the French that [they] would like to discuss co-operating with them'.[101] Although the strategy the British had chosen was slow, it had finally begun to make headway.

At every step, the British became even more apprehensive about US intentions. In the middle of February 1972 the British learned that the US would assist France with operational safety measures.[102] This was something which the French had asked for already in 1964 but were only now receiving. Following Pompidou's visit to Washington in 1970, the US and France had re-launched their joint steering committee on military technology that had been dormant for the later part of the de Gaulle era.[103] The British feared that US-French relations could lead from the establishment of two bilateral relations to three separate bilateral relationships instead of the preferred tripartite collaboration.[104] Such a scenario would of course significantly reduce Britain's role. The British did not blame the French for this potential development, since the French affinity for bilateral relations was established, but the British were worried about the US taking advantage of it. The British had become accustomed to the US taking the lead on many issues, and now when it was up to the British to make progress they were unused to it. This may have contributed to unease and suspicions about the US willingness to let the British pursue its three-way approach.

In the early spring of 1972 Debré was about to state publicly that if faced with 'a great security problem' Britain and France would be close. On the other hand, he also favoured the US presence in West Germany, because he did not favour a West German nuclear force. Such a force, he claimed, would have 'such consequences that a page in our history would be turned'. This was, remarkably, like a call for the status quo. His thinking was also much more concerned with the Germans than the Soviet Union.[105] Heath's vision did not square with Debré's Gaullism, and it was obvious that in order to get somewhere, Heath would primarily have to work through Pompidou and avoid involving the West Germans.

Heath stated his case when he met Pompidou in March 1972. As was his way he referred back to his Harvard lectures from 1967. He said that his views had been made known then and that he had repeated them to Nixon.[106] Pompidou was already acquainted with Heath's lectures. After having read a translation of them by Michel Jobert, his secretary general at the Elysée, he was convinced that he could collaborate with Heath.[107] Clearly, Heath's ideas had the desired effect of making Pompidou amenable to British entry. The question was if he also favoured the implications of Heath's ideas about defence.

Although Heath wanted a European defence it would not have been prudent to reiterate his views publicly during the US presidential election. The last thing his plans needed was to be drawn into the American presidential election.[108] Heath told Pompidou that the 'enlarged European Community would be the most powerful trading bloc the world had ever seen' yet it was vulnerable since an American decision, such as on 15 August 1971, could hit it 'out of the blue' and surprise and upset European policies. He warned that with a person like Connally as President, the EC could be compelled to sign trade and monetary deals under the threat of a US withdrawal. Heath explained that he would welcome greater cooperation in defence as well as in the nuclear field, and he added that he disagreed with Macmillan's policies, and that he instead sought a 'closer relationship' with France after enlargement.[109] Macmillan had wanted Britain to join and lead the EEC while maintaining Britain's special relationship with the US.[110]

The repudiation of Macmillan's European policy was significant and demonstrates that he wanted to follow through on creating a US–EC special relationship and ease out the 'special' ties to the US. In these circumstances it referred directly to the British deterrent and its link with the Anglo-American nuclear special relationship. It demonstrates that Heath intended a complete reorientation of the fundaments of Britain's security policy and consequently the emphasis of its foreign policy allegiance.

Heath understood that 'preparation in the nuclear field required the longest preparatory period of them all'. Since he assumed that France like Britain intended to remain a nuclear power, he hoped that they could pursue the idea that Carrington and Debré had touched on when they last met; 'if the French and British time phasing could be slotted together, there could be useful opportunities for them both' according to Heath.[111] Pompidou agreed to talks – but only that. He did not limit France to talks out of consideration for American sensibilities during the presidential election, but due to concern about the reactions of the West Germans and the Soviet Union.[112]

Pompidou said that his own view on security was 'childishly simple'. In many respects it was similar to Debré's and revolved around the nationhood of Germany, which to Pompidou constituted an 'unknown quantity'. He also feared a German finger on a nuclear trigger. He said that France had 'paid a great price' in having nuclear weapons and although the French deterrent was weak in terms of credibility, it was independent. He pointed out that change had to be initiated by the British. Heath convinced him to instruct their respective Defence Secretaries to continue discussions. They also agreed to publicly deny that they had talked about defence and nuclear collaboration.[113] Both clearly saw the nuclear deterrent as the key to a future European defence effort. The difference was that Heath was ready to forge this entity and Pompidou wanted it to evolve. The British wanted to establish a new Anglo-French interdependence with the assistance of the US. The French of course had to be convinced that this new three-way exchange was possible. In April one senior adviser close to Pompidou told the British that Kissinger had let the French know that Nixon now approved of Anglo-French talks on nuclear cooperation going ahead and that Nixon believed 'that it would be necessary to release Britain from her obligations to the US in order to facilitate this'.[114] This was promising for Heath's vision.

There was, however, one fundamental difference between the French and the British. Namely the interpretation of what was meant by an independent deterrent. The British, as seen above, meant a deterrent that could be fired on its own and that could strike the Soviet Union. The French also meant a deterrent that could be used at their own discretion, but also one that did not depend on the US for technology. Had the British been less anxious about the talks between the French and the Americans on nuclear matters, then these talks could actually have been regarded as favourable French reinterpretations of its nuclear interdependence towards something closer to the British standard.

In May, Heath told the French Ambassador that defence was '[u]nlike those subjects dealt with in the Treaty of Rome, which could be expected to develop along paths already laid down, it would be necessary for deliberate and conscious decisions to be taken on the defence side. This was necessary because weapons had to be ready at a certain time.'[115] Heath had to convince the French not only that defence could not just be allowed to evolve since it was concerned about security, but also that it was inherently different from the other processes of integration. In June 1972 the French Embassy was making enquiries about what kind of venues there were for defence cooperation; asking both about the WEU and the Eurogroup.[116] This was seen as another sign that the French were actively considering working with the British, since they had stayed away from the WEU in 1969, when Britain had made it a venue for its aspirations to join the EEC in the sixties.[117] Either could work as a vehicle for European defence, although the Eurogroup was closer to NATO and the WEU was traditionally dominated by the French.

With Debré still at the rudder of French defence policy, France accepted preparations for talks between military personnel in July. This was assumed to reflect a healthy French realisation that they, like the British, were concerned about the size of the defence budget and especially the costs of their deterrent and that consequently Debré was forced towards the only opening allowed by his political tradition – the bilateral approach.[118] The British had in fact been surprised by how accommodating Debré was.[119] The French did not, however, give an inch to the West Germans. In the summer of 1972 Pompidou was alleged to have said to the Belgian Foreign Minister 'with a bluntness bordering on rudeness' that the French would never accept West German participation in an Anglo-French collaboration on a European nuclear force and therefore nothing could be done.[120] This underlined to the British the importance of not informing other Europeans about the talks.

This British caution did not apply to talks with the Americans, both because they needed the US support for their study on Chevaline, and since the SALT negotiations, further discussed in Chapter 5, could determine the viability of the British deterrent. The pace of the Soviet Union's development of its ABM defence pressured Britain to seek an update to its system by 1975. Otherwise it could not count on having an effective threat against Moscow. In nuclear affairs that was not a lot of time. Even if US diplomacy was successful, SALT might actually make Britain worse off for the reason that the ABMs could remain while the US became committed to limiting its support for the British deterrent. New treaties and the US Congress could prevent even a sympathetic president from helping Britain to update its deterrent.[121] The British were very eager to have close consultations on nuclear relations. This was easier than in economic affairs. They were bound by the intimate continuously on-going intelligence cooperation which directly related to nuclear affairs.

While the US and Britain had a shared perspective on the Cold War both France and Britain were concerned about SALT and their respective budget constraints. The first SALT agreement, which was signed in May, severely restricted the construction of ABM defences and for a few months it seemed as if it gave the British valuable breathing space to analyse necessary requirements.[122] Nevertheless, US diplomacy was not comforting to the security-minded Carrington. When he met his US opposite number, Melvin Laird, in October 1972 he informed him about his apprehensions that the 'set pattern of the last 20 years' was falling apart and that this deconstruction process would be accelerated if it appeared as if SALT, MBFR and the planned European security conference settled superpower issues at the expense of American relations with Europe. Laird told him that Nixon knew of the dangers.[123]

Despite the respite produced by the ABM Treaty, which was concluded satisfying for British security concerns, it was obvious by the summer of 1972 that the research for Super Antelope or Chevaline was very costly; money that had to be wrenched from a reluctant Treasury. The British also considered buying the American-made Poseidon missile instead, or making a combination of both systems named Hybrid (or Stag); but none of them were planned to carry MIRV technology. For the British, these were matters of updating that did not conflict with the possibility of working with the French on the technological development of a completely new successor system.[124] Nevertheless, the update options were all to a lesser or greater degree dependent on collaboration with the US, which made the update a potentially sensitive matter if there was to be a three-way exchange.

Although many factors seemed to favour the British approach on shifting nuclear interdependence, the main problem was that the adopted strategy worked only slowly and time was against it. Ironically, when the ABM Treaty dispelled the immediate concerns to British security the British economic situation grew worse with possible consequences for the spending of the MoD. Trend let Heath know that he thought it wrong of Barber to bring fiscal considerations to bear on the deterrent. For Trend, 'the issue [was] not economic but political'; the independent nuclear deterrent was an 'indispensable... attribute of a sovereign State in our position'.[125] Carrington, Home and Heath were bound to agree.

The MoD took a similar view; the only rationale for a British deterrent was that it was independent. The size of the deterrent was marginal if set against the US nuclear armaments, but its very independence increased Soviet uncertainty about Western responses to aggression. This made the deterrent viable and its use more credible, especially if the US nuclear guarantee wavered and the Soviets sought to try and limit a conflict to Europe.[126] The deterrent stood between Britain and inevitable decline. And Heath's plans were all about avoiding the loss of great power status and influence. European unity only made sense if Britain became a leading member. Any compromise on the way to European unity could only be one of means, not ends. The deterrent could not be compromised away since it would underwrite the final goal of giving Britain a leading position in a united Europe.

Carrington defended the costs of the deterrent claiming that it had been kept 'on the cheap'.[127] This fact had probably spared the nuclear dimension of British defence from a considerable amount of fiscal scrutiny in the past. The research for the update, however, was costing considerably more than originally calculated. Despite the worsening economic situation Carrington, in November 1972, recommended increased defence spending. He reasoned that if the government wanted to strengthen NATO and take the lead in European defence, Britain could not spend less on conventional defence. In fact, it had to be prepared to spend more, especially if it was to bolster the Europeans in case of an American withdrawal.[128] His plans required Britain to spend even more of its GNP on defence, despite the fact that it already spent a greater share of its GNP than France or Germany spent.[129] Worse, Britain had a smaller GNP than either France or West Germany. Given the economic outlook, increased defence spending might not be acceptable to the public so Trend recommended to Heath that they hide the rising costs, after a year or so, by saying that the expected costs were 'merely a continuation of the existing trend'.[130] This was another example of how Heath was forced to hide a policy vital to his European vision.

The economic consideration highlighted the concerns about the deterrent and possible collaboration with others at a gathering of Ministers on 14 December 1972 to discuss how to proceed. Carrington, as always, made a strong case for the relevance of the deterrent, making it clear that the opinion of the Chiefs of Staff was that the 'strategic deterrent was the cornerstone of [British] security' and that Britain should not accept a situation in which France would be the only remaining European nuclear power. Unrepentantly security-minded, he recommended that the British should take no chances and therefore update their deterrent with Hybrid, which made the purchase of US-made Poseidon missiles necessary, although it would involve a considerable amount of

British know-how.[131] This would of course increase the British dependence on the US. More importantly, it would keep British research going.

Home considered the deterrent as growing in importance because of how the superpowers behaved. On the one hand, there was the Soviet build up of conventional forces and on the other an uncertainty about the durability of the American nuclear umbrella. Barber opposed spending based on worst case scenarios. He remained unconvinced that the high levels of expenditure were warranted. The costs only made sense if Britain was to be capable of handling a situation where Britain would be wholly isolated. He wondered if the tactical nuclear weapons on the continent would not be a more effective deterrent – a line of argument which amounted to questioning the basis for an independent deterrent. However, Heath knew that cooperation on tactical weapons would not bring about the cooperation he wanted, so he brushed aside Barber's concerns and supported Carrington's position that it was necessary to keep the deterrent and said he would tell Nixon what they needed for the update.[132]

It was agreed at the meeting that without US support the task of developing a successor generation would be very difficult for two reasons: first, the costs of research and development would be huge even if Britain could collaborate with France; second, without American intelligence about the Soviet ABM defences British security would be greatly impaired. Accordingly, Britain needed American support even if they managed to work with France.[133] In fact the British expected intelligence to remain organised on a national basis for a long time. Hence, this was one part of Anglo-American relations that would not be changed. Instead the Heath government intended to continue the close relationship on intelligence but assumed that the US would be cooperative in sharing information with the rest of Western Europe in order to bolster its effort.[134] For the US to support Anglo-French cooperation, NATO had to seem viable. The Ministers, therefore, wanted to persuade the French to change their attitude towards NATO.[135]

Trend had previously suggested to Heath that a 'reconstructed and reinvigorated NATO' could keep the US in Europe and that they should prevent Nixon from compensating Europe with a deterrent while the US withdrew.[136] His talks with the Kissinger had led him to believe that changes to American diplomacy could be far reaching, a theme developed further in the subsequent chapter. The British wanted to avoid drastic change for two reasons: first, because the US was essential for the development of a credible European nuclear capability according to the tripartite approach; and, second, because the American nuclear commitment to Europe ensured West Germany reliability.[137] Britain already had another trilateral relationship with the US and West Germany within the framework of the Nuclear Planning Group that dealt with the strategic use of tactical nuclear weapons.[138] The US was needed as the glue to keep NATO together and the West Germans in place. Accordingly, Nixon's support was needed to decrease the US dominant role in NATO.[139]

Heath was very concerned that they should not repeat the Nassau situation, by 'presenting the French with a fait accompli' where Britain stuck a deal purchasing Polaris from the US without consideration of French interests. He wanted an increasing degree of openness with the French and told Carrington in November 1972 to explain to Debré the need to update the Polaris system and that this had to be done with the help of the US. The next step towards Anglo-French collaboration on a successor system was a comparison of their timetables for replacement. This was not as straightforward as it might seem. The French method of replacement was fundamentally different from that of the British. The French did not update the system as a whole, generation-wise, but preferred a 'rolling' programme that incorporated new technology continuously, unlike the British who thought in terms of generations of systems. Nevertheless, a 'substantial discussion' with the French on a successor system had to wait until after they knew Nixon's opinion.[140] Heath hoped to elicit this at the next Heath–Nixon Summit in early 1973.

When Carrington met Debré on 20 November, he told him that Britain was looking at a number of options to improve the viability and life span of the existing deterrent and revealed that all depended on US support – even to the extent of buying the American missile Poseidon. He explained the necessity of speeding up the update of the British deterrent and added that Britain intended to try and decide how to do this by the first months of 1973. Debré confirmed that France was interested in working together on a successor system. Debré, as usual, was pessimistic and melodramatic, seeing threats everywhere, which had the benefit that he saw Anglo-French collaboration as imperative.[141] Carrington stressed that it would take between 13 and 15 years to develop a successor system, and they should count backward from 1990. Debré claimed that the French had similar deadlines.[142]

Despite the agreeable meeting it was known that Debré and the French Prime Minister Pierre Messmer were potential Gaullist obstacles to Heath's plans for a European defence. Nevertheless, the government knew that nuclear interdependence was 'the only card' they had to play, which could convince France to return to her full share of European defence.[143] Until Christmas 1972, the trilateral strategy had evolved as planned, yet also as expected at an excruciatingly slow pace. Nevertheless, the very fact that it existed counters the assumptions that the Heath government plunged enthusiastically into European affairs nonchalantly snubbing the US and putting off security considerations. Due to the chosen approach, of a viable European defence inside a reconstructed NATO that kept the US involved and the West Germans in place, change could only come slowly.

Trouble over Poseidon

At the very end of de Gaulle's presidency, French nuclear thinking underwent a change bringing it closer to that of the rest of the West. The planning now centred on the East instead of *tous azimuts*. Pompidou was prepared to say publicly in 1973 that France needed the requirements of flexible response. However, Debré, ever the Gaullist, commissioned a White Paper on defence. Ready in 1972, it said that nuclear weapons could only be used when crucial national interests were at stake. It was conveniently unclear about what these interests were, although Debré's Gaullist interpretation was likely to conflate interest with that of the territory of France.[144]

Clearly, the British were not aware of how incompatible their approach was with that of Debré's. Carrington believed that the French were also concerned about economics and offering Britain a lifeline.[145] The British believed that there was a groundswell of support in the French military and the administration for greater cooperation. Carrington incorrectly assumed that Debré would follow the dictates of the economy.[146] However, Debré remained the problem. If he did not change his mind, he would stand in the way of the British trilateral approach. When Debré met Admiral Hill-Norton, Chief of the Defence Staff, in December 1972, he said that European defence had to be built on 'the two pillars' of France and Britain.[147] This was not good news according to Carrington who believed that if it accepted a solely European two pillar hypothesis Britain would soon find itself at odds with NATO. His opinion was that if the gain was a classical bilateral military alliance with France at the cost of NATO, the British would be worse off than before.[148] This confirms that the Heath government wanted to recreate and not scuttle the Atlantic alliance.

In the long run, the Heath government wanted to create a Western European defence entity that could be in equal and full partnership with the US. The British government hoped to 'exploit [the] economic and military potential' of Europe and establish a 'nucleus' within the EC on which to build a defence identity that would be in 'fair and equal' partnership with the US.[149] The British believed that they had to stay the course and to pursue their strategy. Furthermore, the US had accepted this approach, which meant that there was no way back.

The British realised that there was little enthusiasm for defence cooperation in Europe, but they did not regard it as a hindrance but rather as a symptom of a malaise that a project of this kind could cure. The British intended to wait until after the French elections in the spring of 1973 that could lead to the removal of some of the Gaullists, and only thereafter approach Pompidou.[150] This again shows how much Heath's defence vision and the trilateral plans depended on there being enough time. By the spring of 1973, it was clear that what was required was the sustained will of all three participants over another few years, which meant that plans had to continue after the next British general election. The British impression was that Gaullism was still strong in regard to defence but they believed that Pompidou, who was a key figure for the British plan to succeed, could be gradually moved to cooperation along the lines that the British wanted – with American support for their efforts.[151]

Heath met Nixon again in early February 1973 at Camp David. He told Nixon that he intended to approach the French about defence after the next French election, which he expected to lead to the removal of Debré. Then, Heath claimed, Pompidou would inevitably have to deal with defence because of the strains it was putting on the French economy. These developments, Heath believed, would bring about a new momentum for Anglo-French interdependence.[152]

Nixon welcomed this since he saw that with SALT II the Soviet government would try and limit nuclear capability to the US and to themselves, leaving NATO outside and 'defenceless'. Furthermore, the conventional Soviet forces had made a US trip-wire strategy far less realistic. Hence, independent deterrents became more important. Nixon wished that the British, and possibly also the French, could help in analysing the consequences of détente. He thought it likely that such a study would show that the present NATO was a psychological palliative but that it was ineffective as a military deterrent. He, therefore, supported a restructured NATO as a way to involve France.[153] Accordingly, Nixon and his administration were set on a course that could work in tandem with Heath's vision.

The American Ambassador, Annenberg, reported that the British press had the impression that Heath was reassured after his visit to the US that

Britain would remain a nuclear power. Unlike the days of Kennedy and Macmillan there was no new spectacular deal, since the British government had not yet made up its mind on Poseidon. The media assumed this to be partly due to the costs and in part due to possible cooperation with France.[154] Present were clearly the seeds of the misconception that Britain faced an either-or situation regarding the update of its deterrent. However, as the three-way strategy unfolded the Anglo-American nuclear special relationship continued unimpaired in its supportive role.

In late March 1973, this created a new political problem. Heath learned from Soames that Pompidou had said that there could be no nuclear collaboration with Britain because of its decision to buy the Poseidon missile from the US.[155] Debré turned out to be the hindrance.[156] The British suspected that he had purposely misunderstood Carrington and then misrepresented the British efforts to update their deterrent to Pompidou.[157] Superficially the situation over the update appeared to have the potential to become another Nassau. The British believed that if Pompidou understood that cooperation in this field was still possible, he would appoint another defence minister who would be easier for the British to deal with. Heath quickly sent people over to set the record straight.[158] Pompidou had his own reasons for not reappointing Debré – who symbolised the Gaullists that the more pragmatic Pompidou wanted removed.[159]

This trouble occurred just a few weeks before Kissinger made his call for the 'Year of Europe', a diplomatic initiative, further discussed in the following chapter. Shortly before the launch of his initiative Kissinger met Ambassador Cromer and Trend and took the opportunity to criticise NATO. He also assured them that the discussion about MBFR was not the cover of a 'Vietnamisation of Europe', whereby the US would leave the Western Europeans to fend for themselves. On the contrary, MBFR was a means to meet domestic American criticism of troop levels in Europe. According to him the possible failure of the MBFR talks could be blamed on the Soviet Union, and it would then show 'up the detante [sic] for the sham which it was'. Militarily speaking a failure in the MBFR talks was not a problem either, as long as the Europeans consented to a 'rational defence'.[160] Clearly, the White House expected Western Europe to do more for its own defence whether continued détente was a success or not. However, Kissinger could hardly ask the British to do more. Britain had spent a lot on defence and was the only state which, so far, had presented a strategy, which it had also pursued with considerable vigour.

During the meeting, Trend tried to draw out Kissinger on why he thought that the US benefited from an independent British nuclear deterrent 'as a reinsurance'. Kissinger said that it was an insurance against other kinds of American administrations. He said that the Soviet Union should not be led to believe that to become the 'dominant Power in the world' it only had to 'neutralise...one nuclear rival'. Accordingly, he claimed that a deepened Anglo-French or tripartite collaboration could be 'desirable'. However, given how West Germany and the US Congress would react it was best not to be seen as making any progress or of 'being too specific about what one was doing at all'.[161] A few weeks he told the British that the administration supported independent nuclear deterrents in Europe 'both as a starting point for closer European defence co-operation, and in order that Europe should in the last resort have a nuclear insurance at its own disposal'. However, US assistance depended on overcoming political rather than legal obstacles in the US. He thought a tripartite scheme was likely to be feasible, adding that there were signs that the French themselves wanted to purchase Poseidon-like missiles for their two forthcoming submarines. He encouraged the British to talk about collaboration with Pompidou.[162] Kissinger, who increasingly dominated US foreign policy, allowed the British strategy to continue. He had little choice. The defence of the West had to remain credible to the Western European allies and the US as well as their enemy; yet it was remarkable how the Anglo-American nuclear special relationship was sustained, rather than impaired, by these efforts.

Both the British and the Americans were hoping to engage the French in a tripartite scheme. However, the French held out for a bilateral US-French approach for as long as possible, though they had probably not counted on the Americans making the British aware of this. The British were informed on 20 May 1973, the day before Heath and Pompidou discussed defence issues, by Helmut Sonnenfeldt, of the National Security Staff, who together with Kissinger had been over to Paris. But the Americans did not know if the French were backtracking on the trilateral approach.[163] This signifies how well consultations worked in regard to nuclear affairs which was in stark contrast with the lack of consultations over monetary affairs. In any case, it was an inopportune beginning to the joint Anglo-American efforts to involve the French. It also illustrates that the special relationship approach, with close consultations, between the US and Britain continued to operate and that within the three-way exchange the British and American were closer to each other than either was with France.

On 21 May, Heath and Pompidou for the first time had an extended talk about their respective deterrents and collaboration. Heath told Pompidou that they could not allow the US to link defence to commercial or trade matters, since that could lead to US blackmail of the Europeans.

However, they wanted to keep the US in Europe for the time being and did not want to make it more difficult than necessary for the US to stay in Europe. But if the US was forced to decrease its commitment to Europe because of domestic American political pressures, the French and the British had to discuss what should be done. Pompidou distrusted the superpowers and thought they were trying to save themselves from the ravages of nuclear war. He said that a conventional war in Europe would end in Europe's defeat at the hands of the Soviet Union.[164] This grim view should, nevertheless, have made him open to Heath's arguments.

Pompidou believed that France and Britain alone could not match the Soviet Union's nuclear arsenal. Either the US had to give Europe nuclear weapons or it had to remain in Europe, but he feared that the SALT process would foreclose the possibility of the US sharing its nuclear knowledge with allies.[165] Having eased the Gaullist posture Pompidou wanted to tread carefully. This meant that he preferred NATO to continue to be the centre piece of European defence, which was the retention of status quo of defence and the opposite of what Heath worked for. Heath told Pompidou that he had gone on the record years ago previously in support for a 'Franco/British nuclear deterrent force, held in trust for Europe' as expressed in his Harvard lectures. He stressed that he specifically wanted to avoid a rupture like the one between de Gaulle and Macmillan. Heath made it clear that Britain needed US help to update Polaris, but that this in no way foreclosed any discussions about the future strategic deterrent. He also pointed out the advantages of cooperating with the US.[166] However, it was not the British collaboration with the US that threatened to repeat the de Gaulle-Macmillan rupture but instead the plans for a European defence effort and the suggested pace of achieving it.

Pompidou acknowledged that savings could be made by working with the US, but he remarked that despite the special nuclear relationship Britain's defence budget was still larger than that of France. However, Britain had a technical advantage over France. He conceded that 'their defence interests were identical and their destiny's inseparable' and Heath's worries about a repetition of history were at an end. Pompidou agreed to let their experts in defence and technology look into the possibility of a joint defence effort. Nevertheless, Pompidou was adamant that the agreement should not to be made known to others.[167] It was not the US he worried about, but the impact of cooperation on West Germany. Helmut Schmidt, the West German Finance Minister, and former Defence Minister, had said that an anglo-french nuclear force would without a doubt lead to German neutrality.[168] For his strategy to have any chance of success Heath also had to keep the West Germans in the dark. This could cause difficulties in the future when the nuclear cooperation would be attached to European defence cooperation. The risk was that instead of creating a basis for a European pillar in the alliance Heath was inviting France to join the Anglo-American special relationship at the expense of other allies.

This circumspection did of course not apply to British relations with the US. Heath was reminded of the British obligations to the US by Trend. It would be prudent, Trend argued, to be just as candid in return as the US had been to them just before the Heath–Pompidou Summit.[169] Despite having promised Pompidou to keep their discussion secret, Heath told Nixon everything about the meeting; the decision to let the technicians discuss cooperation, the French obsession with secrecy and fear of the West Germans reaction, and that they were comparing timetables for a possible successor system.[170] Heath was clearly determined to keep both involved, even if this meant a liberal interpretation of pledges to the French.

In the spring of 1973, it finally seemed as if the British strategy to set up a tripartite nuclear relationship could bear fruit. Despite the upset of the Year of Europe initiative, Kissinger like Nixon seemed to believe that renewed European defence efforts were necessary; even if the reason was American self-interest it could be one way to a reconstructed NATO that included France. NATO was also the means with which to make West Germany accept great changes. Heath appeared to think that if he could bring off Anglo-French cooperation while keeping the nuclear link to the US it could be possible to eventually forge a new US-European special nuclear relationship.

Better safe than sorry

As the summer of 1973 approached there were hopeful signs for cooperation. The French informed the British that their planned nuclear tests for 1973 would only test low-yield nuclear warheads in the Pacific and not high-yield warheads. This meant that the British would not have to deploy an extra airborne operation from Lima, Peru, to study the French tests. Britain was in fact obliged to collect intelligence and share it with the US in order to fulfil the Anglo-American agreements to collect information.[171] Since British intelligence observation usually annoyed the French, this new openness was interpreted as a good omen.

Despite this auspicious beginning to the summer, Anglo-French defence relations soon stalled and in June an impatient Heath reminded the French about what they had agreed to.[172] At the end of June, the French blamed internal and foreign reasons saying that the British should not expect an immediate answer to the reminder.[173] The French wanted both sides to sort out their timetables for new weapons systems so that comparisons could be made.[174] Another reason for the slow development was the Nixon–Pompidou Summit in Reykjavik on 31 May and 1 June. The US administration was not convinced that Pompidou had been won for the trilateral approach and believed that Pompidou was more favourably disposed to the British than to them. On the other hand, they thought they could detect French worries about their system and its costs, which could make France more willing to cooperate. Kissinger, having discussed matters with Jobert, now Minister of Foreign Affairs, tempted the French with the possibility of letting French experts come to the US to discuss the capability of their missiles. Trend welcomed this and hoped that the French would agree since it would be an eye opener for the French about the inadequacies of their programmes. He counted on the result being an increased French drive towards Anglo-French collaboration.[175]

At the same time as the British were urging the French to begin constructing the basis for interdependence, the US administration was pressing the British government to make up its mind about what kind of assistance Britain needed for its update. The political climate created by the Watergate scandal made it increasingly difficult for the US administration to get their decisions through.[176] Carrington warned Heath that Pompidou had indicated that Anglo-French nuclear collaboration was in a longer timeframe and that Pompidou wanted to see the likely results of the Conference on Security and Cooperation in Europe (CSCE), MBFR and SALT before committing France. To Carrington this demonstrated that they had to reach a decision about the British update without considering how their successor system would be developed with the French. The preferable option with which to update was the costly Chevaline programme. It was the only option which would keep Britain 'an independent nuclear power in the eyes of Europe' and would impress the French.[177] Even if there was no Anglo-French cooperation on the update, it was only the most expensive programme that had a chance to support and inspire future development by convincing the French about the British ability in the nuclear field. Buying Poseidon would not have the same effect. While security concerns came first, it is evident that the Heath government would choose the update that would guarantee a viable deterrent and which would also allow the possibility to continue with the three-way exchange strategy.

During the spring the British had, according to an agreement at Camp David, been in contact with an American group specially set up to help them. It was led by James Schlesinger, Director of the CIA.[178] The talks initially put the British in a catch-22 situation. The administration's obsession with secrecy prevented the British from talking with the relevant US experts outside the group, for example in the Department of Defense. Instead they had to decide beforehand which solution they preferred. This would then be handed to Nixon, so that the White House could do its so-called 'determination', which would push things through politically. Initially Schlesinger had unwittingly alerted Trend's suspicions by suggesting the use of a new US warhead instead of a British one for either Polaris or Poseidon.[179] It turned out that the Schlesinger's group was 'extremely helpful', in the best special relationship tradition, and tried only to ensure that the British had the best technology available as well as the option of their choice.[180]

The administration's efforts at the British behest could not overcome the fact that the overheated political climate in Washington during Watergate caused grave concerns even among long-standing friends. Especially those like the British, who were already apprehensive due to the necessity to update its nuclear deterrent and its pursuit of a new interdependence. Nevertheless, the Heath government was poised in the summer of 1973 to take as much as possible from the Anglo-American relationship. In June, Kissinger let the British know that there was not necessarily an MIRV limit on submarine-based projectiles that the US could provide.[181] Both Carrington and Heath wanted to find out what the chances were of getting MIRVed missiles before taking a decision, and also the difference between Poseidon and the even newer US missile Trident.[182] These were tempting possibilities but risked fore-closing long-term cooperation with the French on strategic nuclear weapons.

Despite the calls for urgency the issue of an update continued to drift into the autumn. In August, the economic situation reached a stage that made tough saving demands in defence imperative. Carrington protested against the suggested cuts claiming that any cut would jeopardise British ambitions overseas and in Europe, and would endanger or slowdown the update of the deterrent. It would have 'irreparable consequences for our position within Europe and NATO, and would mean going back on everything we have been working for over the past three years. It would involve a wholesale retreat from the policies we announced...on assuming office in 1970...and would make necessary a complete review of all the Government's Defence and Foreign policies'.[183] Cancelling the Chevaline programme would undermine the chances for future Anglo-French cooperation, since the British would not appear to have the same perseverance that the French had demonstrated in their pursuit of a deterrent a decade earlier. Carrington was strongly supported by Home who was adamant that all but the smallest cuts would put at risk the European defence policies. According to Home, the cuts would mean relinquishing the leading role in redesigning European defence and a waste of the work of the Eurogroup. He argued that no other country would step up to fill Britain's shoes; instead it was more likely that, relieved of British pressure, other states would make defence cuts as well.[184] Likewise, the prestige of the Eurogroup would suffer if Britain's fortunes floundered.[185] This meant that if the European defence efforts came about, they might be made on the basis of the WEU instead. On the one hand, it was not necessarily a problem since it was more independent from NATO and from the superpower perspective, which would make it easier for a third force to emerge. On the other, the WEU was France's favoured forum and could mean that France would assert itself at Britain's expense making a US–EC special relationship more difficult to attain. Simultaneously, the US made evermore tempting offers to the British.

During August the US did an about-turn and it now seemed that the US services wanted to press the MIRVed version of Poseidon on the British.[186] It seemed that the issue of MIRV with the Soviet Union in SALT had changed recently so that it might be politically possible for the US to sell the British the complete technology, but that judgement rested with Kissinger.[187] Despite the high cost the British government eventually chose to update its deterrent with Britain's own Chevaline system, which was without MIRV capability.[188] Other options would make British research obsolete depriving Britain of a potential bargaining chip in European defence talks. Other options would also result in an even stronger Anglo-American nuclear special relationship. The British government was also fearful of deals that would recall the interpretation of the deal struck at Nassau, as it was conceived by observers at the time, namely an Anglo-American agreement without due concern for the French.

The Nixon administration's efforts to revise nuclear targeting and the US nuclear strategy eventually began to bear results in 1973. In early 1974 this resulted in what became known as the Schlesinger Doctrine. By this time, Schlesinger was Secretary of Defense. European fears that the US nuclear umbrella was not trustworthy had increased during 1973 to the extent that there was mutual scepticism between the US and Europe according to Schlesinger. As a result, ever greater care was taken to emphasise the protection of Europe with US strategic missiles.[189] The British deterrent did not play a significant part in the US deliberations to form a new nuclear practice. Instead, the new doctrine overran the British three-way exchange strategy. Once the US administration used its prerogative, as the dominant alliance partner, to shape nuclear defence policy there was little the British could do. The doctrine was not a reaction to the British plans but it risked working at cross-purposes with what the British hoped to achieve. The new American approach underlined traditional commitments to Europe.

The creation and shape of the new doctrine illustrated that even though the Anglo-American nuclear special relationship was 'presidential business' the real British contribution in case of war was 'small'. It was, however, certainly large enough to be in 'potential inconsistency with US objectives'. Nevertheless, it was this independence that contributed to its effective deterrence of the Soviet Union.[190] The MoD was aware of the negligible contribution Britain made in comparison to the overwhelming size of the US nuclear force, and it believed that France thought the British deterrent only credible in the defence of the British Isles. However, the MoD held that British EC membership would underline that Britain's national interests were intimately connected to the Western European countries. This would decrease the likelihood that the Soviet Union would pursue war in continental Europe on the assumption that both the US and Britain would stay out of it. Hence, British EC membership was expected to increase deterrence of the Soviet Union, even if Anglo-French cooperation and French re-involvement in NATO developed slowly.[191] Against the background of all the uncertainties and potential possibilities, the choice to press ahead with the Chevaline option is understandable, as it seemed to keep more of British independence. It had to rely on US help, to remain effective, but to a degree possibly acceptable to the French.

Despite the crises in the fall of 1973 – the Arab-Israeli War on Yom Kippur, the oil shocks, and industrial strife in Britain – the Heath government continued to pursue the Chevaline programme and the trilateral approach. However, the domestic economic situation grew so dire that in the beginning of 1974 the able Carrington was moved from the MoD to deal with the domestic situation from the Department of Energy. As usual with his eye on security he declared in February that Britain was facing one of its most difficult post-war situations. He wanted to have the country behind the government and urged a general election at an early date so that the government could deal with the domestic situation.[192] This signals the shift in priorities from vision building to the survival of the government.

However, as late as 16 November, Heath made another attempt to push ahead with the defence efforts with France in a meeting with Pompidou at Chequers. Heath suggested that it was likely that Nixon might cave-in under the combination of political pressures from Watergate and the US Congress and agree to troop withdrawals from Europe. Pompidou pushed these considerations aside claiming that few, if any, of the smaller countries wanted to discuss the matter at the EC Summit in Copenhagen since they were fearful of a transatlantic rift. He also argued that West Germany was more exposed in security terms, than either France or Britain, and not prepared to engage in such security talks. Against this background Pompidou argued that the other EC members were not in a state to contemplate discussions on European defence. Heath acknowledged that it would be difficult to discuss the matter. Pompidou did not think that the situation was quite as melodramatic as Heath and argued that anything more than a symbolic withdrawal was unlikely 'unless the United States were governed by men who had become completely blind to United States interests'.[193] Pompidou believed that even if the EC evolved to create its own defence it would still need to be linked to the US for a considerable time. The insecurity about superpower diplomacy for him meant increased European defence efforts individually and collectively, but primarily in terms of joint procurement efforts.[194] This was so although there were officials in the French administration who had suggested to Pompidou that he should go beyond the 'clandestine' approach to Anglo-French collaboration.[195] Pompidou's view was that the US 'in effect took back with one hand what it had given with the other' when it said that it was alright for France to have nuclear weapons but that these were ineffectual due to inferior intelligence. In other words, the French were unimpressed with the US way of framing the debate of what was required to have a credible deterrent. Besides, he argued, the MIRV technology would continue to change strategic thinking and he did not believe that the US had yet thought through the implications of that technology. Until the consequences were known, France would therefore choose to continue its own strategy of deterrence. He argued that he had been consistent. Nevertheless, he dashed what British hopes remained about a tripartite leap forward, when he said that the present French programme would continue until 1980 and that new possibilities opened up only thereafter.[196]

Heath agreed to the need for the Atlantic link but he wanted to go beyond the status quo and to make an effort that could later engage the rest of the EC. Annoyed, he told Pompidou that whenever and no matter in what way he tried to bring up the matter of common defence efforts he gained the impression that the French suspected him of trying to lure them back into NATO. He assured Pompidou that this was not his intention at all. He had wanted to recreate all relationships. Hence, France's re-involvement would have taken place in a reconstituted alliance. Yet, Pompidou held on to the view that the French and the British could cooperate on armament and armed forces. On the other hand, he argued that they were not yet ready to discuss 'the organization of defence or the co-ordination of means of defence', since France was behind Britain technologically. Heath told Pompidou that as the British had reviewed their nuclear weapons programme to be able to compare it with the French timetable they had come to the conclusion that they should keep their own research on nuclear weapons going. This made cooperation possible at a later stage between their two countries, if the French so desired.[197] This was, of course, a far cry from what Heath hoped for. The events of the summer and autumn of 1973 confirmed Pompidou's preference for the status quo. Consequently, Heath was dissuaded from pursuing the defence initiatives at the Copenhagen Summit.

The tripartite approach had foundered due to Pompidou's scepticism, renewed US efforts to make its nuclear commitments to Europe credible and because further efforts at a tripartite strategy would require a re-election of the Heath government. The US offer of even more modern MIRVed technology had not been consistent with the three-way exchange. In comparison, the British were far more tempted by the deepening of the Anglo-American special nuclear relations than the French were of the trilateral scheme. The Heath government had foregone that opportunity to make a complete renewal of its nuclear independent deterrent for the risk, hitherto unappreciated, of developing the Chevaline programme. The British had hoped that their level of nuclear technology would impress the French, which it did. However, it failed to have the intended effect of bringing the French closer. It turned out that the French government preferred the status quo both in terms of American involvement in Europe and in terms of keeping its own nuclear programme in accordance with its strict interpretation of what it meant by independent.

Hit by the energy crisis and industrial strife, the Britain collapsed back into the Anglo-American special nuclear relationship. It made certain that whatever happened to NATO and future European schemes, its special nuclear relationship with the US was renewed. At the end of 1973, the crumbling Nixon administration also decided to play it safe on defence and to renew the parts of the 1958 agreement on cooperation for mutual defence purposes that was due to be renegotiated.[198] The new US doctrine did underline the importance of the US within the alliance, but it failed to rectify what the three-way exchange strategy had tried to do – namely to re-involve France in allied defence efforts within NATO or under a NATO roof. Instead, the new strategy maintained the status quo in Western Europe generally, as France hoped. Its offer of newer and better technology to Britain showed how, lacking a more original idea of its own, the US preferred to safeguard its position by reinforcing existing ties.

The Chevaline programme and its costs, £1000 million, were only revealed in 1980, and then seemed to be a costly anachronism, as John Baylis has shown.[199] Instead, the programme was the testament of the Heath government's wish to build up a European defence effort with nuclear weapons. Beatrice Heuser hints that that the Chevaline programme to update the British deterrent foreclosed Anglo-French cooperation.[200] It nearly did, but not because it was intended to be an alternative to Anglo-French cooperation, as has been assumed. In fact the programme was sustained in the hope that it would impress the French and safeguard British know-how. It could, perhaps, have been the beginning of Anglo-French interdependence, with security ensured by the involvement of the US in a trilateral approach erected on a very active Anglo-American nuclear special relationship. Instead, the attempt merely brought the US and Britain closer. When the British government decided to focus on the domestic situation, instead of Heath's plans for European integration, it took the precaution of reaffirming the traditional Anglo-American nuclear relationship since it was better to be safe than sorry.

4
Anglo-American Policy Towards European Integration and the Rise of Henry Kissinger

The importance of Kissinger

That American policy towards Europe changed during the Nixon presidency is well known.[1] Yet, as this chapter bears out, the intentions of the Nixon administration towards Europe actually were not consistent. The two previous chapters have dealt with Britain's entry from the more traditional power-political parts of the Anglo-American relationship in the sixties, monetary-economic affairs and military-intelligence affairs. This chapter deals with the influence of Henry Kissinger, Nixon's National Security Adviser and later Secretary of State, on the US adaptation to an enlarged EC. It demonstrates the importance of security thinking over other approaches in the White House and it analyses the Anglo-American efforts to agree on a transatlantic initiative.

Henry A. Kissinger knew that the US had to adapt to a world that was multipolar in a political sense. He recognised that the process of European unification to be inevitable, but he was intensely sceptical of European federalism. As far back as in 1969 he argued that the process of European integration had stalled. Although he believed that the US and Europe had to coordinate their interests, he did not believe that federalism should be an American objective. Nor did he believe that European unification had reached a point where Europe was ready for formal overarching transatlantic plans. He even questioned the US support for British EC membership.[2]

The divergence of opinion between Heath and Kissinger is evident, as Peter Hennessy has demonstrated, by juxtaposing their views on the special relationship.[3] Indeed, such is the standing of Kissinger that in the official documentary publication series *Foreign Relations of the United States*, first ever volume on 'intellectual assumptions' behind an

administration's foreign policy, his views are accorded the same promi-
nence as those of Nixon.[4] Like Heath, Kissinger was greatly to influence
the foreign policy of his country but there are also great differences
between the two. The first and most important is that Heath was elected
to office and Kissinger was chosen to advise an elected person.

Another significant difference is that Heath was what the philosopher Isaiah Berlin called a Hedgehog;[5] he knew one big thing. He had
one political vision. Kissinger on the other hand was forever trying to
square events with a conceptual approach. However, 'the rise of Henry
Kissinger', in the chapter title, refers to the fact that he gradually became
influential, which made all the differences noted above matter. That
this happened, despite everything written about him and by him after
the Nixon–Kissinger years, should not be taken for granted. No one
rises to the top of politics as a result of sheer academic brilliance only.
However, here we are not concerned with the details of the manoeu-
vres that increased Kissinger's influence in his role as National Security
Adviser and which eventually made him Secretary of State.[6] Instead,
what matters is the effect of his rise on British policies and the gradual
realisation on the part of the British government that Kissinger's emergence as the linchpin of US foreign policy meant a reappraisal of US
policies.

The reasons for singling out Kissinger as a major factor are twofold and
simple. First, with his increased importance the difference between his
view of transatlantic affairs and Heath's vision began to matter. Second,
he was in charge of what became known as a failed American diplomatic initiative known as the 'Year of Europe' in 1973, which centred
on the resuscitation of reliable Atlantic practices. This chapter answers
the question: how was Anglo-American policy towards European integration and Heath's vision affected by the US reappraisal of its foreign
policy towards Europe?

In the late sixties the desire to see Britain in Europe was a widespread
Anglo-American wish in both the British establishment and in US
foreign policy circles. In fact, the European diplomacy of the Anglo-
American relationship became even more imperative in the Nixon–
Heath years. Not only because it seemed that Britain had a reasonable
chance to enter the EC but also because the EC Summit at the Hague in
December 1969 had begun to revive the EC and the pursuit of deeper
integration.[7]

Heath eagerly wanted Britain to take part in deepened European integration. This meant that Britain had to become an EC member. In the
process of getting Britain there he made himself very accessible to the

advice of civil servants.[8] He had an almost embarrassingly strong belief in the rationality of governmental processes and practices and he made few administrative changes but he kept a tight reign in the cabinet, which was made up of a collection of loyal colleagues.[9] Nixon preferred a radically different approach and set about reviving the NSC. He preferred to circumvent his cabinet, with the help of the NSC, when he wanted to pursue a specific policy in international affairs. Kissinger, as national security adviser, became chairman of the NSC and hence its key figure. From the outset, Kissinger's influence was great because he was responsible for collecting advice and putting it together for Nixon.[10] Heath worked on a basis of trust and delegated power to colleagues like Geoffrey Rippon, responsible for the EC negotiations. Nixon trusted the US system of government much less than Heath trusted the British system and he was prepared to go much further to channel power and control to himself.

Negotiations on two fronts

Kissinger enforced Nixon's security perspective. The force of the White House's security stance turned out to be crucial during the sensitive EC entry negotiations. That such an important factor in US-European affairs as trade caused relatively few problems to the Anglo-American relationship and British entry was undoubtedly helped by the precedence of the security perspective over economic matters. Kissinger was a vital factor in the upholding Nixon's support for the British EC entry. The process was also emblematic of the thinking and positioning that furthered Kissinger's rise.

In March 1971, Rippon, the British minister in charge of the negotiations for EC entry, travelled to the US. The British understood that the negotiations were being conducted on more than one front, although they were concerned that the Community did not appreciate this.[11] Nixon had promised Heath in December 1970 that the US would avoid causing trouble over issues that might disturb Britain's EC negotiations, but Rippon had to deal with the details of the negotiations and find out what Nixon's promises were worth.

This was especially important because shortly after the Heath–Nixon Summit the US administration claimed that the Community's association agreements with non-EC members were in breach of international trade regulations. On 1 January, Stanley Cleveland, the economic minister at the US Embassy, explained to Con O'Neill, from the FCO, who led the British negotiation team in the Conference of Deputies, that the EC was expanding to a 'world wide trading Empire', which conflicted with the expressed wish of the US to promote a liberalisation of world trade.[12] Britain had supported the US demand for trade liberalisation since the war and, as shown in Chapter 2, the Heath government had promised to continue with this commitment.

Cleveland cautioned the British that the EC preferential trade agreements were a weapon for those in Washington who advocated US protectionism. He hinted that a British 'show of concern' for the US worries would make it easier for those like Nixon, who supported British membership. Con O'Neill would have none of this. He told Cleveland that association agreements had been put in the Treaty of Rome in 1957, without US opposition and that association status for Commonwealth countries had been a part of the British negotiation position since 1961.[13] This was, clearly, a test of whether the White House would live up to its guarantee, given in 1970, that the US would accept some economic costs due to Britain's EC entry.

Imports from the Commonwealth were still subject to 'detailed negotiations' in 1971.[14] Sorting out the American position was therefore seen as being crucial. Rippon believed that he went to the US at the stage when they were at the 'heart of the negotiations'. Before leaving, he told Franco Maria Malfatti, the President of the European Commission, that he was receiving varying responses from different levels of the US government; Nixon 'was firmly in favour of the enlargement' but the Departments of Agriculture and Commerce had a myopic view focused on immediate trading interests. Malfatti agreed that the 'Americans spoke with two voices'; one from the White House and the State Department, the other from the Department of Agriculture. He thought that Clifford Hardin, the US Secretary of Agriculture, 'scarcely seemed able to look further than oranges and tobacco'.[15]

Rippon met Hardin and Maurice Stans, the US Secretary of Commerce on 8 March 1971. He tried to assuage their worries and employed a traditional free-trade argument claiming that enlargement meant a quicker move towards a greater volume of trade to the benefit of all. Stans protested, calling Rippon an 'idealist', which was not meant to be complimentary. He added that '[t]he reality was that the long term interests of the US would not be advanced'.[16]

Rippon found common ground when he talked with Nathaniel Samuels, the US Deputy Under-Secretary for Economic Affairs who shared his concern for the Commonwealth Caribbean countries in America's back yard. Rippon argued that these countries should be given the same chance to export to Britain as they had always enjoyed, a trade that amounted to aid. The British public expected the EC to uphold its 1963 promise in regard to these countries. He also warned that a US complaint to the Community on the issue of the trade arrangements with the Caribbean could spark a crisis in the negotiations.[17]

When Rippon talked with Kissinger the same day he found a more sympathetic attitude. Kissinger 'said that he understood the British position' and asked if there was anything the American administration could do to help, suggesting that staying 'aside' was the best help, to which Rippon readily assented.[18] Kissinger thereby upheld the White House's strategy of support for British entry and portrayed himself as a reliable interlocutor.

Even though Kissinger spoke for the White House he did not yet carry enough weight to suppress dissenting views. A month later Samuels proposed that the OECD should make a call for greater liberalisation of world trade. Rippon thought it a highly inopportune time. The French would suspect the 'Anglo-Saxons' of trying to 'dilute the Community into some kind of free trade area'. He also refused to compromise over the Caribbean issue.[19] The success of Rippon's firm stand undoubtedly depended on the support of the White House.

This dependence also explains why the British government was so careful in handling Kissinger's requests to come to Britain in the spring of 1971, as shown in the previous chapter. It put Britain in an awkward position since it was to take place just before the Heath–Pompidou Summit. The government had to continue to walk a tightrope between pleasing the White House, on which its American support for entry depended, and avoiding appearances of Anglo-American collusion in order not to offend the French.

Alan Milward has shown that the British eventually did not live up fully to their promises to the US to reform the EC trading principles.[20] Apart from the vague British promises to work for liberal trade, it is also clear that that there was no joint political Anglo-American scheme on international trade. Nevertheless, Nixon eventually welcomed association status for the Caribbean countries as this would keep them 'in the Western orbit'.[21] This demonstrates that Nixon put security concerns first even when it caused minor economic problems. In the long run the security focus favoured Kissinger over other realists in the administration, like the Secretary of the Treasury John Connally, who dealt with economic issues and the monetary crisis in the fall of 1971.[22]

Kissinger did not focus on European affairs during the first years of the Nixon administration.[23] As shown in Chapter 2, he was not deeply involved in the monetary affairs that dominated transatlantic relations in 1971–72. He certainly was not very interested or knowledgeable about them. At one instance he complained to the British that although he understood the relevance of economics he found the topic 'boring'.[24] On the other hand, this could merely be his opinion about an area where he was not in charge. However, as seen in the next chapter, he was active in some of the most important European security issues. This, and the fact that he was a close adviser to Nixon accompanying him on his European trip in 1969, contributed to many early contacts with the British.

During the first years of his presidency, Nixon alone had the necessary overview of all US diplomacy and it was he who eventually authorised a study of US-European relations in 1972.[25] Evidently, neither he nor his right hand man Kissinger had a prepared plan for transatlantic relations in 1972. They had little more than the views that each had had expressed before the administration came to office.

Eventually, EC enlargement and related matters, like the Caribbean issue, motivated the administration to begin to think more about its transatlantic policies. Heath and Nixon met on 20 December 1971, after the upheaval caused by the American unilateral monetary measures on 15 August had been sufficiently dealt with by the Smithsonian Agreement. At the meeting Nixon restated that 'the political side' of US-European relations was more important than 'the economic side'. Furthermore, both the British and the Americans accepted that the Caribbean presented a security problem rather than an economic one. Heath said that the British could remain involved in the politics of the area under the pretext of a 'contribution to the area's economic progress'. Kissinger assured Nixon that the US could otherwise grant the necessary trade preferences with an appeal to national security so as to avoid a drift to the left of the regimes in the area.[26] The security perspective prevailed, which made for smooth Anglo-American relations on EC-related issues. It also furthered Kissinger's rise. With entry almost certain, Heath prepared to capitalise on the Anglo-American understanding with a transatlantic initiative.

Heath's thwarted initiative

After the Pompidou–Heath Summit in May 1971, which capped the EC negotiations, Heath informed Nixon that Britain and France had agreed on the goals of the Hague Summit and that he and Pompidou saw eye to eye on 'the future of Europe after enlargement of the Community', where 'Europe should play a role commensurate with its real political and economic capability'.[27]

Pompidou was not an ardent Gaullist. Heath believed that Pompidou's approach to Europe was similar to his own, where the integration would be led by the nation-states rather than an external bureaucracy. Reflecting on this in a meeting with the West German Chancellor Willy Brandt he made a reference to Jean Monnet, the leading man of ideas behind European integration. This was unusual since Heath in matters European preferred to refer to his own Harvard lectures. Heath recalled that Jean Monnet had told him a long time ago that 'the fabric of the community [*sic*] would not stand the strain' of going against the crucial national interest of one single country.[28] Heath thought that the Gaullist approach to the US had been unfruitful and believed that that an inter-governmental approach was the best way forward.

Heath wanted to promote deepened European integration and to tie it to the re-establishment of a special relationship between the US and Europe as equals. His intentions were made clear in a speech to the American Bar association in July in London. On this occasion he again, by reference to his lectures from 1967, said that a united Europe would be an ally of the US.[29] However, subsequent events prevented him from taking the initiative. Until the summer of 1971 Anglo-American relations had in fact been good. Nixon held Heath in high esteem and after the Washington meeting in 1970 much of the press reported that the White House and 10 Downing Street were closer than they had been for years.[30] This was in marked contrast to the relationship that Harold Wilson, Heath's predecessor, had had with the Nixon administration.

However, the White House did not get the chance to hear more about Heath's ideas for a US–EC special relationship during the summer of 1971. The strains over the opening to China, with which the subsequent chapter deals, seems to have led Heath to cancel a visit to the so-called Western White House in San Clemente in California, where he had wanted to talk about the future of the Community.[31] Other issues took their toll on British and American relations, notably the tensions between India and Pakistan that led to war in December 1971.[32] Then, of course, the Nixon monetary measures of 15 August heightened tensions in the transatlantic relationship, to the manifest dislike of Heath. His irritation may also have been due to the fact that this effectively curtailed any chance to proceed with any Atlantic initiative.

Unable to make an appeal for a US–EC special relationship as he had wanted, Heath instead spoke his mind to the Conservative Party in Brighton in October 1971. Angered by the US unilateral actions of 15 August Heath talked about Europe's future needs, instead of talking about a future partnership. He pointed to the risk that Europe might be abandoned by its American partner. He claimed that the American action on 15 August was a sign that the Europeans could not count on the Americans forever. He therefore advocated that Europe should both work to protect its own economy and make provisions for its own defence.[33]

Home, the Foreign Secretary, and the FCO were uncomfortable with Heath's approach.[34] The FCO observed that the US was very busy with all other aspects of its foreign policy.[35] It was possible that the US would simply not have had time to deal with a Heath initiative on transatlantic relations since it was busy with many extra-European diplomatic enterprises. The FCO actually welcomed the low priority that the US gave to European affairs, since this was seen as the continuity of US policies and made any reduction in the number of US troops in Europe less likely. The FCO was sceptical of the French but agreed with Pompidou's view that the US commitment was 'vital' from the security perspective. Nevertheless, it only hoped to postpone troop withdrawals and expected them to begin in 1972. It argued that Britain should work to minimise these withdrawals, while building up a European replacement.[36]

Not only was Heath's speech at the Conservative Party in October 1971 unhelpful and unlikely to help improve relations with the US but he also managed to make relations with the US worse by advising Nixon not to hold a great summit of Western leaders in the autumn of 1971 with the purpose of dealing with the monetary crisis and relations with the East.[37] Nixon, whose idea it was, did not like the criticism. Home consequently had to work in November to limit the damage to the Anglo-American relationship. He urged Cromer, the British Ambassador in Washington, to reassure Kissinger about the durability of Anglo-American relations. Home wanted the White House to understand that not being in favour of Nixon's idea for a grand meeting was in the tradition of good honest Anglo-American relationship advice, and that the British did not see Anglo-American 'relations as strained'.[38] This meant that they actually were.

In effect Home was an insurance policy for the British government's long-term relationship with the US. At this point, more than ever, he signalled the continuity and reliability of British policies. The State Department thought that Home favoured NATO because it was the present incarnation of a 'grand Alliance' ensuring Britain's security, and that he likewise favoured British EC membership as 'essential to withstand increasing Soviet pressure'.[39] This analysis clearly suggested sound security-oriented reasoning on Home's part. Kissinger later claimed that Nixon adored Home.[40] Quite probably Kissinger was a bit in awe of him himself. He was embarrassed to have a conversation with Home disturbed by disturbances in the streets, caused by domestic American protests, when they met at the White House in 1970.[41] Home's view was that EC membership was the 'final break with [the] Imperial past' but not with the US. He hoped to convince both the Americans and the Six that the Anglo-American relationship was to run parallel with the new European commitment.[42] He was undoubtedly aware of Heath's enthusiasm about Europe, a passion that he did not share, but he remained, as always, loyal to the Prime Minister.

In the autumn of 1971 Kissinger was merely a messenger who had to defend the approach of the Secretary of the Treasury, John Connally. Kissinger's task was also to convey Nixon's frustration with the British. He took the opportunity to portray himself as a concerned friend of the British. Kissinger claimed to blame himself for not having informed them about the US deliberations on economic measures, while ingeniously passing the blame on to others by asserting that he himself had not been at the crucial Camp David meeting that set up the August 15 measures.[43] He also made sure that the British knew that the idea of a grand meeting was not his.[44] This merely underlines that it was Nixon not Kissinger who decided on the approach to Europe.

Kissinger's efforts, like Home's, were designed to improve Anglo-American relations. Kissinger pointed to the upcoming Heath–Nixon Summit in Bermuda in December as a chance to resolve Anglo-American disagreements.[45] He confided that he found it difficult to keep the British up to date since he could not even inform 'senior echelons of the United States Administration', meaning Rogers and the State Department, about aspects of the White House's foreign policy plans such as the China initiative.[46] This was the hallmark of Kissinger's personal diplomacy: appearing to share secret confidences with others, thus enhancing the role of the messenger.

At this point the FCO was unimpressed by Kissinger's disclosures. It understood that the State Department was out of the loop but blamed the dysfunctional administrative machinery of the US. Kissinger was merely seen as a part of the White House's attempts to control foreign policy. The FCO thought that the 'old ease and closeness of Anglo-American inter-communication' could be ensured by adjusting to the new White House ways of wresting foreign policy making from the State Department. Nevertheless, the FCO suggested that this adaptation take place after the primary aim of British foreign policy was completed, which was EC enlargement by 1972. Only thereafter would there be need for a new method necessary to avoid the strains of 1971.[47] This shows that the FCO and Number 10 were not pursuing markedly different strategies merely employing different tactics, where the FCO wanted to tread more carefully.

When preparing for the Bermuda Summit, Heath and the FCO agreed to try and reaffirm that the US and Britain had a common interest in a Europe that could 'stand on her own two feet'. They would smooth out small differences such as over the association status of the Commonwealth Caribbean countries. The British hoped to reassure the US that Britain intended to stay 'outward looking' and that they wanted the US to do the same. Heath was set to work for a 'special relationship' in all but name. This meant that the British would try and be closer to the US than any other state.[48] Heath disliked the term the 'special relationship' and believed that it irritated other allies. But in this case, as with so many other policies, he was prepared to adapt the British policy to ensure that his vision would eventually have a chance to come about. He agreed to close Anglo-American consultations as he placed Britain at the heart of Europe.

At the meeting in December 1971, Heath reassured Nixon that Britain did not intend to choose between Europe and the US, by pursuing a ' "Pro-European" policy', at the expense of the US. He argued that the US needed Europe to be strong. This was the kind of security thinking that Nixon appreciated. Heath explained that the Europeans had to go beyond bilateral dealings with the US in order to create a political cooperation of a kind that made the EC a more effective partner able to deal with. Nixon claimed he understood this, and added that it was important that the West remained united, despite increased economic competition.[49]

Kissinger was not equally understanding, and was probably annoyed that Nixon voiced no protest against Heath's rough outline of his plans, which Kissinger recognised was a policy for the long haul, to be pursued with resolutely. It lacked regard for the parts of the special relationship which Kissinger appreciated, namely the interest-based, or mythical, parts.[50] Kissinger claimed that Heath's description at the Bermuda Summit on how European integration would develop a common foreign policy and defence was actually a step away from Kennedy's grand design. Kissinger's, slightly incongruous, reason was Heath's wish that Europe should form a joint policy before talking to the US. However, without a unified European approach there would neither be a pillar equal to the US, nor would Heath's plans be fulfilled. This, as things would turn out, was more than a matter of interpretation; this was the actual difference in Heath's and Kissinger's outlook. A frustrated Kissinger correctly judged Heath's stance to be a crucial alteration of the Anglo-American relationship. He clearly understood what Heath wanted to do, but was not in a position to stop it. Despite the fact that the American administration urged the Europeans to share the burden of defence and even though he was informed about the US tentative support for Anglo-French nuclear collaboration he later portrayed Heath as non-malignant de Gaulle-like figure.[51] However, what Heath wanted were good relations between two equal pillars in the Western camp, a position which hardly amounted to Gaullism; unless one regarded continued support for American hegemony over its European allies as the only reliable position a European ally could have.

Heath's argument alone could not have swayed Nixon, but he did not have to do this in any case. Nixon was already convinced that there would be more centres of powers in the world in the coming decades. In a speech in Kansas City, in the spring of 1971, he had tried to convey the image of a multipolar world, but he found the American media to be unreceptive. He argued that China, Japan and Western Europe were growing into powers alongside the superpowers. This was an unpalatable fact that not many wanted to face up to, and he later remarked that Kissinger, as well, was reluctant to recognise this.[52] As long as Heath played to the security perspective he could push his vision on Nixon, but the events of 1971 had robbed him of the chance to pursue an individual initiative to call for a special relationship between two pillars in the Western alliance. He now had to rely on someone else to push for such an initiative.

Joining Europe

The EC did not have the necessary cohesion to take such an initiative. The EC's foreign policy capability had not matured enough, but at least transatlantic relations had improved sufficiently for a proposal to be successful. By 1972 the White House method of making foreign policy had settled and transatlantic tensions been reduced. Anglo-American relations had also improved.

Despite the lack of concrete agreements, both the British and the Americans were pleased with the Bermuda Summit at the end of 1971. Channels of 'close and continual consultation' were to be established, which the FCO said had to be on all levels including the highest ones.[53] Naturally, the FCO wanted to re-establish lines of communication of the same quality, personal and informal, that Britain had enjoyed over recent decades. These had suffered due to the shift in the generation of diplomats in both Britain and the US and also unintentionally by the White House's efforts to appropriate foreign policy making from the more usual channels of the State Department.

The White House was a bit naïve about its cherished special relationship, as shown when it felt affronted by informal but blunt advice from Heath. Nixon and Kissinger's mistake was that they had bought into the myth of the special relationship as predominantly a relationship between the leading government individuals. Hence, they did not understand that when they by-passed the State Department they also undercut other Anglo-American ties. Consequently, they had to agree with the British in recreating the informal consultation basis of the Anglo-American relationship. The White House was aware that the restoration of relations could be complicated by EC enlargement, but during 1972 Nixon concentrated on his re-election and Heath focused on the run up to actual EC membership.

In 1972 the British government believed that enlargement would be a 'powerful stimulus' for deepening integration.[54] However, it had tried to stir the public with 'a revival of momentum for the European idea' between the parliamentary vote and the date of accession.[55] It was unsuccessful.[56] Heath had also originally wanted the signing of the EC Treaty to take place in London, instead of Brussels.[57] He again had to satisfy his need for action with a speech. This time he chose to make a fervent appeal in Brussels at the signing of the Treaty of Accession in January 1972. He spoke of a future that required 'a strong effort of the imagination' that would inspire 'new measures' beyond the scope of the Treaty of Rome. To him the signing was an 'end to divisions... [and a] beginning of another stage in the construction of a new and greater united Europe'.[58]

Although Britain would only be a formal member a year hence, the EC was gearing up for deepened integration. Pompidou hoped that the EC Summit planned for the fall of 1972 in Paris, to which Britain had been invited, would confirm this drive and his own role as a European statesman.[59] Amongst other things, Pompidou had his eyes on the creation of a political secretariat.[60] This was supposed to deal with international and defence matters, which were areas outside the EC Treaty.[61] Such an institution would be able to coordinate European external policies in a hitherto undreamt of manner. It would avoid linking all matters, in the economic, monetary and trade, to defence and foreign affair fields as the Europeans believed the US desired.

Pompidou's conception of the agenda for the EC Summit mostly appealed to Heath. The only problem was that Pompidou wanted the secretariat to be based in Paris.[62] If a European secretariat for political consultations in foreign affairs came about Heath could not see that that it had to 'conflict with NATO or with the Americans'. According to him, potential conflicts could be avoided by locating it in Brussels.[63] This would make it easier to enmesh the EC in NATO affairs, which, however, would not be to the liking of the French. This said, the British also liked the idea of a secretariat because it would bring continuity to the Council of Ministers and emphasise its role.[64]

In May 1972, Heath reassured the US Secretary of State William Rogers that all EC members except France wanted the secretariat in Brussels, but he said that he did not expect Pompidou to force the matter.[65] However, the proposal was abandoned together with other French proposals at the Paris Summit.[66] By then the wind had gone out of Pompidou's sails. He was frustrated by the lukewarm support given to European integration, and indirectly to him, by the French referendum on enlargement in the spring of 1972.[67] Initially, though, the British government saw the result of the French referendum as an equaliser, bringing the French down to the same level as the other EC member states.[68] The British assumed that this could make it easier for Britain to assume a leadership role in the EC, but they had not counted on the possibility that the referendum could eventually stop the French drive for deepened integration. In any case even a decision to establish a secretariat would have been many away steps from a concerted European initiative on transatlantic affairs.

The October Summit in Paris 1972 was a schizophrenic affair. On the one hand, it reaffirmed the goal to deepen integration and to forge a European Union before the 1980s.[69] On the other hand, the crucial political French enthusiasm waned. In the spring of 1972, Nixon had been pleased to see that Heath and Pompidou were in general agreement. He wrote to Heath saying that the Anglo-French relationship was the key to building 'an enlarged and strengthened Europe' a project that had his 'wholehearted support'.[70]

However, Pompidou was less willing than Heath to push forward with integration against the wishes of his own population. Efforts at greater political coordination became politicised domestically; no appeal to European idealism could change the fact that the French referendum had not been won with a wide margin. Furthermore, as shown in Chapter 2, Anglo-French relations were not helped by the fact that the British government let sterling continue to float during the fall of 1972, instead of tying it to the European currencies as Heath had promised.

Nevertheless, the challenge of creating a union by the end of the decade, which the EC members had set for themselves in Paris, was to be met from 1973 onwards.

In April 1973 Number 10's analysis was that entry had gone quite well. Yet 'the perpetual state of negotiations' in the EC meant that efforts to coordinate Britain's policy towards Europe required more assistance from the FCO. The FCO argued that 'although it [was] true that much of [British] European policy [was] not foreign affairs but an extension of domestic policy, it need[ed] to be backed by more rather than less of the traditional diplomacy'. Heath agreed with the analysis.[71] This shows that adaptation to the ways of the Community was not as straightforward as the Heath government had initially hoped. The EC had not stepped up efforts to deal with transatlantic affairs at the Paris Summit. The Heath government hoped that the pace could perhaps be hastened with a little help from American friends. Only the Nixon administration was in a position to follow up on the initiative that Heath had been unable to make – the call for the creation of two equals in a transatlantic partnership.

The Anglo-American origins of the Year of Europe

The 1973 American diplomatic initiative known as the Year of Europe was not a surprise to the British; was not Kissinger's idea; and was not seen by the British as a problem for Anglo-American or transatlantic relations until Kissinger gave a speech entitled the 'Year of Europe' to the editors of the Associated Press in New York on 23 April 1973.

Kissinger has been linked to many diplomatic successes but the Year of Europe initiative has generally been regarded as one of his failures, although he argued that only the execution not the analysis was at fault.[72] It greatly annoyed Heath, who later compared Kissinger's action of declaring a Year of Europe with no discussions to himself declaring a year of America in Trafalgar Square.[73] However, both Kissinger's and Heath's accounts can be questioned: Kissinger about his analysis; and Heath about not being consulted. In fact the British were consulted, however they did not agree with Kissinger's analysis, and had expected something quite different from the Year of Europe initiative.

For a failed and relatively obscure initiative the Year of Europe has stirred up the emotions of statesmen and contention among academics, who do not even always agree when it ended. Here, also the origin is disputed. Kissinger's account of the beginning of the initiative has generally been accepted. He claimed that the idea of a new radical approach emanated from Pompidou's comments about US-European talks at the top level to an American journalist after a meeting with Kissinger in December 1972. This then led Nixon and Kissinger to dream up the idea of confirming US-European ties with the help of a new Atlantic Charter that would invoke the memory of the charter that had been agreed between Churchill and Roosevelt in 1941.[74]

The use of such an old label illustrates the White House's susceptibility to the mythology of the special relationship, in this case the beginning of the Anglo-American wartime alliance. The basic outlines of the idea reflected Heath's own wish for an initiative that would transfer the meaning of the special relationship from an outmoded and unequal Anglo-American basis to a US-European basis. In fact, the idea for improved US-European relations pre-dated Kissinger's claim, and was more to the liking of Heath.

Nixon had invoked the need for a new partnership between the US and Europe that built on the Kennedy administration's twin pillar design already in his foreign policy report of February 1970.[75] Nixon wanted to be on friendly and equal terms with the enlarged and evolving European Community, and did not believe that 'heavy-handed' US involvement in European affairs would be conducive to this.[76] An equal partnership fitted the Nixon doctrine that required allies to take their share of the burden of defence.[77] As the previous chapter shows the White House support for the British government, when it pursued a European foundation for its deterrent, was in line with this new American foreign policy approach.

The FCO traced the origins of the Year of Europe to Nixon's report on foreign policy to the US Congress in February 1971 and to the Bermuda Summit in December the same year. As seen above, 1971 turned out to be a very inopportune year for overtures to the Europeans. Nevertheless, as the difficulties seemed to have been resolved by the end of the year Heath was able to agree with Nixon's wish for an 'initiative to maintain contact at the highest level "on all issues vital to relations between the United States and Europe"'. Heath also stressed that the British government 'intended to pursue the policy which best served British interests and these included the closest links between the two sides of the Atlantic'. In preparing for the Paris Summit, the British government did precisely that. London looked after British interests and proposed a European fund for regional development, but it did not to push for the establishment of any US-European machinery due to French opposition.[78] Neither Heath nor Pompidou wanted any action that could create transatlantic problems during Nixon's 1972 re-election campaign.

Nixon's favourable view of his meeting with Heath, in December 1971, was evident in his report to Congress in February 1972, when he singled out Heath. Nixon also quoted Heath, saying that the 'new members will now be joining with others in Europe "to work out the common European policies...governing our dealings with the rest of the world, our trade, our finance, and eventually our defense." ' According to Nixon this was 'the end of American tutelage', and the chance 'to establish a new practise in Atlantic unity – finding common ground in a consensus of independent policies instead of in deference to American prescriptions'. Nixon argued that this would work since there was an 'essential harmony of...purposes', which in fact was the reason that the US had promoted European integration.[79] Clearly, Nixon had not reappraised his views regarding Europe since taking office. Hence, he remained sympathetic to the idea of a two pillar Atlantic partnership.

In September 1972, before the Paris Summit, Kissinger made a public comment in London to the effect that if the administration remained in power after the Presidential Election in November 1972 it was likely to make a 'striking new initiative towards Europe'. The White House meant 'to develop a programme for an Atlantic partnership in close co-operation with our European friends'. According to the FCO this actually went beyond what he had told Heath in private during the same visit. However, the FCO believed that it was not until November that the phrase 'the Year of Europe' was widely used in the White House.[80] Even so, it was a month in advance of Kissinger's alleged beginning of the initiative.

So, by the time the political scandal known as Watergate began to unravel in the autumn of 1972, eventually incriminating the White House, the British knew that there would be a European initiative. Home, the Foreign Secretary, welcomed Kissinger's public statement.[81] However, the British had little reason to believe that Kissinger would have a central role in any European initiative. The same month Nixon told Home that the initiative would be planned during the first and second months of his next term.[82] A widespread impression, at the time, was that Nixon wanted 'a broad agreement on the basic aims behind the coming overhaul of the West's trading and military arrangements...[to]...minimise friction' when he said that 1973 would be 'the "Year of Europe" '.[83]

A 1972 analysis of US economic foreign policy towards the EC, requested by Nixon, and put together by the State Department, assumed that the Europeans intended to pursue the aims of the Paris Summit and aim for 'European Union' by 1980. Although the White House expected this process to be 'punctuated by crises' it also expected the EC to make headway. The development towards a union meant that Europe would take on more responsibilities at the same time as it developed 'in close partnership with the US'.[84] There was, of course, some scepticism in the Nixon administration. It was seen as ironic that the EC would commit itself to the creation of a union through economic and monetary means which would create great domestic political difficulties when its members could not even agree on when to recognise Bangladesh.[85]

There were graver doubts. After all, the Nixon administration could not know for certain that the European integration process would be beneficial because the 'direction' of the Community was unknown. Nevertheless, the State Department thought that a favourable outcome was the most likely one. For instance, deepened integration was more likely to create a full economic and monetary union, with a flexible exchange rate, which would be better for the US.[86] Nixon hoped that the united Europe would help with burden sharing, the perennial problem of defence expenses, where the US paid a lot and the European allies considerably less.[87] Consequently, on the eve of EC enlargement, Nixon reaffirmed his administration's commitment to European integration. After a string of diplomatic successes, such as the opening of China and the SALT I agreement with the Soviet Union it may seem that the Year of Europe neatly filled an empty slot. However, as demonstrated in previous chapters, Europe was always on the agenda of the Nixon White House. These efforts were frustrated by monetary disputes and the necessity of dealing with other international events. However, EC enlargement, with the inclusion of Britain, made action imperative.

Kissinger's intimate connection with the Year of Europe initiative tended to reinforce the idea that it was part of his conceptualisation of world affairs and that it was only undertaken because other more important matters had been dealt with. However, it was not self-evident that this should have been his responsibility. William P. Rogers was still Secretary of State and could have taken charge, especially since the Vietnam settlement – Kissinger's main responsibility – was not yet completed in 1972. Furthermore, Nixon had actually considered dispensing with the services of his National Security Adviser in the autumn of 1972 but as long as the Vietnam negotiations continued Kissinger was indispensable. When they were concluded in early 1973 Nixon was mired in the Watergate scandal.[88]

Nixon, jealous of his at the time much admired adviser, would not have liked Kissinger to take the credit for a successful European initiative, but the more Nixon was embroiled in Watergate the more he needed to have favourable limelight. A presidential visit to Europe during the Year of Europe was likely to provide this. Hitherto Kissinger had been best at handling such initiatives, like the one to China, which produced the desired result of a presidential trip.

In the beginning of 1973 when Nixon decided to launch a European initiative, Kissinger had also become more powerful than any of his erstwhile competitors for influence with Nixon. They had either been increasingly marginalised as Secretary of State Rogers, or else they left the administration – as Secretary of the Treasury Connally did. Number 10 was actually surprised that Rogers, who had often been embarrassed by the White House, would want to stay in a second Nixon administration.[89] In the autumn of 1972 a member of the White House staff in confidence informed the British that 'Kissinger was at the height of his power' and that this could cause problems because of Kissinger's reliance on secret diplomacy, which bred distrust. In addition to this the British were informed that Kissinger's independence from the State Department 'had gone too far' with the result that important expertise was not consulted.[90] The warnings were ignored.

Kissinger's stature had obviously grown but it was only in early 1973 that Number 10 began to scrutinise his ideas. The counsel of British Ambassador in Washington, Cromer, held favour at Downing Street. He did not see any problems specifically related to Kissinger and instead he found it natural to see the National Security Adviser as part and parcel of the White House's foreign policy, which he described as 'realpolitik'. Nixon's approach was better suited to dealing with one partner at a time, which actually made it easier to deal with enemies rather than with a group of allies. Helmut Sonnenfeldt, of the NSC staff, almost admitted as much about the White House attitude, when he remarked that discussions between allies could 'involve distasteful questioning of the US judgement'.[91] In hindsight Cromer can be seen as an early believer in the existence of a joint and coherent Nixon–Kissinger approach.

Sir Burke Trend, the Cabinet Secretary, was another person well placed to comment on Kissinger. He had functioned as Kissinger's 'British counterpart' in the 'intermittent bilateral talks' on security affairs during the first three years of the Heath government. During 1973 this role was increasingly filled by Sir Thomas Brimelow, later in the year the new Permanent Under-Secretary at the FCO.[92] Trend understood that Kissinger had a preference for conceptualisation. Already in 1971 Trend guessed that there were 'logical or conceptual links between the various initiatives... in train – SALT, MBFRs, the Berlin discussions, the projected European Security Conference', although Kissinger avoided confirming or denying the existence of 'some comprehensive design'.[93] Despite this, Trend did not make a distinction between Kissinger's and Nixon's views, for good reasons. Kissinger might have tried to bring about such an overarching architecture, but the NSC did not have a specific EC policy; it only developed an ad-hoc approach to certain aspects of Heath's vision such as Anglo-French nuclear collaboration. One reason for the slow construction of a complete Kissinger approach was that Kissinger served Nixon whose foreign policy ideas were dominant for the first years of his presidency. The Watergate scandal would change that.

The *Sunday Times*, as well, believed in late 1972 that the US had given 'little new thought on how to adjust to the fundamental changes set in train within the European Community'.[94] The British government believed that it was not yet clear to the US administration what its initiative would amount to or who would manage it. The White House had talked about changes to US-European relations for some time yet it had made few specific plans. Since the British could not recognise a specific US conceptualisation, they hoped to assist and to inspire the initiative in the best special relationship tradition. One observer thought that Heath was 'particularly eager to review the pending attempts...to revitalize Atlantic relationships'.[95] In fact, Heath had wanted to travel to the US even before EC entry in late 1972.[96]

That the initiative came as Britain entered the EC was no mere coincidence. This is also another argument against the Year of Europe as merely filling an empty slot. The view of the US State Department was that the initiative was linked both to the deepened European integration and to the expansion of the EC, of which Britain was the key new member. Rogers pointed out to Nixon that Heath's visit to the US in February was a good opportunity to begin the 'year of Europe'.[97] This the British knew.[98] And, the Heath government assumed that it could walk in step with the US government when the European initiative was launched.

Heath's own chances to launch a transatlantic initiative were now significantly smaller than in 1971. As the two previous chapters have shown Britain had failed to fix sterling at the time of entry and missed the chance of an early effort to lead Europe towards monetary union. The British government was also increasingly preoccupied with domestic affairs. A US initiative along the lines that Heath envisaged – a twin-pillar partnership – was therefore welcome since it would give added momentum to European integration. In addition, anything that stimulated integration was useful domestically as proof of the wisdom of EC entry.

When Heath and Nixon met in Washington on 1–2 February 1973 Nixon sought 'intimate and deep' collaboration with the British hoping that they could 'keep privately in step' to 'take the lead' in bringing about Atlantic partnership.[99] Heath echoed the two-pillar approach of Kennedy's grand design at the meeting. He told the press that the EC 'was a new type of union', and not the repetition of forging a nation. The nations of Europe would be incorporated within the Community, and increasingly 'act as one'. This would take place via 'constructive dialogue', to cement the relationship between the US and the EC. The dialogue would also make the relationship 'strong and durable... and [helpful in] find[ing] common solutions which meet your needs and interests as well as our own'.[100] In other words, what Heath described was an American-European special relationship. Although Nixon and Heath agreed on the desirability of a new approach Nixon wanted to work closely only with Britain and turned down Heath's request that the US also inform other European governments.[101]

Even though Nixon claimed that he wanted to go beyond the nation-state approach to Western European states, where he dealt with them individually, to a new forum to deal with them together, he was ill suited to deal with the process of changing many bilateral relations to a single one. At this time much of the key parts of the special relationship, such as intelligence and nuclear cooperation, remained intact. Nixon had understood how damaging the American approach to international monetary problems had been to the economic special relationship. In order to avoid alienating Britain he believed the US should hold on to the Anglo-American special relationship until the new Europe was completed. However, it was one thing to quietly sustain the nuclear special relationship and share confidences about nuclear policy. It was another to ask Britain to have close consultation with the US at the same time as the US initiated its new transatlantic diplomacy. Then Britain's special standing with the US could easily become apparent. That could easily result in a misunderstanding with other EC members and expose the British as hypocritical. It required a considerable balancing for Britain to pursue the creation of a single European unit and at the same time support new US policies. Nixon's wish for a cautious approach made it paramount that the US should trust Britain and not draw attention to Britain's still special standing.

Although Nixon did not intend to focus on the actual management of the Year of Europe the person that he chose to deal with it – Kissinger – was even less appropriate for a multilateral approach. Heath's impression was that Kissinger was very loyal to Nixon.[102] At this time

Heath believed that Kissinger was not much more than Nixon's errand boy. It was not until the summer of 1973 that Heath took a greater interest in Kissinger's writings and ideas.[103] By then the divergence between Nixon's and Kissinger's approaches to Europe had dawned on Heath.

Heath could never quite understand that Kissinger regarded Europe in a different light from himself.[104] Kissinger on the other hand never fully grasped the ardour of Heath's Europeanism. Nor did Kissinger understand the degree to which the FCO and Heath worked in tandem. He thought that the FCO led by Home followed a different course from Heath's.[105] This says more about the power struggles within the Nixon administration. Heath's view was always consistent with his Harvard lectures. His views were also congruent with the FCO's view that the US supported British EC membership because it would lead to a united and integrated Europe as a partner to the US.

Kissinger missed what Heath was about. First, Heath did not put more distance between Britain and the US than was necessary. He wanted to be a good European but not at the expense of relations with the US. His vision included a future European partnership with the US, at the time exemplified by the secret Anglo-American efforts to forge Anglo-French nuclear cooperation. Second, Heath was not a Gaullist. However, he was not a pure-supranationalist either. He did not want to give executive powers to the EC Commission. Not because he zealously guarded the prerogatives of the nation-state, but because he saw himself and the other leaders of Europe working together as the most expedient way of constructing a European union.

Heath followed concrete aims, even if his vision was somewhat shrouded in generalities. Kissinger approach was the inverse of Heath's. Heath was a pragmatic as he tried to achieve his specific goals. Kissinger was a realist whose objective was to safeguard what he saw as the national interest of the US. Rather than following a certain goal and adapting policies to that aim Kissinger's instinct was to adhere to a conceptual approach of how everything hung together when dealing with challenges to the US and managing Nixon's aims. Although this approach helped the White House to disentangle the challenges of the seventies Kissinger's realism made him see constancy of purpose in new phenomena. This enabled him to claim that Heath was a new de Gaulle, instead of seeing him as an entirely new factor. This would have mattered little if Watergate had not happened. Because it did, the besieged Nixon left the handling of foreign policy more and more to Kissinger.

Beginning as a domestic affair Watergate became a whirlpool that sucked in all Nixon's political energy. By April 1973, the British realised that Watergate could evolve into a 'crippling' affair for Nixon.[106] A month later, Cromer commented that Kissinger and his NSC staff was 'one of the sectors of the White House machine' working as before.[107] This meant that its relative importance grew. With the rest of the White House busy dealing with Watergate the NSC could still develop policy and work out initiatives. As the political crisis deepened foreign policy making slipped to Kissinger. Another factor that increased Kissinger's influence was Nixon's decision to postpone any trip to Europe until after the summer. Heath believed that the reason for this was the president's frustration with European criticism of the US bombings of North Vietnam in December 1972.[108] It seemed that Nixon's own support for European integration suffered when his impatience with the Europeans increased in the early spring of 1973.[109] In any case, the deferment of the trip meant that Nixon focused on other issues thus shifting the execution of the Year of Europe to Kissinger. He became responsible not only for the Year of Europe but also, because of Watergate, for how it fitted into the administration's foreign policy.

Brimelow, from the FCO, met Kissinger on 5 March in Washington to discuss a transatlantic initiative. At the meeting, Kissinger went no further than Nixon towards involving other Europeans – quite the opposite. The British stated that they were prepared to help inform a study for a European initiative. Kissinger stressed that he wanted 'to place *détente* in a conceptual framework', but also explained that he had 'no clear idea what should be done'. He knew what he did not want, however, and dismissed 'a Grand Design on Europe' since it would not work. Brimelow said that the challenge was to find an 'intellectual framework' that would fit both the EC and NATO. Kissinger said that Nixon wanted 'to achieve his aim of institutionalising the Alliance' and make it safe for change and for the potential weaknesses of his successors. Kissinger wanted to start with Anglo-American consultations and only involve France and West Germany at a later stage.[110]

While Heath agreed that Brimelow could make a separate British study to help the White House efforts he stressed the need to stay attuned to European feelings, so it would not seem as if the British were ' "ganging up" with the Americans against Europe'.[111] This was yet another case where consultations unintentionally reaffirmed special ties. The British study tried to assess how much common Western ground there was for the policy of détente in the future and how more resources could be found for NATO. Nevertheless, the British had considerable difficulties in dealing with the American 'one ball of wax' approach where economic and military matters were put together in one 'global approach'. They were apprehensive of the fact that the US administration might employ this concept in order to achieve a 'linkage' between European concessions over trade and monetary affairs and the American commitment to the defence of Europe. By the time the British put their inter-departmental study together, it was quite clear that Britain could not afford to assign a greater share of its GDP to defence. The diplomacy of détente was believed to limit European motivation for increased defence efforts and the British felt that the greatest question was how to square détente in East–West relations with Western cohesion.[112]

The British gave Kissinger the report shortly before he met with Cromer, Trend and Brimelow on 19 April 1973. Kissinger gave it little attention. Instead of producing a US equivalent he told them that he wanted to focus 'on the presentational aspects of the Atlantic relationship'.[113] He also claimed that he found the tone of the British document a bit too fatalistic.[114] Kissinger believed that Heath found the special advisory role of Britain to the US incompatible with British leadership in Europe.[115] In fact, Heath thought that Britain's special relationship was an affront to the other Europeans.[116] However, the British proposal was oriented to resolve that kind of potential contradiction. It mixed a traditional Cold War security approach with specific intra-Western issues. Most likely, Kissinger's lack of interest in the study was prompted by the British paper questioning whether the interests of two future Western pillars, Western Europe and the US, would be identical in regard to the kind of East–West diplomacy that Kissinger had spent the last four years developing.[117] That the interests of Europe and the US would be very similar had also been Nixon's assumption, but the British were merely pointing to the paradox of the US pursuing a diplomacy of relaxation with the Soviet Union while asking the Western Europeans to invest more in defence. The questions raised by the British were meant to underline the importance of the West sticking together, but also that the future Europe might not be limited to a regional role.[118] The whole British paper was forward looking in a manner that Kissinger had not expected.

Kissinger told the British that he would give a speech on 23 April, and claimed that this would be in line with Nixon's wish to reaffirm Atlantic solidarity. He explained another motivation to act: the need to convince the American public that the US could ' "rely" on Europe', thus shoring up the domestic foundations of foreign policy.[119] This kind of short-term advantages was a far cry from the joint long-term effort that the British had hoped their paper could be the basis of. However, it was not only Kissinger's methods that were different. The ideas of the FCO and Kissinger also diverged.

He informed the British that he would have similar discussions with the French and the West Germans, but added that he would not tell them of his talks with the British or their paper. This new attempt at secretive diplomacy merely underlined to the FCO the 'sharp change' from 5 March when 'the emphasis was on the President's desire to achieve a major act of statesmanship'.[120] In April the emphasis seemed to have switched to soothing the administration's domestic problems, and in this sense Kissinger was loyal to Nixon's needs.

This need to play to the domestic audience had become evident on 15 April when Nixon told the media that he would undertake 'a grand tour' to Europe after the summer. However, this came as a complete surprise to Kissinger.[121] Clearly, Nixon and Kissinger were not communicating with each other about the initiative. The incident underscores that it was still Nixon who ultimately could hold sway, but that more and more of the actual management was made by Kissinger.

Kissinger told the British that what the White House wanted to achieve with the Year of Europe was not a settlement of all outstanding issues but to have them 'clarified' and framed with the help of new principles put in a charter, or declaration. This would involve the global approach and Kissinger added that '[l]inkage was a fact of life'. However, he claimed that an 'overall framework' would increase the US administration's ability to check the consequences of specific negotiations.[122] Evidently, Kissinger was interested in the conceptualisation of the new Atlantic approach, and the domestic effects of it. It answered to more immediate political needs, rather than the evolution of US–EC relations in the long run, and it seemed to take on a more limited form than what the British had expected, omitting any room for British-made visions.

Consequently, when Kissinger was poised to make his speech on the Year of Europe the British were slightly perturbed about the turn of events. Brimelow's study had built on Heath's vision of a united Western Europe that took on an increasing share of the responsibilities of the West. Hence, the major challenge had seemed to be the coordination of US and European foreign affairs. Heath's Europeanism had actually overlapped with Nixon's view of European integration, but when the Year of Europe became Kissinger's to develop, this distanced the initiative from Heath's and Nixon's joint understanding. Clearly, the Year of Europe as a joint Anglo-American effort had failed before the initiative had even begun. All the complications that later stemmed from Kissinger's version of the Year of Europe only served to make the kind of transatlantic relations Heath wanted to see more difficult to attain. This contributed to the ruin of Heath's vision of a cohesive Western Europe in equal partnership with the US.

Kissinger's Year of Europe

On 23 April, Kissinger gave his speech on the Year of Europe at the Associated Press Annual Luncheon in New York. There had been no advance copy for the British.[123] This was not surprising as he finished it shortly before delivering it.[124] It was Kissinger's first formal policy announcement on a major topic and it is surprising that he spent relatively little time on it, only consulting his immediate staff. Kissinger was confident of his own ability. He did not feel the need to consult the State Department. At the time Kissinger was more popular than ever while the rest of the White House was in the throws of the political hurricane of Watergate.[125] Hence, he could count on much attention. Kissinger might have thought that he had followed Nixon's instructions yet his interpretation of the initiative relied on his own ideas. These he believed to be more realistic in the short run. Evidently, he thought that his version of the Year of Europe was in the best interest of the US.

The speech, including Kissinger's interpretation of transatlantic relations, bore a resemblance to his work on transatlantic relations, written nearly eight years earlier.[126] In this, he had rejected the two-pillar approach of the Kennedy administration. He argued that the latter approach, with its emphasis on one single supranational body for Europe, would not be sufficiently flexible for Europe. He thought it more likely that individual Western European countries would at times be closer to the US than to each other. He thought it ironic, and also hence dangerous, if a united federal Europe like the one Monnet promoted would fall into the hands of Gaullists. Instead, Kissinger wanted to build on the Atlantic alliance to maintain the cohesion of the West. He advocated a Europe that was not federal but one which instead had many centres, where the US could link all the issues and play the various centres, national and institutional, of Europe off against each other.[127] What Kissinger recommended amounted to hegemonic domination of its allies. It throws some doubt on the earnestness of the compliant, attributed to him, that he did not know who to call when he wanted to call Europe.

In the 'Year of Europe' speech Kissinger stated that 1973 was the end of an 'era that was shaped by decisions of a generation ago'. Kissinger talked little about partnership and more about Atlantic unity, linking several issues: economic, defence-related and political, claiming that top level discussions involving all the three were the best way to make headway instead of leaving the matters with experts. According to him 'reciprocity' from the EC was necessary in order for European integration to receive continued US support.[128] He also sought an emotional American, as well as European, commitment to shared interests. This became known as an appeal for an Atlantic Charter that impinged on security, economic and diplomatic issues.[129] However, the reference to a charter on top of all the issues Kissinger raised revived the spectre of 'global' or 'one ball of wax' approach, which the Europeans feared. Such an approach suggested that all intricate issues in all fields be dealt with simultaneously. The proposal for a charter would spawn much thinking and drafting with suggestions for either one or several documents, in efforts to cover all areas, on both sides of the Atlantic.

For many, this was the beginning of the Year of Europe, whereas for the British it had already begun with the Heath–Nixon Summit. The British found the alterations to the Year of Europe confirmed and cemented by its public delivery by Kissinger. Nevertheless, the speech was not immediately called an unmitigated disaster by the British. Home made a general welcoming comment to the speech on 27 April, but he underlined both that it was necessary for the EC to give a collective reply and that many of the issues Kissinger linked were already dealt with respectively and in their own pace.[130] Despite its careful response, the FCO realised that the Anglo-American plans for the Year of Europe had come to nothing.[131] The British had to fall back on the EC and to rely on the creation of a second pillar, without the American assistance they had hoped for.

Ambassador Cromer was less disappointed. He tried to explain to London that Kissinger's speech was intended not only for foreign consumption. It was also an attempt to hit back at domestic detractors. It was also not as tough on Europe as it could have been.[132] Since it would merely be seen as an attempt to escape the domestic political problems of the Nixon administration Heath found the timing of Kissinger's speech inopportune. Furthermore, he thought that Kissinger had demonstrated his lack of knowledge about Community affairs. Heath was especially annoyed about a reference Kissinger had made to the EC as a regional actor, since Kissinger, only a fortnight before the speech, had told Heath that the Community had wider responsibilities.[133] Whatever its domestic impact, the speech did have foreign policy consequences, both in terms of content and delivery.

The approach that had served Kissinger so well in dealing with enemies – finding a format of principles on which to base negotiations – was not the ideal technique to deal with friends, as the British and Kissinger himself were to find out. His statement that Europeans had regional considerations and that the US had global ones reflected the kind of bluntness that might have impressed enemies but it infuriated Europeans. If Kissinger had looked at Europe less from the security angle and had studied economic affairs, it would also have been obvious to him that his claims were far from the truth. However, economics, which was after all what the US–EC affairs had hitherto often been about, was not Kissinger's strongest suit. Because of Kissinger's realist outlook, his view of European integration tended to be different from what the British were used to and they accordingly had to make quite an effort to interpret what Kissinger actually wanted.

While Kissinger was running the show he tried to appear flexible when talking to the British representatives. This was not entirely spurious. He did not know how to bring his version of the new transatlantic alliance about in practical terms. Since Kissinger's speech was 'framed in very general terms', Trend could not figure out how the British should respond to the idea of an Atlantic Charter.[134] He warned that Britain should not reject Kissinger's initiative since the consequences could strengthen isolationism in the US. He also argued that Britain should refrain from leading a European effort in response to Kissinger's speech, because even if Britain could accept the economic costs of linkage it might be too much for others, like the French. Heath, who, despite having seen what he had hoped to be a carbon copy of his own ideas, in the form of an initiative, hijacked and significantly altered, nevertheless, agreed.[135]

Kissinger and Heath both wanted a future transatlantic relationship to be based on trust and informality, which both saw as necessary to keep the West together. Kissinger wanted the Euro-American transatlantic relationship to be like the Anglo-American relationship of the sixties, with one dependent junior partner, who offered advice and remained loyal. Heath, on the other hand, wanted to recreate the original special relationship – one between equals. The difference, in practice, was that Heath wanted consultations after each had had held their own counsel; where the European on their part first agreed between themselves and only then discussed issues with the US. Whereas Kissinger wanted the Europeans to give counsel to the US on its leadership of the West, and additionally to let the US have its say in European affairs. This would emphasise that the West was led by one single power – the US – and not by a duo.

On 10 May 1973, Kissinger met Trend and Greenhill, the Permanent Under-Secretary at the FCO. They agreed that unless there was a renewed commitment to Western unity transatlantic tensions would eventually lead to a full blown crisis in the future. Trend and Greenhill suggested that Kissinger should pursue the idea expressed in his speech and conduct 'preliminary discussions' with Britain, West Germany and France while studiously avoiding references to France's involvement in NATO.[136] They did not want to have the update of the nuclear deterrent or the British three-way strategy on nuclear cooperation for re-involving France in European defence mixed up with and disturbed by the new US policy. Kissinger promised a message for the European Heads of government from Nixon, which never materialised.[137] This is further evidence of Nixon's lack of involvement.

The crux was that the British had been set on engaging France; Kissinger's speech had not made that easier. When Heath met Pompidou, on 21 May 1973, Heath told him of his misgivings about Kissinger's initiative.[138] If Heath thought Kissinger had misread the workings of the EC the French, according to the FCO, were even more critical. Paris did not think the Europeans had any obligations to the US for being protected by the American nuclear umbrella. The French held that the US defence of Europe was in the interest of the US.[139]

As seen in the previous chapter, Pompidou had been misinformed in the spring of 1973 about Britain's nuclear weapons planning, having repaired that damaging factor to Franco-British relations Heath now wanted to avoid further problems. He admitted that Nixon had told him a year earlier that he intended some kind of action on transatlantic affairs. He also told Pompidou that the Year of Europe was the result of a long-standing White House wish to deal with transatlantic relations. Nixon had informed Heath about his ideas about transatlantic relations a year earlier and again informed him how the approach was developing when they met in February 1973. Since then, according to Heath, the proportions of the Watergate affair had become such that the scandal could impede Nixon's foreign policy commitments. He was now afraid that the Year of Europe would seem like a diversionary manoeuvre designed to draw attention away from American domestic issues. Most dangerous of all, however, was Kissinger's wish to conceptualise relationships, in this case with 'linkage', and find suitable policies afterwards. Heath proposed that the Europeans should decide what they wanted from the Americans, and then find the best approach in each of the various fields.[140] Clearly, he intended to oppose Kissinger's efforts to link all the issues of trade, monetary and defence affairs.

Since the EC had settled its course for the coming ten years, Heath suggested that they should display their confidence to the US. Pompidou completely agreed that Kissinger's 'global view' of putting all the issues together was undesirable. As Heath said, they could not allow trade and monetary affairs to be linked to defence, since that would make it possible for the US to constantly use its defence of Europe as a reason for European concessions. Heath found that in the long run Europe's dependence was unhealthy.[141] Pompidou, however, was unwilling to take up Heath's suggestions that they look at transatlantic relations and defence arrangements. Pompidou also turned down the idea that the Nine should prepare any papers on US–EC relations. The British put this down to a French desire to have 'freedom of action' at the US-French Summit that was to be held at Reykjavik ten days later.[142]

Already prior to the meeting Kissinger had realised that the relations with the French were fraught. One French minister had called his approach the beginning of a 'super Yalta'. Kissinger protested to Michel Jobert, now the French Minister for Foreign Affairs, whom he met on 17 May arguing that in that case he would have involved the Soviet Union too. He admitted, though, that he could have prepared the initiative better. However, he claimed that the administration intended to use the remaining '3½ years' of the Nixon administration to work on the Atlantic alliance. He argued that if the US had wanted to blackmail Europe it would not need a new initiative to do so. While saying that the US was not opposed to French autonomy, he added that many had noticed that US policies were similar to his published writings and that his analysis of Europe was 'well-known, and the President knew when he hired me'.[143] However, while this may have been the case, no one has argued that Nixon hired Kissinger because he wanted to implement Kissinger's ideas. On the contrary, Kissinger was hired to allow Nixon to have maximum control of foreign policy.

By the beginning of June, it had become clear that there had been a series of misunderstandings between the French and the Americans at their summit in Reykjavik. This prompted Heath to make a move.[144] There was neither a process of consultations in place between the Europeans nor between the Europeans as a group and the US. As the British government had come to realise, consultations with allies had not been the Nixon administration's strength. Getting a process in place was made difficult by suspicions among all the Europeans, including the British, about 'Dr. Kissinger's methods and...secretive handling' of the Year of Europe. On 20 June, Heath told the British government that they had to save the Year of Europe so that there would not be further domestic American pressure of withdrawals from Europe. He regarded Kissinger's wish 'for a single declaration of principles as unrealistic'.[145] The French would never agree to a NATO declaration that involved EC affairs.

Kissinger was undoubtedly right that Heath's plans of turning Britain European showed that he was both obstinate and daring.[146] Heath cared desperately about his vision and he therefore tried to make use of the already failing Year of Europe initiative. As he said at the time he rejected the idea that individuals were unimportant and decision-makers interchangeable.[147]

The phase the Year of Europe was used less in the summer and when Heath and Home met Jobert on 2 July Heath remarked that it seemed as if the US had ended the idea of a Year of Europe. Jobert believed that the concept, if not the phrase, remained. He told them that Kissinger had recently given him a draft for a charter on which Kissinger wanted comments. Jobert was then made privy to the outlines of the British solution of two declarations. He said that France did not seek any declarations but would not object if others devised them since 'if the...documents said nothing, it would not really matter having them'.[148]

In the summer of 1973 the Year of Europe turned even sourer and Heath came to see the American approach as 'tactless and ham-handed'.[149] He was also frustrated that the US could not tell the difference between NATO and the EC. At one point he exclaimed to his American friend Walt Rostow, with White House connections, that '[f]or the last 25 years Britain had been divesting itself, largely to please the Americans, of imperial responsibilities and creating a Commonwealth of independent countries. The result was of little benefit and of some liability to the United Kingdom.' He claimed that the American present experience of no longer being 'No. 1' was a decline of a similar kind and that the US had to wake up to this reality. To him the refusal of the Americans to recognise that the 'twin pillar' West was coming into reality was fundamentally irritating.[150] A despondent Heath thought that decline was spreading throughout the West.

Home too was annoyed, but with Heath. He feared that Heath's comments would reach the White House and that he would have to mend relations with the US. Especially bad was a reference to how the US prepared better for talks with their enemies than their friends. He pointed out to Heath that the Year of Europe speech was to a high degree for domestic consumption, to which Heath remarked '[w]hich is precisely why it has gone wrong!'.[151]

The main reason that Heath came to dislike the Year of Europe was that Kissinger's secretive tactics were imported into a multilateral context, which disrupted British relations with France and his friend Michel Jobert. On 1 July, the day before Home and Heath had met Jobert, Ambassador Cromer had received a White House draft version like the one Kissinger had given to Jobert.[152] Jobert had been led to believe by Kissinger that he was an exclusive recipient, but Heath and Home did not know when they met Jobert that Britain too was in the possession of a copy of the draft.[153] Towards the end of July, Jobert found out that the British had also received a copy before the meeting. He grew distrustful and blamed Home for not telling him.[154] But this criticism was unfounded. The draft Cromer had received had not yet reached London when Jobert met Heath and Home.[155] Jobert at first thought that the British had gone behind his back and was deeply hurt and at first he 'shrugged off' the British explanations.[156] 'His unjustified suspicions were only dispelled with difficulty' at the end of July.[157] Kissinger later maintained that Jobert on purpose accused the British and the Americans of collusion, with the intention of causing difficulties in the Anglo-American relationship.[158] However, that was not how Heath saw it. Greenhill, the Permanent Under-Secretary at the FCO, observed that '[t]he one thing Kissinger and the French seem to have in common is a penchant for highly selective and unorthodox bilateral dealings'.[159]

The British regarded Kissinger's draft as 'a high opening bid'.[160] Throughout July the British worked on coordinating the Europeans.[161] A considerable part of the efforts to work out a response from the Nine took the form of a document on European identity. The deliberations about this took place within the framework of the Political Committee of the European Political Cooperation, the EPC, where the respective political directors of the member states' foreign ministries sat. Brimelow was the British representative.[162] The pace of the work was slow. Instead of jumping at Kissinger's challenge as a healthy institution, confident of itself and its status would have done, the EPC viewed Kissinger's initiative as an unwelcome test. As such, it increased the pressure on a community which was already dealing with its first enlargement as well as its attempts to live up to the goals from the Hague and Paris Summits while at the same time experiencing an increasingly adverse economic reality.

Kissinger's Year of Europe threatened Heath's vision of an outward looking Community endowed with a foreign policy based on the two-pillar approach. Instead of carefully building upon the security foundation of the Atlantic alliance it carelessly blended security and economic affairs. This undermined the possibility of transforming the transatlantic relationship into a special relationship similar to what the Anglo-American relationship had been in the past. Kissinger's success in keeping the US Departments at bay meant a loss of valuable advice and 'historical memory'. It meant lost opportunities in finding information through informal channels, and having discussion at lower levels that tied in with what had been agreed at the top levels.[163] Instead, he exposed himself to all the diplomatic signals that should normally have been filtered by large sections of the Nixon administration. Rogers told Home in June 1973 that he would have handled matters differently since he was not a 'one ball of wax' man. He also told Home that the State Department had worked on four separate versions of an Atlantic declaration in order to meet Kissinger's suggestion of an Atlantic Charter. He claimed that the State Department product was 'grandiose' and adaptable to a NATO setting or a meeting with the Nine.[164] Kissinger had shown little interest in any of these.

At the end of July, Heath's attempt to rescue the Year of Europe went from bad to worse. Heath told Nixon that the Community's foreign ministers were hard at work on a 'European Identity' from which to launch their response to the US.[165] This sparked a stark response from Nixon, who was very frustrated by the slowness of the European response. He vented his frustration on Heath in a 'very frank' reply, telling him that that if the initiative failed Europe would 'be the loser'. Of course, there was also the matter of his trip to Europe being unnecessarily delayed. Nixon wanted his trip to Europe to be 'a major symbolic and substantive act' that would give momentum to their common enterprises. He wanted meetings with the North Atlantic Council and the Community to have real results, but instead it seemed, he complained, as if the Europeans were stringing the US along. He was 'flexible' about the number, shape and form of the document or documents, but did not want them to be the foundation for a bargaining position.[166] One observer at the British Embassy thought that Watergate had made Nixon much more sensitive and more easily provoked.[167] Nixon was not up-to-date on Kissinger's management and he did not understand how the British perceived Kissinger. Neither did he understand that the British regarded the American draft as exactly the kind of document Nixon himself did not want to see. However, Nixon like Kissinger was also interested in the immediate political benefits that the Year of Europe could bestow.

On 30 July there was a tense meeting at the White House where Kissinger met with Trend and Brimelow. Kissinger explained his and

Nixon's great frustration at having to face a European draft of the charter presented as a 'fait accompli'. Kissinger was exasperated by all the various proposals on how to conduct the discussion of reaffirming the Atlantic alliance, only to end up with what he thought was an 'adversary relationship'. He had expected 'the sort of relationship the US had had with Britain in the past' with the Europeans, not the 'insulting' lack of consultations of the Europeans over the draft Charter.[168] Ironically, that 'sort of relationship' was exactly what Heath had wanted to import into US–EC relations with the help of previous Anglo-American experience.

Trend told Kissinger that the US 'had asked for a coordinated European response'. Kissinger argued that he had meant a 'coordinated Atlantic response'. He had wanted to focus on the three major powers in Europe. Above all, he blamed the French, and Brimelow fell in with this criticism but tried to explain that 'Europe was trying on a very modest scale to coordinate foreign policy'. He then went on to explain that the Europeans had had a 'procedural deadlock' over how the Community should handle the charter, the role of the European Commission, and a possible Nixon visit. This deadlock was news to Kissinger, who added that Nixon had not asked to meet the Community. In contrast, the British had wanted to deal with the Year of Europe through the machinery of cooperation among the Nine. Trend believed that Kissinger was 'trying to get the machine to work faster than it was capable of'.[169] The willingness of the leading European states, Britain, France and West Germany, to continue to exchange information bilaterally with the White House while they tried to harmonise reactions to the American ideas had been unpopular with the other EC members.[170]

That Kissinger had never bothered to grasp the functions of the EC now showed. The US State Department thought that the 'British support for the integration process [was]...closely tied to the fortunes of Heath and the Conservative Party'. However, looking at Britain's domestic situation it believed that Britain had made a 'great gamble' by joining the Six, since membership exposed the British economy to greater competition.[171] The essence of EC affairs was still economics, a field that did not interest Kissinger. Only now did he realise that he had not appreciated that the Europeans could be confident in this area and remain sensitive about political affairs. In July, he claimed that had he understood what the European reaction would be, he would never have mentioned its regional role. On the contrary, he would have welcomed a Europe that helped the US by undertaking 'global responsibilities'.[172] At the meeting with Trend and Brimelow it became clear that Kissinger found the responsibilities of the EC incomprehensible.

At one point Kissinger exclaimed that 'the "Year of Europe" was over' as far as the White House was concerned and that it was now up to the Europeans if it would amount to anything. He later admitted that the speech 'was one of the worst mistakes that he had made' and that he had not understood that efforts at European Union took precedence over the individual responses of the national governments. He claimed that the US intention had been 'to build Atlantic unity' not 'to build Europe'. Trend, taking the Heath line, claimed that both could be achieved, which Kissinger disagreed with.[173] Kissinger had sought a situation where transatlantic unity was preserved under US hegemony.

Kissinger remained firmly opposed to the twin-pillar idea, just as he had been in the mid-sixties. Instead, he had advocated a weak Europe, with many centres. In such a constellation, the US could link all the issues and play the various centres, national and institutional, of Europe against each other. Nonetheless, he wished to see a common Atlantic foreign policy, but under US auspices.[174] Undoubtedly, this was very attractive to his view of the US role but exactly why such a constellation would not make greater demands on the US in terms of time spent on diplomatic coordination and sheer costs was unclear. In any case Kissinger's ideas would have stymied the developments that Heath wished to see. Kissinger, however, agreed to wait and see if anything came out of the Copenhagen EC Summit.[175]

US hegemony reasserted

The EC Summit was eventually held only in December. This delayed a possible visit by the US President. The American leader was, however, engulfed in the Watergate scandal. One of its repercussions was to make the Europeans less keen on a presidential visit.[176] The affair also made the Europeans doubt as to whether Nixon would be able to stick to any agreements signed. The FCO actually believed that the Watergate affair affected the mind frame of both Kissinger and Nixon.[177]

At his meeting with Trend and Brimelow, at the end of July, Kissinger left it to the Europeans to make something out of the Year of Europe. It was now up to them to make something out of the initiative. Kissinger was disappointed with the initiative and his frustration spilled over on the Anglo-American relationship. Although, at the time, Heath was on the same side of the Atlantic to attend the Commonwealth Conference in Canada, there was little he could do. Heath was annoyed with the failure of the Year of Europe as a US-led initiative. Yet, he also had to take into account the necessity to maintain good relations with the US. A crucial reason, as seen in the previous chapter, was the need to update the nuclear independent deterrent. He was prepared to say that he understood the frustration that Kissinger had expressed. Heath attributed these to Britain having become an EC, which had caused procedural problems. However, he did not want to deal with Kissinger; instead, he sought to reassure Nixon directly that he did not want the Atlantic relationship to be damaged.[178]

In a letter to Nixon, Heath expressed shock both at Kissinger's comments, during the National Security Advisers meeting with Trend and Brimelow, and with Nixon's own letter on 26 July. Heath stressed that he did not seek any 'loosening of the close ties' of the Anglo-American relationship. He explained his opinion that the US reappraisal of its European policy had been paradoxical because the US was about to shift its stance on European integration, just when the result that he and Nixon had talked about – 'an equal partnership' – was materialising. Heath wrote that he was sure that this was not Nixon's intention. He appealed to his sense of history by comparing the difficulties of coordinating the EC members with the problems the US had itself had in the beginning of its existence.[179] On this issue at this time there was a Nixon–Kissinger policy. There was only a single view in the White House; to await the results of the European deliberations.

During the autumn there were negotiations on both US–EC and NATO declarations. The joint EC proposals which emerged in September were full of the kind of trivialities the White House did not want.[180] This meant that the high hopes invested in the Year of Europe first by Heath and later in a different way by Kissinger devolved into something much more mundane than either had hoped for. In late September, when Kissinger had finally been promoted to Secretary of State, Anglo-American tempers had cooled. Meeting Kissinger the same month Home acknowledged that the Community had suffered from its lack of 'real machinery at the lower levels', and that it yet had to work out its political identity. He added that the new procedures of the EC were something which everyone had to 'learn to work with'. Kissinger said that the White House had not appreciated how quickly the American relations with Britain, that 'had never been treated as a foreign Government', had been transformed, or that 'Europe as a unit' should be taken 'literally' so soon. He added that there was no reason to have signed a charter that was 'a controversial issue'. That would merely contradict its original purpose. He was amenable and repeated that Nixon wanted to go to Europe, possibly in the coming year. At the same time he assured Home that the visit was destined above all to strengthen the Atlantic alliance and was not for motivated by domestic reasons. Nixon wanted to sign a charter, or charters, but only with someone of equal stature.[181] Whether or not Heath's ideas would come about it was clear that the EC could not be ignored.

In October the Yom Kippur War broke out, bringing with it an oil crisis, which shifted the focus of the planned EC Summit, which was to be held in Copenhagen. As a result transatlantic declarations were not given adequate attention. Meanwhile, the White House continued to sink deeper into the Watergate affair, to the point where it incapacitated Nixon. For these reasons and in the light of the British government's concerns for its domestic situation, Heath could not work with Nixon to reaffirm the twin-pillar partnership within the alliance.

Nevertheless, work continued on an Atlantic declaration grounded in NATO. Although Kissinger had agreed to await the results he later accused the Europeans of not completing a proper follow up.[182] Evidently, the dynamism had gone out of the Year of Europe and of any efforts to redesign the transatlantic relationship in any fashion. The worst fears of the Europeans were avoided. There was no linkage of all issues in the form of an Atlantic Charter or any other form. There was not even a single charter. Kissinger's hopes for an emotional revival through the means of declaration had backfired. Instead, there were two parallel attempts leading nowhere. The NATO Atlantic declaration was eventually signed but after Heath's premiership had ended. It lacked the importance that the Nixon White House had wanted to accord it. By the time it was signed, shortly before Nixon left office, it had already been overridden by events according to Kissinger.[183] It was merely a confirmation of traditional relations.[184] On the other hand, the result of the work on a European identity when it appeared in December 1973 was a lacklustre document that demonstrated that the Nine were concerned with other matters. It failed to become the basis for a US–EC declaration.[185] Neither declaration reflected Heath's hopes for the recognition of the ambition to have two equals within the West.

The FCO's conclusion was that the Year of Europe had effectively come to an end in October 1973 and that the things the British and Americans had in common – language, assumptions and habits of cooperation, all the parts of the Anglo-American relationship that Heath had called 'natural' – 'create[d] a more fertile soil for misunderstandings than a genuinely adversary relationship'.[186] On 12 December 1973, Kissinger, as US Secretary of State, was able to put forward his view of how the administration regarded on the past year, and the Year of Europe, as well as transatlantic relations for the future in a speech to the Pilgrim Society in London.

In his speech, Kissinger underlined the importance of Anglo-American bonds. He claimed that the US administration's worry had been that the Atlantic alliance would be weakened by a new generation that was disconnected from the ties forged in the early years of the Cold War. Therefore, the administration had sought to reinvigorate US-European relations with the Year of Europe. He argued that European unity was a fact to which the US raised no objections; however, this 'unity must not be at the expense of Atlantic Community', and he complained that the behaviour of the EC had tended to emphasise differences rather than Western unity. He said that the US was an 'old ally' that should be trusted to have a say much earlier in the processes where Europe dealt with transatlantic affairs. Summing up he *said* he hoped Britain, 'though the loosening of some of our old ties have been painful at times', as a new EC member could use its experience and transfer 'the same special confidence and intimacy' characteristic of Anglo-American relations to the new US-European relationship, because the US was now 'prepared to offer a unifying Europe a "special relationship"' to foster Western unity.[187] This was not a late conversion to Heath's view but a reference to the special relationship as Kissinger saw it; a relationship between the US and a reliable, and yet, junior partner. It was consistent to Kissinger's doubts about the pace of European integration that he had held since the sixties. While he recognised that the world was becoming multipolar politically he was not prepared to assist in forging a pole in Europe with all attributes. He believed that forcing through European unity would risk common Atlantic interests, especially in dealing with the East. He willingly recognised that Europe and the US had common interests but felt that these were best served by avoiding overly formal communications. Instead he preferred the continuation of many and more informal communications, as in the past. This had more than a touch of the 'mythical' aspect of special relations.

During the first years of the Nixon presidency Kissinger had helped to give the US new leverage with the East by means of triangular diplomacy between the US and China and the Soviet Union. Perhaps, with his systemic realism, Kissinger was apprehensive that a second pole within the West, which was independent in economic, military and political terms, would allow the East to drive a wedge between the US and Europe as the US had successfully done between China and the Soviet Union. In the short term at least, with the West in fear of decline, Kissinger argued that his approach to Europe was the safest in terms of the Cold War.

Since helping Rippon to deal with the US administration's reaction to the EC negotiations, Kissinger had proved a strong supporter of the traditional special relationship as he saw it, with Britain as a reliable junior partner in a loyal and advisory capacity. Kissinger's reference to importing the best of the special relationship to the US-European relationship was akin to Heath's but overshadowed by Kissinger's determination to ensure American hegemony for as long as possible. As an approach, he found this more realistic and one which he could uphold in his new capacity as Secretary of State.

Heath's chance to shape the Year of Europe had been fatally undermined. In this process Britain's chances of leadership in Europe decreased, as well as its chances to work for any approach, either British or American, which aimed at improving transatlantic relations. Heath's chances to change the reappraised US policy towards Europe to a semblance of his own idea had also been dealt a severe blow by the failure of the EC to live up to the challenge of the Year of Europe. Nor would he have a chance to influence the US further.

The 1974 General Election did not give any party a majority. Heath defiantly tried to bring together a coalition government between the Tory and the Liberal parties. The leader of the Liberals, Jeremy Thorpe, was like Heath keen to 'safeguard the membership' and opposed Wilson's planned renegotiation of the EC treaty.[188] In the end, Heath's soundings came to naught and he was seen as a bad loser who clung to power.[189] Wilson returned to Number 10 and brought back a traditional view of the Anglo-American relationship compatible with Kissinger's, who was comforted by the attitude of the new British government.[190] At this point, Kissinger counted for more than Nixon did.

The Watergate affair forced Nixon from office but long before that it had helped to undermine the outlook that Heath and Nixon shared. With little time to spend on new foreign policy initiatives Nixon's and Heath's shared understanding disintegrated and with it the Anglo-American coordination that would have supported Heath's vision. This had effects on both the reappraisal of US policies towards Europe and on European integration. The EC both goaded a reappraisal of American foreign policy towards Europe but eventually the EC's integration was also influenced by the revision of American foreign policy. Initially, during the Nixon–Heath years, the EC enlargement, and especially the inclusion of Britain, was a major factor in launching an American policy reappraisal. Instead of bringing forth an initiative of equal Euro-American partnership, as Heath wished, the Nixon administration's reappraisal of American policies towards Europe unnecessarily provoked

the Europeans and damaged the sensitive process of political coopera-
tion on foreign affairs in the EC. Kissinger's management of the Year of
Europe spelled the end to a coordinated Anglo-American policy towards
European integration.

Kissinger had loyally tried to bring about a face saving European trip
for Nixon in 1973. This did not prevent him from interpreting the Year
of Europe according to his own ideas. Once a trusted interlocutor for
the British with the centre of the Nixon administration's foreign policy
making – the White House – he stayed on in the next US administration
in a strengthened position, as Secretary of State. The FCO's conclusion,
after the Year of Europe began to disintegrate, was that Anglo-American
relationship required the same kind of 'systematic approach' with which
Britain dealt with Europe 'to the extension that Kissinger [would] allow'
it.[191] Clearly, his reappraisal of the transatlantic policies had led to the
restoration of the kind of traditional Anglo-American relationship of
the late sixties, which excluded the possibility of Heath's vision of a
partnership of equals.

In his first book, *A World Restored*, on European diplomacy at the end
of the Napoleonic wars Kissinger stated that a statesman was one who
realised what the future would hold but who was unable to relate it to
his people. Therefore the statesman had to overcome the difference in
what his compatriots understood from the past and the plans he had to
realise.[192] Perhaps he came to feel that he himself became a statesman
in part by adapting the US to an emerging multipolar world, one that
in regard to Europe had to be delayed for the sake of Western security.
Applying Kissinger's dictum to Heath it cast him as a tragic hero, who
failed to bridge the gap not only between his vision of European integration and the experience of the British people, but also between his
vision and the new European foreign policy regime in the White House.

5
Anglo-American Diplomacy: Cold War Warriors and Détente

The Heath government and the Cold War

When the era of East–West relaxation began in the early seventies Britain positioned itself as sceptical of Cold War détente. This was surprising, given Britain's long-standing support for détente efforts, attempts almost as long as the Cold War itself.[1] The previous chapter focused on inter-allied diplomacy. This chapter looks outwards: on international security and diplomatic relations with the Cold War enemies. The chapter explains why the Heath government shifted Britain's Cold War stance. It also analyses the effect of détente on the foreign policy of the Heath government and on Anglo-American relations. Like most aspects of the Cold War affairs East–West diplomacy had profound consequences for inter-allied relations. For example, the very nature of the post-war special relationship had been shaped by the Cold War. While studying the impact of European détente on Heath's plans it becomes necessary to relate Anglo-American relations to simultaneous changes in the Cold War.

The evolution of the Cold War itself conditioned possible changes to the special relationship and the chances for ambitious schemes, such as Heath's. The Cold War, despite the actions of key decision-makers like Heath and Kissinger, continued to define the special relationship, and that efforts at international relaxation could in fact work at cross purposes to European integration.

Heath's ideas had several foreign policy implications: not only for the special relationship but also for the transatlantic relationship. These relationships were linked to the Cold War and vice-versa. The plans of the Heath government also had implications for the Western stance in the Cold War. Since Heath wanted to change the special relationship it is easy to assume that he would have used détente in Europe to lessen the US grip on the special relationship. Actually, détente constituted a danger to the plans of the Heath government. This chapter shows how Heath pursued his ideas of European integration in the era of US-led détente.

Hitherto the contradiction between détente and foreign policy of the Heath government has not been fully appreciated. In the happy world of progressive beliefs processes like European détente and the development of the EC go hand in hand. This chapter takes issue with such streamlined narratives. Britain's lack of enthusiasm for détente during the early seventies period has often been put down to its relative decline. Some contemporary observers, such as the political journalist Andrew Roth, even implied that Heath merely gave tit-for-tat support for Nixon's Cold War policies, such as over Vietnam, in return for US support for British EC entry.[2] While EC membership was central to Britain it is an overly simplistic argument. The political scientists Christopher Hill and Christopher Lord argue that even though the Heath government was slow to commit itself to European détente this was compensated by being the first after the US to help open China.[3] However, as demonstrated below the way China was opened was not an ad-hoc diplomacy on Britain's part. The process of détente and the opening of China in particular indicate that the Heath government, in fact, had its own ideas about other foreign policy issues than Europe.

Building on Kissinger's recollections, Lord and Hill argue that the formation of a united European standpoint in the EPC, in preparation for the East–West Conference on Security Cooperation in Europe, the CSCE, was the result of Heath's and Kissinger's 'shared ... analysis' of the dangers of European states pursuing separate détente policies.[4] The previous chapter indicates that even such agreement, on one key question, does not necessarily correspond to agreement about other important matters – like transatlantic relations.

Brian White has looked a bit further at the reasons for Britain declining to play a supporting role for US détente efforts already in the late sixties.[5] He also notes that the British government became more sceptical of détente in 1970–71. Referring to the then Defence Secretary, Lord Carrington, he acknowledges that there was a fear of competitive détente where the government felt that there was a risk that the process of East–West might become uncontrollable.[6] This answer, however, is unsatisfactory and begs the question; why a British government chose to adopt a critical stand about all détente efforts after three decades of general support for East–West relaxation.

The origin of the British government's new stand is actually to be found in the rationale dictated by Heath's vision. In his 1967 Harvard lectures Heath stated that it was a paradox that NATO and the Western European Union had discussions on policy towards the Soviet Union, but not the EEC, especially since such an EEC forum for discussions was suggested in the Fouchet plan from the early sixties.[7] The EPC, created after the 1970 Davignon report, was a successor to the failed Fouchet plan. The EPC proposed that the six EC members should work to speak in unison on matters of international concern.[8] When the EPC began to function in 1970 it immediately had to deal with the new West German détente known as *Ostpolitik*.[9] Clearly, the Community had begun the foreign policy coordination that Heath had called for. The Heath government, however, could only look on from the outside. Britain was a NATO member but not an EC member. The Heath government had to consider West Germany's détente initiative in view of Britain being an EC applicant. There was a risk that the harmonisation of European foreign policy was accelerating too rapidly for the British, who were still outside the EC.

The Heath government's first concern was not a new foreign policy towards the Soviet Union but a viable defence, especially a credible independent nuclear deterrent. Matters of East–West relaxation also had to compete for attention with a number of contested issues, like Rhodesian independence and arms sales to South Africa.[10] The Foreign Secretary Sir Alec Douglas-Home (hereafter Home) and the deeply patriotic Heath were both firm Cold War warriors.[11] They would not take any risk with Britain's security and both regarded the Soviet Union as a potential aggressor. Heath envisaged Europe as an equal partner to the US within the Atlantic alliance. His vision did not entail détente however. It assumed a world where the Cold War situation was similar to what it had been in the early sixties. If East–West tensions were to be reduced the Heath government wanted the circumstances to be such that European integration would benefit.

However, as Heath concentrated on European affairs, he left much of the task of handling East–West relations in the experienced hands of Home. Home's views were similar to those of Sir Denis Greenhill, the Permanent Under-Secretary at the FCO. Greenhill argued that détente was a way for the Soviet Union to strengthen its position without 'abandoning its long-term aims'. Nevertheless relaxed tensions, he argued, could be used 'to solve concrete problems'. He recommended that the first priority should be to 'set Western Europe's house in order: a strong and unified Western Europe may be the only long-term basis for better East-West relations'.[12] With this Number 10 could only concur.

Home was a suitable choice as Foreign Secretary (actually Foreign and Commonwealth Secretary). At least if Heath wanted to reassure the Americans of the continued reliability of British foreign policy whilst Heath tried to realise his European plans. The US State Department believed that Home was a politician who sought to minimise the differences on foreign policy between the major parties in Britain.[13] Home's standing with the Americans was valuable to Number 10 since it was not certain that Nixon and Heath would develop a good working relationship during their time in office.

After the General Election, Heath moved quickly to establish himself as an avowed Cold War warrior. In July 1970, after Nixon's April expansion of the War in Vietnam to Cambodia, Heath commended Nixon's decision. He 'expressed the view that it had been a great success'.[14] During Nixon's brief visit to the Prime Minister's country residence, Chequers, in October 1970 Heath told Nixon that the US was 'making an important contribution' to the War in Vietnam. A receptive Nixon said that the US would withdraw from Vietnam under condition that it left behind a viable South Vietnam. Any projection of a US '"defeat" could not be allowed. Because if the US "failed" they "could forget Israel – and that goes for Western Europe too"'.[15] He meant that a failure in Vietnam would translate into a mood of isolationism among Americans which would make interventions elsewhere impossible.

Heath agreed adding that the US needed to 'withdraw from Vietnam in good order' otherwise the Soviet Union would harden its attitude towards Europe.[16] He shared Nixon's belief in this extended domino theory, where failure to contain communism in one part of the world could have repercussions thousands of miles away. Heath's support for the American presence in South East Asia was not given simply in return for US support for Britain's EC application. Even Kissinger, Nixon's arch-realist foreign policy adviser, was, by the end of 1970, convinced that Heath was 'solid in his support of' Nixon's policy on Vietnam.[17]

At no point did Heath try to distance Britain from the American involvement in Vietnam. A plausible rationale for criticism could have been some kind of British pro-European principle. However, Heath was intent on not distancing Britain from the US any more than necessary. In fact the Heath government was likely to favour most Western overseas commitments, because in Heath's view Britain's European future involved overseas responsibilities.[18] Heath and his government would prove themselves to be staunch Cold War warriors, more so than any other ally, because only in this way was it possible to safeguard Heath's vision of a Europe that became increasingly involved in international affairs.

The intended benefit to the US of London's tough Cold War stand was supposed to be Britain as a trustworthy partner. The relationships of the US with the other two major European powers were not the best. Relations with France were improving but problems stemming from France's partial withdrawal from NATO remained. Willy Brandt, the West German Chancellor, and the driving force behind Ostpolitik, gave the Nixon White House headaches. In contrast, Britain was a reliable ally and one with which the Nixon administration would hopefully discuss détente.

London did want reduced East–West tension but without an expansion of the Soviet 'influence' or at the price of 'formally endorsing the Soviet Union's claim to absolute hegemony East of the Elbe'.[19] Another reason was that much of Britain's influence both globally and in Europe, where British troops were committed, depended on its Cold War role. Uncontrolled East–West relaxing of tensions could annul any benefit in international standing that Britain derived from its overseas defence commitments. It could also risk the cohesion of the West and especially Western Europe. Europe had to engage in a safe and single kind of détente if it was to emerge as an outward looking and equal partner to the US. The separate détente of any ally, like Ostpolitik or American superpower relaxation, could jeopardise the plans of the Heath government.

The Heath government takes a tough stance towards the East

Ostpolitik did not only worry the British. It also caused Nixon concern.[20] He did not rely on the advice of Wilson, Heath's predecessor, who had assured the US about Brandt's reliability.[21] In August 1970, Brandt signed the Soviet-German Treaty, which recognised the post-war borders of East Germany.[22] In order for West Germany to ratify the treaty, the status of Berlin had to be determined. Doing that involved the occupying powers: the Soviet Union, the US, Britain and France because West Germany had no legal right to negotiate. The negotiations gave the US a chance to influence the pace of Ostpolitik.[23] The White House understood that a failure would lead to the US being blamed for the collapse of Ostpolitik.[24] This it did not want. It was a testament to the stasis of the Cold War that the German question still laid at the heart of détente in Europe decades after the Cold War had begun.

That the German question was still the main concern of East–West relaxation in Europe suited Heath's plans. On the one hand, the Heath government needed continued good relations with West Germany to ensure EC entry and to be able to develop the Heath's vision at a later stage. But on the other hand, Ostpolitik could not be allowed to undermine European integration. The British Ambassador to Bonn, R. W. Jackling, argued that Brandt needed to remain 'strongly interested in European integration' to embed Ostpolitik. Brandt had stated that his country could 'only safely seek an opening to the East if it keeps its feet firmly embedded in NATO and the European Communities'.[25] Hence, Brandt was thought to support EC enlargement, which favoured London's plans. Accordingly, Ostpolitik, the policy that occupied the top slot on the West German government's foreign policy agenda, complemented the top foreign policy item of the Heath government – EC entry.

East–West diplomacy and European integration were evidently connected. Nevertheless, it was not certain that they would work like two connected cogwheels where motion in one would turn the other forward. Anglo-German relations were important, not least because of the negotiations for EC membership and the Community's future. There were already concrete defence reasons in the form of the British Army on the Rhine, The BAOR, which amounted to 50,000 British troops stationed in West Germany. Furthermore, there were politico-economic reasons. The British believed that West Germany's 'clear economic preponderance within the EEC' would increase its importance as a key player in the EC.[26] Hence, Britain needed to foster good relations with West Germany as an EC partner. Consequently, Britain had to support Ostpolitik and be cooperative on the issue of Berlin. However, Berlin would also offer an unexpected opportunity to demonstrate Britain's tough Cold War stance to the US.

After a pause during the summer, the four occupying powers were to begin a new series of meetings on the status of Berlin on 30 September 1970. On 29 September, the Russians provoked the Western allies. The Russian controller at the Berlin Air Safety Centre informed the British that two of the air corridors to Berlin would be closed for two hours in the early morning of the following day.[27] This was precisely the kind of incidents that showed that the status of Berlin had to be settled.[28] Such incidents had taken place two times previously, in the sixties. The British argued that the Western powers should respond in the same manner as in the past – by military probes – to assert their access to Berlin. After talking to Heath, Home gave the go-ahead pending the agreement and participation of at least one of the two other Western allies: France and the US. Initially, Nixon had settled for a protest to the Soviet Union, but when he learned of the British proposal he agreed and so did the French. The flights went through without any problems. The British thought 'that the Russians [were] prepared to play a dangerous as well as silly game' and hence 'firmness' was necessary when negotiating over Berlin.[29] The British initiative and hard line duly impressed the Nixon administration.

This demonstration was also important in view of the Soviet Foreign Minister Andrei Gromyko's forthcoming visit in October to Britain. It was the first visit since 1965 when Wilson had been Prime Minister. This time the FCO wanted to avoid any sudden Wilson-like interventions on Vietnam and Heath was advised not to propose mediations.[30] European security easily filled the agenda. It was a contentious issue since the Soviets blamed Britain for taking the lead in Western criticism of the Soviet invasion of Czechoslovakia in 1968.[31] The Heath government did not pander to efforts at détente by recanting British critique. Instead, when Gromyko pushed for a European security conference, Heath indicated that Berlin was a good example of a case where something tangible could be done to improve East–West relations.[32] Gromyko tried to convince the British to take a larger view and argued that an all European security conference would be beneficial.[33] However, when quizzed by Home on what such a gathering would accomplish his answers were mostly rhetorical such as a claim that Britain already supported the 'status quo' in Europe.[34] What the British really supported was a strong West that would further European integration.

The aim of the British approach to East–West relations was initially to walk in step with the Americans, who the British assumed shared their scepticism about détente. The State Department was aware that Home, as late as the spring of 1970, had expressed the view that it was not 'worthwhile having a conference on European security' since there was 'nothing specific such a conference could constructively act on'.[35] It was an early indication of a new British scepticism about détente. William P. Rogers, the US Secretary of State, and Home had discussed the Soviet suggestion for a European Security Conference in the summer of 1970, debating whether it, lacking the substantive issues, was a propaganda exercise. Rogers's view was that the Russians seemed more committed to the SALT.[36] The Nixon administration's attempt at superpower détente including a SALT agreement required a degree of flexibility that Britain had not prepared for. Home, in fact, risked appearing as too sound on East–West relations. Clearly, an Anglo-American tandem ride to détente was not a foregone conclusion.

The question was how the US would react to a Britain that did not share the American approach to détente. The Heath government wanted to tread carefully in regard to East–West relaxation and that included superpower détente. Britain had to support Ostpolitik, a détente initiative not favoured by the US. At the same time British détente scepticism could be seen as a rigid position, unhelpful to the American desire for superpower détente. While the British action over Berlin demonstrated a tough traditional Cold War position it also represented a reactive diplomacy. It had not been enough to clarify Britain's position to the US.

In September, Home told Rogers that they 'all had welcomed Herr Brandt's Ostpolitik' but he threw doubts on whether the Soviet Union genuinely wanted a relaxation of tensions. This was especially important, argued Home, since SALT would raise doubts in Europe about whether the US would stay in Europe.[37] The US did not appreciate the British scepticism. Instead it was misinterpreted. The NSC drew Nixon's attention to the possibility of the British dissenting and speculated that Gromyko's visit to Britain could be a sign that Britain wanted 'to play an active role in improving East-West relations'. The NSC also believed that the British had already resigned themselves to 'a conference on European security' in the future.[38] The White House assumed that British foreign policy continued to accord high priority to the 'relaxation of tensions between East and West'.[39] Therefore it did not appreciate the new British détente scepticism and assumed that Britain was tempted to play a separate role, alone or with another Western European state, in East–West diplomacy.

When Nixon made his brief visit to Britain, in October 1970, he praised the British response to the Soviet Union's intimidations over Berlin because it showed that the Western powers had not gone 'soft'. He told Heath that the necessity for good personal contact between the leaders of Britain and the US was 'probably greater than it had ever been' since many global issues required a common outlook.[40] Home confirmed that American and British differences in regard to the European security were only 'marginal and tactical'.[41] The Americans began to realise that the British were not preparing a separate détente diplomacy. This was soon confirmed by Heath's decision not to make immediate use of an invitation to go to the Soviet Union.[42] It was clearly not the action of someone who intended to take independent détente initiatives, nor was it the action of someone who wanted to accelerate the détente process.

Although the US was duly reassured about Britain's reliability the question of Ostpolitik remained. The US, unlike France and the Soviet

Union, did not fear German revanchism. The State Department also understood that British foreign policy was not based on a fear of a revival of 'German militarism' either.[43] However, Ostpolitik might still lead the US where it was not prepared to go. The Americans feared that Ostpolitik was a potential way for the Soviets to disaggregate the Western allies, for example Western Europe from the US.[44] Kissinger argued that Ostpolitik, at the very least, could undermine the Nixon administration's efforts to maintain the size of its military commitment to Europe.[45] The NSC assumed that the British analysis was the same as its own; that the Soviet Union wanted 'Europe quiet in order to free Soviet hands as Moscow deals with China and consolidates its Middle East position and...as always, disuniting the West'.[46] Accordingly, the Americans favoured Anglo-American coordination on questions of East–West relaxation in Europe such as Ostpolitik and the proposed European security conference.

The FCO remained sceptical of the conference. Heath was advised to tell Nixon at their next summit, in December 1970, that there was not yet enough progress 'to justify going to a European Security Conference'.[47] The British did not want the conference on European security to go ahead until discussions on the Berlin question had been resolved and until 'an understanding' on the basics of an 'inner-German settlement' had been reached.[48] The British analysis was intended to demonstrate to the US that Britain was not eager to advance East–West relaxation.

At the December summit, Nixon voiced his concerns. He told Heath that the West Germans had been warned that it was 'a mistake to risk real friends for new friends'. Yet, Nixon was not prepared to stop Ostpolitik, but he would not encourage it either.[49] Kissinger added that it might still come to constitute a danger.[50] Therefore, West Germany had to be embedded 'into a Western Europe in both political and military terms'.[51] This fitted with Heath's plans. Nixon also said that the military strategy of massive retaliation was no longer credible. This increased the need for more conventional forces; a need he thought Europe ought to fill.[52] This was also compatible with Heath's vision of a united European defence cooperation. Kissinger told Heath that they needed 'to avoid a differentiated detente [*sic*] in which the Soviets bought themselves time by making a selective relaxation with particular allies'.[53] On this position, the Americans and the British agreed as well. Heath again reassured the Americans that he did not intend to visit Moscow any time soon.[54] He also expressed doubts about the Soviet Union's intentions. In fact, he was so concerned that he expressed apprehension about the implications of SALT and said that it seemed to him that the Soviet Union sought 'strategic superiority'.[55] Even though the Heath government reiterated the new British scepticism about East–West relaxation it agreed with the US on the general approach to détente in Europe and Heath successfully portrayed Britain as the US most reliable ally. The Heath government was prepared to sustain the Anglo-American Cold War special relationship until a new US–EC relationship was in place. Still, the British could not uphold the relationship alone the US also had to remain a steadfast ally.

In February 1971, Walter Annenberg, the US Ambassador to London, reported that Heath and his key advisers were worried about the Soviet Union's military build up. He was certain that the US could count on Britain as long as it was 'assured and reassured that British national interests and [the] defense needs of Western Europe' were duly considered. Clearly, the Americans were becoming aware that there was a considerable amount of apprehension behind Britain's tough Cold War stand. Annenberg believed that Anglo-American relationship remained 'stable' but reminded Washington that Heath was 'unsentimental about the "natural relationship" ' and that the Heath government should be dealt with in a straightforward manner. He also thought that 'Heath's claim that Britain [was] a middle power of the first rank [would] be severely tested during the year' not only in relation to international security but also in the economy, the standard of living, and relations with the Community. The Heath government faced choices that, according to Annenberg, would decide Britain's 'course for years to come'.[56] According to this analysis, the success of Heath's policies would have considerable consequences for the value of Britain as a US ally: failure, following the same logic, could alter the American desire for Anglo-American détente coordination.

Throughout the spring, Ostpolitik continued despite the West German government's awareness of the White House's dislike of its diplomacy.[57] After having proved its Cold War credentials to the White House, Britain could give its support for the West German diplomatic efforts, without the US suspecting European collusion on détente. Later, during a visit to Bonn in April 1971, Heath was able to enlist Brandt's support for the EC negotiations.[58] Nevertheless, the Heath government's ability to link its stand on Ostpolitik with its image as a reliable Cold War partner to the US did not slow down the progress of détente. Instead, West German, and possibly French efforts on the question of Berlin, together with Kissinger's diplomacy, gave the process added impetus during the spring.[59] Actually, the British role in the working out of an agreement was probably not negligible.[60] The result came just as the US was changing its monetary policies. On 3 September 1971 the four powers approved the Quadripartite Agreement on Berlin. After West Germany in turn ratified a series of treaties, in the spring of 1972, a major obstacle to further détente was removed.[61]

During the year British misgivings about détente increased. In March 1971 with the Heath government's worried about the size and purpose of the growing Soviet strategic force Whitehall called for better intelligence on these matters, which meant close cooperation with the CIA.[62] Heath agreed to a joint study and collaboration with the US.[63] This was another instance of close consultations on security affairs and in sharp contrast to the lack of consultations at the same time in the area of monetary policy. The Heath government's anxiety about détente actually made it more, and not less, prone to uphold the traditional Cold War Anglo-American special security relationship. Every time Britain and the US cooperated on security matters, such as intelligence, it strengthened the traditional Anglo-American special relationship even if no specific agreement, public or otherwise, was made.

In August 1971, with the Berlin question seemingly resolved, Number 10 geared up to what it knew would follow after continued SALT talks – a European Security Conference. Heath wanted to know if Britain was ready for this and how Britain should adapt its tough standpoint.[64] His main concern was whether détente, in the long run, was compatible with his plans. In the short run, the immediate questions about détente processes would test the Anglo-American commitment to a joint approach.

'Soviet Westpolitik', China and the difficulties of achieving Anglo-American cooperation

By the summer of 1971 the British FCO believed that Soviet détente overtures, or 'Soviet Westpolitik' as the FCO called it, had a lot to do with European integration. This would explain their wish for an 'all-European Conference'. According to the FCO, European integration made the Russians anxious: they feared that the EC could become dominated by West Germany and attract the Eastern European countries. They had a recurrent 'nightmare that a politically united Western Europe, dominated by [West Germany] and backed by the United States, might try to bring about German reunification'. The Soviet approach to détente was seen, by the FCO, as designed to limit European integration by

offering 'all-European' venues for action. The Russian shift of emphasis 'from "security" to the "co-operation" aspect' in the Soviet proposals
for a conference was seen as an indication of this. Furthermore, the
actual content of the conference remained conveniently vague – for the
Russians. The British believed that the Russians were eager and wanted
the talks on MBFR separate so that it could not be made into another
precondition like the Berlin settlement.[65] If the FCO's analysis of the
Russian plans was correct then these constituted a potential hindrance
to the creation of a united Western Europe.

Kissinger was also apprehensive about Soviet motives. At this stage
Anglo-American discussions about détente had more of a consultative nature and did not represent fully fledged British involvement in
superpower détente. Kissinger had been deeply involved in the SALT
discussions with the Soviet Union during the spring. In June 1971 he
conveyed his views to Thomas Brimelow, Deputy Under-Secretary at the
FCO.[66] Kissinger claimed that by acting antagonistically towards the US
and conducting détente towards Europe the Soviet Union thought it
possible to reduce the American troops in Europe. Brimelow thought
that the Russians regarded détente as a regional rather than global concept. By this was meant that Soviet expansionism outside Europe was
not checked. Kissinger agreed that for the Soviet Union détente only
had an instrumental value.[67] Despite shared opinions, Anglo-American
Cold War coordination, nonetheless, suffered in the fall of 1971, not
only as a result of the Nixon administration's new economic policies,
but as a consequence of Kissinger's success in another area altogether.

The US initiative, in the summer of 1971, to establish relations with
China overshadowed any Anglo-American concord. The opening to
China disturbed plans harboured by the British FCO. Since 1970 it had
worked towards a full exchange of Ambassadors with China and also
forewarned the US that this meant that Britain could not support the
old American stand towards China. The Americans then made the FCO
delay its move. As the State Department later recognised the July 1971
'announcement of the President's visit ... undercut' the British designs.
Nonetheless, it thought the British reactions 'highly exaggerated'. However, it appreciated that the news of Nixon's coming trip had thwarted
a British opportunity to play 'a central role in a critical foreign policy
problem'.[68] The way the US opened up China struck a blow to Anglo-
American relations. It also deprived the Heath government of a foreign
policy initiative other than EC membership. Here was again an example
of a lack of US consultations, but this time over an issue that went to
the heart of the special relationship. Then again the White House had

not done anything that the Heath government had not wanted to do itself. Yet, doubts arose about the trustworthiness of the Nixon administration and its conduct of Cold War diplomacy. If it was prepared to upstage Britain, then what other sacrifices was the US prepared to make in pursuit of superpower détente?

Not surprisingly, the Heath government persevered with its tough stance towards the Soviet Union and in September 1971 it seized upon another opportunity to demonstrate it. After much preparation, Home, on 24 September, expelled 90 Soviet intelligence agents working in Britain. The Soviet counter-measures were surprisingly mild, although Anglo-Soviet political relations became significantly frostier.[69] Although a prodigious feat, the action was not risk free. It led to rumours in France that the British were trying to slow down the détente process. This was particularly inopportune time as Brezhnev was about to visit Paris.[70] Heath, always concerned about maintaining good relations with France, wrote to Pompidou explaining the British actions. It turned out that Michel Jobert, Secretary-General of the French President's staff, rather admired the action and that Pompidou himself understood it.[71] That the Heath government took such a risk with French reactions might merely indicate how necessary the action was. It also shows that Heath had no qualms about positioning Britain as the Western state least keen on improving East–West relations.

At this point Britain was less interested than France in détente, although this was not obvious to the US. Yet, France was not the adamant leader on East–West relations that it had been in the sixties.[72] Pompidou's view of East–West affairs was close to Nixon's apprehensions about Soviet intentions as the Americans had actually noted already in 1969,[73] something which Georges-Henri Soutou's research confirms. He argues that Pompidou feared that the whole of Germany would take the Cold War position of Finland, and that consequently of Western Europe would follow, and adapt its foreign policy to the wishes of Moscow. Soutou also argues that Pompidou was more honest with the US than any other ally. One reason could have been his desire for France to be the leader of the EC and its interlocutor with the US. However, Pompidou unlike Heath tried to establish a durable Franco-Soviet relationship and, in 1970, he went to Moscow. There he spoke of his support for the US presence in Europe but added that he would not return France to the NATO fold.[74] How Pompidou expected France to be the Americans' foremost partner while adhering to the Gaullist doctrine of not reintegrating France into NATO is unclear. Besides scepticism of West Germany and the Soviet Union the French were also sceptical of the intentions of the US. Thus, Nixon had promised Pompidou, in 1969, that there would be no superpower condominium saying that the existence of only two superpowers was 'not healthy', which led to his calling for a strong France and a strong Europe.[75] Even though Pompidou was not advocating a détente diplomacy that excluded the US, the Nixon administration was concerned that Heath would be led astray by, what the US London Embassy saw fit to describe as, his 'mystical and emotional attraction to France'. By December 1971 the US Embassy in London found that '[t]he prospect of European Association has already cast its influence over other aspects of British foreign policy', and that Britain could follow French leads on questions of European security and East–West relations.[76]

The US Embassy in London noted that American policies towards China, as well as the Soviet Union, together with the economic measures of 15 August 1971 had given the British second thoughts about the special relationship. The US Embassy believed that many in the British establishment had originally 'more or less taken for granted that [the special relationship] would probably continue informally regardless of public posturing'. Heath, in particular, had put great stock on his relationship with Nixon but was now more likely to make cool calculations. The Embassy never fully grasped Heath's ideas although it saw the connection between Heath being upset at the damage to his plans and his speech at the Conservative Party conference in Brighton, in the fall of 1971, where he had explained that 'Europe could no longer depend on US help as it has in the past'.[77] However, the Americans fretted needlessly about Britain following a French lead on détente.

The Heath government had no intention of following a French lead on détente because it did not want to spur on any détente process, least of all a European security conference, which they thought would play into the hands of the Soviet Union. The FCO expected 1972 to be a more difficult year than 1971, because of the EC enlargement and the first meetings about 'the future of European security'.[78] This actually meant that Britain would have to take extra care to maintain good relations with the US. It wanted the White House to understand that this did not mean any lessening of Britain's support for the transatlantic alliance according to the FCO. All the NATO members wanted the US to stay in Europe, including France, even if it was unwilling 'to draw the right conclusions' about its own re-involvement in NATO.[79]

The British believed that, although the Europeans were grateful for Nixon's steadfast support for NATO, they were concerned about the future, about SALT, about isolationist tendencies in the US Congress, about MBFR, and about alliance strategy. Nevertheless, as long as it got the transatlantic relationship right the British did not believe that Europe had anything 'to fear from détente'. This required normal NATO consultations before decisive agreements between the US and the Soviet Union.[80]

To ensure this and to explain British apprehensions about Soviet détente the British had to restore Anglo-American relations at the summit in Bermuda in December 1971. The Smithsonian Agreement on international monetary reform went a long way towards smoothing the past for a successful summit. Nonetheless, there was no shortage of questions to deal with in Bermuda. For instance, in the weeks prior to the summit war erupted between India and Pakistan with the consequent creation of Bangladesh.[81] Topics such as this eventually consumed a great deal of the energy at the summit, even though Britain played only a minor role during the crises. However, Heath believed that Kissinger had wanted to involve Britain in the India–Pakistan war. At this stage of his presidency, Nixon was still in full command of foreign policy. During the summit he found out that Heath disapproved of Kissinger's conceptualisation of policy and the handling of the crisis, which Kissinger believed required British participation. Nixon quickly put an end to Kissinger's insistence on this necessity.[82] Straightforward talk helped to re-establish good relations between Heath and Nixon and quickly improved Anglo-American relations.

At the summit, in December 1971, the British and the Americans agreed that the spring of 1973 was the earliest time for convening a European Security Conference.[83] However, they shared a mutual incomprehension about Soviet motives for the conference, especially as many tangible questions were to be dealt with separately in the MBFR talks.[84] Rogers, the US Secretary of State, explained that MBFR was potentially quite useful for domestic American purposes as a means with which to counteract isolationist demands for cutting US defence spending abroad.[85] Home wondered what the Russians would make of the insistence of putting 'the free movement of people and ideas' on the conference agenda.[86] Heath took the opportunity to explain that his plans were compatible with a joint transatlantic approach to détente. First, he tried to allay American anxieties about Britain joining a separate European détente effort by claiming that he 'did not subscribe to the view that European Unity would lead to confrontation across the Atlantic'. In the future, he said, there would have to be political organisation of Europe in terms of foreign policy, and an eventual contribution to defence, but he added that the US and Britain should keep in close contact about this development.[87] He presented his vision as a means to keep the West united as détente progressed, which, of course, necessitated close Anglo-American consultations.

Nixon accepted the implications of Heath's vision.[88] He understood the 'temptation for Europe to play the role of a third force in the world, which it indeed would be'. He also believed that 'it was essential that Europe and the United States should co-operate closely'. Therefore, he appreciated the role that Britain intended to play inside the EC. This was especially important in view of isolationist trends in the US that emanated from concerns due to trade and defence costs in particular. To prevent the same trend of isolationism from appearing in Europe, and strengthening the existing current in the US he argued that there had to be 'a kind of relationship which would enable the close co-operation to continue', to avoid 'economic crisis and recession'.[89] As shown in the previous chapter the two leaders intended to coordinate their respective approaches to transatlantic affairs. In their joint statement, Heath and Nixon reaffirmed the close relations between their two countries. They also said that they would work to maintain this after Britain's entry into the EC, presenting this as a step towards strengthening the Atlantic alliance.[90] This demonstrates their wish that the Anglo-American special relationship would evolve into a US–EC special relationship.

Anglo-American cooperation was the smoothest way of achieving Heath's desired move of the special aspects of the Anglo-American relationship to a US-European level. Heath much preferred cooperation over confrontation. Even though EC membership would change the Anglo-American relationship, he believed that a 'healthy relationship can withstand change'.[91] At least one commentator, at the time, argued that Heath's focus was not exclusively on European affairs per se, but that he was also an atlanticist and that his concept of Europe remained that of the Atlantic alliance of the 'twin pillars'.[92] Nixon mirrored Heath's aspirations for the development of the transatlantic relationship in a toast at the summit. He warmly welcomed '[a] united Western Europe, with Britain part of it, [as] a fundamental goal of American policy', and hearing it 'speak with one voice'.[93] It was thought that Nixon had managed to restore relations with Britain.[94] Good personal relations always mattered to the special relationship. However, the special relationship did not depend solely on Nixon's and Heath's ability to get along, but the success of Heath's plans was very dependent on their relationship. Efforts had been made both by Heath and

Nixon and their mutual understanding went beyond an improvement in Anglo-American relations.

At the end of the summit, Heath informed the press that he shared the American position on a possible European security conference.[95] It was the slowest possible approach to détente. It meant that the conference could progress only after Ostpolitik was successfully completed. In the meantime the British and the Americans would have enough time to coordinate their approach to détente in Europe. They could work together to ensure that Europe remained cohesive. This would ensure that Heath's vision was not put at risk by separate détente efforts.

European integration and détente

At the Brandt–Nixon Summit at the very end of December 1971 the West Germans were surprised 'by the importance which the President evidently attached to the relationship between the enlarged Europe and the United States'.[96] Yet, by fulfilling Heath's wishes, Nixon eventually had to disappoint Pompidou, who had expected to be the key interlocutor for the US with the new enlarged EC.[97] Evidently, the White House was committed to its agreement with Heath. For the Heath government the next stage was to ensure that France's view of détente was compatible with Heath's vision.

France was for the European security conference but it was not keen on MBFR;[98] partly because participation would limit France's independence,[99] and partly for defence reasons. Pompidou believed that it could be the beginning of the slippery slope towards conventional force reductions, which the West could ill afford, or worse – to a US withdrawal from Western Europe. He feared a détente that was limited to Europe, which, in effect, could result in a regional superpower agreement over the heads of the Europeans.[100] Consequently, the French refused to join NATO discussions on a common approach to MBFR but the British were also concerned about the risks that MBFR entailed. The annoying aspect of the French position was that it favoured the aspect of détente in Europe where the US and the British were cautious – the conference.

However, all the key actors desired a common Western approach to the conference. West Germany hoped the conference would underwrite the achievements of Ostpolitik and likewise it favoured MBFR as a means to reduce the risk for East–West tension.[101] The US wanted a viable Western Europe united enough to withstand Soviet temptations. Pompidou was not Gaullist enough to want to exclude the US and like Heath he wanted to avoid having the Soviet Union and the US deciding Europe's fate over their heads. While Heath wanted the Europeans to work out their position he also desired agreement with the US as the basis for a future equal partnership between the US and Europe. This made it necessary for Britain to work for a comprehensive Western approach both within the EPC and within NATO, but France was not active in NATO.

After Brezhnev's state visit to France in the fall of 1971, Maurice Schumann, the French Foreign Minister, told Home that the Soviet Union desired a stable Europe but that it would not sacrifice Eastern Europe to achieve this. Nevertheless, Schumann believed that over time the West could slowly attract the Eastern European countries, away from Moscow's domination. However, he warned the British 'that any policy towards the Russians which was based on trusting them would amount to giving in to them'.[102] The element of distrust was something which Heath and Home could recognise. Nonetheless, the French suggestion that the conference be called the Conference on European Security and Co-operation ostensibly indicated East–West relaxation rather than distrust of the Soviet Union.[103] As Pompidou told Heath, when they met in March 1972, it reflected the French desire to use the 'virtues of liberty' to foster the possibility of change in Moscow's European satellites. He, also, stressed that this would take a long time. He favoured a conference that dealt with 'the political and human conditions necessary for [the] creation of security in Europe and not deal with problems of relative disarmament', like MBFR.[104] He explained his suspicions about MBFR, which could make 'Germany into a kind of neutral area in Europe and thus isolate Germany from the West'.[105] He added that France did not have a problem with, what he thought was the Soviet reason for the conference, namely acceptance of the 'status quo' on the post-war borders in Europe. He agreed that the US would not be ready for the conference before 1973.[106] Pompidou's wish to have the MBFR outside the conference was perfectly compatible with the British and Americans views. Likewise, his doubts about substantial or quick results from the conference also reflected British and American misgivings.

After his meeting with Pompidou, Heath informed Nixon that the French expected the results of the conference to be meagre.[107] By maintaining close contacts at the top, between Number 10 and the White House, the British hoped to improve consultations and prevent distrust from emerging. Anglo-American contacts were particularly close before Nixon's visit to the Soviet Union, scheduled for May 1972. Nevertheless, they were not as intimate as Heath would have liked. Unlike the situation in the autumn, he was now conciliatory and suggested that Nixon could stop over in Britain on his way to or from Moscow.[108] However, at the same time, problems in Vietnam mounted. On 4 May, the Secretary of State Rogers told Heath that if the situation in Vietnam grew worse, Nixon would 'take strong measures'. He added that Nixon expected his visit to the Soviet Union to take place despite the escalation in Vietnam.[109] Heath assured Nixon that Home would tell the Soviet Ambassador that Britain wanted the Soviet Union to put 'the maximum possible pressure on Hanoi to use this opportunity to put an end to the war'.[110] Number 10 evidently tried to re-establish consultations with the US about Cold War diplomacy in the traditional Anglo-American special relationship manner.

The British involvement in the preparations for Nixon's visit to Moscow appeared to symbolise the Anglo-American intimacy. Heath was asked by Nixon to assist him in his preparations for the visit by talking with Rogers about MBFR and 'a conference on European security and cooperation'.[111] Given Nixon's scant regard for Rogers his request had an ersatz-like quality, as if he wanted to give the impression of close consultations, without being bothered by them.[112] Despite some adaptation to the Nixon White House's way of making foreign policy the British found it difficult to accept that the State Department was out of the process to the degree that it was. It actually assumed that Rogers would be in charge of the CSCE and MBFR partly as a compensation for not being greatly involved on China.[113] The British received a list on what issues the Americans were doing briefs.[114] Yet, Kissinger demonstrated the Nixon administration's increasingly extraordinary approach to Anglo-American consultations when he told Cromer, the British Ambassador, that Heath should disregard advice coming from US officials, including Rogers, that referred to any reopening of the Geneva conference on Vietnam.[115] While Nixon clearly welcomed the British wish for closeness he seemed to think that he could satisfy Number 10, at least partially, with ritual rather than the real thing. Most likely, Nixon did not want to be inconvenienced, either by the British or by the State Department, when he engaged in his favourite pursuit of making foreign policy, but he wanted to take care that the British were not alienated.

The SALT I Treaty was concluded on 26 May during the US-Soviet Summit. It was satisfactory to Britain, since it reduced the number of ABMs, keeping the British nuclear deterrent relevant. The SALT I Treaty was the showpiece of Nixon and Kissinger's détente diplomacy. According to William Bundy, it may also have been the high point of détente efforts, as far as the White House was concerned.[116] Nevertheless, the success of superpower détente raised expectations about continued détente in Europe.

After the summit, Nixon drew Heath's attention to the Summit communiqué, which stated that the Russians and the Americans agreed that the talks on possible MBFR should be conducted in parallel with the preparations for the CSCE. Nixon claimed the talks 'can do some good if they are carefully prepared and very concrete'. He had suggested a timetable, to begin after the EC Summit in the late fall, to the Russians for preparations on a multilateral basis. He wanted Heath's support to ensure that the alliance was not 'being split by generalities'.[117] Heath's wish for a cohesive approach to détente and good relations with the US made him agree to Nixon's request. He pointed out, however, that there were inherent contradictions in 'the prospect of detente [*sic*] . . . it [was] . . . a heavy responsibility on democratic Governments to hold their domestic public opinion together and keep attention fixed upon the realities of power'. His concerns reflected the necessity of squaring Britain's security with European integration. He wanted to keep the Western alliance intact and suspected that the Russians wanted to 'confuse public opinion' in Europe so that it could 'drive a wedge between the Allies'.[118] It was now becoming essential to ensure that détente did not take precedence over European integration.

Britain wanted détente 'but not at the expense of further European integration'.[119] The Heath government was also not prepared to pay the price of a disintegrating alliance to achieve further European integration, which would cancel out the aim and benefits of two equal partners within the West. Accordingly, the British were concerned with the presentational aspect of a reduction in East–West tensions. Or, as Heath told Brandt, in the spring of 1972, it must not only look as if it was only the East that was 'interested in producing a peaceful life for the Europeans'.[120] Every move further along the path of East–West relaxation moored Britain to the traditional Anglo-American Cold War relationship, especially after the US became more restrictive on détente. The challenge, for the British, with the next step in European détente, the CSCE, was to make it a catalyst for the transfer of traditional areas of Anglo-American cooperation onto a European footing.

Ultimately, the Heath vision also depended on the actions of the other superpower – the Soviet Union, which had not even recognised the EC officially. Russian disregard for the EC was founded on the assumption that it was an economic arm for the West in the Cold War. This supposition held that the US would continue to exercise hegemony over

Western Europe, hence the idea that the EC would evolve from an economic organisation to a united Western Europe was alien to the Russians. Nevertheless, it would be wrong to think that the Soviet Union did not understand the potential of the EC to become more than an economic entity. Though reluctant to recognise it, Brezhnev did what he probably thought was the next best thing and recognised the Community as 'a fact of life' in a speech on 20 March 1972. He also denied that Soviet actions and the CSCE were designed to thwart the EC.[121] However, to his dismay he got little response from Europe.[122]

Heath's initial reaction to Brezhnev's acknowledgement that the EC existed, however, was positive. It was a sign of 'a realistic and businesslike attitude to the Community'.[123] Heath wanted to react to Brezhnev's speech as it contributed to the high profile with which Heath wanted to endow the EC. He considered making it the springboard for a foreign policy speech or initiative of his own.[124] However, he was held back by the fact that Britain was, after all, not yet formally a full member of the EC. For some months afterwards, the Heath government expected Brezhnev's speech to be followed by some Soviet initiative. But there was no further initiative to act upon.[125] Nonetheless, the British Embassy in Moscow stressed that if the EC commented on Brezhnev's speech it should not allow for a reply that accepted the EC as 'a purely economic grouping', which, it was believed, the Soviet Union wanted to limit it to.[126] The Soviets admission of realities was made to assuage the West German Conservative Party, the CDU, in order to make it more likely that the Moscow Treaty of 1970 between the Soviet Union and West Germany was ratified by the German parliament, the *Bundestag*. The Soviets believed the Treaty would practically recognise East Germany. Furthermore the new Soviet stance paved the way for the East's economic grouping, the COMECON, to communicate directly with the EC. This would discipline the Eastern European countries and prevent them from talking to the EC separately.[127] In any case, little could be gained by a lone British response, and accordingly Britain took no action to meet Brezhnev's speech.

In September 1972, Helmut Sonnenfeldt, of the NSC staff, cautioned Kissinger about the changes in the Soviet Union's policy towards the EC. The Americans were well aware of the Russian dislike of the EC. Sonnenfeldt interpreted this new line to mean that the Russians had not changed their views of the EC but had decided that their former negative stance did not pay any dividends. He argued that the Soviet Union still sought to limit the evolution of the EC towards political integration and what it saw as EC protectionism. However, the Soviet

Union would refrain from causing problems that might derail their much desired CSCE, which they would like to make a permanent forum for discussing East–West economic issues.[128] Unlike the Heath government the White House was not concerned that the CSCE would hinder European integration.

In June 1972, the Quadripartite agreements on Berlin as well as West Germany's treaties with Poland and the Soviet Union became effective.[129] The CSCE and MBFR were now at the top of the Anglo-American détente agenda. The White House was also aware of the need to reassure the Europeans about the continued SALT II talks. The fear was that these talks would result in the two superpowers agreeing to limit a nuclear conflict to Europe. The consequence would be that the Western European allies would loose their trust in the US nuclear guarantee.[130] To avoid a revolt of their allies the Americans needed to involve them through consultations. A continued close relationship with the British was part of that approach and in the middle of September 1972 Kissinger stopped by in London, on a return trip from Moscow. The British saw this as an attempt to maintain the process of consultations with Western European allies that had begun in late 1971. By know the British understood that they had to communicate their views to both the State Department and the White House. Their trust in Kissinger was limited, although he was seen as part and parcel of the White House. They knew that for Kissinger European integration was not a priority and believed that anything he was told could easily reach the French ears. Therefore, they sought to reiterate their belief that they could work out US–EC problems and stress that Britain was working for 'good relations with the United States'. Nevertheless, they were not certain that Kissinger was interested in talking about the EC's external relations, in which case they wanted to persuade Kissinger to take a greater interest in Community matters.[131]

However, détente easily filled the agenda. Kissinger told the British that the Russians had pushed for agreement on 22 November as a starting date for preparations for the CSCE so that it could begin in June 1973. He said that this approach worked for the US, with the MBFR negotiations running roughly parallel, beginning in the fall of 1973 and at a different location.[132] Home asked 'about the fundamental Soviet aim in a CSCE, was it to weaken the Western will to resist?' Kissinger said that he believed the Russians wanted to create a feeling of safety in Europe that would lead to suggestions for 'alternative security organisations' on an all-European basis.[133] That was something that both the US and the British wanted to avoid.

As a consequence the US and Britain, which now appreciated the White House's role in foreign policy, worked closely together, in the best Cold War special relationship style during the autumn. In September 1972, there was a session on the CSCE and MBFR kept secret from other allies as well as US Agencies, including the State Department. Kissinger made a substantial analysis on MBFR available. The White House representatives stressed that Washington was not keen on either the CSCE or the MBFR but that the administration wanted 'to nail down MBFR negotiations' for domestic reasons. They did not want the Russians to be able to get out of them no matter what happened with the CSCE. The MBFR negotiations were expected to take a considerable amount of time but have the benefit of forcing NATO members 'to look at defence problems in their widest aspect and face up to...deficiencies'.[134] This was an encouraging perspective for the British who wanted the other European allies to work constructively and to spend more on defence. However, the British thought that whereas 'the CSCE, properly handled, could be relatively harmless, MBFR[s] were potentially dangerous'. The British restated their belief that Europe should bear a greater burden of its own defence but that it was difficult to argue this when there was talk about European force reductions at the same time.[135]

They would stick with this position all through the Anglo-American preparations for the Year of Europe, described in the previous chapter. The European predicament was potentially the opposite of the American. The Nixon administration needed MBFR talks to strengthen its position against its domestic isolationists whereas in Europe increased defence spending could be difficult to sell to European electorates in view of on-going MBFR negotiations. Nevertheless, the British viewpoint did not cause any friction in the autumn of 1972.

At the end of September 1972, Home went to Washington to reaffirm the continued good relations with the Nixon administration. It seemed certain that there would be an election victory for the incumbent President in the presidential election. From Rogers, he learned that the US did not yet want to settle on a specific date for the start of the CSCE negotiations.[136] Home did not urge the US on. During the same visit, Kissinger told him that the Chinese were apprehensive about what the CSCE and the MBFR would do to the US presence in Western Europe.[137] The Chinese did not want the pressure on their communist rivals, the Soviet Union, to be lessened and Kissinger exclaimed 'that China was one of the better NATO allies!' He added that the Chinese held Heath in high regard and read his speeches on Europe welcoming the British entry into the Common Market.[138] Nixon explained that the Chinese fear of the Soviet Union 'made them pro-NATO, pro-Europe'. He also assured Home that he had not weakened in his Cold War resolve and that he knew that 'the Russian animal was still dangerous for the West', hence he 'would not withdraw any American forces from Europe without a *quid pro quo*'.[139] Home left the meeting convinced and impressed by this last statement.[140]

After the 1972 EC Summit in Paris, Nixon wrote to Heath saying that he 'was pleased to note the many signs at the meeting that the Community [was] moving with resolve and new elan toward the high goal of European Union'. Nixon reiterated his continued support 'with undiminished enthusiasm'. He was particularly pleased with Heath's efforts to improve transatlantic relations, and especially Heath's 'clear perception of the overriding importance of the political relationship between America and Europe', an insight that Nixon regarded as 'an invaluable asset'.[141] He wanted a common EC foreign policy so that would put it on the same level as the US, the Soviet Union, China and Japan.[142] Nixon appreciated Heath's tentative steps towards the establishment of a US–EC special relationship, which would contribute to a united Western approach to détente and prevent the process from going too far too quickly.

The White House believed that '[d]espite doubts, concerns, and even suspicions, the US security relationship with Western Europe' would stay based on the legal obligations of the North Atlantic Treaty and the nuclear guarantee, with continued consultations in NATO on matters of Western security such as SALT, the CSCE and the MBFR talks.[143] In December 1972, after Nixon had been re-elected, Rogers tried to convince NATO of the American continued commitment to Europe. Rogers said that the US worked on the conviction 'that an intimate and co-operative bond with Western Europe is at the very centre of all our international relationships. No policy objective in the coming years [would] be more important to us than to preserve and strengthen that bond.' The US wanted to work well both with NATO and the 'enlarged European Community' since the 'enlarged Community [was] the major new fact on the European scene'. He quoted Nixon who, after the EC Summit, had said that 'It is, and has always been, my own deeply held view that progress towards a unified Europe enhances world peace, security and prosperity'.[144]

The British FCO agreed with the centrality of NATO. According to the FCO the '[m]ilitary and political partnership with the United States' was crucial if they were to achieve a lasting reduction of tensions with the Soviet Union. However, the FCO also wanted to take precautions against any superpower impulse to engage in détente over the heads of the Europeans. It wanted the EC to work towards the aim of preserving 'the political independence of Western Europe'. Therefore, the FCO proposed 'that the Community's "European identity" should be developed with regard to Eastern Europe' and that Britain should pretend to be more optimistic than was warranted in order to bring this 'Community solidarity' about. This would have the benefit of helping to 'deter the Americans from deals with the Russians at European expense' just as it would help to prevent the Soviets from meddling in 'the internal development of the Community'.[145] A European identity was also necessary to make the EC cohesive enough for a special relationship with the US.

However, the US already had a special relationship of sorts with an equal – the Soviet Union. In an off hand remark, at a scholarly conference, on 10 December 1972, Sonnefeldt noted that 'the US and the Russians had a special relationship because of the special problems of being super-powers'.[146] Evidently equality qualified for a special relationship. This was not the kind of relationship the US and Britain had at the end of 1972. Britain was a junior partner which remained close to American security thinking.

Anglo-American closeness in 1972 was in part due to the lessened US interest in détente and their common scepticism of the CSCE. Nonetheless, it was not clear whether European views were compatible with the lessened Anglo-American enthusiasm for détente. One observer wrote, in late 1972, in regard to the CAP, that British interests were closer to the American than the European ones. This made it difficult for Britain to act as an 'honest broker' since the accusation of being a Trojan horse could be raised when Britain became a formal EC member on 1 January 1973.[147] The same argument could be raised over the British government and détente when it tried to create a transatlantic special relationship. However, Heath had not choice. If he was to achieve his vision Britain had to work with the US in the preparations for détente in Europe. Britain could not pursue a détente of its own, regardless of whether there was a Soviet initiative to act upon or not. Following a separate French lead, had there been one, would only have resulted in giving France the leading role in Europe. France, however, wanted the US. But it was Britain, which had to work within both NATO and the EPC in order to achieve a cohesive Europe that could work with the US. While it is possible to doubt Nixon's sincerity in his attempt to involve Britain before his talks with the Soviets it is clear that Anglo-American détente coordination increased after SALT I. The White House both understood

Heath's desire for a US-European special relationship and it was itself moving closer to Britain's scepticism of détente.

The Anglo-American approach to détente

During the autumn of 1972 Anglo-American relations were close enough for Heath to have toyed with the possibility of proposing to Nixon that he make a state visit to Britain.[148] This did not come off and Heath's own visit to the US was postponed until the following year when Britain was an EC member. Heath would have preferred to meet Nixon once more before EC entry so that he would not have to take into consideration that the EC should speak with one voice.[149] Having successfully managed to situate Britain as a friend of both Brandt's détente and the US efforts on East–West relations, Heath now had to coordinate Anglo-American relations in regard to what was supposedly the emerging new Europe. As seen in the last chapter, the US diplomatic initiative on the Year of Europe involved dealing with US-European relations, but Heath also had to delve into the larger diplomatic gambit of continued détente processes in Europe.

Like Nixon, Kissinger saw Heath's visit, in February 1973, as the most important of all Nixon's upcoming meetings with European leaders. He claimed that Heath and the rest of Europe expected the US to take the initiative and lead détente.[150] The White House was intent on, as Kissinger put it, a 'new concept and common direction' and on playing 'a key role in the development of detante [sic], which rests to a great degree on US-Soviet relations; we need some room for maneuver [sic] but within the framework of agreed Western goals'.[151] This was the essential sticking point, since Heath saw a united Western Europe as such a goal.

At this time the CIA completed an analysis for the NSC on American relations with Europe that was somewhat different from Kissinger's viewpoint and closer to that of Heath. It welcomed a 'unified self-reliant Western Europe', and cited Western Europe's solidarity in the preparations for the CSCE as a good example of what could be achieved if the US and Europe moved towards a US-European 'special relationship'. This was the policy that the CIA preferred, since US and European interests were not identical but because they had common interests in many areas, hence 'both parties ... [could] act separately as well as jointly but it [did] not permit either to act without regard for [their] common concerns'. The CIA warned against harming this possibility by frightening the Europeans to cooperate by America concluding deals with the Soviet Union over their heads.[152] Kissinger preferred a different route to

Western unity: he wanted to minimise the diplomatic freedom of the Western Europeans. He claimed that Western Europe and the US might need to forge a united détente strategy to avoid a 'race to Moscow'. However, according to Kissinger, the White House required allied support to develop a workable strategy in MBFR. He suggested that Heath should be reassured that the US was not about to do any 'bargain with the USSR at Europe's expense'.[153] The US wanted its European allies to agree to a US-led détente. The White House, like Number 10, wanted to avoid competitive détente. Accordingly, the White House thought it necessary that Britain should feel secure, especially since Britain and the US now shared a common perspective of the necessary Cold War diplomacy.

This was evident from Britain's continued support for the US involvement in Vietnam. During the Christmas of 1972 the intensified efforts to end the war in Vietnam was the chief preoccupation of the White House.[154] This decreased the Nixon administration's attention to European affairs. Therefore, the FCO wanted to remind Nixon that it was 'of the greatest importance that the United States should play the role for which the President would wish to be remembered'. They were certain that Nixon had 'no wish to go down to history as the President who presided over the dissolution of the Atlantic Alliance'. The British were clearly concerned that the momentum which Anglo-American coordination had created, with Nixon favouring moves towards the establishment of a transatlantic partnership, would be lost. Nevertheless, the FCO assumed that Nixon's foreign policy still supported European integration. Hence, Britain would follow the US lead on détente. Despite professing the need for one European voice, Heath wanted to assure the White House that Britain would remain an 'interlocuteur' of use on world affairs and European policy.[155] This meant that Britain reaffirmed its intention to continue the Anglo-American Cold War special relationship until an Atlantic partnership was completely established.

It is conceivable that détente could have given Europe a period of relaxed tensions during which the West could work for the emergence of a united Western Europe, but Heath and his Cabinet saw a risk in détente. Handled in the wrong manner it risked having the opposite effect by weakening Western European cohesion thus undermining efforts to build a united Western Europe.

For détente to be beneficial it could not endanger any existing security arrangements. By 1973 the CSCE and the MBFR were no longer merely talked about they were soon to become reality and despite the increased Anglo-American coordination the British feared that these talks would 'rouse in Western Europe excessive wishful thinking about detente [*sic*]'. The US Secretary of State Rogers's speech to NATO in December had not been enough to assuage European anxieties. The worst scenario was a stronger Soviet Union and a fragmented West, with a reduced US commitment to Western Europe. The British priority was 'to maintain the stability... of the Alliance', but the longer term aim was 'to secure the emergence of a Western European defence entity with sufficient political coherence and military capability to aspire to a fair and equal partnership with the United States in an Atlantic alliance'.[156] This was congruent with the defence plans that Britain tried to bring about with the French as described in Chapter 3.

The British view was that any MBFR '[r]eduction should be seen as a product of détente and not as a means to it' with due regard for 'the principle of undiminished security'.[157] However, the British were slightly more optimistic about the CSCE, which they believed could help the alliance if its members worked well together. However, the British impression was that the Soviets were only interested in a quick conference with difficult questions put off to the future.[158] The FCO believed that the CSCE should be used to accentuate differences between East and West, which in turn would dispel wishful thinking about what détente could achieve. This could help strengthen the unity of the West at a crucial time and further the government's European plans. In other words, the CSCE presented an opportunity to exploit détente for the purpose of European integration.

Accordingly, the British and the Americans agreed on the need for allied cohesion. At the Heath–Nixon Summit, methods for reining in the smaller NATO states at the CSCE were discussed. Home thought that these might otherwise be led astray by the Soviet Union in the 'atmosphere of general euphoria and detente [*sic*]'. Rogers agreed with this.[159] Nixon reflecting similar concerns told Heath that it was important to avoid a European scramble under the cry of 'peace at any price' which could cause isolationism.[160] This also reflected the Nixon administration's intention, after having achieved its primary aims with SALT I, to be more restrained about further détente. To Nixon, 'MBFRs, SALT II, CSCE, the Middle East, and so forth' were all a ruse intended to keep 'the prospect of some further deal with the Soviet Union continuously dangling just ahead in order to keep the Soviet Government in play and at the same time to fend off, month by month, Congressional pressure for United States troop reductions in Europe'.[161] Since both the US and Britain were set on exploiting détente, Nixon's tactics could create the breathing space needed to develop Heath's ideas.

Rogers claimed that the Soviet Union believed that the Germans were the 'potential successors' of the US in Europe.[162] This was not the legacy that Nixon wanted. Although future administrations might lack his determination Nixon told Heath that they could be 'practically sure – that we will stay in Europe so long as I am here'.[163] That implied that the assurance only held until the next presidential election. Nixon, with the help of the Year of Europe initiative, wanted to forge a bond with Europe that future US administrations could not easily dissolve. For this reason there had to be allied agreement on the CSCE, the substance, and accordingly the risks, of which were still unclear.[164] Heath told Nixon that the CSCE was probably originally a Soviet method for dealing with the German problem. Brandt's Ostpolitik had taken care of that – leaving the proposal empty. Kissinger expressed his view that the Soviet Union's aim was to 'undermine NATO by every means they could'. He argued that the CSCE might be an attempt to 'lull the West into a false sense of security, which the Soviet Government would then exploit in their interests elsewhere'. Naturally, the British and the Americans could not let the CSCE be turned into a vehicle for that. Nixon, therefore, wanted the West to have control over what the CSCE negotiations would involve.[165] The British favoured this, since this was the only way to ensure that it would be the West which reaped the benefits from the conference.[166]

Nixon warned 'that the Soviet Government might be systematically preparing to attack the United States or NATO or China'. He had been critical of NATO but he would not allow the MBFR negotiations to risk the viability of NATO. Nevertheless, he claimed that Britain was the only ally with whom the US could talk about these matters.[167] Heath believed that Nixon understood that almost any cut agreed at the MBFR talks would be detrimental to the alliance.[168] Nixon's position had a reassuring effect on the British. Heath's willingness to foster good transatlantic relations while remaining a candid interlocutor probably helped foster the impression of more continuity than Heath intended. He was ensnared by his own conviction that a US–EC special relationship had to be created while at the same time avoiding an instantaneous dramatic change in the Anglo-American relationship. Such a rupture would not be conducive to his aims.

The continuity and closeness of Anglo-American relations were confirmed by the British involvement in drafting a text for a US-Soviet statement on the non-use of nuclear weapons. Not a new idea as such, except this time the Soviet edge was directed against China.[169] Brimelow, the Deputy Under-Secretary of the FCO, was greatly involved in the US drafting of a proposal. Britain risked being brandished a Trojan horse, if its assistance was found out. However, the consultations were in line with Nixon's wish for consultations and also provided the setting in which Kissinger told the British about his plans for the Year of Europe initiative.[170] By allowing the British to help the US could also allay British worries about US-Soviet condominium over the heads of the Europeans. Nixon, in fact, hoped to find some way of amending the existing draft to be acceptable yet not mean 'anything very much at all'. He believed that the treaty could be a tranquiliser to help the American people overcome the trauma of Vietnam, which he claimed would take one year.[171]

Nixon was also candid about the developments in Vietnam. He told Heath that the North Vietnamese had not given up their goal of a united Vietnam but he expected 'the settlement to hold for two years'.[172] The eventual Number 10 analysis of this was that the phrase should be understood to mean that the US did not expect a challenge to the South for another two years, but it did not refer to the possible success or failure of such a challenge.[173] A few months later Kissinger confided to the British that '[he] had no illusion that the Vietnam agreement would stop the course of history'.[174] Vietnam was still an issue that separated Britain from other Western European states. The FCO believed that Britain had gained credibility with the Nixon administration 'for the restraint...shown over Vietnam' where Britain was 'seen as America's staunchest and most dependable ally'. Its view was that the US regarded 'the European nations as weak, selfish, indecisive, and suspicious of US motives, and hence a pretty unrewarding lot to try and manage'.[175] That Britain had a special standing was reflected by the White House's belief that Nixon could talk 'more freely' with the British than any other European allies. Kissinger believed that, despite Heath's preference for the term the natural relationship, '[t]here continue[d] to be a special relationship'.[176] This had implications for the American wish that the British should help to further the forging of one cohesive identifiable partner on the other side of the Atlantic ready to shoulder greater responsibilities. There were those, like Nixon and the CIA, who understood that this meant that Europe would emerge as a fully fledged partner. There was also Kissinger who hoped for greater European cohesion but under the aegis of American leadership.

Heath deemed his visit to the US to be a success.[177] He was right. Britain was seen as a loyal ally and the US had moved closer to the British position on détente. Both the US and Britain were now intent on exploiting détente to further the cohesion of the West. It seemed no less as if the traditional Anglo-American relationship had been adapted to the era of East–West relaxation, with the effect that the relationship deepened. This did not appear to conflict with Heath's plans, however, as he and Nixon still agreed on the overall goal of a US-European partnership. Only in April would Kissinger's speech on the Year of Europe reveal that his interpretation was more oriented towards inter-allied management than Cold War diplomacy. Nevertheless, the process of Cold War détente and the inevitable factor of international affairs – unexpected events – would demonstrate how well the British and the US had actually adapted their Cold War relationship.

The near destruction of the special relationship

As always, Britain's approach to the French had to be consistent with Anglo-American relations and that was, as the last chapter showed, a great challenge for 1973. By the summer of 1973 the preparations for the CSCE were drawing to a close. Britain therefore needed to anchor its approach to its European partners. France refused participation in the MBFR, but in regard to the CSCE the EPC managed successfully to bring the EC members together.[178] It was particularly difficult to handle the French given their suspicions of both the US and the Germans. The British were in the potentially awkward position of being privy to the Soviet-US discussions on an Agreement on the Prevention of Nuclear War. When Pompidou met Heath in May 1973 the French President wondered whether the US and the Soviet Union were trying to devise a way to protect themselves from a nuclear conflict. Nonetheless, Pompidou was not alarmed about the US doing something rash in regard to the defence of Europe. There would be reductions of the conventional troops to satisfy the domestic US critics, like Senator Mansfield, he believed. But the Americans would have to keep its forces in Western Europe to make certain that Europe had a functional defence and to ensure that they kept their fingers on the nuclear weapons it had placed in Europe.[179] Pompidou's composure indicated that he did not anticipate any drastic changes in the transatlantic relationship. Even though Heath and Pompidou had different views as to how long and to what extent the US should stay in Europe, they agreed that Europe needed the US for its defence in the seventies. Heath said that they should not 'make it more difficult for those in the US Administration who sought to maintain the US defence position in Europe'.[180]

Heath needed the French support to achieve a joint Western approach with the US over European détente and for his efforts to push the EC towards greater responsibilities for the defence of Europe. Exactly what these efforts would be also depended on the development of the détente processes. However, there was also a possibility that the French tactic of trying to break up the two sides of the Cold War by bilateral schemes would resurface and obstruct EC cohesion. Most EC members believed that integration and détente could be pursued simultaneously. Only France considered putting détente before integration, although France ultimately did not cause a rift in the EC over détente.[181] Instead, British reactions to the Year of Europe contributed to the transatlantic quarrel in the middle of 1973. After the summer the French expressed their appreciation that the British had not acted as Trojans but that they had turned out to be sound Europeans.[182] The inter-allied diplomacy that the British engaged in during the spring and summer of the 1973 was not conducive to their attempt to simultaneously reaffirm the joint Anglo-American approach to the Cold War.

In March 1973, before his Year of Europe speech, Kissinger met with Brimelow, of the FCO. Kissinger told him that 'whether [they] liked it or not the "*détente*" band wagon was already rolling' and it was given ample help by the Russians. He believed that with Ostpolitik the Soviets had achieved their aim of ratification of the existing borders in Europe. Their new goal for the CSCE was to establish the mirage of détente. The Soviets hoped this would create a climate conducive to US troop withdrawals and simultaneously prevent a European replacement of US capabilities skewing 'the future balance of power ... in favour of the Soviet Union'.[183] It was a case of competitive exploitation. The Soviet Union using the next phase of détente was exactly what the US and Britain had agreed to prevent.

For the British the difficulty was in transferring their détente scepticism to other Europeans who were more enthusiastic. The FCO, under Home, had a favourable view of an idea emanating from Number 10. The idea was that they could use the formulation contained in the NATO Ministerial Communiqué from Rome, May 1970, about 'freedom of information and freedom of movement' in order 'to put the Russians on the defensive'.[184] This was, as seen above, also an idea that the French had taken up.

The White House remained sceptical and believed that '[t]he idea of freer movement: of people and information [was] a worthy goal' but that it was unlikely to be possible 'to talk the Soviets out of their empire in East Europe'.[185] The White House actually believed that the British were 'somewhat more sanguine about' the CSCE than the US was. The White House, due to its own doubts about the CSCE, still wanted to have it over rapidly.[186] Kissinger eventually grew impatient with the British stand

over his Year of Europe initiative and what he regarded as their intransigence, exemplified by their insistence on a very restricted position on
MBFR. In August he told NSC colleagues that he was frustrated with
the British at one point exclaiming: 'They can't milk us for everything
in the name of special channel [*sic*].'[187] However, he was probably just
venting his frustration. He had no wish to impair the Anglo-American
special relationship, where Britain remained a junior partner, or to cause
a transatlantic disagreement about détente.

The US and Britain differed about how long the conference should
last. Heath thought that the Russians wanted the MBFR to follow a short
CSCE. This, he believed, was congruent with the American desire for
NATO to hurry the beginning of the MBFR negations since this would
help in keeping the domestic isolationists at bay.[188] However, the British
believed that a short CSCE conference would play into the hands of the
Soviet Union, which wanted a short conference for its own reasons. The
British were anxious that the US would be tempted by the expediency
and try and get the conference over with quickly. The danger was that
the Americans, with the rest of Western Europe in tow, might fall into
a Soviet trap which would give the Soviet Union what it wanted. The
Soviet Union, and not the West, would then have been able to exploit
the conference. The preparations for the CSCE ended in early June 1973.
The first stage followed a month later and was a swift affair. This gave
only practical guidance to proceedings and was in contrast to the second
stage where much of the real work was done. The British need not have
worried about the conference. It began in the middle of September and
would last until July 1975 long after the Heath government had ended
and Nixon had left office.

The time just before the conference got under way took place against a
foreboding backdrop. In early May, Kissinger caused Heath great worry.
Kissinger had told the British Prime Minister that the Russians were
thinking about 'taking out the Chinese nuclear capability by a preemp-
tive [*sic*] attack'.[189] This would extend the Brezhnev Doctrine to China.
However, the British dismissed the possibility of a pre-emptive surgical
strike against China as unlikely. It was seen as a Russian card to pressure
the Americans to agree to a treaty on the non-use of nuclear weapons,
since an actual strike would undo the Soviet Union's détente efforts.
An auxiliary explanation was that Kissinger overstated the dangers especially to European nuclear powers, which were otherwise anxious about
'their freedom of action', so as to be able to justify and go ahead with
the Agreement on the Prevention of Nuclear War with the Soviets.[190]
The US-Soviet treaty was the main item during Brezhnev's visit to the

US in the summer of 1973. There was neither a Sino-Soviet conflict nor enough progress on SALT II to stir the Europeans, nor did the Europeans need to fear an Asian nuclear conflict or a superpower condominium.

Nevertheless, Kissinger claimed to still be alarmed about the Sino-Soviet situation in July. He said that the US had refused the Soviet Union crucial information on estimates of the Chinese nuclear forces. Kissinger 'could not see that Europe could survive with the whole of the Far East under Soviet domination'. As the situation momentarily intensified in July Kissinger asked Heath whether the British and the Americans could prepare contingency planning together.[191] The White House tried to show how quickly it reverted to traditional Anglo-American consultations at the first sign of a chill in the Cold War. Given the diplomatic wrangles over the Year of Europe initiative, which went from bad to worse in July, as described in the previous chapter, a fright could perhaps also remind the British as to where their security allegiance lay.

By the autumn, when the Year of Europe had become the responsibility of the Europeans, both the US and Britain wanted to restore the Anglo-American relations but an unexpected, yet, real test of Britain's allegiances emanated from tensions in another part of Asia – the Middle East. As seen in previous chapters, the Yom Kippur War, or October War, in 1973 and the subsequent oil shocks were greatly problematic to all Western countries and also to grand designs such as Heath's. In fact, the October War nearly had the side effect of wrecking the Anglo-American special relationship.

In an attempt to regain territories and to avenge Israel's victory in 1967 Egypt and Syria coordinated an attack on Israel on Yom Kippur, 6 October, which surprised nearly the whole world, including the White House. Britain was not directly affected. The US, in contrast, was soon far more deeply involved. After three days of fighting Israel pleaded with the US for supplies on which Israel's defence depended.[192] By the time the war broke out Nixon was becoming deeply involved in Watergate and the crisis management was done by others, notably by Kissinger, from September 1973 Secretary of State, and by James Schlesinger, the Secretary of Defense.[193] The US–Israel relationship was very nearly close enough to qualify for specialness and Kissinger and Schlesinger did not hesitate to aid Israel. However, Kissinger remained conscious of the fact that the US was running up to the limitations of détente. Nonetheless, the way to solve the situation was through discussions with the Soviet Union. These talks were crucial to ending the conflict and saving East–West relaxation and were more important than informing the NATO allies. This could not but sour alliance relations.[194] In addition, the American crisis management disturbed Anglo-American attempts at coordination of their détente policies.

During the crisis, Britain refused to live up to Kissinger's expectation of being a reliable junior partner to the US. Unlike the talk about a Sino-Soviet conflict the very real October War was a chill in the Cold War that would demonstrate the restrictions on the Anglo-American relationship. Sudden events in the Cold War that involved the two superpowers exposed the lesser importance of great powers like Britain. Even if inevitable it was not popular with Heath. In many crises, Britain and the US had stood shoulder to shoulder but now Britain like France was critical about the lack of American pressure, during the preceding years, on Israel to seek a diplomatic solution. They also feared that the Arabs would use the oil weapon, which would reduce economic growth in Europe. Consequently, the Heath government refused to act on behalf of the White House. On 13 October, Home rebuffed Kissinger's attempt to make Britain responsible for a UN Security Council Resolution that called for a ceasefire in circumstances that seemed less than promising.[195]

Not only were the British less cooperative about diplomacy than the White House had hoped, it also refused to assist in the transport of US aid to Israel and Heath would even criticise US conduct. Heath, like the nearly all NATO's leaders in Europe, refused the American use of bases and air-space for its air-lift to Israel that began on 14 October. Heath argued that both sides were to blame and that it was not in Britain's interest to take sides. Kissinger took this very badly.[196] The aid came, though anyway. But by 24 October the concerted US-Soviet efforts to end the conflict had gone too far. An overexcited Kissinger drew the worst possible conclusions from a Soviet suggestion that it could act unilaterally, and send Soviet forces, if necessary, to achieve an end to hostilities and uphold a ceasefire. With limited instruction from Nixon, Kissinger and key group of officials decided to demonstrate the US resolve against such a development. The following day not only the Soviets but also allies and the media realised that all US military commands were moved to a higher level of readiness DEFCON III, above the normal IV but below II – being ready for imminent war. No other ally had been consulted or told that it was meant as a diplomatic signal to the Soviets.[197] Heath and Home were taken unaware by the US alert, although the British military had heard about it in the early morning. Heath believed 'that the American action had done immense harm...both in this country and world wide'. He was concerned about Nixon who was tormented by Watergate, or his men – Schlesinger and Kissinger rushing to take rash action.[198] To Kissinger's anger Heath publicly rejected supporting the nuclear alert.[199]

The British failure to live up to Kissinger's expectations came close to permanently fracturing Anglo-American relations. Not because a new US–Israel relationship trumped the Anglo-American relationship. Britain was not unique in its reaction on the contentious issues of transport and the US alert. It actually remains doubtful whether the contentious American alert helped to bring about a ceasefire that held. But the war ended on 28 October.[200] Like the other NATO members Kissinger also realised the problems of association with Israel in the eyes of the oil-producing Arab countries. Initially he had, unsuccessfully, urged the air-lift to Israel to be as discreet as possible.[201] It was not a question about Israel replacing Britain as a trusted partner but to Kissinger it was a question about loyalty.

Accordingly, the State Department, now headed by Kissinger, considered how the British could be punished for its behaviour during the conflict. It looked into what kind of measures the US could take to make clear the American 'dissatisfaction with [the British] performance as an ally'. Any US reaction had to 'be weighed carefully' since it could lead to the 'erosion of the close working relationship' the US had with Britain. The punishments ranged from a slap on the wrist, such as giving the British Ambassador an oral demarche. More dramatic measures were considered like publicly siding with Spain on Gibraltar, or striking at the Heath government's European policies by convincing the other EC members to make an EC regional policy unfavourable to Britain. The most extreme measure under consideration was a cancellation of the Anglo-American nuclear and intelligence agreements. The detrimental effects of many of the contemplated measured made them improbable. In fact, many of the proposed punishments were so intertwined that the State Department found it difficult to make clear delineations between them. It quickly realised that the more severe the action the greater the risk that Britain would be alienated permanently. This would decrease the possibility for the US to 'influence future British actions'. It also did not want to give the impression that the Nixon administration 'overreacted'.[202] Clearly, even if Kissinger had wanted to punish Britain, the consequences were soon deemed to be too costly to the US. Under the conditions of the Cold War and in view of the need to have good relations with the EC a break with Britain was intolerable. Due to this Cold War conditioning of what could be done the US collapsed back into the Anglo-American special relationship.

That the US had overreacted in the crisis was in fact the British analysis.[203] After all, Britain was still Americans' best friend in Europe. The State Department's considerations reveal that contrary to the assumptions of many in the American administration, and of Heath as well, the Anglo-American relationship was deeply embedded. Agreements and other policies were not easily changed without considerable risks. To a greater degree than the US and the British appreciated the Cold War set the limits on how much and how rapidly the relationship could change. It was also evident that different parts of the Anglo-American special relationship could not be disaggregated. Hence, there was no easy separation between what Heath called the 'natural' and the special parts of the relationship. If Heath had not held on to the Anglo-American Cold War special relationship, with the purpose of fostering a joint Anglo-American approach to détente, the difficulties of separating 'special' from 'natural' relations would probably have surfaced earlier. The necessities of the Cold War alone could not have rammed the relationship back together but these requirements stayed the hand that considered severing a few ties. During the autumn both the US and Britain moved to restore Anglo-American relations.

Restoration

In the fall of 1973, it became clear that the CSCE and MBFR would not be quickly resolved. Heath thought that 'the US would be prepared to give the Russians what they wanted without getting what the Europeans needed on liberalisation'.[204] The British wanted the two détente processes to take a long time. Nevertheless, the Heath government would have to win the next general election in order to use the CSCE as it had envisaged. Time was needed for the British strategy of getting concessions from the Soviet Union on human rights and to create a stable period in which to build the European integration. In order to ensure that the extended period of CSCE negotiations was beneficial the Heath government had wanted to return to its balancing act between the US, and NATO, and the EC already after the summer. Britain had accordingly sought an agreement on European identity. Before the Yom Kippur War, the British had also intended to inform the Nixon administration that it was in the British 'national interests to help the Americans cope' with its American domestic political problems of new isolationism by ensuring that they agreed on the approach to the MBFR.[205] This would have been in line with the Anglo-American Cold War relationship as it had developed since the beginning of the Nixon–Heath years. It would also have gone some way towards meeting Kissinger's wishes on the question of MBFR and it would have been a step to improve relations after the disagreements over the Year of Europe.

The rift over the Yom Kippur War aside, Kissinger and the White House had come to understand that the British preferred drawn out negotiations in the CSCE, where the West would 'keep making demands, rather than negotiating a minimal and early conclusion' to the conference. Unlike the Americans the British wanted to use the conference to demonstrate 'the intransigence of the Soviets'.[206] However, the US believed that the MBFR cuts suggested for NATO really worried the British. The British thought it unwise to commit the West to cuts without knowing the result of later phases of the MBFR. Therefore, Kissinger had planned to reassure the British just before the rift over conflict in the Middle East happened.[207] Clearly, both the US and Britain, albeit for different reasons, had been intent on shoring up the special relationship in the fall of 1973. Kissinger wanted to restore the relationship. Heath wanted to keep it so as to be able to pursue his vision. The British later clarified to the US that they wanted the second phase of the MBFR to be unclear lest it upset the efforts at 'future European defence arrangements'.[208] Clearly, Heath's ideas were still the organisational principle for the Heath government's Cold War policies. However, success for these depended on the response they got from the other allies. In this regard none was as important as France.

When Heath met Pompidou in the middle of November 1973 he sought to explain the idea of using détente for the purposes of European integration. He suggested the use of a text, accompanying the text on European identity vis-à-vis the US, on European identity vis-à-vis the Russians and the Eastern Europeans. This was to reflect the ideas from the Paris Summit that the EC should try and 'formulate "common medium and long term positions"'. Although the EC had not kept to a joint position on the whole of East–West affairs it had done so on the CSCE. The British argued that '[t]he experience of the CSCE' had already shown how much more weight they carried when acting together. The British wanted the EC members to 'preserve their independence vis-à-vis the Soviet Union and eventually to see the... relationship with the Soviet Union replaced by something more constructive'. The idea was to build on Heath's EC accession speech, which had said 'that "Europe is more than Western Europe alone"', in order to devise a policy towards the Eastern European states that would make them less dependent on the Soviet Union, and show that European integration was not a process 'directed against them'.[209]

As the 'next step...for the Nine', Heath envisaged 'a common policy toward the relationship between' the East and the EC. This would awaken the Community members to 'the real position of the Soviet Union'. Pompidou agreed and said that such a common policy was in the members' interests. It would tie West Germany to the EC thus ensuring common security in regard to the German problem. He was concerned about the German question and reminded Heath that although he liked and trusted Brandt, 'only ten years had separated Herr [Gustav] Stresemann from Adolf Hitler'.[210] Although Pompidou's enthusiasm for the European project had waned since the French referendum on enlargement and the Paris Summit in 1972, he realised that West Germany had to be tied closely to the Western fold.

The October War had pushed the British government closer to Europeans than it otherwise would have been. Britain had, despite disagreement with the US on the Year of Europe initiative, kept traditional and close contact on matters of security with the US until the October War began. The British government was naturally aware that its plans for Anglo-French nuclear cooperation were dependent on transatlantic understanding not confrontation. Likewise, US help with the update of the British deterrent required that the security concerns of the Anglo-American special relationship were not put in jeopardy.

In a speech on 28 November 1973, Heath tried to clarify his position to American correspondents. He called for a greater American effort to distinguish between the two Europes, that of the NATO alliance, where the US was a key member, and the Community, where it was not. Clearly, Heath still hoped to be able to exclude the US from influencing the internal processes of the EC. Heath also said that federalism could not be transplanted from the US experience to Europe, which unlike the North American continent had 'ancient nation states', but he assured his audience 'that in the end it would be a British approach to unity in Europe'. This presumably meant a level of intra-governmentalism acceptable to France, as well as Britain. Britain should also lead the EC, alone, or together with France and West Germany, towards deeper integration and an evolving union. Although, he admitted that the process might not move as quickly as he had hoped. For example, defence would not be on the agenda of the EC Summit in Copenhagen. And, as was his way he referred to his Harvard lectures saying 'that the French were not yet ready for the idea he had put forward to them'.[211] This was a coded reference to the progress on an Anglo-French nuclear force on which to build a European defence. The speech demonstrated that his ideas as encapsulated in the Harvard lectures had stayed with him over the years, and been the outline for his ideas about what Britain should be inside the EC. As seen above, he had often referred to them in private conversations with other Western leaders in order to achieve things but as the programme envisaged in the lectures had been slowed down he admitted this publicly.

On 12 December 1973, Kissinger delivered a speech to the Anglo-American Pilgrim society in London, as discussed in the previous chapter, where he admonished the Europeans saying that the US would continue to support European unity but 'not...at the expense of the Atlantic Community'.[212] For Kissinger, the crisis highlighted the precarious state of European external relations and confirmed his stand in favouring a strengthening of the transatlantic bonds over support for deepened European integration.[213] During Kissinger's visit Home wanted to clarify that the EC had to 'travel at the pace of its slowest member in dealing with the world outside', which in this case was France. Nevertheless, according to Home, there were good signs that the French were taking a more cooperative stance on defence and in regard to relations with the US. Home also wanted to clarify that it was the British who had originally suggested the paper on a 'European Identity' that the newly enlarged Community were working on. Although the US was not supposed to be involved, Home was prepared to show Kissinger the draft in strictest confidence.[214] Home also stated in public that Europe was not an extra Force but an added force at the US's side.[215] This was said to persuade Kissinger that he had the Europeans where he wanted them. At the same time it was vaguely consistent with the Heath's claim that even as equals Europe and the US would face the same enemy. So when unable to pursue Heath's plans the government turned back to the confidences of the traditional Anglo-American relationship. This to some extent undermined the ardent Europeanism of Heath where the Europeans were supposed to work out their joint positions vis-à-vis the US. However, the British did so in order to be able to continue its European plans at a later stage. The British government was not prepared to abandon its plans for Europe even if they moved painfully slow, just like the MBFR and the CSCE.

On the agenda of the Copenhagen Summit, 14–15 December, was the development of a European identity. It was in accordance with the ambitions from the Hague and the Paris Summit, and came as a response to the Nixon administration's the Year of Europe initiative. In October 1973 the West Germans had contact with the French and were now prepared to discuss a European defence identity within the alliance context because Brandt had become convinced that US withdrawals from Europe were inevitable and would come soon. Heath favoured talks beginning among the Nine but he also wanted to make sure they kept the existing alliance stable until a new identity came about.[216] Work on the European identity had been given added impetus by the Middle East crisis. It indicated the need to develop common views on foreign affairs and then speak with one voice; however, it left security affairs squarely to the NATO realm. The project of a European identity was eventually completely overshadowed by the EC members' more immediate need to deal with the oil crisis.[217] Perhaps it, like the new Atlantic declaration discussed in the last chapter, also suffered from a lack of momentum after the Heath government lost power in 1974. It was replaced by a Labour government under Harold Wilson, who was prepared to accept Britain's role as a junior partner in the special relationship, just like Kissinger had wanted.

Nixon commented on the domestic crisis in Britain where the oil crisis had given added strength to miners' claims who went on strike in the winter of 1973–74. As he poignantly put it, 'Without coal you are dead.'[218] And so it was, Heath's plans for European integration grounded to a halt but the Cold War Anglo-American special security relationship remained. When the Heath government fell, in March 1974, it ended British efforts at European integration and an equal partnership based on American involvement.

During the four Nixon–Heath years both the Americans and the British tried to safeguard Western security but no traditional Anglo-American outlook emerged easily; instead there were misunderstandings. The British constantly tried to work on both sides of the Atlantic to guarantee a cohesive West. This was in the interest of Heath's vision that needed a Europe that put integration before East–West relaxation. Britain helped to make progress in the EPC towards European policy coordination on détente in Europe, which was taken by some in the US as an example of what could be achieved in a US–EC special relationship. Nevertheless, the White House preferred to control détente to be able to pursue a superpower détente and, after the SALT I treaty, in order to ensure that no ally was led astray in pursuit of a separate détente effort. It seemed that the US thought that steps towards détente should be the privilege of those that were equals like the US and the Soviet Union. Allies like West Germany, or Western Europe for that matter, should follow the US lead. Yet, a strong West required a stronger Europe, which would have to become more independent and closer to an equal of the US, something which Nixon understood.

Nixon believed regions to be the way of the future. Although he valued the consultative aspect of the special relationship, at least when it suited him, he was prepared to forego the special relationship with

Britain in favour of a transfer of special ties to Europe. He thought, however, that the transfer of special ties would take time and that it should not interfere with his remaking of American foreign policy. Notwithstanding Nixon's support for Heath, the Nixon administration had difficulties in understanding Britain's approach to détente.

The British were actually more sceptical of détente than the Americans. But the White House did not recognise this and feared that Britain was considering following a French approach to East–West relaxation. Even when they moved closer to each other's views after SALT I, the Americans thought the British more relaxed about the CSCE. In fact, the British wanted to exploit détente in Europe both for the benefit of the West but also as a means to create an EC foreign policy towards the East.

At first glance it may seem like American relations with Israel superseded Anglo-American relations during the October War. Kissinger, at the time in full control of the US foreign policy, wanted the British to follow his lead. As during the conflict between India and Pakistan, the British looked to its own interest, and refused to be a tool to the White House. When the joint Nixon–Heath approach ended the Anglo-American Cold War relationship remained. Even a severe crisis in the relationship only highlighted how deeply entrenched the security relations really were and how these remained even when consultations sometimes flagged and parts of the traditional institutional relationships had disappeared or been replaced by a foreign policy directed from the White House. The rift over the October War in fact exposed the degree to which Anglo-American relations were conditioned by the Cold War. The entanglement of special relations made a US break with Britain counterproductive. Like Britain, the US still got more than it gave, from the Anglo-American special relationship.

Conclusion

> What follows is not intended to imply praise or blame or even
> to explain – that must await the retrospective judgement of dis-
> passionate historians.[1]
>
> The FCO, in 1973, stating the purpose of
> analysing a contemporary initiative.

At the time of President Nixon's resignation, in 1974, an article in *The
Times*, which seemed to reflect much of informed opinion, claimed that
the ' "special relationship" is dead'.[2] The contemporary judgement was
that the Anglo-American relationship had nearly been extinguished during the Nixon–Heath years. Later assessments of the special relationship
have usually chosen to confirm this view or, in view of new findings,
often ignored contradictions and discounted the period as an anomaly
best dealt with briefly and in passing. However, others, especially those
who have had access to the primary sources, have in part come close
to many of the points made in this book. When added together, however, the partial insights do not fit either with the usual descriptions of
the Nixon–Heath years in the literature. This book has shown that it is
necessary to invert the position of the Nixon–Heath years in narratives
about the post-war special relationship and to give the period due attention. Far from being an anomaly, the period was formative for the special
relationship with a simultaneous impact on transatlantic relations.

The first part of the conclusion looks at advantages of reconsidering the Anglo-American relationship between 1970 and 1974 to the
study of the special relationship. The succeeding section demonstrates
the necessity of appreciating the centrality of Heath's ideas for Britain
and European integration as well as his understanding with Nixon. The
last section addresses the main question and looks at reasons for why

Heath's transfer of special ties to a US–EC basis failed and what this meant to the special relationship and Anglo-American relations. Before venturing on to reviewing old assumptions about the Nixon–Heath years it is helpful to recapitulate the major tenets of Heath's vision and the Nixon administration's initial policy towards Britain and Europe.

Heath sought to modernise Britain and reverse British decline. He intended to remould British society along continental lines in order to copy the success, especially the economic growth, of the EC members. The post-war winding up of the British Empire would have been worth it if he could replace this basis for British claims of great power status and endow Britain with a leading role in Europe. Hence, he desired the completion of a united Europe by the end of the seventies, in other words a veritable Western European super-state. This required changes in a number of areas where British policies were closely aligned, by treaty or convention, to the US. His ambitious solution was to make a seamless adaptation of the Anglo-American special relationship to an American-European, or specifically US–EC, special relationship. The Nixon administration also tried to accrue transatlantic relations a place of priority. In contrast to its wish to radically alter other US foreign policies the Nixon administration continued traditional American support for European integration and sought to strengthen the NATO alliance. Like the Heath government in Britain the new American administration wanted to prevent American power from decreasing but it also wanted to ensure that there was no Western decline.

Britain and the US shared more views than the wish to avoid decline. In order to benefit from studying the shared views it is necessary to revise some common assumptions about the Nixon–Heath era. The first misconception is that Britain and the US drifted apart between 1970 and 1974. When studied briefly this episode of the Anglo-American relationship has been made to point in the negative direction cited from *The Times*. This way of seeing things is problematic. There never was a single and constant American policy towards Britain and European during the Nixon administrations nor was the British policy towards the US the same during the whole of the Heath government either. A brief recapitulation of the highs and lows makes this evident.

Despite setbacks and a few debacles the Anglo-American special relationship never died or went away. Relations were good when Heath came to power and quickly became even better after the first two meetings in 1970 between Heath and Nixon. Their views overlapped and Nixon was won for Heath's vision. The special relationship was regarded as exceptionally good until the summer of 1971 exposed the differences between the American and the British interpretations of their mutual obligations. Heath reacted to the unilateral American economic decisions of 15 August, by pushing plans for European integration on his own and against the US. Relations were restored at the Nixon–Heath Summit in December 1971. Nixon wanted to maintain good relations and Heath retracted his confrontational attitude and between 1972 and the spring of 1973 Anglo-American relations improved and the Heath government pursued Heath's plans with renewed support from the US. In the spring of 1973, after Watergate, Nixon gradually lost control of foreign policy making. Instead, Henry A. Kissinger, Nixon's National Security Adviser, became responsible for the diplomatic initiative known as the Year of Europe. He set the US on a new course towards Britain and Europe. As a result Anglo-American relations plummeted in the summer of 1973, made even worse by their disagreement about how to manage the latest Middle East conflict – the October War of 1973. However, neither the US nor Britain could afford to severe the ties of the special relationship and both sides moved to improve relations in the autumn of 1973. However, any chance for renewed American support for a US–EC special relationship ended with the Heath government losing power in 1974 and Nixon resigning from office. Nevertheless, the years 1970–74 were not simply a long litany of continuously worsening Anglo-American relations.

Another misconception is that little happened in the Anglo-American relationship in the Nixon–Heath years, which is why little attention has been given to the period. When an event, or in this case the transferral of special ties, fails to occur the predicament is that the non-occurrence might not be recognised. For example, there were no major changes to the Anglo-American relationship such as a decision to create a new Anglo-French nuclear interdependence or a decision to update the British deterrent with an American system similar to the Polaris deal between Britain and the US in the early sixties. This, however, is to confuse the result with the intention. Just because little seemed to happen does not mean that British and American policies were geared towards the status quo or less. The pursuit of Heath's vision and changes to the American foreign policy towards Europe led to tremendous activity in the nuclear, security, economic and diplomatic areas.

Anglo-American affairs during the early seventies have been obscured by the many great changes to international affairs in the early seventies such as Cold War détente and the breakdown of the international monetary system. The very complexity of the changes to international affairs in the early seventies may have contributed to the limited study of the Nixon–Heath years. For researchers, there are other important issues to focus on in this period. Disentangling Anglo-American relation, in which little seemed to happen, has not been a priority. Nevertheless, in view of the amount of change the fact that the special relationship survived at all is a call for more research of this period. A more mundane reason for there being little research on the Anglo-American relations in the Nixon–Heath years is because the period has been wedged between the post-war decades for which archive material was accessible and the eighties, a period where there for a long time appeared to be more reason to study the Anglo-American relationship.

One advantage of studying the special relationship in the Nixon–Heath years is that it helps to reveal the limitations of the so-called functional interpretation of the special relationship. Such an interpretation relies too much on the desire to emulate political science. Such functional interpretations are difficult for two reasons: first, because the special relationship is not a constant easily traced over time. For example, it was originally proposed as an equal partnership between Britain with her Empire and the US. Second, the idea of the special relationship with 'mythical' attributes, such as instinctive loyalties on both sides, cannot be discounted merely because some features of Anglo-American relations are intangible and difficult to measure. Building up special ties and sustaining them are not only a question about signing treaties but also about establishing practices and creating a common past. The alleged closeness between Britain and the US meant that the term 'special relationship' became automatically associated with the Anglo-American relationship. Because the relationship was supposed to be about more than agreements and since it was unequal the conventional interpretation was that Britain, the previous hegemon, had the privilege of offering the US, the new hegemon, advice as a loyal, trusted junior Cold War partner. The analysis was based on the Anglo-American relations of the late fifties and early sixties but by the sixties this myth of the special relationship was widely accepted. Many, like Kissinger, coming to the relationship as an academic observer, thought the special relationship should remain like that. There were also those, of whom Heath was one, who argued that the special relationship amounted to nothing more than a set of agreements. It is necessary to understand both perspectives in order to make sense of Anglo-American misunderstandings and disagreements.

Another advantage of studying Anglo-American relations together with European integration is that the importance of individuals is underscored. The long-term view of Britain and European integration emphasises the state as a unitary actor at the expense of individuals who yield power only temporarily. According to the long-term view the Heath government took up the preparations for negotiations where the Wilson government left off in the summer of 1970 and pursued EC membership because there was nowhere else for Britain to go. Usually, the long-term view pays relatively little attention to details, making little distinction between the organisation that Britain tried to join in 1961–63, 1967, and that which it eventually joined in 1973. Even if, as seems likely, there was no viable alternative for Britain than EC membership, a successful entry does not inevitably follow from necessity. The long-term view is often associated with a systemic idea of international relations, where if Britain wanted to join the EC it had to distance itself from the US. This is then viewed either as a part of clever British plan to keep the special relationship or as a means to end the relationship and become fully European depending on which long-term policy one believes will prevail. The international system is very likely to limit what can be achieved. It may be a truism but the restrictions need to be neither based on a world of unitary actors nor understood by the actors – be they states or statesmen. The long-term view implies that a Labour government, under Harold Wilson, would also have been able to bring Britain into the EC. The likelihood of that aside, it is a claim in which little distinction is made between what Heath and Wilson wanted from EC membership. But, as this book has shown Heath's ideas about Britain in Europe were very distinct. Had Britain been unsuccessful in its attempt to join the EC, or if Britain had been successful under a Wilson government, the Nixon administration might have reacted differently to the outcome depending on whether Britain had had a Labour instead of a Conservative government.

* * *

Heath's vision of Britain in Europe and a US–EC special relationship are central to the new understanding of the Nixon–Heath years. By studying Heath's ideas and his understanding with Nixon it becomes possible to make sense of the vacillating Anglo-American relationship between 1970 and 1974. Among academics who recognise Heath's ambition, his ideas have often been underestimated mainly because they failed. Among many others, both contemporaries and researchers, it is overlooked because it failed spectacularly in the sense that it was not even evident that he had a comprehensive vision. The Conservatives were unable to campaign on promises of a Britain flourishing in the EC in the

British General Election of 1970. Instead, the issue that caught the people's and the pundits' imagination was the Heath government's plans to modernise the British economy, which was associated with market liberalisation. Four years of economic turmoil obscured the fact that it was the Heath's wish to see a strong Britain at the centre of a united Europe, which was the overriding goal of the Heath government rather than any specific economic ideology.

The debate about Heath's enthusiasm for European integration has often been about when he was won for Europe. Instead the key question should be about how Europe became useful to his political ambitions. In practical politics idealism is not easily distinguished from self-interest. Regardless of what part of Heath's experience one chooses to stress it is evident that his enthusiasm had an element of idealism, perhaps based on his cultural tastes. Nonetheless, his advocacy for British EC entry in the late sixties served an instrumental purpose – for him and for Britain. He believed that British society could continue to thrive by adhering to the traditional 'one nation' policy of the Conservative Party of serving the welfare of the British people as a whole. He was also profoundly patriotic and believed that Britain still had a role to play internationally. Accordingly, Britain should keep the influence of a great power. For this, not only economic growth but also the leverage and influence that came with leading a large grouping in the world such as the EC was needed. Heath, lacking an ideological '-ism' as a guiding light, required a single aim around which to organise the pragmatic politics of his party. This need became especially urgent when he became leader of the Conservative Party in 1965 and it was then Europe came to constitute the basis for his vision.

Whereas Harold Wilson intended to use EC membership to shore up the British economy and rescue the role Britain had thitherto played in the post-war era, Heath was far more ambitious. His conception of power was akin to that of a statesman in the nineteenth century. In this, but in few others, he resembled de Gaulle. Heath wanted to ensure that the EC moved swiftly from an economic grouping to a political union, not by handing power over to Brussels, but with the means of a kind of inter-governmental approach. He regarded personal diplomacy as the most efficient method of accelerating integration and assumed that he would be able to accomplish a united Europe by working together with the leaders of the major member states, France and West Germany. He thought that he understood the mistakes that had been made during the first application. He believed that he could accommodate France since his goal was different from those of Wilson and Harold Macmillan, the Prime Minister during the first attempt to join the EEC. Heath was prepared to go further than his predecessors because he intended to become more than a British statesman. He also sought to become a great European statesman.

Heath was not a political philosopher and when he developed his ideas about Britain in Europe he borrowed heavily from the ideas about European integration and transatlantic relations of others. Nearly all of the ideas he drew on had been prevalent when he had negotiated for British entry. Amongst others he borrowed from Harold Macmillan, Jean Monnet, and from the Kennedy administration. While the separate ideas were not original, Heath's overall vision was. Heath agreed with Macmillan's view that British membership would make the EEC more outward looking but he did not share Macmillan's belief that Britain could be a force alongside Europe and the US, nor that the special relationship could be maintained. Unlike de Gaulle and Macmillan, he thought the nation-state as an independent actor passé although he retained a conviction about the qualities and benefits of British identity. The future, he believed, would instead belong to closely knit unions in the international system.

Like Monnet, whose ideas were reflected in the Kennedy administration's idea about a twin-pillar West, Heath believed that Europe had to be a partner of the US. Heath's interpretation, which built on Kennedy's, was that the partnership should be completely equal. This meant that the EC would have to become a fully fledged political union, with its own defence, and not subordinated to the US. Heath wanted to help bring about an equal partnership by transferring, special relations, to a US–EC basis and in so doing to assist his efforts to carve out a leading role for Britain in the EC.

In his Harvard lectures from 1967, Heath was as precise as was politically wise or practical about his vision. However, he did not publicly state 'this is my vision' nor did he press the overarching European dimension of his ideas on the British people. Nevertheless, his ideas remained valid during his four years in government. His ideas were not rhetoric aimed to convince the broader public but a blueprint for his future actions. By themselves the Harvard lectures had the effect of convincing Pompidou, the French President, that he could work with Heath. And between 1970 and 1974 Heath continuously referred back to his lectures at important summits with key foreign leaders. Nixon, especially, was a frequent recipient of Heath's insights.

Heath's ideas were actually in tune with the thinking that went on inside the FCO at the end of the sixties. The FCO was well acquainted with Kennedy's grand design and did not believe that membership was incompatible with good Anglo-American relations. Heath agreed. The FCO was concerned about the effect Wilson had had on the special relationship since it believed that the Nixon administration's assent was crucial to ensure British entry. Heath was seen as capable of restoring relations with the US and make EC entry possible. The convergence of the views of the FCO and the ideas of Heath enabled good cooperation between officials and Number 10. The difference was that the FCO focused on attaining EC entry and Heath on what would come after. The question for Britain was if the Nixon administration would prove as cooperative as the FCO.

Why would the Nixon administration consider Heath's version of ideas which were ten years old? Like Heath, Nixon thought that the world was becoming one of regions, that is multipolar. As a realist Nixon did not believe he could prevent this evolution only make certain that it was beneficial to the US. The Nixon administration intended to re-establish the economic pre-eminence of the US. As a result it wanted its allies to do more for their own security. This became known as the Nixon Doctrine. Consequently, the administration wanted a viable Atlantic alliance but also a stable Atlantic community. Nixon realised that Britain adrift outside any major customs area would contribute to the lessening of Britain's power and increase the risk of Britain becoming a problem for its allies. He believed that an enlarged EC, with Britain as a member, would be more amenable to agreements, satisfying to the US, on trade and monetary affairs and responsible on matters of security. EC cohesion was thought likely to increase the Europeans' willingness to accept more of the costs for their own defence and pave the way for NATO reform.

This explains the American support for British entry but not for Heath's ideas. Nixon had always supported European integration. Accordingly, Heath's reference to an Atlantic partnership between equals resonated with Nixon. The administration was already aware, before Heath came to power, that the EC Summit at the Hague in 1969 meant that European integration was about to deepen further, which raised question marks about the benefits to the US of an EC that was both stronger and larger. Nixon accepted the implications of Heath's vision because it fitted the requirements of the Nixon doctrine. And as long as Britain remained reliable, and kept its views on market liberalisation and the need to remain involved overseas, Heath's version of the future EC was preferable to potential alternatives less attuned to the needs for agreement within the West. Nixon was not sentimental about the special relationship and would not let it stand in the way for his support for greater European integration. He admired Heath's statesmanship and ability to tackle Britain's problems but ultimately his support for the plans of the Heath government was based on the national interest of the US. A US–EC special relationship would be more valuable to the US than an Anglo-American special relationship. Furthermore, Britain was not likely to remain loyal to the US if Heath's European plans were thwarted. This is not to suggest that Nixon expected Britain to do the work of a Trojan horse inside the EC as a US proxy. Nevertheless, Nixon would not have gone as far in his support if he had not been assured that Britain still viewed a number of key transatlantic issues, like the need for security, in the same light as the US.

Once the membership negotiations began the Nixon administration immediately offered muted support since any overt American pressure on the Six would have been counterproductive. Nixon supported Heath's vision from 1970, until he lost control over foreign policy making in 1973. However, Nixon believed that the transfer of special ties would take longer than Heath did and by the summer of 1973 he was frustrated with Heath's eagerness to forge ahead. But between 1971 and 1973 Nixon offered the same kind of muted support for the transfer of special ties that he provided during the negotiations for entry. For example, he gave Heath leeway in his attempt to create a new Anglo-French nuclear interdependence. Since the transfer encompassed altering Britain's nuclear interdependence, and by implication affected the interest of the US, a secretive approach was at least as much in the US own interest. When Anglo-American relations were restored after the misunderstandings and disagreements of the summer and fall of 1971 Nixon also endorsed the general outline of Heath's vision when talking to foreign leaders. He also supported the official dimension of Heath's efforts in his report to Congress in February 1972. Where he singled out Heath and quoted him to the effect that the US should realise that Europe had evolved into an entity ready to shoulder more responsibilities than in trade only. According to Nixon a new way of reaching agreements across the Atlantic was necessary. He assumed that support for Heath's plans and good Anglo-American relations was the best way to ensure that the EC or a European union remained a friend and ally of the US. Because to him European integration was not meant to further American domination; it was to strengthen the West. It is not certain that Nixon would have been as impressed with Wilson as he was with Heath or that he would have given Wilson the same support during the EC negotiations as he gave to the Heath government. Clearly,

Heath's approach was crucial for American support for British entry and European integration.

*   *   *

The question addressed in this book is: how did the Heath government try to disentangle Britain from its traditional post-Second World War special relationship with the US in pursuit of a viable European union by the end of the seventies? The analysis of the failure to transfer special ties helps us to understand the consequences to the Anglo-American special relationship and transatlantic relations. There are probably many reasons for the failure of Heath's vision: both for the collapse of the overarching aim of making Britain first among equals inside the EC and for the breakdown of its constituent parts, like the plan to remould British society and economy in the likeness of Western Europe societies. This book looks at the reasons for the failure of Heath's vision that are found in the attempt to transfer special ties to a US–EC foundation. In this section these reasons are related to each other and the consequences for the Anglo-American special relationship and transatlantic relations. Before venturing onto how Heath's vision was inextricably linked to American diplomacy we have to look at the cohesiveness of the Heath government's approach and to interpret the British strategy.

In order for a Prime Minister to successfully alter long-term foreign policy it helps if he is in agreement with the Foreign Office. As Foreign and Commonwealth Secretary Heath had chosen Sir Alec Douglas-Home, it was a decision that signalled continuity and reliability to both the US and the FCO. Heath's and Home's views were not identical but in the attempt to fulfil Heath's vision their approaches complemented each other. Heath's approach to the US was straightforward. On the one hand, he believed that Britain's privileged position with the US was an annoying affront to other American allies and incompatible with the goal of US–EC equality. On the other, he wanted good, but not special, relations between the US and Britain. Home was certain that Britain still benefited from the special relationship. Nevertheless, he understood that foreign policy changes were required if Britain was to become a leading member of the EC. In so far as he pursued a slightly more US-oriented policy approach than Heath it was on the need to sustain efforts to prevail in the Cold War. Ironically, it turned out that Home was more inflexible on the Cold War than the Americans who were engaging in superpower détente.

In contrast to the US, where the White House pre-empted potential disagreement by appropriating foreign policy making from the US State Department, Number 10 Downing Street instead relied on the FCO to aid Heath's foreign policy ideas. Like Heath, the FCO assumed that if Britain's powers declined further and if Britain remained outside the EC then Britain's relevance to the US would soon dwindle. Since Home and the FCO wanted to maintain Britain's great power status, or as Heath put it, a middle power of first importance they concurred with Heath's ideas.

The British strategy was that of an ambitious weaker ally. As the weakening partner, Britain could extort assistance from its stronger ally – the US. This had been done in a piecemeal fashion during the sixties. Heath presented his ideas as a permanent solution requiring only one major American exertion on Britain's behalf – assisting in the transfer of special ties from Britain to Europe. Accordingly, Britain had to alter Anglo-American relations by withdrawing from the special relationship. However, it had to be ended in an amiable way. The cabinet was not prepared to take any risks with Britain's security. Proceeding slowly in order to avoid unnecessary risks was therefore essential. While Heath had learnt the need for swift negotiations, the slowness of the negotiations for EEC entry between 1961 and 1963, in order to enter the EC the pace of his approach to the transfer of special ties, in pursuit of his vision, was similar to the first deliberations of the first attempt to join the EEC.

The increased pace of European integration between the Hague Summit in 1969 and the Paris Summit of 1972 made Heath all the more eager to see Britain enter the EC soon, before new obstacles to entry arose and before the EC changed in a direction contrary to his plans. Furthermore, it was possible that another US President might be less accommodating than Nixon who agreed to support his vision. Consequently, Nixon's support actually increased the pressure to initiate the vision. Accordingly, as soon as membership seemed certain, Heath quickly instigated the next step of his vision – the transfer of special ties. Furthermore, substantial change like the creation of a European monetary cooperation and a European defence would take time. Consequently, it was best to begin as soon as possible both in order to capitalise on the favourable relationship with Nixon and since it would take time to make new agreements to which special ties could safely be transferred.

Heath assumed, wrongly as it turned out, that special ties, such as agreements on nuclear interdependence and monetary and political cooperation, could be disaggregated from each other and from 'natural' bonds, such as language and culture, and new agreements easily made with France and within the EC. He did not merely intend to exchange phraseology – the 'special relationship' with the 'natural relationship' – as a way to put his own stamp on the relationship. He wanted changes in the Anglo-American economic relationship, in particular the monetary links, and in the nuclear special relationship. Heath was only silent on intelligence cooperation probably because he expected these to be the slowest to change and since talking about them openly would have been regarded as irresponsible. Heath also wanted to bring about a new practice in transatlantic diplomacy, preferably by means of a public initiative which would both herald the creation of US–EC equality and help make it take place.

The Heath government's attempt to disentangle Britain from the special relationship resulted in a paradox. The strategy ultimately failed in every aspect as the Heath government tried to create a natural relationship with the US and relocate special ties to a US–EC basis. Nearly every step Britain took to smoothly transfer special ties from the Anglo-American relationship to a new footing in fact deepened Anglo-American cooperation. Thus, the result at the end of the Nixon–Heath years when Heath's vision had ground to a halt was not only an intact Anglo-American relationship but a relationship confirmed and moored to the sixties' interpretation of Britain as a junior partner.

The separate failures demonstrated in each chapter all point to one main consequence – the confirmation of the existing Anglo-American special relationship. The Heath government failed to liberate sterling from the economic special relationship and pursue a European monetary cooperation. The US, alone, began the process that would lead to the disorderly transformation into a non-system of international monetary affairs. The change was like a shift of paradigm. With the new non-system the American interest in a European currency dwindled. The Heath government was unable to maintain a fixed exchange rate and at the same time expand the economy to make the British economy ready for EC entry. The oil shocks later forced the EC to abandon its plans from the 1973 Paris Summit of monetary union. In regard to this Britain's failure to join in the efforts at European Monetary Cooperation might not have mattered but the failure to return to a fixed exchange rate soured relations with France. Britain's was unable to re-peg its currency for over a decade and had again to rely on American goodwill.

The Heath government failed to make arrangements for a new nuclear interdependence with France that would underwrite a future European defence effort. The Americans hoped that the British initiative might re-involve France in NATO. France suspecting this proved unwilling to come to any agreement on nuclear arms with Britain. The British did hope that it would be able to cooperate with the French, not necessarily through NATO, but with the alliance intact. The immediate crux was the Britain's need for American aid with an update for its existing deterrent while Britain at the same time tried to initiate Anglo-French cooperation, with American aid, on a successor system. French reluctance and new American nuclear strategic planning undercut the British efforts. In the hope of eventually being able to impress the French at a later date the Heath government left a legacy of high spending in research and development. But in order to maintain the British deterrent, Britain collapsed back into the nuclear special relationship.

Heath's wish for a diplomatic initiative, either British or American, that would mark the official beginning of an equal US–EC partnership failed. Initially the British and the Americans agreed to coordinate a new transatlantic initiative. The transatlantic initiative came about in the form of the American diplomatic initiative, the Year of Europe. Kissinger's security-oriented diplomacy of 1973 contributed to stalling the emergence of a multipolar world as far as Europe was concerned. His diplomacy allowed for the continuation of existing bonds such as the special relationship. He implemented the initiative and in his hands the Year of Europe came to represent the opposite to the transatlantic equality that Heath and Nixon had agreed on. Kissinger probably hoped to ensure the cohesion and security of the West in the short term. Although the Year of Europe became deeply unpopular, on both sides of the Atlantic, and failed to produce any significant document it symbolised an American foreign policy towards Europe, more clearly concerned with the US own interests and primarily with security. American hegemony was reasserted, which meant a confirmation of the view that special relations should be an unequal venture, regardless of whether it was with the British or the Europeans.

The Heath government also failed to exploit Cold War détente in favour of Heath's ideas. The Heath government was sceptical of détente since it feared that détente would be more popular than integration in Europe. The US engaged in its separate superpower détente. It discreetly involved Britain in Cold War consultations, which confirmed the traditional nature of their relationship. Meanwhile Britain sought to ensure that neither the Americans' nor the Western Europeans' attempts at détente got out of hand. The Heath government hoped in due course to be able to use détente to further EC cooperation on foreign policy but the main consequence of the Nixon–Heath years was that the desire to keep the West united and secure, which eventually drove Britain and the US closer. All the chapters demonstrate that the failure of Heath's vision made both Britain and the US collapse back into a special relationship.

This outcome was unexpected since it had been assumed that special ties were transferable. Heath and Nixon expected changes to the international affairs, though not sudden new obstacles like the oil crisis, just like they assumed that the pace of European integration would increase. It is possible to speculate about how the Heath's vision could have succeeded by asking a number of what ifs; what if Anglo-French nuclear cooperation had come about, what if the EC had fulfilled its plans for a common currency and increased integration, and so forth? Instead let us consider another possibility: what would have happened if there had been a sudden rupture in Anglo-American relations at an early stage, akin to the disagreement over the crisis management of the October War, in 1973?

Assume the concerns of the actors, such as about security and the need to avoid decline, to be the same. Assume that all other events and obstacles would have taken place. Then, probably the outcome would have been that the tenacity and necessity of the special ties between the US and Britain would have become evident much earlier on. The point is not that the special relationship was inescapable. It is unlikely that Heath would have altered his ideas or that Nixon would have changed his views about the need to get Britain into the EC and ensure that the EC was friendly towards the US. The miscalculation about the tenacity of the special ties and difficulties of transferring them would merely have been evident at an earlier stage. Another way of disaggregating and transferring special ties might then have been set up but the success of that strategy, like the chances of success for the strategy actually chosen under other conditions, remains hypothetical.

The fact remains that altering Anglo-American relations was a key element for Heath's plans to succeed. While a number of the reasons for the failure of Heath's vision are to be found in the relationship such a list is by no means exhaustive. Further research will undoubtedly be able to find additional reasons in the politics between the EC members. Nevertheless, the reasons for the failure that stem from Anglo-American relations are more directly linked to the consequences since failures in Anglo-American relations had more of a direct impact on the special relationship than other failures. Some of the reasons for the failure of Heath's vision and the endurance of the Anglo-American special relationship cut across the chapters. The advantage of the thematic chapters is that we are able to discern patterns specific to the Nixon–Heath years and connections between issue-areas that might otherwise escape us. The analysis below draws on the patterns and helps to facilitate the explanation.

The immediately discernible pattern is the importance of Heath's ideas. Since his plans were based on the world of the sixties it became difficult for the Heath government to incorporate changes in the underlying conditions such as the end of the Bretton Woods system, and a new Cold War diplomacy. Heath's plans were also sensitive to the actions of individuals. Heath, Nixon and Kissinger were not merely reflections of their offices or the necessities of their states. They were important because of the office they held from which they were able to exercise their own ideas as well as interpretation of events. Kissinger's idea to reassert US hegemony over Western Europe was not applied because his idea was more recent than Heath's vision, which it was not, but because he came to control American foreign policy as a result of the Watergate affair. Kissinger preferred a confederal Europe of several centres of power that would involve the US and allow it to influence and control any major steps the EC would take. A view which was ironic in view of his alleged famous compliant that he did not know whom to call when he wanted to talk to Europe. Kissinger and Nixon shared an appetite for secretive and unorthodox diplomacy which also affected the attempt to reshape transatlantic relations. Kissinger's handling of the Year of Europe met with frequent complaints due to him seeming to negotiate with allies as he did with the enemies of the US.

Another pattern is the difficulty of establishing continuous Anglo-American consultations, which was by no means the fault of the British. Nixon preferred to hold on to the consultative tradition of the special relationship for as long as he could, but there was no Anglo-American policy making on global issues. This is illustrated by an Asian example. The Nixon administration welcomed the Heath government's stance on the Vietnam War. The British support represented continuity and reliability which was the hallmark of Anglo-American agreement during the Cold War. But when the White House prepared the opening of China, which would influence the whole structure of the international system, Britain was not privy to the White House's plans. Britain never was the key to any part of Nixon's new American foreign policy except the enlarged EC. When the British were involved, as when Kissinger asked for British assistance in security issues relating to the Cold War, they never contributed to more than a part of the overall American policy. Sometimes the White House took British advice seriously but sometimes only gave the impression of doing so. This may be in the nature of continuous consultations but at some points, especially over China and the new American economic foreign policy in the summer of 1971, discussions with the British were wholly dispensed with. Some in the Nixon administration even blamed the British, wrongly, for increasing pressure on the dollar in August 1971. One of the few times when the Heath government was greatly involved, in the preparations for the transatlantic initiative that would become the Year of Europe, its influence waned when the Year of Europe came under Kissinger's control. The chequered American behaviour on policies probably corresponded to the Nixon administration's view that the Anglo-American special relationship was a junior yet advisory relationship. Nearly every time the Americans asked for consultations the British, who needed good Anglo-American relations, immediately acquiesced. This of course strengthened the traditional interpretation of the relationship.

The American adherence to the sixties interpretation of the special relationship haunted Heath's attempts to explain the difference between what he regarded as special and natural ties. The British were set on continuous consultations with Heath seeking a meeting with Nixon before British EC entry in 1973 in order to be able to confirm a common outlook on transatlantic relations before Britain had to consider the viewpoint of the EC in Anglo-American talks. While Heath did not want to maintain special relations he did want good relations with the US. However, after the Year of Europe, in 1973, the British realised that sharing a language and a tradition of foreign policy cooperation actually seemed to increase the risk of misunderstandings between each other. Different expressions carried different weights and suggested changes to past conventions could easily be exaggerated or be seen as a let down. When the Anglo-American relations worsened in 1973 it can be said that the natural relationship, with the supposed benefits of a common language and culture, helped to fell the transfer of special ties.

Another pattern that counteracted Heath's efforts was the changes in the foreign policy of the US and France. The Nixon Doctrine, the unilateral economic actions on 15 August 1971, and the way British diplomatic efforts were brushed aside during the opening of China heralded an American foreign policy made primarily in the interest of the US. Not all of this was intentional on the part of the White House. It was to some extent a consequence of solving domestic problems with foreign policy means. The Nixon administration used foreign policy, like the opening of China and Mutual Balanced Arms Reductions, to avert isolationism and to assuage domestic American political issues, such as over the economy. These concerns reduced the American consideration for its allies and increased the need for American control of the rest of the West. As a result the emergence of another centre of power in the West became less desirable. Such a centre might not allow the US the necessary freedom in deals with the Soviet Union or in the new monetary non-system. Although far from Nixon's original intention in regard to Britain and Europe it was the result.

France, the country of the greatest importance for Heath's vision, apart from the US, also changed its foreign policy in regard to Europe in the middle of the Nixon–Heath period. Compared to the sixties US-French relations got better during the Nixon–Heath years. Unfortunately for Heath the improvement probably stemmed from President Pompidou's wish for France to be the leading power in an enlarged EC. Heath always believed that Britain could become the leader of the EC, alone or together with the other major states of Europe. He did not fully appreciate to what extent France represented possible competition for leadership in the EC. Otherwise he would not have tried so hard and so long to bring about Anglo-French nuclear interdependence. Pompidou never had to come into conflict with Heath about the leadership of the increasingly integrated Europe. Neither the Nixon administration nor the French people, as the French referendum on enlargement indicated, gave Pompidou the support he sought for his European designs. However, the British inability to participate in the European monetary schemes was a disappointment to Pompidou. Most likely the British failure to re-peg sterling after the float of 1972 was an important factor in his scepticism about cooperation in other areas. Britain being earnestly European during the Year of Europe in 1973 did not help the plans for nuclear cooperation. The oil shocks and subsequent energy crisis resulted in different British and French reactions to the American leadership during the Energy Conference in 1974 similar to the choices made after the Suez crisis of 1956. France and Britain went separate ways: France turned away from the US due to American strength and dominance and Britain turned towards the US, and accepted US leadership.

In contrast to the changes in the international conditions, the institutional bonds that bound Britain and the US during the many great changes of the Nixon–Heath years proved surprisingly enduring. Neither Kissinger nor Heath despite their opposing views on Europe intended to suddenly and swiftly severe the special relationship. Kissinger wanted to keep it. Heath, Home, and the other key members of his government Anthony Barber, the Chancellor of the Exchequer, and Geoffrey Rippon, the Chief negotiator with the EC, all sought to keep the Nixon administration informed during the negotiations. For the British the talks with the Americans amounted to a second front in the negotiations. Keeping the US in favour of British entry was essential to ensure a situation favourable for concluding the negotiations and for preparing the Americans for the next steps of Heath's plans. After the negotiations were completed the British continued to avoid a rift with the US. But the patience on both sides of Atlantic was tempted in a time of crisis, but in both cases relations were ameliorated by institutional judgements.

Sudden events, like the August 15 measures in 1971 and the October War in 1973, were not only disruptive but also revealing. When the outraged Heath complained about the US actions in the fall of 1971 and spoke out against the US Home and the FCO worked to defuse Anglo-American tensions. By the summer of 1973, however, the entire Heath government appreciated how interconnected different ties were. It stymied its critique of the US Year of Europe initiative in 1973 because Britain was dependent on American goodwill for its nuclear plans. Institutional caution was not reserved for the British. Kissinger's irritation with the British government's lack of support for his crisis management during the October War in 1973 led to an enquiry into how the British could be punished for its obduracy. The State Department's suggestions were framed in such a manner that they actually indicated how intermingled Anglo-American ties were. Measuring out a reprimand would be difficult and all but certainly counter-productive. It also demonstrated that the ties of the special relationship were difficult to disaggregate.

Though similar, the calculations of the FCO in the fall of 1971 and of the State Department in 1973 were not the sign of close Anglo-American institutional cooperation. Home and the FCO had initially not understood the extent to which American foreign policy was conducted from the White House by Nixon with the help of Kissinger. Home thought that the State Department was responsible for US foreign policy. When the British eventually adapted to the ways of the Nixon administration the British remained unaware about the differences between Kissinger and Nixon.

Time was also an intangible factor that worked contrary to Heath's efforts. The Heath government took office at a time of rapid changes to the international economy and in the Cold War. There was no orderly change of the international monetary system despite several attempts. Far more threatening was that disorderly change that beckoned in the form of West German *Ostpolitik* and superpower détente. East–West relaxation made coordinated Western conduct in the Cold War all the more important. The Heath government was loath to take any risk with British security and the choice of a low-risk strategy to pursue Heath's vision meant slow progress. However, the chosen strategy was clearly at odds with the pace of developments in the international monetary system and in the Western approach to détente.

The Cold War by itself, or what can be said to amount to called Cold War conditioning, also limited the chances of remaking the special relationship. Despite East–West relaxation the Cold War enforced the need for Britain to maintain its links to the US. Britain needed American aid to update the British nuclear deterrent, if Britain was to be secure and remain a great power. It also required the US to work for a cohesive West to avoid détente efforts spiralling out of control. Nevertheless, the Cold War perspective also indicates where the Heath government and the Nixon administration were successful in terms of the international system. Without British EC membership Britain's international relevance and influence would almost certainly have diminished. It would have ended up, at least temporarily, going-it-alone partially forced to play a maverick role in international affairs to safeguard its interests. Hence, with Britain in the EC the US had a tidier Atlantic community and the possibility of Britain as a potentially destabilising factor to transatlantic affairs was avoided.

The reassertion of American hegemony made up for the slow down of European integration and failure to bring about a second pole within the West. A favourable view of Kissinger's actions during 1973 could argue that Kissinger's remaking of American foreign policy towards Europe in the wake of great changes to international affairs in the Cold War at least ensured a united West in the short term, in contrast to the East where two poles emerged, which could be pitted against each other. But his actions alone were nearly sufficient to curb Heath's vision.

Perhaps the policies of the Heath government would have been better understood if Heath had spoken earlier and more frequently and more clearly about his ideas of Britain at the heart of united Europe. It becomes easier to understand that the enthusiasm for Europe in the British political establishment suffered if one considers the failure of Heath's vision. The lack of a clear idea of what to do with membership contributed to Britain's difficulties with its commitment to the EC, which fuelled Britain's reputation as an awkward partner. Britain would have to continue walking the tightrope between the US and Europe. However, his vision was understood by the key actors in the US and France. Furthermore his key idea of an equal US–EC partnership was not altogether new.

What was mainly new was his way of achieving it. In a sense Heath's vision was both before and after his time. The ideas of US-European equality were a decade old by the time Heath and Nixon got into power. Both thought a united Europe would eventually emerge but the many events and changes during the Nixon–Heath years delayed plans for further European integration and also prevented the transfer of special ties which Heath and Nixon had agreed on. Heath's mistake was rigidity in the face of altered conditions and new obstacles. He tried to achieve all his plans at the same time. Had the transfer been partially successful it would perhaps have made for a more balanced transatlantic relationship in the long run and possibly a more confident Europe. What is also clear is that his vision depended on American assent. At least if a second pole was to emerge in a West that was stable internally and also secure in the international system. In hindsight, with a view to the later evolution of the EC into the EU, Heath's ambition for equality between the US and Europe appears understandable and prescient. While Heath's vision was not such a comprehensive phenomenon as EC membership, it may be that future histories of Atlantic relations will discuss the failure of Heath's vision as a missed opportunity.

Notes

Introduction

1. Some key works are, in particular, J. Ellison, *The United States, Britain and the Transatlantic Crisis, Rising to the Gaullist Challenge, 1963–68* (Basingstoke: Palgrave Macmillan, 2007) and also H. Parr, *Britain's Policy Toward the European Community: Harold Wilson and Britain's World Role, 1964–1967* (London: Routledge, 2006); R. Roy, *The Battle of the Pound: The Political Economy of Anglo-American Relations 1964–1968* (PhD thesis LSE, unpublished, 2000); and T. Schwartz, *Lyndon Johnson and Europe: In the Shadow of Vietnam* (Cambridge: Harvard University Press, 2003).
2. When Churchill spoke about a special relationship in Fulton, Missouri, otherwise a speech most famous for foreseeing the Cold War it was about a relationship between the US and Britain with its Commonwealth and Empire. See J. Dumbrell, *A Special Relationship: Anglo-American Relations in the Cold War and After* (Basingstoke: Macmillan Press Ltd, 2001), p. 7.
3. Reprinted by permission of the publisher from Old World, New Horizons: Britain, Europe, and the Atlantic Alliance, by Edward Heath, pp. 2, 6, 9–12, 18–19, 26, 29–30, 49, 53, 66–68, 72–76, Cambridge, Mass.: Harvard University Press, Copyright © 1970 by the President and Fellows of Harvard College. This note, pp. 11, 67–68.
4. Heath, *Old World*, pp. 19–20.
5. J. Frankel, *British Foreign Policy 1945–1973* (London and New York: For The Royal Institute of International Affairs by Oxford University Press, 1975), p. 157. For the influence of Churchill's ideas on Labour, see amongst others Saki Dockrill, *Britain's Retreat from East of Suez: The Choice Between Europe and the World?* (Basingstoke and New York: Palgrave Macmillan, 2002), pp. 15–16. That Labour and the Conservatives shared the same views, see W. Kaiser and G. Staerck (eds), *British Foreign Policy 1955–64 – Contracting Options* (New York: Macmillan Press Ltd, 2000), p. xiv. A work that is accordance with the insights of Anne Deighton.
6. See, amongst others, F. Logevall and A. Preston (eds), *Nixon in the World, American Foreign Relations, 1969–1977* (New York: Oxford University Press, 2008); and W. P. Bundy, *A Tangled Web: The Making of Foreign Policy in the Nixon Presidency* (London and New York: I.B. Tauris, 1998).
7. D. Dinan, 'Building Europe: The European Community and the Bonn-Paris-Washington Relationship, 1958–1963', in H. Haftendorn, G.-H. Soutou, S. S. Szabo, and S. F. Wells Jr. (eds), *The Strategic Triangle: France, Germany, and the United States in the Shaping of the New Europe* (Washington, DC, and Baltimore: Johns Hopkins University Press, 2006), pp. 37, 40–41; J. G. Giauque, *Grand Designs and Visions of Unity: The Atlantic Powers and the Reorganization of Western Europe, 1955–1963* (Chapel Hill: University of North Carolina

Press, 2002), pp. 106–108; P. Winand, *Eisenhower, Kennedy and the United States of Europe* (New York: St. Martin's Press, 1993), pp. 245–264.

8. G. Lundestad, *The United States and Western Europe since 1945 – From 'Empire' by Invitation to Transatlantic Drift*, 2nd Ed. (Oxford: Oxford University Press, 2003), pp. 55–59.

9. R. Boardman and A. J. R. Groom, *The Management of Britain's External Relations* (London: Macmillan, 1973), pp. 1, 21; O. J. Daddow, *Britain and European Integration since 1945: Historiographical Perspectives on Integration* (Manchester: Manchester University Press, 2004), pp. 80–82.

10. TNA/FCO/7/1808, 'Nixon to the US Congress 1970'; see also R. M. Nixon, *The Memoirs of Richard Nixon* (New York: Grosset & Dunlap, 1978), pp. 48–52.

11. A. P. Dobson, *The Politics of the Anglo-American Economic Special Relationship* (Brighton: Wheatsheaf Books Ltd, 1988), pp. 233–235.

12. Acheson was a supporter of European unity. See Daddow, *Britain*, pp. 80–82. He did, however, unlike President Kennedy proposal that the EEC and the US should become equal partners. See Winand, *Eisenhower*, pp. 194, 239–249.

13. Boardman and Groom (eds), *Management*, pp. 1, 21, footnote 2; G. K. Fry, *The Politics of Decline, An Interpretation of British Politics from the 1940s to the 1970s* (New York: Palgrave Macmillan, 2005), p. 1; J. Baylis, *Anglo-American Defence Relations, 1939–1984: The Special Relationship* (London: Macmillan, 1984), pp. 102–103.

14. Boardman and Groom (eds), *Management*, pp. 1, 21, footnote 2, 3; Acheson gave the speech with the phrase on 5 December 1962, and the comment on it on 26 April 1970.

15. On the debates about decline, see for example R. English and M. Kenny, 'British Decline of the Politics of Declinism', *British Journal of Politics and International Relations*, Vol. 1, No. 2 (June 1999), pp. 252–266; J. Tomlinson 'Inventing "Decline": The Falling behind of the British Economy in the Post-war Years', *The Economic History Review*, New Series, Vol. 49, No. 4 (November 1996), pp. 731–757 ; Fry, *The Politics*; G. L. Bernstein, *The Myth of Decline; The Rise of Britain since 1945* (London: Pimlico, 2004).

16. J. Campbell, *Edward Heath* (London: Jonathan Cape, 1993), p. 163; Tomlinson, 'Inventing "Decline": The Falling Behind of the British Economy in the Postwar Years', p. 732. See also Fry, *The Politics*.

17. For the longer perspective of decline, see, for example, A. Orde, *The Eclipse of Great Britain: The United States and British Imperial Decline 1895–1956* (Basingstoke: Palgrave Macmillan, 1996); C. Barnett, *The Audit of War: The Illusion and Reality of Britain as a Great Nation* (Basingstoke: Macmillan, 1986); P. Kennedy, *The Rise and Fall of the Great Powers: Economic Change and Military Conflict from 1500 to 2000*, 2nd Ed. (London: Allen & Unwin, 1989).

18. J. W. Young, 'The Heath Government and British Entry', pp. 259, 283; and C. Hill and C. Lord, 'The Foreign Policy of the Heath Government', in S. Ball and A. Seldon (eds), *The Heath Government 1970–74 – A Reappraisal* (London and New York: Longman, 1996), pp. 285, 314.

19. Oliver Daddow argues that there are two main schools on Britain and European integration, but he suggests that there is also undergrowth of post-revisionist approaches. See Daddow, *Britain*, pp. 87–88, 92–94, 97, 174.

20. Anthony Seldon, 'The Heath Government in History', in Ball and Seldon, *The Heath Government*, pp. 1–2. According to Anthony Seldon there are at least four interpretations.

21. For a contrasting view, see M. Holmes, *The Failure of the Heath Government*, 2nd Ed. (Basingstoke and London: Palgrave Macmillan, 1997), p. x.

22. Young, 'The Heath Government and British Entry', pp. 260–261.

23. By the time of the third attempt to join the Community the three executives of the EEC had been merged, allowing for the reference to the EC, despite the British insistence on using the EEC acronym.

24. See, for example, C. Bell, *The Diplomacy of Detente: The Kissinger Era* (London: Martin Robertson, 1977) or G. A. Andrianopoulos, *Western Europe in Kissinger's Global Strategy* (Basingstoke: Macmillan, 1988).

25. Alex Danchev has tried to pin down the term 'special relationship' and has searched for criteria of what is meant by special – with little success, see A. Danchev, 'Special Pleading', in K. Burk and M. Stoker (eds.), *The United States and the European Alliance since 1945* (Oxford and New York: Berg, 1999), pp. 277–279.

26. Max Beloff has argued convincingly, however, that is necessary to consider the impact of myths on diplomacy, since myths may be created consciously. See M. Beloff, 'The Special Relationship: An Anglo-American Myth', in M. Gilbert (ed.), *A Century of Conflict 1850–1950: Essays for A. J. P. Taylor* (London: Hamish Hamilton, 1966), pp. 151–158, 170.

27. According to Christopher Hill decision-makers came to believe that they could balance between Europe and the US. C. Hill, 'The Historical Background: Past and Present in British Foreign Policy', in M. Smith, S. Smith and B. White (eds), *British Foreign Policy: Tradition, Change and Transformation* (London: Unwin Hyman, 1988), p. 44.

28. A. P. Dobson, *Anglo-American Relations in the Twentieth Century* (London: Routledge, 1995), p. 139.

29. Ibid., p. 141.

30. See P. Finney (ed.), *Palgrave Advances in International History* (Basingstoke: Palgrave Macmillan, 2005); Elman and Elman (eds), *Bridges and Boundaries: Historians, Political Scientists and the Study of International Relations* (Cambridge, Mass., and London: The MIT Press, 2001).

31. For reflection on history and methodology see, H. Butterfield, *The Whig Interpretation of History* (Harmondsworth: Penguin, 1973); J. L. Gaddis, *The Landscape of History: How Historians Map the Past* (Oxford and New York: Oxford University Press, 2002); P. Gardiner, *The Philosophy of History* (London and New York: Oxford University Press, 1974); N. Ferguson (ed.), *Virtual History: Alternatives and Counterfactuals* (New York: Basic Books, 1999); Fischer, *Historians' Fallacies: Towards a Logic of Historical Thought* (London: Routledge and K. Paul, 1971); M. Trachtenberg, *The Craft of International History: A Guide to Method* (Princeton: Princeton University Press, 2006).

32. Baylis, *Anglo-Americans*, pp. 166, 174.

33. B. Heuser, *NATO, Britain, France and the FRG: Nuclear Strategies and Forces for Europe, 1949–2000* (London: Macmillan, 1997), pp. 159–160.

34. Hill and Lord, 'The Foreign Policy of the Heath Government', p. 309.

1.   Heath's European Ideas as a Response to British Decline and Nixon's New American Foreign Policy

1. The abbreviation 'the EC' is used here when referring to the Community in the early seventies instead of 'the EEC', which was only one of the communities. The executives of the EC (the ECSE, the EAEC and the EEC) were merged on 1 July 1967, three weeks after Britain's second application, establishing a single European Commission. This inspired the use of the abbreviation the EC for the European Communities. US documents consistently refer to the EC from 1969 to 1974. The British do not however.
2. E. Heath, *The Course of My Life: My Autobiography* (London: Hodder & Stoughton, 1998), pp. 381–382; K. Cooper, *I Challenge Ted Heath Pamphlet* (Vaxholm: 1974), pp. 2–3.
3. W. Sendall, column, *The Daily Express*, 20 December 1971.
4. *The Times*, 21 December 1971.
5. Heath, *The Course*, p. 472.
6. H. A. Kissinger, *White House Years* (London: Weidenfeld & Nicolson, 1979), p. 965. For a recent analysis of the consequences of de Gaulle on Anglo-American relations, see J. Ellison, *The United States, Britain and the Transatlantic Crisis, Rising to the Gaulllist Challenge, 1963–68* (Basingstoke: Palgrave Macmillan, 2007).
7. A. Milward, *The United Kingdom and the European Community, Volume 1: The Rise and Fall of a National Strategy 1945–1963* (London and Portland, Or.: Whitehall History Publishing in association with Frank Cass, 2002), p. 3. His view should be contrasted with Dockrill's view that there was a sense of continuity in Britain after the war with its institutions intact. See S. Dockrill, *Britain's Retreat*, p. 8.
8. J. Campbell, *Edward Heath* (London: Jonathan Cape, 1993), p. 163; J. Tomlinson 'Inventing "Decline"'. See also Fry, *The Politics*.
9. The lectures were given at Harvard, in the series of Godkin Lectures, in March 1967 and were published in 1970. Heath, *Old World*.
10. B. Heuser, *Nuclear Mentalities? Strategies and Beliefs in Britain, France and the FRG* (Basingstoke and New York: Macmillan, 1998), pp. 28–30.
11. J. G. Giauque, *Grand Designs*, pp. 106–112.
12. B. W. E. Alford, *British Economic Performance, 1945–1975* (Cambridge and New York: Cambridge University Press, 1995), pp. 84–86.
13. H. Parr, *Britain's Policy*, pp. 185–186.
14. C. Wrigley, 'Now You See It, Now You Don't: Harold Wilson and Labour's Foreign Policy 1964–70', in R. Coopey, S. Fielding, and N. Tiratsoo (eds), *The Wilson Governments 1964–1970* (London and New York: Pinter Publishers, 1993), pp. 131, 133.
15. Parr, *Britain's Policy*, pp. 185–187, 202–203.
16. Dobson, *Politics*, pp. 211–212.
17. J. Coleman, *A 'Special Relationship'?: Harold Wilson, Lyndon B. Johnson and Anglo-American Relations 'At the Summit', 1964–68* (Manchester: Manchester University Press, 2004), p. 171.
18. Schwartz, *Lyndon*, pp. 75–76, 231–233.

19. Roy, *The Battle*, pp. 329–331.

20. Ibid., pp. 328, 331–332.

21. P. Lynch, 'The Conservatives and the Wilson Application', in O. Daddow (ed.), *Harold Wilson and European Integration – Britain's Second Application to join the EEC* (London and Portland: Frank Cass, 2003), p. 66.

22. TNA/PREM/13/2113, 'Attitude of H.M.G to NAFTA'; Parr, *Britain's Policy*, p. 90. The issue was also debated in the press: Arthur Schlesinger Jr., 'Why I Support Free Trade', in *the Evening Standard*, Thursday, 16 May 1968 in TNA/PREM/13/2095. Even before the application to join the EEC, the creation of a NAFTA was considered a second best in the Prime Minister's office.

23. TNA/PREM/13/2113, 'Attitude of H.M.G to NAFTA'.

24. Ibid.

25. Parr, *Britain's Policy*, p. 146.

26. Ibid., pp. 185–187, 202–203. Wilson was advised in 1961 that without EEC membership the special relationship would die.

27. Parr, *Britain's Policy*, pp. 194, 202. Wilson's critics argued that he 'muddied discussion of the principle of EEC membership' according to Parr, in which she may be right.

28. P. Catterall, 'Conclusions: The Ironies of Successful Failure', in Daddow (ed.), *Harold Wilson*, p. 249.

29. Parr, *Britain's Policy*, p. 191.

30. J. Ellison, 'Dealing with de Gaulle: Anglo-American Relations, NATO and the Second Application', in Daddow (ed.), *Harold Wilson*; James Ellison, 'Defeating the General: Anglo-American Relations, Europé and the NATO Crisis of 1966', *Cold War History*, Vol. 6, No. 1 (February 2006), pp. 102–104.

31. Ellison, 'Defeating the General', pp. 183–184.

32. P. Ludlow, 'A Short-Term Defeat: The Community Institutions and the Second British Application to Join the EEC', in Daddow (ed.), *Harold Wilson*, pp. 147–148.

33. M. Pine, 'British Personal Diplomacy and Public Policy: The Soames Affair', in *The Journal of European Integration History*, Vol. 10, No. 2 (2004), pp. 75–76.

34. Coleman, *A 'Special'*, pp. 44–45.

35. Baylis, *Anglo-American*, pp. 137, 152, 158.

36. Dumbrell, *A Special Relationship*, p. 138; Baylis, *Anglo-American*, p. 138.

37. Heuser, *Nuclear Mentalities?* pp. 28–30.

38. C. Bluth, 'British-German Defence Relations, 1950–80: A Survey', in K. Kaiser and J. Roper (eds), *British-German Defence Co-operation: Partners within the Alliance* (London: The Royal Institute of International Affairs, 1988), pp. 17–18, 21–24.

39. J. Ellison, 'Defeating the General', pp. 103–104. At the time the FO was set 'on riding "the Atlantic and European horses in double-harness"'.

40. P. Busch, *All the Way with JFK?: Britain, the US, and the Vietnam War* (Oxford: Oxford University Press, 2003), pp. 11–19, 204; Schwartz, *Lyndon*, pp. 32–33.

41. Dockrill, *Britain's Retreat*, p. 181; D. Healey, *The Time of My Life* (London: Michael Joseph, 1989), p. 293.

42. Coleman, A *'Special'*, pp. 82–85. Coleman, Dockrill, Dumbrell and Schwartz agree in this analysis.
43. B. White, *Britain, Détente and Changing East-West Relations* (London and New York: Routledge, 1992), pp. 117–120.
44. Coleman, A *'Special'*, p. 170.
45. R. R. James, *Ambition and Realities: British Politics 1964–1970* (London: Weidenfeld & Nicolson, 1972), pp. 111–113.
46. A. Roth, *Heath and the Heathmen* (London: Routledge and K. Paul, 1972), pp. xiv–xv.
47. Heath, *The Course*, p. 61.
48. L. Iremonger in John P. Mackintosh (ed.), *British Prime Ministers in the Twentieth Century* (London: Weidenfeld & Nicolson, 1978), p. 150.
49. Armstrong in Kaniah, Michael David, ' "The Heath Government" – Witness Seminar in Contemporary Record', *The Journal of Contemporary British History*, Vol. 9, No. 1 (Summer, 1995), pp. 188–219.
50. Heath, *The Course*, pp. 54–56.
51. LSE\Seventies, Interview Madron Seligman. See Heath, *The Course*, pp. 59–61; and Campbell, *Edward*, pp. 32–34.
52. Heath, *The Course*, p. 138.
53. Ibid., pp. 153, 161.
54. Ibid., pp. 171, 175; Campbell, *Edward*, pp. 93–94.
55. Heath, *The Course*, p. 192; Campbell, *Edward*, p. 97; Roth, *Heath*, pp. 111–113, Roth's account is suggestive. He also plays on the fact that all post-war Prime Ministers, except Home, had like Heath been anti-Chamberlain, and R. A. Butler who did lose the chance for leadership in 1957 had been pro-Chamberlain.
56. Heath, *The Course*, p. 201.
57. Ibid., pp. 257–258.
58. Ibid., pp. 267, 275.
59. Roth, *Heath*, p. 184.
60. Heath, *The Course*, pp. 73–76, 144–145.
61. Roth, *Heath*, p. xiv.
62. Heath, *The Course*, p. 235.
63. It should be noted that Heath was part of the pro-European movement. See Daddow, *Britain*, pp. 87–88, 92–94, 97.
64. Campbell, *Edward*, pp. 133–134; and LSE\Seventies, Interview Madron Seligman.
65. Young, 'The Heath Government and British Entry', pp. 260–261.
66. Iremonger in Mackintosh (ed.), *British Prime Ministers*, p. 149.
67. Campbell, *Edward*, pp. 193, 267.
68. Ibid., pp. 263, 266–267.
69. Ibid., p. 263.
70. Heath, *Old* World, pp. 18–19.
71. LSE\Hetherington, 10/15, Points from a meeting with Edward Heath, 29 June 1965, dictated 3 July. Section 3, pp. 2–3.
72. Young, 'The Heath Government and British Entry', pp. 260–261. Consider, for example, the Carrington-led study of a new basis for British greatness completed in 1965.
73. LSE\Seventies, Interview Lord Home.

74. Heath, *Old World*, p. 26.
75. Ibid., p. 1. These were later collected in a slender volume *Old World, New Horizons – Britain, The Common Market, and the Atlantic Alliance* published in 1970.
76. Heath, *The Course*, p. 201.
77. Heath, *Old World*, pp. 2, 29–30.
78. Ibid., p. 6.
79. Ibid., p. 7.
80. Ibid., p. 9.
81. Ibid., pp. 9–10.
82. Ibid., p. 11.
83. Ibid., pp. 54–55, 58.
84. Ibid., p. 12.
85. Ibid., p. 66.
86. E. Heath, 'Realism in British Foreign Policy', *Foreign Affairs/Council on Foreign Relations*, Vol. 48, Nos. 1–4 (October 1969–July 1970), pp. 39–51.
87. Heath, *Old World*, p. 22.
88. Ibid., p. 66.
89. Ibid., pp. 66–67.
90. Ibid., p. 67.
91. Ibid.
92. Ibid., pp. 72–73.
93. Ibid., p. 74.
94. Ibid., p. 84.
95. Ibid., pp. 72–74, 84.
96. R. Oakley and P. Rose, *The Political Year 1970* (London: Pitman Publishing, 1970), p. 52.
97. Ibid., p. 59.
98. A. Deighton, 'The Labour Party, Public Opinion, and the "Second Try" in 1967', in Daddow (ed.), *Harold Wilson*, p. 52.
99. TNA/PREM/15/030, Opinion Research Centre survey on 'Britain and the common Market' for Conservative Central Office. In June 1966 the percentage of the public in favour was 66 per cent, in August 1970, it was 32 per cent.
100. Oakley and Rose, *The Political Year*, p. 65.
101. Heath, *The Course*, pp. 301–302; Oakley and Rose, *The Political Year*, pp. 141–142.
102. Heath, *The Course*, p. 302; Holmes, *The Failure*, pp. x–xi.
103. Campbell, *Edward*, pp. 266–267.
104. James, *Ambition*, pp. 233–234.
105. Ibid., p. 239.
106. Ibid., p. 278; LSE\Seventies, Interview George Brown.
107. Campbell, *Edward*, pp. 278–279. On polling day, however, Lord Carrington, later Chairman of the Conservative Party and Secretary of Defence in the Heath government, approached Heath and told him that he was expected to stand down as Leader if they lost, see Heath, *The Course*, p. 307.
108. Campbell, *Edward*, p. 282; James, *Ambitions*, p. 267. It gave the Conservatives a strong overall majority of 30 seats. It was the greatest move to a party since 1945 – 4.7 per cent, 46 per cent of votes cast, and in absolute

numbers 13,144,692 more than Labour's 13,066,173 in 1966. Under normal peace time conditions, it was the greatest swing in the size of majority since 1906.

109. Campbell, *Edward*, p. 299.
110. Ibid., pp. 297, 299.
111. Oakley and Rose, *The Political Year*, p. 65.
112. Heath, *The Course*, p. 320.
113. Ibid., p. 283.
114. Ibid., pp. 310–311.
115. LSE\Seventies, Interview Lord Home.
116. Ibid.
117. D. R. Thorpe, *Alec Douglas Home* (London: Sinclair-Stevenson, 1996), pp. 47, 64–65, 88–89, 105–106.
118. HarperCollins©1976Home. Quote in this note Home of the Hirsel, Alec Douglas-Home, *The Way the Wind Blows: An Autobiography by Lord Home* (London: Collins, 1976), p. 222. See also Roth, *Heath*, p. 186; Thorpe, *Alec*, pp. 390–392.
119. Campbell, *Edward*, pp. 335–336.
120. Thorpe, *Alec*, pp. 88, 106–107, 169.
121. Heath, *The Course*, p. 468; LSE\BOAPAH, Interview with Lord Home, pp. 19–20.
122. LSE\Seventies, Interview Lord Home.
123. Ibid.
124. LSE\BOAPAH, Interview with Lord Home, p. 20.
125. TNA/FCO/7/1839, 'Anglo / United States Relations, by the FCO, 23 September 1970'.
126. TNA/FCO/7/1808, 'Press guidance for use unattributely in reply to questions – President Nixon's Report to Congress on US Foreign Policy in the 70's' and 'Letter to Mr. De Courcy Ireland from C. L. G. Mallaby, 18 February, President Nixon's Report to Congress on US Foreign Policy in the 70's'.
127. TNA/FCO/7/1427, 'The Implications for Anglo/US Relations of Britain's European policies', from P. Craddock to Mr Holland, 14 November 1969.
128. Heath, *Old World*, pp. 67–68.
129. TNA/FCO/7/1839, 'Anglo / United States Relations, by the FCO, 23 September 1970'.
130. Ibid.
131. Ibid.
132. Ibid.
133. TNA/PREM/15/1376, 'Priorities for British Interests, 1970/1', p. 1.
134. TNA/PREM/15/1376, 'Diagrammatic Map of the United States Interests Overseas'
135. TNA/PREM/15/1376, 'Letter, seen by PM on "Priorities for British interests Overseas", from the Foreign Secretary, 18 March 1971'.
136. TNA/PREM/15/1376, 'To the Secretary of State for Defence from the Prime Minister, 15 July 1970'.
137. TNA/PREM/15/7 1970, First Cabinet Meeting, 'Handwritten note by the Prime Minister'.

138. TNA/PREM/15/64, Foreign Policy, 'Foreign Policy Issues, DOP 70-3, Annex A, Detailed Comments, 30 June 1970'; and 'To Secretary of State, from Denis Greenhill June 1970, Summary of H.M.G Foreign Policy', p. 7.
139. TNA/PREM/15/62, Note from W. A. Nield to Heath, 19 June.
140. Ibid.
141. Ibid.
142. TNA/PREM/15/62, Message from Geoffrey Rippon to Heath, 30 October 1970.
143. TNA/PREM/15/62, Annex 'Opening statement for 30 June'.
144. Campbell, *Edward*, p. 354.
145. The EUI Archives\Oral History Project *Voices on Europe*, Crispin Tickell, Interview, 1988.
146. TNA/PREM/15/62, Political Unification – The Davignon Report, Heath given analysis end of October 1971.
147. Campbell, *Edward*, p. 357.
148. TNA/PREM/15/368, Record of the Prime Minister's meeting with SGR. Malfatti, President of the Commission of the European Communities, at 6.15 p.m. on Wednesday, 3 March 1971.
149. TNA/PREM/15/368, Record of a meeting held at the Foreign and Commonwealth Secretary's Office, 16 February at 4 p.m.
150. TNA/PREM/15/351, Note from Heath.
151. TNA/PREM/15/359, Record of the Prime Minister's meeting with M. Monnet on 11 November 1970.
152. H. Kissinger, *Years of Upheaval* (London: Weidenfeld & Nicolson, 1982), p. 138.
153. F. Duchêne, *Jean Monnet: The First Statesman of Independence* (New York and London: Norton, 1994), pp. 324–326, 335, 338.
154. TNA/PREM/15/369, Letter from the FCO to P. J. S. Moon, 'Options for British External Policy If Our Application for Membership of the Community Fails', 8 March 1971, probably seen by Heath.
155. TNA/PREM/15/369, 'Options for British External Policy If Our Application for Membership of the European Communities Fails', summary.
156. TNA/PREM/15/369, Letter from the FCO to P. J. S. Moon, 'Options for British External Policy If Our Application for Membership of the Community Fails', 8 March 1971.
157. TNA/PREM/15/711, 'The Implications for Anglo/US Relations of Britain's European Policies' – 'summary'. by the FCO Planning staff, 1970 early/mid.
158. Ibid.
159. Ibid.
160. Ibid.
161. Bundy, *A Tangled*, pp. 5, 545.
162. Nixon, *The Memoirs*, pp. 3, 13, 34, 40.
163. Bundy, *A Tangled*, pp. 5, 8
164. I. Morgan, *Nixon* (London and New York: Oxford University Press, 2002), pp. 2, 42.
165. See R. Perlstein, *Nixonland – The Rise of a President and the Fracturing of America* (New York: Scribner, 2008); and R. Morgan, *Richard Nixon and the Quest for a New Majority* (Chapel Hill: University of North Carolina University Press, 2004).

166. Morgan, *Nixon*, p. 65.
167. FRUS, *Foreign Relations, 1969–1976, Foundations of Foreign Policy 1969–1972, Vol. 1* (Washington: United States Government, Printing Office, 2003), Notes on the FRUS volumes 1 and 2. Address by Richard M. Nixon to the Bohemian Club.
168. Ibid.
169. Ibid., pp. 5–7.
170. Ibid., p. 7; 2. Address by Richard M. Nixon to the Bohemian Club.
171. Ibid., pp. 12–14; 3. Article by Richard M. Nixon – Asia after Viet Nam.
172. Nixon, *The Memoirs*, p. 343.
173. Hanhimäki, *The Flawed Architect: Henry Kissinger and American Foreign Policy* (Oxford and New York: University of North Carolina University Press, 2004), pp. 21–22 represents the careful analysis. Bundy, *A Tangled*, p. 52, charges Nixon with playing politics. See also R. Dallek, *Partners in Power – Nixon and Kissinger* (New York: HarperCollins, 2007), pp. 80–82.
174. Nixon, *The Memoirs*, p. 341.
175. W. Isaacson, *Kissinger: A Biography* (London: Faber and Faber, 1992), p. 136; H. Kissinger, *White*, pp. 10–16.
176. Bundy, *A Tangled Web*, p. 52.
177. Morgan, *Nixon*, p. 128.
178. Isaacson, *Kissinger*, pp. 195–197.
179. H. Kissinger, *A World Restored* (London: Gollancz, 1973), p. 1.
180. Ibid., pp. 54–55.
181. FRUS, *1969–1976, Vol. 1*, 4. Article: 'Central Issues of American Foreign Policy', from *American Foreign Policy: Three Essays*, originally published in 1969.
182. Ibid., pp. 36–37.
183. TNA/FCO/7/1808, 'Nixon to the US Congress 1970'.
184. Bundy, *A Tangled*, p. 68. The speech that was later named the 'Nixon Doctrine.
185. TNA/FCO/7/1808, 'Nixon to the US Congress 1970'.
186. Coleman, *A 'Special'*, p. 163.
187. Kissinger, *White*, pp. 91–92.
188. NSC/Box 942, Memorandum for the President, Brief for meeting with Prime Minister Wilson 27–28 January 1970, p. 1.
189. *Daily Express*, 26 January, by Wilfred Sendall.
190. NSC/Box 942, Memorandum for the President, Brief for meeting with Prime Minister Wilson 27–28 January 1970.
191. NSC/Box 1023, Memcon Nixon – Prime Minister Wilson. Conversation between President Nixon and Prime Minister Harold Wilson, Sir Burke Trend and Henry A. Kissinger, 27 January 1970.
192. Ibid.
193. *The Financial Times*, 26 January 1970.
194. WHSF – Ronald Ziegler, Presidential Trips, Feb 3 – March 3, 69, speaking notes Q and A: 'Current Press interest London'.
195. LSE\Hetherington, 16/29, Points from a meeting with President Nixon and Dr Henry Kissinger, February 25, 1969.
196. NSC/Box 942, Facts book United Kingdom, DoS, January 1970.

197. Ibid.
198. Ibid.
199. Ibid.
200. Bundy, *A Tangled*, p. 57.
201. D. Dinan, *Europe Recast – A History of European Union* (Boulder and London: Lynne Rienner, 2004), p. 127.
202. NARA/NSSM/box H-164 folder NSSM 79 1 of 2, 'UK Accession to the European Community', 13 October 1969, by Henry Kissinger.
203. NARA/NSSM/box H-164 folder NSSM 79 1 of 2, NSSM 79 and 91 'Enlargement of the European Community: Implications for the US and Policy Options'.
204. Kissinger, *Years*, p. 137.
205. NARA/NSSM/box H-164 folder NSSM 79 1 of 2, Memorandum for Dr Kissinger, from C. Fred Bergsten and Helmut Sonnenfeldt, 7 November 1969.
206. NARA/NSSM/box H-164 part 2 of NSSM 79, Department of State Study Paper 'Enlargement of the European Community and Implications for the U.S.'.
207. Ibid.
208. Ibid.
209. NARA/NSSM/box H-164 folder NSSM 79 1 of 2, NSSM 79 and 91 'Enlargement of the European Community: Implications for the US and Policy Options'.
210. NARA/NSDM/68 in box H-217, NSDM 68, July 3, 1970, by Henry Kissinger to The Sec of State, the Sec of Def, etc.
211. NARA/NSSM/box H-164 part 2 of NSSM 79, Department of State Study Paper 'Enlargement of the European Community and Implications for the U.S. with Annexes'.
212. NARA/NSSM/box H-164 folder NSSM 79 1 of 2, NSSM 79 and 91 'Enlargement of the European Community: Implications for the US and Policy Options'.
213. NARA/NSSM/box H-164 part 2 of NSSM 79, Department of State Study Paper 'Enlargement of the European Community and Implications for the U.S. with Annexes'.
214. NARA/NSSM 79 and 91, 'Enlargement of the European Community: Implications for the US and Policy Options'.
215. NARA/NSSM/box H-164 folder NSSM 79 1 of 2, NSSM 79 and 91, 'Enlargement of the European Community: Implications for the US and Policy Options'.
216. Heath, *The Course*, pp. 307–308.
217. TNA/PREM/15/62, Telegram from Ambassador Freeman to Heath, No. 1896, 20 June 1970.
218. TNA/FCO/7/1812, A note 'President Nixon's Visit to Chequers, 3 October'.
219. TNA/PREM/15/1540, Letter to the Permanent Under-Secretary from Sir Con O'Neill, 30 October 1970, probably seen by Heath underlined.
220. J. R. Schaetzel, *The Unhinged Alliance: America and the European Community* (New York: Harper & Row, 1975), pp. 48–52, 58.
221. Winand, *Eisenhower*, p. 147.

222. TNA/PREM/15/1540, Letter to the Permanent Under-Secretary from Sir Con O'Neill, 30 October 1970.
223. TNA/FCO/7/1812, A message from Greenhill to Freeman [October].
224. Dumbrell, *A Special Relationship*, p. 73.
225. Heath, *The Course*, p. 308.

2. Monetary Catharsis: Anglo-American Economic and Monetary Affairs

1. A. Cairncross, 'The Heath Government and the British Economy', in Ball and Seldon, *The Heath Government*, p. 108.
2. Campbell, *Edward*, pp. 301–303; E. Dell, *The Chancellors: A History of the Chancellors of the Exchequer, 1945–90* (London: Harper, 1996), pp. 373–374.
3. LSE\Seventies, Interview Timothy Kitson.
4. C. Schenk, 'Sterling, International Monetary Reform and Britain's Applications to Join the European Economic Community in the 1960s', *Contemporary European History*, Vol. 11, No. 3 (2002), p. 345.
5. Roy, *The Battle*, p. 323.
6. Bernstein, *The Myth*, pp. 32–37, 208–209; F. J. Gavin, *Gold, Dollars and Power: The Politics of International Monetary Relations, 1958–1971* (Chapel Hill and London: University of North Carolina Press, 2004), pp. 166–171; Alford, *British*, pp. 18–19, 66–80; C. Schenk, *Britain and the Sterling Area: From Devaluation to Convertibility in the 1950s* (London and New York: Routledge, LSE, 1994).
7. H. James, *International Monetary Cooperation since Bretton Woods* (New York and Oxford: Oxford University Press, 1996), pp. 203–209, 228.
8. Bernstein, *The Myth*, pp. 208–209.
9. Dell, *The Chancellors*, p. 358; and TNA/PREM/15/368, Draft Reply to EEC Question No. 5, secret.
10. Dell, *The Chancellors*, p. 358; Roy, *The Battle*, pp. 313–323; and NARA/State Department Files. RG 59, Lot file Records relating to the UK 1962–74, Entry 5603, Part 1, Box 2, Folder ECIN 6B EC Monetary Union 1971, Memorandum, The Economic and Financial 'Problem' in the British Negotiations, Confidential, Cleveland, December, 1970, Economics and the EEC.
11. Schenk, 'Sterling', pp. 361, 366.
12. Ibid., pp. 363–364, 367–369.
13. Bernstein, *The Myth*, pp. 36–37; and A. Cairncross, 'Economic Policy and Performance', in R. Floud and D. McCloskey (eds), *The Economic History of Britain since 1700, Volume 3: 1939–1992*, 2nd Ed. (Cambridge: Cambridge University Press, 1994), pp. 54–61.
14. Heath, *Old World*, pp. 49, 53.
15. Heath, 'Realism'.
16. EUI Archives, Oral History Project, Edmund Dell interview.
17. LSE\Seventies, Interview Anthony Barber.
18. Lord Croham comments in Kaniah, Michael David, ' "The Heath Government" – Witness Seminar in Contemporary Record', *The Journal of Contemporary British History*, Vol. 9, No. 1 (Summer, 1995), pp. 188–219.
19. Cairncross, 'The Heath', pp. 109–110.

20. LSE\Seventies, Interview with Robert Carr.
21. Campbell, *Edward*, pp. 311–313.
22. Fry, *The Politics*, pp. 218–219.
23. TNA/PREM/15/42, Notes for the Record, Secret, Economic Policy. Milton Freedman visits, 18 September 1970.
24. TNA/PREM/15/42, Prime Minister, Note on Note from Brian Reading, signed R. T. Armstrong, 29 September 1970. Seen by Heath on 30 September. And to Mr Reading, 30 September 1970, from R. T. Armstrong the PM's comments. The model was the Phillips Curve.
25. TNA/PREM/15/50, Note for the Record, meeting between Sir Eric Roll and the Prime Minister, 24 November 1970.
26. L. V. Boyd, *Britain's Search for a Role* (Westmead, and Lexington, Mass., US: Saxon House – Lexington Books, 1975), pp. 17–18, 19. TNA/PREM/15/62, 'The Reasons why Britain should join the Common Market'.
27. TNA/FCO/7/1840, Brief for the 'Visit of the Prime Minister to Washington – Britain and the European Communities, 17–18 December, 1970', 11 December 1970.
28. Boyd, *Britain's Search*, p. 71.
29. Ibid., p. 61.
30. Dinan, *Europe*, pp. 111–112.
31. Dell, *The Chancellors*, pp. 374–376.
32. TNA/PREM/15/814, Memorandum by Brian Reading, 'Preparing for Europe – The Government's Economic Strategy, 10 November 1971.
33. Ibid.
34. TNA/FCO/7/1828, Record of a meeting between the Foreign Secretary and Commonwealth Secretary and the United States Secretary of State held at Dorney Wood on Saturday, 11 July 1970.
35. Ibid.
36. Ibid.
37. TNA/PREM/15/1275, Note of the Prime Minister's Private talk with Mr William Rogers, US Secretary of State, 12 July 1970 at Chequers. Delivery of a Letter from President Nixon to the Prime Minister, 7 July 1970.
38. NARA/59 State Department General Records Subject Numerical Files 1970–73 box 814, ECIN 3 EEC 6-1-70, Letter from Robert J. Schaetzel, to Hillenbrand Ass Sec of State for European Affairs, Brussels 30 June 1970, – change of commission and British negotiations.
39. NARA/State Department Files. RG 59, Lot file Records relating to the UK 1962–74, Entry 5603, Part 1, Box 1, Folder EI General Policy Plans Programs 1970. Memorandum Confidential to EUR – Mr Hillenbrand 2 November 1970, from – EUR/BMI Mortimer D. Goldstein – on Heath's Progress and the First Week of Parliament, information memorandum.
40. NARA/State Department Files. RG 59, Lot file Records relating to the UK 1962–74, Entry 5603, FT 2 General Reports & Statistics 1971, Part 4, Memorandum, 9 October 1970, to: EUR Mr Hillenbrand, from: BMI Mortimer D., Goldstein, subject: British Plans for New Agricultural Policy.
41. TNA/PREM/15/62, To M. Moon, from W. A. Nield, 4 December 1970, and 59 State Subj Num Files 1970–73 box 2648, Pol 7 UK 9-1-70 Telegram, from: Embassy London, Secretary Roger's Cabinet Room Meeting with Sir Alec Douglas-Home 17 December: Part II, British Agricultural Policy.

42. *The Times,* 21 December 1970, 'A US assault on Europe's farm policy' by Anthony Thomas.
43. NARA/State Department Files. RG 59, Lot file Records relating to the UK 1962–74, Entry 5603, Part 1, Box 1, Folder EI General Policy Plans Programs 1970. Memorandum Confidential to EUR – Mr Hillenbrand 2 November 1970, from – EUR/BMI Mortimer D. Goldstein – on Heath's Progress and the First Week of Parliament, information memorandum.
44. Ibid.
45. Ibid.
46. TNA/PREM/15/1810, Visit of United States Secretary of State 11/12 July 1970 – Steering Brief, confidential, and Steering Brief – The Prime Minister's Main Objectives for Heath's Chequers meeting with Nixon, and President Nixon's objectives.
47. TNA/FCO/7/1812, Minute, Prime Minister, Mr Rippon – Nixon's Visit: Membership of the European Communities. And 'Nixon's Visit: Membership of the European Communities', by J. A. Robinson, 25 September 1970.
48. TNA/FCO/7/1815, Records of a Meeting between the Prime Minister and President Nixon at Chequers on Saturday 3 October.
49. Ibid.
50. Ibid.
51. TNA/PREM/15/714, Draft letter from the Prime Minister to HM the Queen, On October visit of Nixon.
52. TNA/PREM/15/62, To the Prime Minister, from the Chancellor, 10 December 1970, Economic Implications of Entry into the EEC. And Attached to the above, to Mr Ryrie, Top Secret, signed F. E. Figgures.
53. Ibid.
54. Ibid.
55. TNA/FCO/82/66, North America Department; Prime Minister/President Meeting, 29 November 1971.
56. TNA/PREM/15/53, From the Treasury to Robert T. Armstrong from W. S. Ryrie, 23 October 1970, comments on the Cromer Memorandum.
57. NARA/State Department Files. RG 59, Lot file Records relating to the UK 1962–74, Entry 5603, Box 2, Folder ECIN 6B EC Monetary Union 1971, Memorandum, The Economic and Financial 'Problem' in the British Negotiations, Confidential, Cleveland, December, 1970, – Economics and the EEC.
58. TNA/PREM/15/62, Summary of the Report of the Werner Group.
59. TNA/PREM/15/62, Telegram, No 1197, from Soames, to the FCO, 23 November 1970, on De Gaulle's funeral Contains Carrington on Defence talk.
60. TNA/PREM/15/214, Note of a meeting held at 10 Downing Street, 7 December 1970.
61. NARA/State Department Files. RG 59, Lot file Records relating to the UK 1962–74, Entry 5603, Box 2, Folder ECIN 6B EC Monetary Union 1971, Memorandum, The Economic and Financial 'Problem' in the British Negotiations, Confidential, Cleveland, December, 1970, – Economics and the EEC.

62. TNA/FCO/7/1840, Brief for the 'Visit of the Prime Minister to Washington-steering brief 17–18 December, 1970', 11 December 1970.

63. TNA/FCO/7/1840, Brief for the 'Visit of the Prime Minister to Washington-Britain and the European Communities, 17–18 December, 1970', 11 December 1970.

64. NARA/59 State Department box 2657 Subject Numerical 70–73, Secret, White House, Memcon, subject: Meeting between President Nixon and Prime Minister Heath, 17 December 1970, The President's Office, and NSC/box 1024, Secret, Memorandum of conversation, Meeting between Nixon, Heath, Trend and Kissinger, 17 December 1970, the President's Office.

65. NARA/59 State Department box 2657 Subject Numerical 70–73, Secret, White House, Memcon, subject: Meeting between President Nixon and Prime Minister Heath, 17 December 1970, The President's Office, See list for participants.

66. NARA/NSC/box 1024 Secret, Memorandum of conversation, Meeting between Nixon, Heath, Trend and Kissinger, 17 December 1970, the President's Office.

67. Ibid.

68. Ibid.

69. NARA/59 State Department box 2657 Subject Numerical 70–73, Secret, White House, Memcon, subject: Meeting between President Nixon and Prime Minister Heath, 17 December 1970, The President's Office.

70. Ibid.

71. Ibid.

72. NARA/NSDM 68 in box H-217, 3 July 1970, NSDM 68, US Policy Toward the European Community.

73. NARA/NSC/box 942 Secret, Memorandum for the President, from: HAK, subject: The Visit of Prime Minister Heath December 17–18.

74. NARA/State Department Files. RG 59, Lot file Records relating to the UK 1962–74, Entry 5603, Box 2, Folder ECIN 6B EC Monetary Union 1971, Memorandum, The Economic and Financial 'Problem' in the British Negotiations, Confidential, Cleveland, December 1970, Economics and the EEC.

75. W. Grant, *Economic Policy in Britain* (Basingstoke: Palgrave, 2002), pp. 84–85.

76. NARA/State Department Files. RG 59, Lot file Records relating to the UK 1962–74, Entry 5603, Box 2, Folder ECIN 6B EC Monetary Union 1971, Memorandum, The Economic and Financial 'Problem' in the British Negotiations, Confidential, Cleveland, December 1970, Economics and the EEC.

77. Roth, *Heath*, p. 219; and *The Times*, 21 December 1970, by F. Emery Heath.

78. *The Times*, 18 December 1970, 'Firm Nixon backing for Britain in EEC', by Fred Emery.

79. NARA/State Department Files. RG 59, Lot file Records relating to the UK 1962–74, Entry 5603, Part 1, Box 3, FT 2 General Reports & Statistics 1971, 11 February 1971, to: Stanley M Cleveland, from: John C. Griffith United Kingdom Affairs.

80. Roth, *Heath*, p. 221; Dell, *The Chancellors*, p. 380.

81. NARA/State Department Files. RG 59, Lot file Records relating to the UK 1962–74, Entry 5603, Part 1, Box 1, Folder AGR 2 General Reports & Statistics 1971, to: EUR – Mr Springsteen, 3 February 1971, from: EUR/BMI John C. Griffith on Basle Agreement, Economics. Folder AGR 2 General Reports & Statistics 1971.

82. NARA/State Department Files. RG 59, Lot file Records relating to the UK 1962–74, Entry 5603, Part 1, Box 2, Limited Official Use, 16 February 1971, to: E/IFD Mr Weintraub, from: E/IFD Matilda Milne, subject: Extension of the Basle Agreement on the Sterling Balance.

83. NARA/State Department Files. RG 59, Lot file Records relating to the UK 1962–74, Entry 5603, Part 1, Box 2, Folder ECIN 6B EC Monetary Union 1971, from Stanley M. Cleveland Minister For Economic and Commercial Affairs 26 February 1971, to 'Mort' Mortimer D. Goldstein, Esq. Director EUR/ BMI Department of State – Agriculture. Figgures persuaded Volcker that his tactics did not go down well.

84. TNA/PREM/15/368, Letter from C. C. C. Tickell, FCO (Lancaster), with attached minute by J. A. Robison, to P. J. S. Moon, for the attention of Heath, 7 January 1971.

85. EUI Archives, Oral History Project, Interview with Crispin Tickell.

86. TNA/PREM/15/372, Record of a conversation between the Prime Minister and the President of the French Republic at the Elysée Palace in Paris on Friday 21 May 1971, at 10.00 a.m.

87. TNA/PREM/15/372, Record of a conversation between the Prime Minister and the President of the French Republic at the Elysée Palace in Paris on Friday 21 May 1971, at 16:00 hours.

88. TNA/PREM/15/372, Records of Conclusions – of the meeting between the President of the French Republic and the Prime Minister of the United Kingdom held at the Le Palais de'Elysée, Paris, on Thursday 20 and Friday 21 May 1971.

89. Government White Paper; 'The United Kingdom and the European Communities', Her Majesty's Stationary Office, July 1971.

90. NARA/State Department Files. RG 59, Lot file Records relating to the UK 1962–74, Entry 5603, Part 1, Box 3, FN 12 Balance of Payments 1971, to: E – Mr Trezise, from: E/IFD – Sidney Weintraub, subject: Meeting with Mr Brian Griffiths on International Constraints on Invisibles. Invisible earnings were £500 million in 1969 and £600 million in 1970.

91. Roth, *Heath*, p. 223.

92. LSE\Seventies, Interview Anthony Barber.

93. Bernstein, *The Myth*, pp. 178–179; and James, *International*, pp. 179–181.

94. Heath, 'Realism'.

95. James, *International*, p. 224.

96. TNA/PREM/15/375, Note for the Record, meeting between Lord Cromer and the Prime Minister in London 18 June 1971.

97. Ibid.

98. D. Kunz, *Butter and Guns: America's Cold War Economic Diplomacy* (New York: The Free Press, 1997), pp. 195–196; and James, *International*, p. 208.

99. Kunz, *Butter*, pp. 195, 201.

100. Gavin, *Gold*, p. 192.

101. Kunz, *Butter*, p. 198; and Cairncross, 'The Heath', p. 130.

102. TNA/PREM/15/722, Telegram from Cromer, No. 1934, 4 June 1971, seen by Heath 6 June. And MY I. P. T. 'A free summary of Secretary Connally's speech in Munich 28 May'.
103. Gavin, *Gold*, p. 193.
104. TNA/PREM/15/722, Telegram from Cromer, No. 1934, 4 June 1971, seen by Heath 6 June. And MY I. P. T. 'A free summary of Secretary Connally's speech in Munich 28 May'.
105. TNA/PREM/15/385, Message from Brian Reading, 6 May 1971.
106. TNA/PREM/15/385, Message from Brian Reading, 11 May 1971.
107. TNA/PREM/15/385, Letter from the Chancellor to the Prime Minister, 11 May 1971, and Telegram from the Prime Minister to the Ambassador, Lord Cromer, signed Douglas-Home, 18 May 1971.
108. TNA/PREM/15/385, Letter from Lord Cromer to the Foreign Secretary, 11 May 1971.
109. TNA/PREM/15/832, Letter from Barber to Heath, 12 July 1971, 'Repayment of IMF Debt'.
110. Gavin, *Gold*, p. 194.
111. Ibid.
112. Ibid., pp. 194–195; Kunz, *Butter*, p. 203. See TNA/PREM/15/838, A message to Heath from R. T. Armstrong, 26 January 1972.
113. TNA/PREM/15/838, Letter from A. M. Bailey to R. T. Armstrong, 13 January 1972. It is possible that Connally somehow mixed up the British standard requests in the process of repaying loans.
114. TNA/PREM/15/309, Draft Reply by the Prime Minister to President Nixon's Letter of 15 August; and Letter from the Department of Trade and Industry, from the Secretary of State's Private Secretary P. H. Twyman, to R. T. Armstrong, 19 August 1971.
115. TNA/PREM/15/309, Attached to the letter above 'International Monetary Situation', by Lord Cromer 15 August 1971, written in London.
116. Ibid.
117. TNA/PREM/15/309, From the Treasury, W. S. Ryrie, to R. T. Armstrong, 17 August 1971. See also TNA/PREM/15/309, added analysis 'Measures to Counter Speculative Inflows', 17 August 1971.
118. Kunz, *Butter*, p. 207.
119. TNA/PREM/15/309, Telegram from Peter Gregson to the Prime Minister, seen by Heath 23 August 1971.
120. NARA/RG 59, Records relating to the UK 1962–74, Entry 5603, Box 3, FN 2 General Reports & Statistics 1971, Discussion memorandum, 13 September 1971, UK concerns over job development tax credit in NEP, Participants; Julius Katz (see doc), and RG 59, Lot file Records relating to the UK 1962–74, Entry 5603, Box 3, FN 2 General Reports & Statistics 1971, 19 August 1971, to: EUR Russell Fessenden, Acting, from: EUR/BMI Scott George, subject: Effects of President's New Economic Program on the UK.
121. NARA/NSC/box 950, additional folder one Heath Visit Bermuda December 1971, 1 of 2 and Heath visit Bermuda folder nr 2 exists folder Heath – Presidential Trip, United Kingdom Reaction to NEP.
122. NARA/RG 59, Lot file Records relating to the UK 1962–74, Entry 5603, Box 3, FN 2 General Reports & Statistics 1971, 19 August 1971, to: EUR Russell

Fessenden, Acting, from: EUR/BMI Scott George, Effects of President's New Economic Program on the UK.
123. Ibid.
124. TNA/PREM/15/309, To the Prime Minister, 20 August 1971. On Chancellors talks with the Six.
125. J. Connally with M. Herskowitz, *In History's Shadow: An American Odyssey* (New York: Hyperion books, 1993), pp. 244–245.
126. TNA/PREM/15/712, Cutting from the *New York Times*, 22 October.
127. Roth, *Heath*, p. 224.
128. TNA/PREM/15/361, A note from C. C. C. Tickell, Private Secretary to the Chancellor of the Duchy of Lancaster, to Sir Con O'Neill and HM Ambassador in Washington and others, on 'The United States and the EEC', 15 October 1971. And a message from C. C. C. Tickell to P. J. S. Moon, seen by Heath, 18 October.
129. TNA/PREM/15/361, A letter from Lord Cromer to C. C. C. Tickell, 21 October 1971.
130. NARA/RG 59, Lot file Records relating to the UK 1962–74, Entry 5603, Box 1, folder AGR 2 General Reports & Statistics 1971. Department of State Information Memorandum 19 October 1971, to D– Mr Samuels, from EUR – Martin J. Hillenbrand – Elements of British Economic Thinking.
131. TNA/PREM/15/310, Telegram from Washington, number 3677, 4 November 1971, 'International Monetary Situation'.
132. TNA/PREM/15/310, Note for the Record: 'International Monetary Situation' Note of a meeting held at 10 Downing Street on Wednesday 3 November 1971, at 4.30 p.m.
133. TNA/PREM/15/310, A note from PLG, on discussions between the Chancellor and the Prime Minister, 18 October 1971.
134. TNA/PREM/15/812, Letter from the Chancellor to the Prime Minister, 23 November 1971.
135. TNA/PREM/15/812, A note from William Nield to Armstrong for the attention of the Prime Minister, record of conversation with Financial Times journalist Freddie Fisher, 18 November 1971.
136. TNA/PREM/15/812, Letter, in telegram No. 851, 24 November, from the Prime Minister to President Nixon.
137. TNA/PREM/15/812, A note, by RTA, the Chancellor and the Governor of the Bank of England meeting the Prime Minister, 7 December 1971.
138. TNA/FCO/73-133, A Letter from J. A. N. Graham to the Permanent Under-Secretary, 'Relations with the US', 9 September 1971.
139. Kunz, *Butter*, pp. 105, 208–211.
140. TNA/FCO/82/66 A note, 'Bermuda Meeting between the Prime Minister and President Nixon 20–21 December 1971', secret.
141. TNA/FCO/82/66 A note, 'Bermuda Meeting between the Prime Minister and President Nixon 20–21 December 1971–Relations between the United States and the enlarged EEC', secret.
142. TNA/FCO/82/66, A brief for the Bermuda meeting 'Relations between the US and the enlarged EEC – Points for the Prime Minister to Make', undated.
143. Ibid.
144. S. Pollard, *The Development of the British Economy, Fourth Edition, 1914–1990* (London: Edward Arnold – Hodder & Stoughton, 1992), pp. 306–308.

145. TNA/FCO/82/66, A note, 'Bermuda Meeting between the Prime Minister and President Nixon 20–21 December 1971–Relations between the United States and the enlarged EEC', secret.

146. NARA/NSC/box 950, folder one Heath Visit Bermuda December 1971, 1 of 2 and Heath visit Bermuda folder nr 2 exists folder Heath – Presidential Trip Telegram from London 'Bermuda Meeting: International Economic Issues Agenda Item'.

147. NARA/NSC/box 950, folder one Heath Visit Bermuda December 1971, 1 of 2 Heath visit Bermuda folder nr 2 exists folder Heath – Presidential Trip British Balance of Payments.

148. TNA/FCO/82/71, Record of a plenary meeting between the UK and US Delegations, lead by the Prime Minister and President Nixon, at Government House, Bermuda, at 2.30 p.m. on Tuesday, 21 December 1971.

149. Ibid.

150. Ibid.

151. TNA/FCO/82/183, 'Bermuda Meeting: Part I – General'

152. TNA/FCO/82/71, Record of a plenary meeting between the UK and US Delegations, lead by the Prime Minister and President Nixon, at Government House, Bermuda, at 2.30 p.m. on Tuesday, 21 December 1971.

153. NARA/WHSF subject files 1969–1974 OA box 9 folder CF OA 159 CF TR 43 Briefing book for the President's meeting with British Leaders Bermuda 20–21 December 1971.

154. TNA/FCO/82/71, Record of a plenary meeting between the UK and US Delegations, lead by the Prime Minister and President Nixon, at Government House, Bermuda, at 2.30 p.m. on Tuesday, 21 December 1971.

155. TNA/FCO/82/71, Record of a conversation between the Foreign and Commonwealth Secretary and Mr William Rogers, Unites States Secretary of State, at the Princess Hotel, Bermuda, at 10.30 a.m. on 21 December 1971.

156. TNA/FCO/82/71, Record of a plenary meeting between the UK and US Delegations, lead by the Prime Minister and President Nixon, at Government House, Bermuda, at 2.30 p.m. on Tuesday, 21 December 1971.

157. TNA/FCO/82/183, 'Bermuda Meeting: Part I – General'.

158. TNA/FCO/82/71, Note of a meeting at the Princess Hotel, Bermuda at 2.30 p.m. on Monday, 20 December 1971. Present Barber, Connally, Volcker, Neale, Bailey.

159. *The Guardian*, 21 December 1971 by Adam Raphael.

160. *The Guardian*, 22 December 1971 by Adam Raphael.

161. *The Daily Telegraph*, 23 December by HB Boyne. 'Main British aim won at Bermuda'.

162. Cairncross, 'The Heath', pp. 131–132.

163. NARA/59, State Department Subject Numerical Files 70–73 box 2658, Pol 1 UK-US 1973 Airgram 14 February 1972, Embassy London, subject: Annual Assessment for the United Kingdom.

164. Dell, *The Chancellors*, pp. 386–387.

165. LSE\Seventies, Interview Anthony Barber.

166. Campbell, *Edward*, pp. 522–523.

167. *The New York Times*, 'Excerpts from Interview with Prime Minister Heath', by Anthony Lewis, 27 February 1972.

168. D. H. Aldcroft and M. J. Oliver, *Exchange Rate Regimes in the Twentieth Century* (Cheltenham and Northampton: Edward Elgar, 1998), pp. 146–148.
169. TNA/PREM/15/812, Telegram from Washington, No. 1643, 13 May, 'International Monetary Reform'.
170. N. W. C. Woodward, Nicholas, *The Management of the British Economy, 1945–2001* (Manchester, New York: Manchester University Press, 2004), pp. 140–141.
171. TNA/PREM/15/813, Note for the Record, 'Floating the Pound', 4 July 1972, secret.
172. Kunz, *Butter*, p. 212.
173. TNA/PREM/15/813, Note for the Record, 'Floating the Pound', 4 July 1972, secret.
174. LSE\Seventies, Interview Anthony Barber.
175. TNA/PREM/15/813, Note for the Record, meeting between Barber and Heath, and Treasury advisers at 10 Downing Street, Thursday, 21 June 1972 at 4.30 p.m. signed R. T. Armstrong, 3 July.
176. TNA/PREM/15/813, 'Message from the Prime Minister to President Nixon', 241430 June 1972.
177. TNA/PREM/15/813, Note for the Record, 'Floating the Pound', 4 July 1972, secret.
178. TNA/PREM/15/813, Explanatory note by the Treasury, 'EEC Margins Scheme: International Obligations', seen by Heath, 27 June 1972.
179. TNA/PREM/15/813, Telegram from Soames, Paris, No. 839, 23 June.
180. TNA/PREM/15/813, Unofficial translation 'Text of letter from the President of France to the Prime Minister'.
181. TNA/PREM/15/813, Telegram from Mitchell, Washington, No. 1979, 23 June, top secret.
182. Kunz, *Butter*, p. 213. And FRUS, *1969–1976, Vol. III*, Foreign Economic Policy 1969–1972; International Monetary Policy, 1969–1972, 234. Memorandum from Secretary of The Treasury Schultz to President Nixon.
183. FRUS, *1969–1976, Vol. III*, Foreign Economic Policy 1969–1972; International Monetary Policy, 1969–1972, 242. Editorial note.
184. TNA/PREM/15/813, Letter from Cromer to Heath, 17 July 1972.
185. TNA/PREM/15/813, Telegram from Cromer to Heath, No. 1978 'Personal for the Prime Minister', 23 June.
186. TNA/PREM/15/813, A note by RTA, 7 July 1972.
187. TNA/PREM/15/813, A letter from A. M. Bailey to Robert Armstrong, 24 July 1972.
188. TNA/PREM/15/813, Letter from Cromer to Heath, 17 July 1972, seen by Heath.
189. PREM Note for the Record, meeting between the Prime Minister and the Governor of the Bank of England, 10 Downing Street, 5.00 p.m., Monday 26 June 1972.
190. *The New York Times*, 'Excerpts from Interview with Prime Minister Heath', by Anthony Lewis, 27 February 1972.
191. TNA/PREM/15/875, Handwritten letter from the R. T. Armstrong to Christopher [Soames?], 13 June 1972.
192. Ibid.

193. TNA/PREM/15/813, Letter from Soames to Sir Alan Neale, 1 August 1972, 'The EEC, International Monetary Reform and EM'.
194. TNA/PREM/15/875, Letter from Soames to R. T. Armstrong, 10 July 1972.
195. TNA/PREM/15/875, Note for the Record, Discussions between M. Jobert, M. Raimond of the Secretariat General at the Elysée, later joined by M. Jean-René Bernard and Soames in Paris on Wednesday 12 July 1972, 13 July 1972.
196. TNA/PREM/15/870, Note for the Record, Discussions between M. Jobert, M. Raimond of the Secretariat General at the Elysée, later joined by M. Jean-René Bernard and Soames in Paris on Wednesday 12 July 1972, 13 July 1972, secret.
197. TNA/PREM/15/1457, Letter from Barber to Heath, 10 October 1972.
198. TNA/PREM/15/905, Record of a Discussion between the Prime Minister and the French Foreign Secretary [M. Schumann] at Chequers, Thursday, 24 August 1972.
199. TNA/PREM/15/1457, Handwritten note from RTA to Heath, 9 October 1972.
200. Lord Croham comments in Witness seminar 'The Heath Government', in *Contemporary Record*, *The Journal of Contemporary British History*, Vol. 9, No. 1 (Summer, 1995), pp. 197–198 and TNA/PREM/15/1457, A note from R. T. Armstrong to the Prime Minister, 12 October 1972.
201. TNA/PREM/15/1457, A note from R. T. Armstrong to the Prime Minister, 12 October 1972 .
202. Dinan, *Europe*, pp. 142–143.
203. TNA/PREM/15/1269, Telegram from Nixon to Heath 'European Summit', No. 3297, 8 November 1972.
204. Ibid.
205. Dell, *The Chancellors*, p. 393.
206. TNA/PREM/15/1269, Telephone Conversation between the Prime Minister and President Nixon, Wednesday, 8 November 1972.
207. TNA/PREM/15/1457, Letter from Heath to Pompidou, 13 December 1972.
208. TNA/PREM/15/1979, A record from a meeting between Arthur Burns, Chairman of the United States Federal Reserve Board and Heath, Tuesday, 9 January 1973 at 5.00 p.m.
209. NARA/NSC/box 942, Letter from Arthur F. Burns to HAK, 21 February 1973, from: Arthur F. Burns, Chairman of the Board of Governors Federal Reserve System. Suggestion on Heath talking points.
210. *The Financial Times*, 9 January 1973, 'Anglo-American relations to be fully reviewed' by Paul Lewis.
211. TNA/FCO/82/301, Extract, point 4.
212. TNA/FCO/82/291, Draft Steering Brief (Part II) – Washington meeting 1973.
213. NARA/59, State Subj Num Files 1970–73 box 2649, Pol 7 UK 1-1-73 Outgoing Telegram Dep of State, subject: Roger's Meeting with Alec Douglas Home part II US–EC relations, 1 February.
214. NARA/NSC/box 942, Secret, Memorandum for the President, from: HAK, subject: Your Meeting with Prime Minister Heath Thursday 1 February and Friday 2 February at Camp David. Briefs.
215. Ibid.
216. Ibid.; and Dell, *The Chancellors*, p. 397.

217. TNA/FCO/82/301, Letter from Heath to Pierre Trudeau, 15 February 1973.
218. NARA/NSC/box 942, Memorandum for the President, from: Peter Flanigan, subject: Heath visit: Economic Issues.
219. NARA/NSC/box 942, Talking points for the President for the visit of Prime Minister Heath, Economic Issues, Special Role of UK in international trade and monetary affairs.
220. TNA/FCO/82/301, Extracts from speech by the Rt. Hon. Edward Heath, British Prime Minister, at the National Press club, Washington, DC, 1 February 1973.
221. Ibid.
222. *The Observer*, 4 February, Article, by Michael Braham.
223. Kunz, *Butter*, p. 214. The Anglo-American view was an increased use of SDRs.
224. TNA/PREM/15/1457, A report from the Treasury 'Exchange rate policy', 6 February 1973.
225. TNA/PREM/15/1457, A note on 'Exchange rate policy' from J. B. Hunt to R. T. Armstrong, 8 February 1973, top secret.
226. Kunz, *Butter*, p. 215.
227. TNA/PREM/15/1982, Telegram from Heath to Nixon, CABWH001/24, March 1973.
228. NARA/HAK/box 53, Monetary Crisis March 1973 and NAC Summit Brussels June 1974. Top Secret, Memorandum for Theodore L. Eliot Jr Executive Secretary Department of State, 9 March 1973. Messages from World Leaders; Includes Top Secret, Message to Prime Minister Heath 3 March 1973.
229. Ibid.
230. Kunz, *Butter*, pp. 215–216, 222.
231. TNA/PREM/15/1519, A note on a report from J. B. Hunt to Heath, 14 March 1973.
232. Dell, *The Chancellors*, p. 396.
233. TNA/PREM/15/1519, A note from RTA to Heath, 21 June 1973, secret.
234. S. Rosenberg, *American Economic Development* (Basingstoke: Palgrave Macmillan, 2003), pp. 186–187.
235. TNA/PREM/15/1461, Letter from Cromer to Heath, 26 June 1973, and Handwritten note from RTA to Heath, 28 June 1973.
236. Dell, *The Chancellors*, p. 398.
237. TNA/PREM/15/1461, Note for the Record – Foreign Exchange Markets and Exchange Rates, not of a meeting held at 10 Downing Street on Friday 5 July 1973 at 10.15 a.m.
238. TNA/PREM/15/1461, Note of a Meeting held at 10 Downing Street on Monday 9 July 1973 at 7.00 p.m.
239. TNA/PREM/15/1461, Note for the record – Foreign Exchange Markets – Note of a meeting held at 10 Downing Street on Wednesday 25 July 1973 at 10.30 a.m.
240. TNA/PREM/15/1461, Note for the record – Foreign Exchange Markets – Note of a meeting held at 10 Downing Street on Wednesday 26 July 1973 at 4.30 a.m.
241. TNA/PREM/15/1461, A note for Heath by RTA, 13 August 1973, secret.

242. TNA/PREM/15/1461, Extract from meeting: Prime Minister, Chancellor of the Exchequer and Governor of the Bank of England at Chequers, 30 August 1973.
243. TNA/FCO/7/1841, Brief for the 'Visit of the Prime Minister to Washington-International Oil Supplies, 17–18 December, 1970', 10 December 1970.
244. TNA/PREM/15/1090, A note to the Permanent Under Secretary, 'Oil', from J. R. A. Bottomley, 29 December, secret.
245. TNA/PREM/15/1762, Letter from the FCO to Lord Bridges, 10 Downing Street, 7 June 1972.
246. TNA/PREM/15/1982, Telegram from Heath to Nixon, No. 1269, 'Middle East', 15 June 1973.
247. Kunz, *Butter*, pp. 235–236.
248. TNA/PREM/15/1982, Telegram from Heath to Nixon, No. 2081, – a personal message, 15 October 1973, secret.
249. Woodward, *The Management*, p. 141.
250. Symposium 'The Trade Unions and Fall of the Heath Government', chaired by Hugo Young, Contemporary Record, Vol. 2, No. 1 (Spring, 1988), pp. 41–42; and Dell, *The Chancellors*, p. 399.
251. Dell, *The Chancellors*, p. 398.
252. TNA/PREM/15/2041, A message to EEC posts, on line to take at Copenhagen Summit on issues 'other than the Middle East and energy', undated – December 1973.
253. TNA/PREM/15/2041, Draft Confidential Conclusions on subjects other than the Middle East and Energy.
254. TNA/PREM/15/2041, A note on the Copenhagen Summit: Kissinger's Proposal on Energy, from the FCO, seen by Heath, 13 December 1973.
255. TNA/PREM/15/2041, Draft of conclusions from the Copenhagen Summit.
256. TNA/PREM/15/2041, A message to diplomatic postings, No. 3908, 18 December 1973.
257. TNA/PREM/15/2041, Telegram from Kissinger to Home, 20 December 1973.
258. Kunz, *Butter*, p. 238.
259. TNA/PREM/15/2041, Telegram from Nixon to Heath, 6 January.
260. TNA/PREM/15/2178, Letter from Home to Heath, 1 January 1974.
261. TNA/PREM/15/2178, Letter from P. H. Grattan, FCO, 3 January 1974.
262. TNA/PREM/15/2178, Letter from Earl D. Shom, Charge d'Affaires ad interim to Heath, 9 January 1974, 1974. With the attached message from Nixon to Heath.
263. TNA/PREM/15/2178, Telegram, No. 58 from Home to Diplomatic posts, 9 January 1974.
264. TNA/PREM/15/2179, Telegram from Sykes, Washington, No. 516A, 'Washington Energy Conference', 9 February 1974.
265. TNA/PREM/15/2178, A message to Heath from Nixon, February 1974. And Letter to the FCO, from Bridges, 10 Downing Street, 4 February 1974.
266. TNA/PREM/15/2235, Message from Heath to Nixon, 7 February 1974.
267. TNA/PREM/15/2235, Message from Nixon to Heath, February 1974.
268. TNA/PREM/15/2179, Letter from C. T. E. Ewart-Biggs, 22 February 1974.
269. Dobson, *The Politics*, pp. 227–228.
270. Roy, *The Battle*, pp. 321–323.
271. Seldon, 'The Heath Government in History', p. 10.

3. The Anglo-American Nuclear Special Relationship and New Interdependence

1. TNA/PREM/15/139, 'The Current Sate of the Polaris Force', top secret (parts retained).
2. Baylis, *Anglo-American*, p. 173; and Dumbrell, *A Special Relationship*, p. 142.
3. Heuser, *NATO*, p. 160.
4. Heuser, *NATO*, p. 199; Dumbrell, *A Special Relationship*, pp. 141–142; and Baylis, *Anglo-American Defence Relations*, p. 172.
5. Heuser, *Nuclear Mentalities*, pp. 40–41.
6. Heath, *The Course*, pp. 226–227.
7. Heath, *Old World*, pp. 4, 72–73.
8. Roth, *Heath*, p. 215.
9. Heath, *Old World*, pp. 67–68, 72–76.
10. Peter Carrington, *Reflect on Things Past: The Memoirs of Lord Carrington* (London: Collins, 1988), pp. 221–222.
11. TNA/PREM/15/788, A note from PJSM to Trend, 1 March 1971.
12. Hill and Lord, 'The Foreign Policy of the Heath Government', p. 312.
13. Carrington, *Reflect*, pp. 221–222.
14. NARA/RG 59, Lot file Records relating to the UK 1962–74, Entry 5603 [box 3] Secret, 29 September 1969, Letter to: G. Warren Nutter Assistant Secretary for International Security Affairs, from: Martin J. Hillenbrand Assistant Secretary for European Affairs – US-UK French nuclear collaboration.
15. TNA/PREM/15/1276, Steering Brief 'Visit of the United States Secretary of State 11/12 July 1970'.
16. NARA/RG 59, Lot file Records relating to the UK 1962–74, Entry 5603 [box 3], Limited Official Use 28 October 1969, FBX Mr Tanguay, BMI M. D. Goldstein; UK Conservative Party Discussions with the French. Anglo-French Nuclear Cooperation/EEC.
17. TNA/PREM/15/35, Statement on Defence Policy: Lord Balniel, Wednesday, 28 October 1970.
18. D. Hurd, *An End to Promises: Sketch of a Government* (London: Collins, 1979), p. 50.
19. TNA/PREM/15/35, Letter from A. R. M. Jaffray, MoD, W. S. Ryrie, PS Chancellor of the Exchequer, 4 November 1970.
20. NARA/RG 59, Lot file Records relating to the UK 1962–74, Entry 5603, Box 2, Folder ECIN 6 – UK Entry into the EC General – August 1971 Memorandum from Mortimer D. Goldstein, EUR/BMI, to Mr Hillenbrand, 2 November 1970.
21. TNA/PREM/15/35, Letter from A. R. M. Jaffray, MoD, W. S. Ryrie, PS Chancellor of the Exchequer, 4 November 1970.
22. TNA/PREM/15/38, United States Request to Establish a Missile Monitoring Facility in the Phoenix Islands, 10 July 1970, Defence Department.
23. Kissinger, *White*, pp. 210–212.
24. TNA/PREM/15/38, United States Request to Establish a Missile Monitoring Facility in the Phoenix Islands, 10 July 1970, Defence Department.
25. TNA/PREM/15/38, Annex B Background Note on the United States Request for a Missile Monitoring Facility in the Phoenix, FCO July 1970.

26. TNA/PREM/15/38, Letter from Joseph N. Greene, Jr. Charge d'Affaires the US Embassy, to Sir Denis Greenhill, Permanent Under Secretary FCO, 15 July 1970.
27. TNA/PREM/15/38, Information from Home to Heath, 27 July 1970, U.S. Request for a Missile Monitoring Facility in the Phoenix Group of the Gilbert and Ellice Islands Colony. Seen by Heath 31 July, secret. And at the beginning of August Britain agreed to the request. See TNA/PREM/15/38, Letter from D. V. Bendall, the FCO, Willam J. Galloway the US Embassy, 5 August 1970.
28. TNA/PREM/15/718, A note by P. J. Moon, 21 September 1970.
29. TNA/PREM/15/718, PM/70/106 'Facilities for the USA', seen by Heath 21 September 1970 (parts retained), signed by Home.
30. TNA/PREM/15/718, Annex 'Facilities made available to the United States Force and Information exchange, co-operative, reciprocal, shared and joint-planning arrangements' (pieces of which is retained).
31. Ibid.
32. Baylis, *Anglo-American*, p. 165.
33. TNA/PREM/15/718, Annex 'Facilities made available to the United States Force and Information exchange, co-operative, reciprocal, shared and joint-planning arrangements' (pieces of which is retained).
34. TNA/PREM/15/213, Letter to Carrington from Heath, 25 October 1970, secret.
35. TNA/PREM/15/35, Letter from A. R. M. Jaffray, MoD, W. S. Ryrie, PS Chancellor of the Exchequer, 4 November 1970, with Lord Carrington's proposed text for the debate on Defence White Paper. Attached; Defence Debate – House of Lords, Thursday 5 November 1970.
36. NARA/RG 59, Lot file Records relating to the UK 1962–74, Entry 5603, Box 3, FN 4 Agreements incl. Burden Sharing AD – 70 etc. 1971, Office Memorandum, 18 October 1971, to: S/PC – M. Goldstein, from US NATO – George Vest, subject: Study of UK-US Relations: Working Paper No. 5.
37. NARA/RG 59, Lot file Records relating to the UK 1962–74, Entry 5603, Box 3, FN 4 Agreements incl. Burden Sharing AD – 70 etc. 1971 Confidential, London Embassy, 18 October 1971, to: Mortimer D. Goldstein, Esq, S/PC at State in DC, from Robert J. Murray – Political-Military Attache.
38. S. Duke, *The Elusive Quest for European Security: From EDC to CFSP* (Basingstoke and New York: Macmillan, 2000), pp. 55–56.
39. Heuser, *Nuclear Mentalities?* p. 108.
40. Bluth, 'British-German' p. 24.
41. TNA/PREM/15/788, 'Minute from the Prime Minister to Sir Burke Trend'.
42. Heuser, *NATO*, p. 159.
43. TNA/PREM/15/788, Brief by Trend for Heath 'European Defence Co-operation', 6 November 1970.
44. TNA/PREM/15/788, European Defence Co-operation – Paper by the FCO for Discussion with the Prime Minister and Defence Secretary, 1970 with cover below.
45. TNA/PREM/15/788, Record of tête-à-tête conversation between the Secretary of State for Defence and M. Michel Debré on Friday, 20 November 1970.
46. TNA/PREM/15/788, 'Minute from the Prime Minister to Sir Burke Trend'.
47. TNA/PREM/15/788, Anglo-French Collaboration, 15 February 1971.

48. Heath, *The Course*, p. 488.
49. NARA/HAK/box 63, Message Department of State, 15 December 1970. US–British consultations on the use of nuclear weapons, including US weapons used in anti-submarine warfare and currently located in Great Britain.
50. TNA/PREM/15/787, Telegram from the Hague, No. 139, 21 April 1971.
51. TNA/PREM/15/788, Message from Trend to Heath 'European Defence Co-operation', 23 February 1971.
52. TNA/PREM/15/788, A memorandum from Home to Heath, 'Anglo-French Defence Collaboration and European Defence Co-operation', 3 March 1971.
53. TNA/PREM/15/788, A memorandum from Trend to Heath, 'Anglo-French Defence Collaboration', 4 March 1971.
54. Seldon, 'The Heath Government in History', p. 65.
55. TNA/PREM/15/788, A memorandum from Trend to Heath, 'Anglo-French Defence Collaboration', 4 March 1971.
56. Ibid.
57. TNA/PREM/15/1359, Letter from Solly Zuckerman to Heath, 17 July 1970.
58. TNA/PREM/15/1359, A note from R. T. A. to Heath, 19 July 1970.
59. Bluth, 'British-German Defence Relations', p. 11.
60. TNA/PREM/15/787, A note from Home to Heath, PM/71/43, 'Anglo-French Nuclear Defence Collaboration', 19 April 1971.
61. Winand, *Eisenhower*, pp. 312–313.
62. TNA/PREM/15/787, A note from Home to Heath, PM/71/43, 'Anglo-French Nuclear Defence Collaboration', 19 April 1971, secret.
63. T. Terriff, *The Nixon Administration and the Making of US Nuclear Strategy* (Itacha and London: Cornell University Press, 1995), pp. 19–20, 41–42.
64. NARA/NSSM 123 in box H-182 NSSM – 123 2 of 2, Top Secret, 25 Mar 1971, from: the Deputy Secretary of Defense, to: HAK, on US-UK Nuclear Relations.
65. NARA/NSSM 123 in box H-182 NSSM – 123 2 of 2, Top Secret, from: HAK, to Sec State, Sec Def, Director CIA, 17 April 1971, subject: US-UK Nuclear Relations.
66. NARA/NSSM 123 in box H-182 NSSM – 123 2 of 2, Memorandum for Eliot, 4 June 1971, from Jeanne W. Davis Staff Secretary, subject: Due Date for Response to NSSM 123.
67. NARA/NSSM 123 in box H-182 NSSM – 123 2 of 2, Top Secret, Urgent, 10 July 1971, Memorandum for HAK, from: Helmut Sonnenfeldt, subject NSSM 123: US-UK Nuclear Relations.
68. TNA/PREM/15/787, Telegram from Cromer, No. 1466, 29 April 1971.
69. TNA/PREM/15/787, Letter from Sir Burke Trend, Cabinet Office, to Denis Greenhill, the FCO, 3 May 1971.
70. TNA/PREM/15/787, Note for the Record, a meeting with Trend, Greenhill, Thomson, R. T. Armstrong and Heath, 3 May.
71. N. Ashton, *Kennedy, Macmillan and the Cold War: The Irony of Interdependence* (Basingstoke: Palgrave Macmillan, 2002), p. 148.
72. TNA/PREM/15/1272, Letter from the FCO to P. J. S. Moon, 10 Downing Street, 15 April 1971.
73. TNA/PREM/15/1272, A note to Heath, 16 April 1971, seen by Heath 18 April.

74. TNA/PREM/15/787, Note for the Record, a meeting with Trend, Greenhill, Thomson, R. T. Armstrong and Heath, 3 May.
75. TNA/PREM/15/787, Telegram from Home to Cromer, No. 1352, 'US/French Nuclear Collaboration', 12 May 1971.
76. TNA/PREM/15/1272, Telegram from Washington to the FCO, No. 1608, 10 May 1971, seen by Heath 13 May.
77. TNA/PREM/15/787, A note from Soames to Home, 'Anglo-French Defence Co-operation', 9 June 1971.
78. TNA/PREM/15/1272, Telegram from Washington to the FCO, No. 1608, 10 May 1971, seen by Heath 13 May.
79. NARA/RG 59 Lot file Records relating to the UK 1962–74, Entry 5603, Box 3, FN 4 Agreements incl. Burden Sharing AD –70 etc 1971, Confidential To Mr Armistead I. Selden, Jr, Principal Deputy Assistant Secretary, International Security Affairs, Department of Defense from Mr George S. Springsteen, Deputy Assistant, Secretary for European Affairs 6/21/71 – Reciprocal Defense procurement from UK.
80. TNA/PREM/15/1272, Telegram to FCO (Flash), No. 1876, 1 June 1971.
81. TNA/PREM/15/1272, Handwritten note, 2 June 1971, seen by Heath same day.
82. NARA/NSSM 123 in box H-182 NSSM – 123 2of 2, Top secret, Memorandum for the President, from: HAK, subject: US-UK Nuclear Relations.
83. Ibid.
84. NARA/NSSM 123 in box H-182 NSSM – 123 2of 2, Top Secret, NSSM 123 US-UK Nuclear Relations – Analytical Summary.
85. NARA/NSSM 123 in box H-182 NSSM – 123 2of 2, Top secret, NSDM, to: Sec State, Sec Def, The Chairman Joints Chiefs of Staff, subject: US-UK Nuclear Relations.
86. NARA/NSSM 123 in box H-182 NSSM – 123 2of 2, Top Secret, NSSM 123 US-UK Nuclear Relations – Analytical Summary.
87. Ashton, *Kennedy*, pp. 167–168, 180–183.
88. NARA/NSSM 123 in box H-182 NSSM – 123 2of 2, Top Secret, NSSM 123 US-UK Nuclear Relations – Analytical Summary.
89. TNA/PREM/15/1272, Memorandum from Trend to Heath, 'The Kissinger Visit', 28 June 1971, seen by Heath 29 June, secret.
90. Ibid.
91. Ibid. and TNA/PREM/15/37, Summary of Discussion following the Defence Secretary's presentation of NATO strategy to the Prime Minister on Wednesday 25 November 1970, Secretary of State's Office, 26 November 1970.
92. TNA/PREM/15/787, Draft Letter from HM Ambassador in Washington to Dr Kissinger, approved by Heath.
93. Bluth, 'British-German', pp. 17–18, 22.
94. Heuser, *NATO*, p. 105; and TNA/PREM/15/787, Letter from R. J. Andrew, the MoD, to R. T. Armstrong, 6 May 1971.
95. TNA/PREM/15/787, Handwritten note to Heath, 25 January 1972, seen by Heath same day.
96. TNA/PREM/15/389, 'Brief for Meeting between Prime Minister and M Debré: 22 September, 1971'.
97. TNA/PREM/15/389, Meeting between the Defence Secretary and the French Minister of Defence at the Ministry of Defence on 22 September 1971.

98. NARA/59 State Department box 2657, Pol UK-US 2-8-71 Top Secret, 7 December 1971, from: Martin J Hillenbrand Ass Sec Bureau of European Affairs, Memorandum for Mr Henry A. Kissinger, subject: Briefing the British Regarding Our Special Defense Programs with the French. It was in fact vaguely reminiscent of the nuclear trio that de Gaulle had proposed in 1958.

99. TNA/PREM/15/787, For Heath by Trend, draft brief above, about 'Anglo-French Nuclear Co-operation' and the US, 28 January.

100. TNA/PREM/15/787, Note from Burke Trend to Heath 'Anglo-French Nuclear Collaboration', 17 February 1972, seen by Heath 18 February.

101. TNA/PREM/15/787, Anglo-French Nuclear Co-operation, general aims, Brief 1972.

102. TNA/PREM/15/787, A note from R. Press to Sir Burke Trend, 'US/French Nuclear Talks', 16 February 1972.

103. TNA/PREM/15/1272, Telegram from Washington to the FCO, No. 1560, 5 May 1971, seen by Heath 6 May.

104. TNA/PREM/15/787, Letter from R. J. Andrew, the MoD, to Lord Bridges, 'US/French Nuclear Talks', 17 February 1972, seen by Heath 19 [?] February.

105. TNA/PREM/15/787, Telegram from Soames, No. 230, 17 February.

106. TNA/PREM/15/904, Record of part of a conversation between the Prime Minister and the President of the French Republic at Chequers at 10.30 a.m. on Sunday 19 March 1972.

107. Heath, *The Course*, pp. 361–362.

108. TNA/PREM/15/904, Record of part of a conversation between the Prime Minister and the President of the French Republic at Chequers at 10.30 a.m. on Sunday 19 March 1972.

109. Ibid.

110. Giauque, *Grand Designs*, p. 111.

111. TNA/PREM/15/904, Record of part of a conversation between the Prime Minister and the President of the French Republic at Chequers at 10.30 A.M. on Sunday 19 March 1972.

112. Ibid.

113. Ibid.

114. TNA/PREM/15/787, Letter from C. T. E. Ewart-Biggs, British Embassy Paris, to C. N. Rose, the FCO, 19 April 1972, secret. The adviser was Pierre Juillet.

115. TNA/PREM/15/787, A note on a meeting between Heath and the French Ambassador M. De Courcel, 30 May 1972, secret.

116. TNA/PREM/15/788, A note from C. C. C. Tickell 'European Defence Co-operation', 22 June 1972.

117. Duke, *The Elusive Quest*, p. 55.

118. TNA/PREM/15/1357, A note from Soames, to Carrington, 18 July 1972, seen by Heath, 22 July, top secret.

119. TNA/PREM/15/1359, A memorandum from Trend to Heath, 16 June 1972.

120. Ibid.

121. TNA/PREM/15/787, Brief; The scope for possible cooperation between the British and French strategic nuclear forces.

122. TNA/PREM/15/1379, 'Strategic Nuclear Options', 2 November 1972.

123. TNA/PREM/15/1278, Meeting between Defence Secretary and US Secretary of Defense, 27 October, 1972.

124. TNA/PREM/15/1379, 'Strategic Nuclear Options', 2 November 1972.
125. TNA/PREM/15/1359, A memorandum from Trend to Heath, 16 June 1972.
126. TNA/DEFE/5/192/45, MoD, Chiefs of Staff Committee, 'The Rationale for the United Kingdom Strategic Nuclear Deterrent Force', 25 April 1972.
127. TNA/PREM/15/789, Memorandum [with above] 'European Defence and British Defence Policy – Memorandum by the Secretary of State for Defence', 3 November 1972.
128. Ibid.
129. Ibid.
130. TNA/PREM/15/789, A memorandum from Trend to Heath, 'European Defence and British Defence Policy'.
131. TNA/PREM/15/1359, Extract from Note of a Meeting of Ministers, 14 November 1972.
132. Ibid.
133. Ibid.
134. TNA/PREM/15/711, Paper on Implications for Anglo-United States Relations of Britain's European Policies attached to letter from FCO to No. 10, Prime Minister's Visit to Washington, 8 December 1970.
135. TNA/PREM/15/1359, Extract from Note of a Meeting of Ministers, 14 November 1972.
136. TNA/PREM/15/789, A memorandum from Trend to Heath, 'European Defence and British Defence Policy'.
137. TNA/PREM/15/789, Note of a Meeting Ministers held at 10 Downing Street on Wednesday 14 November 1972.
138. Bluth, 'British-German', p. 26.
139. TNA/PREM/15/789, Note of a Meeting Ministers held at 10 Downing Street on Wednesday 14 November 1972.
140. TNA/PREM/15/1359, Extract from Note of a Meeting of Ministers, 14 November 1972.
141. TNA/PREM/15/1357, A memorandum to Lord Bridges, 'Anglo/French Nuclear Collaboration', 21 November 1972, seen by Heath 25 November.
142. Ibid.
143. TNA/PREM/15/789, Note of a Meeting Ministers held at 10 Downing Street on Wednesday 14 November 1972.
144. Heuser, *NATO*, pp. 106–110; and Heuser, *Nuclear Mentalities?* pp. 106–109.
145. TNA/PREM/15/1357, Letter from R. J. Andrew, the MoD, to Lord Bridges, 9 January 1973.
146. TNA/PREM/15/789, Note of a Meeting Ministers held at 10 Downing Street on Wednesday 14 November 1972.
147. TNA/PREM/15/1357, Chief of Defence staff Admiral Hill-Norton 'Conversation with M. Debré 12 December, 1972'.
148. TNA/PREM/15/1357, Letter from R. J. Andrew, the MoD, to Lord Bridges, 9 January 1973, seen by Heath same day.
149. TNA/FCO/82/293, Brief for Washington 'European Defence', 17 January 1973, secret.
150. Ibid.
151. Ibid.
152. TNA/PREM/15/1359, Record of a Discussion at Camp David on Friday 1 February 1973, 'British Nuclear Deterrent'.

153. Ibid.
154. NARA/59, State Subj Num Files 1970–73, Box 2649, Pol 7 UK 1-1-73, Telegram unclassified, Feb 73, subject: Heath visit to Washington – London Times Reports that British Received Assurances of Nuclear Defense Exchanges.
155. TNA/PREM/15/1357, Message from R. T. A. to Robert Andrew, the MoD, 28 March 1973.
156. Heuser, *NATO*, p. 160.
157. TNA/PREM/15/1357, Letter from C. M. Rose, the FCO, to Lord Bridges, 31 March 1973.
158. TNA/PREM/15/1357, Message from R. T. A. to Robert Andrew, the MoD, 28 March 1973.
159. S. Berstein and J.-P. Rioux, *The Pompidou Years, 1969–1974* (Cambridge and New York: Cambridge University Press, 2000), p. 88.
160. TNA/PREM/15/1359, Personal Record of a Discussion in the British Embassy, Washington DC on 19 April, 1973.
161. TNA/PREM/15/1359, A memorandum from Trend to Heath 'Discussions with Dr. Kissinger', 24 April 1973.
162. TNA/PREM/15/1360, Extract Record of Meeting Sir B. Trend/Dr Kissinger 10 May 1973.
163. TNA/PREM/15/1357, A note from Denis Greenhill to R. T. Armstrong, 20 May 1973.
164. TNA/PREM/15/1357, Record of a conversation between the Prime Minister and the President of the French Republic at the Elysée Palace, Paris, During the Morning of Monday 21 May 1973.
165. Ibid.
166. Ibid.
167. Ibid.
168. Heuser, *NATO*, p. 161.
169. TNA/PREM/15/1357, Memorandum from Trend to Heath, 'Nuclear Deterrent: Anglo-French Co-operation', 25 May 1973.
170. TNA/PREM/15/1357, Telegram from Heath to Nixon.
171. TNA/PREM/15/1364, Message from Carrington to Heath, 23 May 1973, 'French Nuclear Weapon Tests 1973'.
172. TNA/PREM/15/1357, A note 'The Nuclear Deterrent', 15 June 1973.
173. TNA/PREM/15/1357, 'Transcript of a telegram from Paris to FCO Dated 25 June 1973', seen by Heath 27 June.
174. TNA/PREM/15/1357, Letter from E. E. Tomkins to R. T. A., 2 July 1973.
175. TNA/PREM/15/1360, A memorandum from Trend to Heath, 11 June 1973.
176. TNA/PREM/15/1360, Letter from Carrington to Heath, 13 July 1973.
177. Ibid.
178. TNA/PREM/15/1359, Record of a Discussion at Camp David on Friday 1 February 1973, 'British Nuclear Deterrent'.
179. TNA/PREM/15/1359, A memorandum from Trend to Heath, 5 March 1973.
180. TNA/PREM/15/1359, Letter from R. J. Andrew to Trend, 14 March 1973.
181. Ibid.
182. TNA/PREM/15/1360, Letter from Carrington to Heath, 8 June 1973.
183. TNA/PREM/15/1360, Letter from Carrington to Heath, 17 August 1973.

184. TNA/PREM/15/1360, Letter from Home to Heath, 30 August 1973, advance copy seen by Heath 29 August.
185. Bluth, 'British-German', p. 25
186. TNA/PREM/15/1360, A memorandum from Trend to Heath, 31 August 1973, seen by Heath 1 September.
187. TNA/PREM/15/1360, Notes on a meeting held in the Pentagon at 11:00 hours 29 August 1973.
188. Heuser, *NATO*, p. 76.
189. Terriff, *The Nixon*, pp. 1–2, 48, 228–229, 231, 236.
190. NARA/NSSM 123 in box H-182 NSSM – 123 2 of 2, NSSM 123 US-UK Nuclear Relations – Analytical Summary.
191. TNA/DEFE/5/192/45 MoD, Chiefs of Staff Committee, 'The Rationale for the United Kingdom Strategic Nuclear Deterrent Force', 25 April 1972.
192. Carrington, *Reflect*, pp. 262–264.
193. TNA/PREM/15/2093, Record of part of a conversation between the Prime Minister and the President of the French Republic at Chequers during the later afternoon of Friday, 16 November 1973.
194. Ibid.
195. TNA/PREM/15/2040, Memorandum from C. D. Wiggin to Mr Cable 'Defence and France – Note in Conversation with Monsieur Gergorin in Brussels on 11 December'.
196. TNA/PREM/15/2093, Record of part of a conversation between the Prime Minister and the President of the French Republic at Chequers during the later afternoon of Friday, 16 November 1973.
197. Ibid.
198. NARA/NSSM 123 in box H-182, NSSM – 123 2 of 2; Secret, Memorandum for the President, 17 December 1973, from Kenneth Rush – subject: Continuation of Certain Provisions of the US-UK Agreement for Cooperation on the Use of Atomic Energy for Mutual Defense Purposes.
199. Baylis, *Anglo-American*, p. 182.
200. Heuser, *NATO*, p. 160.

4. Anglo-American Policy Towards European Integration and the Rise of Henry Kissinger

1. Dumbrell, *A Special Relationship*, p. 184.
2. *FRUS, 1969–1976, Vol. 1*, 4. Essay by Henry Kissinger.
3. P. Hennessy, *The Prime Ministers: The Office and its Holders since 1945* (London: Allen Lane, 2000), pp. 350–351.
4. *FRUS, 1969–1976, Vol. 1, Foundations of Foreign Policy*, General introduction 3 June 2003, and introduction to Foundations of Foreign Policy 1969–1972.
5. I. Berlin, *The Proper Study of Mankind: An Anthology of Essays* (London: Chatto & Windus, 1997), p. 437.
6. On Kissinger's rise and influence, see the biographies by Hanhimäki, *The Flawed*; and W. Isaacson, *Kissinger*. For a machiavellian interpretation, see S. Hersh, *The Price of Power: Kissinger in the Nixon White House* (New York: Summit Books, 1983).

7. Dinan, *Europe*, pp. 129–130.
8. J. Ramsden, 'The Prime Minister and the Making of Foreign Policy', in Ball and Seldon (eds), *The Heath Government*, pp. 35–36.
9. Hennessy, *The Prime Ministers*, pp. 336–337, 344–345.
10. Hanhimäki, *The Flawed*, pp. 11–12, 24.
11. TNA/PREM/15/369, Message from C. C. C. Tickell to Sir Con O'Neill, 'President Pompidou and the EEC negotiations', 16 March 1971.
12. TNA/PREM/15/364, Telegram, No. 4, 1 January 1971, 'The United States and Commonwealth Association with the EEC', signed by Home; and D. Hannay (ed.), *Britain's Entry into the European Community: Report by Sir Con O'Neill on the Negotiations of 1970–1972* (London and Portland, Frank Cass, 2000), p. xxi.
13. TNA/PREM/15/364, Telegram, No. 4, 1 January 1971, 'The United States and Commonwealth Association with the EEC', signed by Home.
14. LSE\Seventies, Interview Geoffrey Rippon.
15. TNA/PREM/15/364, Record of private conversation between the Chancellor of the Duchy of Lancaster and the President of the European Commission Foreign and Commonwealth Office, 3 March 1971.
16. TNA/PREM/15/369, Record of Conversation between the Chancellor of the Duchy of Lancaster and the United States and Secretaries of Agriculture and Commerce, Washington, 8 March, 1971, at 09:30 hours.
17. TNA/PREM/15/369, Record of meeting between the Chancellor of the Duchy of Lancaster and the Deputy Under Secretary for Economic Affairs and other State Department Officials, State Department, Washington, 8 March 1971, at 11:30 hours.
18. TNA/PREM/15/369, Record of private conversation between the Chancellor of the Duchy of Lancaster and the Assistant to the President of the United States for National Security Affairs, the White House, Washington, 8 March 1971.
19. TNA/PREM/15/371, Call on the Chancellor of the Duchy of Lancaster by Mr Nathanial D. Samuels, Deputy Under Secretary for Economic Affairs at the State Department, FCO, 26 April 1971.
20. A. Milward, *Politics and Economics in the History of European Union* (London: Oxford University Press, 2005), pp. 99–102.
21. TNA/PREM/15/1540, Extract Record of Conversation Heath Brandt in Germany Thursday 1 March 1973. See also Milward, *Politics*, pp. 79–80, 102–13.
22. Isaacson, *Kissinger*, pp. 356, 474–475; TNA/PREM/15/898 Record of meeting of Heads of Mission from Community posts 3 May 1972.
23. For an opposing view, see G. A. Andrianopoulos, *Western Europe in Kissinger's Global Strategy* (Basingstoke: Macmillan, 1988), pp. 164–165.
24. TNA/PREM/15/1379, Personal Record of a Discussion in the British Embassy, Washington DC on 19 April, 1973.
25. NARA/NSSM 164 in box H-194 National Security Memorandum 164, 'United States Relations with Europe' by Henry Kissinger, 18 November 1972, secret.
26. The National Security Archive, Washington DC Kissinger transcripts 414, 'Memorandum for the President's file' Nixon-Heath meeting, 20 December 1971.

27. TNA/PREM/15/373, Message from Heath to Nixon, April.
28. TNA/PREM/15/371, Extract from Record of PM's meeting with Herr Brandt on 6 May 1971, secret. Brandt suggested making this clear to the British public.
29. TNA/PREM/15/717, Speech by the Prime Minister to the Assembly of the American Bar Association, Grosvenor House, London, 19 July 1971.
30. TNA/PREM/15/711, 'The Visit of the Prime Minister and Secretary of State to Washington 16–18 December, 1970 – Summary', from Ambassador Freeman, seen by Heath 25 January 1971. And Letter from Freeman to Home, 8 January 1971.
31. Dobson, *Anglo-American*, p. 142, footnote p. 181. This story only surface in US press, although John P Dobson refers to it in passing. Dobson's reference is 'H. Brandon, "The Private World of Richard Nixon" *The New York Sunday Times Weekly Review*, 12 November 1972'.
32. Bundy, *A Tangled*, p. 269.
33. TNA/PREM/15/712, Cutting from *New York Times*, 22 October.
34. TNA/PREM/15/712, Note to Heath, 22 October 1971.
35. TNA/PREM/15/712, Memorandum 'Future Relations with the US', from the FCO to P. J. S. Moon, not singed but underlined parts, 3 November.
36. Ibid.
37. TNA/PREM/15/712, Telegram, No. 3360, 11 October 1971, top secret and TNA/PREM/15/712, Telegram from Cromer, response to the one above, No. 3781, 12 November.
38. TNA/PREM/15/712, Telegram from Home to Washington, No. 2879, 12 November.
39. NARA/59, State Subj Num Files 1970–73, Box 2648, Biography and Home's view on major foreign policy issues, secret.
40. Kissinger, *White*, p. 932.
41. W. Hyland, *Mortal Rivals: Superpower Relations from Nixon to Reagan* (New York: Random House, 1987), p. 18.
42. TNA/PREM/15/712, Telegram from Home to Washington, No. 2831, 5 November.
43. TNA/PREM/15/712, Telegram from Cromer, response to the one above, No. 3781, 12 November.
44. TNA/PREM/15/712, Letter from Cromer to Greenhill, 13 October 1971.
45. TNA/PREM/15/712, Telegram from Cromer, response to the one above, No. 3781, 12 November.
46. Ibid.
47. TNA/PREM/15/712, Steering brief, from H. T. A. Overton, 25 November 1971, secret. (2nd draft).
48. TNA/PREM/15/714, Steering brief 'The Prime Minister's main objectives'.
49. TNA/PREM/15/2089, FCO analysis 'IV Supporting Documents – Meeting between the Prime Minister and President Nixon in Bermuda on 21 December, 1971', secret.
50. Kissinger, *White*, pp. 934–935.
51. Ibid., pp. 964–965.
52. M. Crowley, *Nixon in Winter: The Final Revelations* (London: Random House, 1998), pp. 100–101.

53. TNA/FCO/82/183, Letter from H. T. A. Overton, FCO, 7 January 1971, with a copy of US State Department telegram summary of the Summit.
54. TNA/PREM/15/869, Memorandum undated, Spring 1972.
55. TNA/PREM/15/880, A note from R. T. Armstrong to J. A. N. Graham FCO, 27 July 1971.
56. Fry, *The Politics*, pp. 215–216.
57. TNA/PREM/15/880, Letter from the FCO, to P. J. S. Moon, 27 October 1971.
58. TNA/PREM/15/880, Prime Minister's Speech on the Signature of the Treaty of accession, 22 January 1972.
59. Dinan, *Europe*, pp. 141–142.
60. TNA/PREM/15/869, Memorandum undated, Spring 1972.
61. TNA/PREM/15/898, Meeting of heads of Mission from Community posts, 5.15 p.m., 3 May 1972.
62. TNA/PREM/15/869, Memorandum undated, Spring 1972.
63. TNA/PREM/15/904, Record of Conversation between the Prime Minister and the President of the French Republic at Chequers at 5.20 p.m. on Saturday 18 March 1972.
64. TNA/PREM/15/869, Memorandum undated, Spring 1972.
65. TNA/PREM/15/898, Extract, Record of a Conversation held in No. 10 Downing Street between the Prime Minister and the US Secretary of State Mr William P. Rogers at 4.00 p.m. on Thursday, 4 May 1972.
66. TNA/PREM/15/886, Note for the Record, meeting between Dr Sicco Mansholt and Heath, at Chequers 8 October 1972.
67. Dinan, *Europe*, p. 141.
68. TNA/PREM/15/898, A note to Heath, 11 May 1972.
69. Dinan, *Europe*, pp. 142–143, 337.
70. TNA/PREM/15/904, Letter from Nixon to Heath, 29 March 1972.
71. TNA/PREM/15/1529, A memorandum from J. J. B. Hunt to RTA, 12 April 1973.
72. Hanhimäki, *The Flawed*, p. 261. In his memoirs Kissinger regrets the outcome of the Year of Europe initiative, see Kissinger, *Years*, pp. 192–194.
73. Heath, *The Course*, p. 493.
74. Bundy, *A Tangled*, p. 415; and Kissinger, *Years*, p. 130.
75. See C. Hiepel paper unpublished 'Kissinger's "Year of Europe"—a challenge for the EC and the Franco-German relationship'. Paper to be presented at the conference 'Beyond the customs union: the European Community's quest for completion, deepening and enlargement, 1969–1975' in Groeningen.
76. FRUS, *1969–1976, Vol. 1, Foundations of Foreign Policy*, 56. Editorial note (Minutes of NSC meeting; NSC, Secretariat Files, NSC Meeting Minutes, Originals, 1970).
77. Ibid., p. 60. Report by President Nixon to the Congress, Washington, 18 February 1970.
78. TNA/PREM/15/2089, FCO Analysis 'the Year of Europe, III Record of Events', secret, October 1973.
79. US Foreign Policy for the 1970's – The Emerging Structure of Peace – A report to the Congress by Richard Nixon, President of the United States, 9 February 1972, p. 18.

80. TNA/PREM/15/2089, FCO Analysis 'the Year of Europe, III Record of Events', October 1973.
81. TNA/PREM/15/2089, FCO Analysis 'the Year of Europe II Analysis', October 1973.
82. TNA/PREM/15/2089, FCO Analysis 'the Year of Europe III Record of Events', October 1973.
83. *The Financial Times*, 'Trade looms large in Heath-Nixon talks', 23 December 1972, by John Elliott.
84. NARA/WHCF/Whitman box folder EC-CIEP 2of 2, Annex – US-EC Relations An Assessment.
85. Ibid.
86. Ibid.
87. US Foreign Policy for the 1970's – The Emerging Structure of Peace – A report to the Congress by Richard Nixon, President of the United States, 9 February 1972, pp. 18, 20, 22.
88. Hanhimäki, *The Flawed*, p. 260.
89. TNA/PREM/15/1272, Handwritten note to Heath, 16 March 1972.
90. TNA/PREM/15/1273, Talk with Mr Hyland of the White House Staff, by Malcolm Mackintosh, 15 September 1972.
91. TNA/PREM/15/1540, Letter from Cromer to Greenhill, 19 January 1973, probably seen by Heath.
92. TNA/PREM/15/2089, FCO Analysis 'the Year of Europe, III Record of Events', October 1973.
93. TNA/PREM/15/1272, Memorandum from Trend to Heath, 'The Kissinger Visit', 28 June 1971, seen by Heath 29 June.
94. *The Sunday Times*, 'Heath-Nixon talk on US fears about Europe', 3 December 1972, by Henry Brandon.
95. *The Times*, 'US visit by Mr. Heath likely before EEC entry', 1 December 1972, by Fred Emery.
96. *The Sunday Telegraph*, 'Heath poser over Nixon EEC policy', 24 December 1972.
97. NARA/NSC/box 942 Secret, Memorandum for the President, from: William P. Rogers, subject: The Heath visit, Thursday February 1 and Friday February 2 at Camp David. Brief.
98. TNA/FCO/82/301, Comments on the official visit to Washington of the Prime Minister, by Cromer, 22 February 1973.
99. TNA/PREM/15/2089, FCO Analysis 'the Year of Europe II Analysis', October 1973.
100. TNA/FCO/82/301, Extracts from speech by the Rt. Hon. Edward Heath, British Prime Minister, at the National Press club, Washington, DC, 1 February 1973. In TNA/PREM/15/1542 A note of a meeting between Walt Rostow and Heath, 18 June 1973 at 5.45 p.m.
101. TNA/PREM/15/2089, FCO Analysis 'the Year of Europe II Analysis', October 1973, secret; and TNA/PREM/15/2089 FCO Analysis 'the Year of Europe III Record of Events', October 1973, secret.
102. Heath, *The Course*, p. 492.
103. TNA/PREM/15/1983, A message from RTA to A. A. Acland, 30 July 1973. Then a list of the Kissinger's works was drawn up and recommendations for readings made.

104. Heath, *The Course*, pp. 492–493.
105. Kissinger, *Years*, p. 143.
106. TNA/PREM/15/1992, Telegram from Cromer, No. 1373, 24 April 1973.
107. TNA/PREM/15/1992, Letter from Cromer to Heath, 4 May 1973.
108. TNA/PREM/15/1529, Note for the Record Heath Soames meeting Monday 29 January 1973.
109. See Burr, and Wampler draft paper 'With Friends Like These'; ref Nixon-McCloy meeting 1973 March. Paper to be presented at the conference 'Beyond the customs union: the European Community's quest for completion, deepening and enlargement, 1969–1975' in Groeningen.
110. TNA/PREM/15/2089, FCO Analysis 'the Year of Europe III Record of Events', October 1973.
111. TNA/CAB/164/1232, A note from Trend to Heath, 16 March 1973.
112. TNA/CAB/164/1232, The Next Ten Years in East-West and Trans-Atlantic Relations – Assumptions and questions; and TNA/PREM/15/2089, FCO Analysis 'the Year of Europe III Record of Events' and 'Doc 4, The Next Ten Years in East-West and Trans-Atlantic relations – Summary of Paper Given to Dr. Kissinger on 16 April, 1973', October 1973.
113. TNA/PREM/15/2089, FCO Analysis 'the Year of Europe III Record of Events', October 1973.
114. TNA/CAB/164/1233, Record of a Meeting in the British Embassy, Washington on Thursday, 19 April 1973.
115. Kissinger, *Years*, p. 140.
116. Hennessy, *The Prime Ministers*, p. 350.
117. TNA/CAB/164/1232, The Next Ten Years in East-West and Trans-Atlantic Relations – Assumptions and questions. And TNA/PREM/15/2089, FCO Analysis 'the Year of Europe III Record of Events' and 'Doc 4, The Next Ten Years in East-West and Trans-Atlantic relations – Summary of Paper Given to Dr. Kissinger on 16 April, 1973', October 1973.
118. Ibid.
119. TNA/CAB/164/1233, Personal Record of a Discussion in the British Embassy, Washington DC, on 19 April 1973, by Cromer, 24 April.
120. TNA/PREM/15/2089, FCO Analysis 'the Year of Europe III Record of Events', October 1973, secret.
121. TNA/CAB/164/1233, Record of a Meeting in the British Embassy, Washington on Thursday 19 April 1973; and TNA/PREM/15/2089 FCO Analysis 'the Year of Europe III Record of Events', October 1973, secret.
122. TNA/CAB/164/1233, Record of a Meeting in the British Embassy, Washington on Thursday 19 April 1973.
123. TNA/PREM/15/2089, FCO Analysis 'the Year of Europe III Record of Events', October 1973.
124. P. Winand, 'Loaded Words and Disputed Meanings. The Year of Europe Speech and its Genesis from an American Perspective', in J. van der Harst (ed.), *Beyond the Customs Union: The European Community's Quest for Completion, Deepening and Enlargement, 1969–1975* (Brussels, Paris and Baden-Baden: Bruylant, L. G. D. J and Nomos Verlag, 2007), pp. 297–317.
125. Bundy, *A Tangled*, p. 416.
126. Winand, 'Loaded Words'.

127. Henry Kissinger, *The Troubled Partnership: A Re-appraisal of the Atlantic Alliance* (Garden City: Doubleday, 1966), pp. 242–243.
128. TNA/PREM/15/2089, FCO Analysis 'the Year of Europe II Analysis' and 'Doc No. 6 – Speech by Kissinger 23 April 1973', October 1973.
129. Hanhimäki, *The Flawed*, pp. 348–349. TNA/PREM/15/2089 FCO Analysis 'the Year of Europe II Analysis' and 'Doc No. 6 – Speech by Kissinger 23 April 1973', October 1973.
130. TNA/PREM/15/2089, FCO Analysis 'the Year of Europe III Record of Events', October 1973.
131. TNA/PREM/15/1541, Telegram from Cromer, No. 1370, 23 April 1973, seen by Heath 25 April.
132. Ibid.
133. TNA/PREM/15/1541, Record of a conversation between Heath and Pompidou at the Elyseé Palace, Paris on Monday, 21 May 1973, at 10.00 a.m.
134. TNA/PREM/15/1541, A Memorandum from Trend to Cromer, 2 May 1973, seen by Heath 3 March.
135. TNA/PREM/15/2089, FCO Analysis 'the Year of Europe III Record of Events'.
136. TNA/PREM/15/1541, Extract Record of meeting between Kissinger and Trend, 10 May 1973.
137. TNA/PREM/15/2089, FCO Analysis 'the Year of Europe III Record of Events'.
138. TNA/PREM/15/1541, Record of a conversation between Heath and Pompidou at the Elyseé Palace Paris on Monday, 21 May 1973, at 10.00 a.m.
139. TNA/PREM/15/2089, FCO Analysis 'the Year of Europe III Record of Events'.
140. TNA/PREM/15/1541, Record of a conversation between Heath and Pompidou at the Elyseé Palace, Paris on Monday 21 May 1973, at 10.00 a.m.
141. Ibid.
142. TNA/PREM/15/2089, FCO Analysis 'the Year of Europe III Record of Events'.
143. The National Security Archive, Washington DC Kissinger Transcripts 727, Memcon, Meeting between Kissinger and Jobert, 17 May 1973.
144. TNA/CAB/164/1233, A note from Heath to Trend, 8 June 1973, secret.
145. TNA/PREM/15/2089, FCO Analysis 'the Year of Europe III Record of Events'.
146. Kissinger, *Years*, p. 142.
147. *The Observer*, Article, interview by Kenneth Harris, 24 June 1973.
148. TNA/PREM/15/1542, Note for the Record meeting between Jobert, French Foreign Secretary, and Heath and Home, London, 2 July 1973, 5.00 p.m., secret; and TNA/PREM/15/2089, FCO Analysis 'the Year of Europe III Record of Events'.
149. TNA/PREM/15/1542, Note for the record meeting between Heath and Mr van der Stoel, the Dutch Ambassador, 27 June 1973.
150. TNA/PREM/15/1542, A note of a meeting between Walt Rostow and Heath, 18 June 1973 at 5.45 p.m.
151. TNA/PREM/15/1542, A note from RTA to Heath, 29 June 1973.
152. TNA/PREM/15/1542, Letter from Greenhill to Trend, 4 July 1973, secret.
153. TNA/PREM/15/2089, FCO Analysis 'III Record of Events', October, secret.
154. TNA/PREM/15/1543, Letter from Palliser to J. O. Wright, FCO, 24 July 1973.
155. TNA/PREM/15/1543, Message to Paris, piece.
156. TNA/PREM/15/1543, Telegram from Paris, 31 July 1973.

157. TNA/PREM/15/2089, FCO Analysis 'III Record of Events', October, secret.
158. Kissinger, *Years of Upheaval*, p. 187.
159. TNA/PREM/15/1542, Letter from Greenhill to Trend, 6 July 1973, secret.
160. TNA/PREM/15/2089, FCO Analysis 'III Record of Events', October, secret.
161. TNA/PREM/15/2089, FCO Analysis 'III Record of Events', October, secret.
162. The EPC was an administrative construct from 1970 that built on the effort of Etienne Davignon and his report, the Luxembourg report or Davignon report. It was at tentative step towards greater European political cooperation in terms of harmonization of their foreign policy outlooks rather than fully fledged co-operation. See I. Megan, 'The declaration on European identity of December 1973. The effect of a transatlantic debate and the result of a team spirit among European diplomats', Paper to be presented at the conference Beyond the customs union: the European Community's quest for completion, deepening and enlargement, 1969–1975 in Groeningen.
163. TNA/PREM/15/2089, FCO Analysis 'II Analysis', October, secret.
164. TNA/PREM/15/1542, A memo from Acland to Butler, 12 June 1973, seen by Heath 14 June.
165. TNA/PREM/15/1543, Message from Heath to Nixon, 25 July 1973, secret.
166. TNA/PREM/15/1543, Message from Nixon to Heath, 26 July 1973, secret.
167. TNA/FCO/82/311, Letter from Sykes to Brimelow, 13 August 1973, secret.
168. TNA/CAB/164/1235, Record of meeting at 3.00 p.m. on 30 July 1973, at the White House, Washington DC.
169. Ibid.; Kissinger focus was on the three major states, and he virtually ignored the minor EC members. See Winand, 'Loaded Words.'
170. TNA/PREM/15/2089, FCO Analysis 'III Record of Events', October, secret.
171. NARA/WHCF/Whitman box folder EC-CIEP 2 of 2, Annex – US-EC Relations An Assessment.
172. The National Security Archive, Washington DC Kissinger transcripts 776, Memcon, Kissinger's meeting with Robert Gaja, Roberto Ducci, and Egidio Ortona, 16 July 1973.
173. TNA/CAB/164/1235, Record of meeting at 3.00 p.m. on 30 July 1973, at the White House, Washington DC.
174. Kissinger, *The Troubled*, pp. 242–243.
175. TNA/CAB/164/1235, Record of meeting at 3.00 p.m. on 30 July 1973, at the White House, Washington DC.
176. Kissinger, *Years*, p. 193.
177. TNA/PREM/15/2089, FCO Analysis 'II Analysis', October.
178. TNA/PREM/15/1544, Draft Message from Heath to Nixon, August.
179. TNA/CAB/164/1235, Message from Heath to Nixon, August 1973.
180. W. Cromwell, *The United States and the European Pillar: The Strained Alliance* (Basingstoke: Macmillan, 1992), p. 84; and TNA/CAB/164/1235, Record of meeting at 3.00 p.m. on 30 July 1973, at the White House, Washington DC.
181. TNA/FCO/82/310, Record of Conversation between Home and Kissinger US Monday 24 September.
182. Kissinger, *Years*, p. 192.
183. Ibid., p. 194.
184. See Burr and Wampler, 'With Friends Like These'.
185. See Hiepel, 'Kissinger's "Year of Europe" '.

186. TNA/PREM/15/2089, FCO Analysis 'the Year of Europe II Analysis', October 1973.
187. TNA/FCO/82/309, Kissinger's Address to the Pilgrim Society, Official Text, The US Embassy London, 13 December 1973.
188. TNA/PREM/15/2069, Note for the Record, 3 March 1974.
189. Campbell, *Edward*, pp. 617–618.
190. Hanhimäki, *The Flawed*, p. 350.
191. TNA/PREM/15/2089, FCO Analysis 'the Year of Europe II Analysis', October 1973.
192. TNA/PREM/15/1983, Dr Kissinger's ideas, Memorandum with a reference from the end of Kissinger's book *A World Restored*, probably underlined in the margin by Heath, end of July 1973.

5. Anglo-American Diplomacy: Cold War Warriors and Détente

1. White, *Britain, Détente*, pp. 179, 182.
2. Roth, *Heath*, p. 219.
3. Hill and Lord, 'The Foreign Policy of the Heath Government', p. 309.
4. Ibid.
5. White, *Britain, Détente*, pp. 124–125. See also J. P. D. Dunbabin, *International Relations since 1945: A History in Two Volumes* (London and New York: Longman, 1994), pp. 305–306.
6. White, *Britain, Détente*, p. 127.
7. Heath, *Old World*, p. 58.
8. Duke, *The Elusive*, pp. 57–58; and Dinan, *Europe*, pp. 99–100.
9. Dinan, *Europe*, p. 143.
10. Hill and Lord, 'The Foreign Policy of the Heath Government', pp, 292–297.
11. Heath, *The Course*, pp. 115, 156.
12. TNA/PREM/15/64, Memorandum from Greenhill to Home, June 1970.
13. NARA/59, State Subj Num Files 1970–73 box 2648, POL 7 5-1-70, Bio. on Alec Douglas-Home.
14. NARA/59, State Department Subject Numerical Files 70–73 box 2658, Pol 1 UK-US 1973, Telegram secret, Jul 1970, from Am Embassy, to sec state, – Heath and the threats to the West.
15. TNA/FCO/7/1815 Record of a Meeting between Heath and Nixon, 3 October 1970, top secret.
16. Ibid.
17. NARA/NSC/box 942, Memorandum for the President, from: HAK, subject: Your Meeting with Prime Minister Heath Thursday 17–18 December at Camp David 1970.
18. Roth, *Heath*, p. 196; and Hurd, *An End*, pp. 40–41.
19. TNA/PREM/15/64, Position Paper No. 3 'European Security'.
20. R. L. Garthoff, *Détente and Confrontation: American-Soviet Relations from Nixon to Reagan* (Washington: Brookings Institution, 1985), pp. 107–109.
21. NARA/NSC/box 1023, Memcon Nixon – Prime Minister Wilson 27 January 1970, Secret, Memcon, 27 January 1970, the Oval Office, The President, PM Wilson, Trend, Kissinger.

22. Dunbabin, *International*, 1945, p. 276.
23. Helga Haftendorn, Soutou, George-Henri, Szabo, Stephen S. and Wells Jr., Samuel F. (eds), *The Strategic Triangle: France, Germany and the United States in the Shaping of the New Europe* (Washington DC: Woodrow Wilson Center Press and Baltimore: Johns Hopkins University Press, 2006), p. 24. Introduction.
24. The National Security Archive, Washington DC, Kissinger transcripts 178, Senior Review Group Meeting, Monday, 31 August 1970.
25. TNA/FCO/33/1547, Memorandum from R. W. Jackling, British Ambassador to FGR to Home, 29 June 1970.
26. TNA/FCO/33/1547, Letter from Jackling to Greenhill, 11 November 1970.
27. TNA/FCO/7/1813, Brief 'Ostpolitik, Berlin and European Security', 3 October 1970.
28. H. Haftendorn, 'German Ostpolitik in a Multilateral Setting', in H. Haftendorn (eds), *The Strategic Triangle*, p. 202.
29. TNA/FCO/7/1813, Brief 'Ostpolitik, Berlin and European Security', 3 October 1970.
30. TNA/PREM/15/194, Brief Heath Gromyko meeting October 1970, seen by Heath, 25 October.
31. Ibid.
32. TNA/PREM/15/194, Record of Heath Gromyko meeting, on Wednesday, 28 October at No. 10 Downing Street.
33. Ibid.
34. TNA/PREM/15/194, Record of a conversation between Home and Gromyko at the FCO at 11.00 a.m. on Tuesday, 27 October 1970.
35. NARA/59, State Subj Num Files 1970–73, box 2648, POL 7 5-1-70, Telegram secret, 16 May 1970, from: 'Action' Am Embassy London, subject: Douglas-Home Meetings with Secretary and Under Secretary, discussion.
36. TNA/FCO/7/1828, Record of a meeting between Home and Rogers at Dorney Wood on Saturday, 11 July 1970.
37. TNA/FCO/7/1836, Record of conversation between Home and Rogers at the State Department at 3.20 p.m., 23 September, 1970.
38. NARA/NSC/Box 446, Memorandum for the President, from: HAK, Subject: Your Visit to England, Saturday 3 October 1970.
39. NARA/NSC/Box 941, Fact book on UK.
40. TNA/FCO/7/1815, Record of a Meeting between Heath and Nixon, 3 October 1970.
41. TNA/FCO/7/1814, Secretary of States talks with United States Secretary on 3 October 1970, to Cabinet 6 October.
42. TNA/PREM/15/194, Record of Heath Gromyko meeting, on Wednesday, 28 October at No. 10 Downing Street.
43. NARA/59, State Subj Num Files 1970–73 box 2648 POL 7 5-1-70, Bio. on Alec Douglas-Home, secret.
44. Bundy, *A Tangled*, pp. 116, 120–121.
45. The National Security Archives, Washington D.C. Kissinger transcripts 214, Summary of Conversation – Rockefeller residence, 2 December 1970.
46. NARA/NSC/box 446, Memorandum for the President, from: HAK, Subject: Your Visit to England, Saturday 3 October 1970.

47. TNA/FCO/7/1840, Brief 'East-West Relations' visit of Heath to Washington 17–18 December 1970, 5 December 1970.
48. TNA/FCO/7/1840, Brief 'East-West Relations' visit of Heath to Washington 17–18 December 1970, 1 December 1970.
49. NARA/NSC/box 1024, Memorandum of conversation press Nixon, Heath, Sir Burke Trend and HAK, 17 December 1970.
50. NARA/59, State Department box 2657 Subject Numerical 70–73 Pol UK-US 2-3-70 White House, Memcon, subject: Meeting between President Nixon and Prime Minister Heath, 17 December 1970.
51. TNA/FCO/33/1547, Abstract from Record from Meeting between Heath and Nixon at the White House 17 December 1970.
52. NARA/59, State Department box 2657 Subject Numerical 70–73 Pol UK-US 2-3-70 White House, Memcon, subject: Meeting between President Nixon and Prime Minister Heath, 17 December 1970, The President's Office.
53. NARA/59, State Department box 2657 Subject Numerical 70–73 Pol UK-US 2-3-70 White House, Memcon, subject: Meeting between President Nixon and Prime Minister Heath, 18 December 1970, Camp David.
54. Ibid.
55. NARA/59, State Department box 2657 Subject Numerical 70–73 Pol UK-US 2-3-70 White House, Memcon, subject: Meeting between President Nixon and Prime Minister Heath, 17 December 1970, The President's Office.
56. NARA/59, State Department Subject Numerical Files 70–73 box 2658 Pol 1 UK-US 1973 Airgram secret, 11 February 1971, from: Am Embassy London, subject Annual Assessment for the United Kingdom.
57. Bundy, *A Tangled*, p. 116.
58. Roth, *Heath*, p. 223.
59. Dunbabin, *International*, p. 278.
60. White, *Britain, Détente*, p. 122.
61. Dunbabin, *International*, pp. 278–279.
62. TNA/PREM/15/1218, Memorandum on 'Soviet Strategy', signed J. A. Thomson to Trend, 4 March 1971.
63. TNA/PREM/15/1218, A note from Trend to Moon, 12 March 1971.
64. TNA/PREM/15/1522, A note from Moon to Barrington, FCO, 24 August 1971.
65. TNA/PREM/15/1936, FCO analysis by A. D. Wilson 'Soviet Westpolitik', 30 July 1971. See also Garthoff, *Détente*, pp. 127–128.
66. For an overview of Kissinger and the preparations for SALT see Hanhimäki, *The Flawed*, pp. 128–130.
67. EUI Library \ The Declassified Documents Reference System, DDRS. (Infotrac by Thomson and Gale)\, US files, Memcon, Kissinger Brimelow and others, the FCO, 24 June 1971.
68. NARA/NSC/box 950, folder one Heath Visit Bermuda Dec 1971, 1 of 2 Telegram from London to Rogers, P1QRQPZ, December 1971.
69. C. Keeble, *Britain the Soviet Union and Russia* (Basingstoke: Macmillan, 2000), p. 280.
70. TNA/PREM/15/1935, A note to Heath, 5 October 1971.
71. TNA/PREM/15/1935, Telegram from Soames, No. 1263, 22 October, secret.

72. F. Bozo, 'A French View', in R. Davy (ed.), *European Détente: A Reappraisal* (London: SAGE Publication, 1992).
73. NARA/NSC/box 1024, Memorandum of conversation President Pompidou 24–26 February 1969.
74. H-G. Soutou, 'President Pompidou, Ostpolitik, and the Strategy of Détente', in H. Haftendron (eds), *The Strategic*, pp. 230, 234–235, 239–240, 252.
75. NARA/NSC/box 1024, Memorandum of conversation President Pompidou 24–26 February 1969.
76. NARA/NSC/box 950, folder one Heath Visit Bermuda Dec 1971, 1 of 2, Telegram from London to Rogers, P 081409Z part 2, December 1971.
77. Ibid.
78. TNA/FCO/82/67, Steering Brief Fourth draft, Bermuda, secret.
79. TNA/FCO/82/66, Steering Brief – third draft, Bermuda, secret.
80. Ibid.
81. Bundy, *A Tangled*, pp. 288–289, 536–537.
82. P. Hennessy, *The Prime Ministers*, p. 351.
83. TNA/FCO/73/140, Record of plenary session between the UK and US Delegations, with Heath and Nixon, at 2.30 p.m., Tuesday, 21 December 1971.
84. The National Security Archive, Washington D.C. Kissinger transcripts 414, Memorandum for the President, Nixon-Heath meeting, 20 December 1971.
85. TNA/FCO/44/533, Record of a conversation between Home and Rogers, Bermuda 3.00 p.m., Monday, 20 December 1971.
86. TNA/FCO/73/140, Record of plenary session between the UK and US Delegations, with Heath and Nixon, Tuesday, 21 December 1971.
87. Ibid.
88. NARA/NSC/box 950, Memorandum from Kissinger to Ziegler, time of Bermuda meeting.
89. TNA/FCO/73/140, Record of plenary session between the UK and US Delegations, with Heath and Nixon, Tuesday, 21 December 1971.
90. TNA/FCO/82/71, Press statement 'Bermuda Statement', Tuesday, 21 December 1971.
91. *The Times*, 'America told British entry will change relationship', 21 December.
92. TNA/FCO/44/533, Peter Jenkins, Article 16, December 1971.
93. NARA/NSC/box 950, Heath visit Bermuda folder nr 2 exists folder Heath – Presidential Trip Memorandum for HAK, subject: President-Heath Talks: Themes for a Toast, 10 December 1971.
94. *The New York Times*, 21 December.
95. TNA/FCO/82/71, Bermuda, Heath's press conference, 22 December 1971.
96. TNA/FCO/82/71, Memorandum from T. L. A. Daunt, 'Nixon-Brandt Meeting', 31 December 1971.
97. Soutou, 'President Pompidou', pp. 239–240.
98. TNA/PREM/15/388, Record of Home Schumann meeting, 3.30 p.m. 11 November 1971.
99. Bozo, 'A French view', p. 66.
100. Soutou, 'President Pompidou', pp. 233, 238–239, 241.
101. Haftendorn, 'German Ostpolitik', pp. 221–222; C. Bluth, 'A West German View' in Davy (ed.), *European Détente: A Reappraisal* (London: SAGE Publication, 1992), pp. 44–45.

102. TNA/PREM/15/388, Record of Home Schumann meeting, 11 November 1971.
103. Ibid.
104. TNA/PREM/15/904, Record of conversation between Heath and Pompidou at Chequers, 10.30 a.m. Sunday, 19 March 1972.
105. TNA/PREM/15/1555, Record of a conversation between Heath and Pompidou at the Elysée Palace, Morning of Monday, 21 May 1973.
106. TNA/PREM/15/904, Record of conversation between Heath and Pompidou at Chequers, 10.30 a.m. Sunday, 19 March 1972.
107. TNA/PREM/15/1269, Letter from Heath to Nixon, 22 March 1972.
108. TNA/PREM/15/1274, A telegram, message from Heath to Nixon, May.
109. TNA/PREM/15/1274, Extract of a record of a conversation between Heath and Rogers at 4.00 p.m. on Thursday, 4 May 1972.
110. TNA/PREM/15/1269, Telegram from Heath to Nixon, 10 May 1972.
111. TNA/PREM/15/1274, Letter from Annenberg to Heath with oral message from Nixon in connection to Rogers' visit, 3 May 1972, message.
112. TNA/PREM/15/1274, Telegram from Cromer, Washington, No. 1060, 24 March 1972, seen by Heath 31 March.
113. TNA/PREM/15/1276, Steering brief, 1st revise, Rogers visit 4 May 1972.
114. TNA/PREM/15/1274, Telegram from Cromer, Washington, No. 1060, 24 March 1972, seen by Heath 31 March.
115. TNA/PREM/15/1274, Telegram from Cromer, Washington, No. 1677, 'for eyes of Prime Minister only', 17 May, top secret.
116. Bundy, *A Tangled*, pp. 347, 526.
117. TNA/PREM/15/1269, Telegram from Nixon to Heath, 8 June 1972.
118. TNA/PREM/15/1269, Message from Heath to Nixon, after 8 June.
119. TNA/PREM/15/1522, Brief for meeting with M. Pinay, 13 January 1972.
120. TNA/PREM/15/1522, Part of Heath Brandt talks, 1 May 1972.
121. TNA/PREM/15/1219, Extract from Brezhnev's speech to the 15 Soviet Trade Unions Congress on 20 March 1972, NATO.
122. TNA/PREM/15/1219, Telegram from Helsinki, No. 495, 31 August 1972.
123. TNA/PREM/15/1219, Extract from Heath's interview with the DPA on 18 March 1972.
124. TNA/PREM/15/1219, A note from No. 10 to Alexander, the FCO, 4 September 1972
125. TNA/PREM/15/1219, Extract from Brezhnev's speech to the 15th Soviet Trade Unions Congress on 20 March 1972, NATO.
126. TNA/PREM/15/1219, A telegram from Moscow to the FCO, 6 September 1972.
127. T. Yamamoto, 'Détente or Integration: EC Response to Soviet Policy Change Towards the Common Market, 1970–1975', *Cold War History*, Vol. 7, No. 1 (2007), pp. 75–94.
128. The Rise of Détente, Document Reader for the International Conference, 'NATO, the Warsaw Pact and the Rise of Détente, 1965–72, 19720905_Memo, Memorandum for Mr Kissinger from Sonnenfeldt, 5 September 1972.
129. White, *Britain, Détente*, p. 122.
130. NARA/NSSM 164 in box H-194 Secret, Memorandum for HAK, from: Walter J. Stoessel Jr Ass Sec for European Affairs, NSSM 164 US Relations with Europe.

131. TNA/FCO/82/196, FCO Brief Kissinger's UK visit after Moscow trip, 14–15 September 1972.
132. TNA/FCO/82/182, Record of Discussion between Trend and Kissinger and later also Heath, summary, 14 September 1972.
133. TNA/FCO/82/196, Record of a conversation between Home and Kissinger at the FCO 4.00 p.m. on 14 September 1972.
134. TNA/PREM/15/1365, A memorandum from C. C. C. Tickell to Brimelow, 'Anglo/American talks on CSCE and MBFR – 22 September', 27 September 1972.
135. Ibid.
136. TNA/FCO/82/195, Record of Conversation between Home and Rogers at 3.00 p.m. on Wednesday 27 September 1972, secret.
137. TNA/FCO/82/195, Record of meeting between Home and Kissinger at the White House, 29 September 1972, secret.
138. Ibid.
139. TNA/FCO/82/196, Home talk with Nixon at the White House 4.00 p.m. Friday, 29 September 1972.
140. TNA/FCO/82/195, Extract from CM 72 Meeting held 6 October.
141. TNA/PREM/15/1269, A telegram, message from Nixon to Heath sent on 7 November received the day after.
142. Heath, *The Course*, p. 392.
143. NARA/NSSM 164 in box H-194 Secret, Memorandum for HAK, from: Walter J. Stoessel Jr Ass Sec for European Affairs, NSSM 164 US Relations with Europe.
144. TNA/FCO/82/199, Piece, Mr Rogers's speech to the NATO Council, NATO.
145. TNA/PREM/15/2093, Memorandum 'The External Relations of the European Community: Relations with the Soviet Union and Eastern Europe', 30 November 1972.
146. TNA/FCO/82/182, Message from J. A. N. Graham, British Embassy Washington, to H. T. A. Overton, North America Department, FCO, 18 December 1972.
147. *The Financial Times*, 'How America sees the outside world', David Watt, 17 November 1972.
148. TNA/FCO/82/199, Letter from Cromer to Robert Armstrong, 8 December 1972.
149. TNA/FCO/82/199, Letter from Robert Armstrong to Antony Acland, 12 December 1972.
150. NARA/NSC/Box 942, Memorandum from Kissinger to Nixon, 31 January 1973.
151. Ibid.
152. NARA/NSSM 164 in box H-194, Secret from: CIA 3 January 1973, Memorandum for HAK, subject: NSSM 164 US Relations with Europe.
153. NARA/NSC/Box 942, Memorandum from Kissinger to Nixon, 31 January 1973.
154. Bundy, *A Tangled*, pp. 361–363.
155. TNA/FCO/82/291, Draft steering brief Washington meeting 1973, secret.
156. TNA/FCO/82/293, Brief Nixon Heath talks on 1 and 2 February 1973 'European defence', 17 January 1973, secret.
157. Ibid.

158. Ibid.
159. TNA/FCO/82/301, Record of Conversation between Home and Rogers at 2.45 p.m. Thursday 1 February 1973 at the State Department.
160. TNA/PREM/15/1365, Record of Discussion between Heath and Nixon 'East-West Relations', at 4.00 p.m. Friday, 2 February 1973 Camp David.
161. TNA/PREM/15/1365, Record of Discussion between Heath and Nixon 'Hullabaloo', at 4.00 p.m. Friday, 2 February 1973 Camp David.
162. TNA/FCO/82/301, Record of a conversation between Home and Rogers at 10.30 on Thursday 1 February 1973.
163. TNA/PREM/15/1365, Record of Discussion between Heath and Nixon 'Hullabaloo', at 4.00 p.m. Friday, 2 February 1973 Camp David.
164. TNA/FCO/82/301, Record of a conversation between Home and Rogers at 10.30 on Thursday, 1 February 1973.
165. TNA/PREM/15/1365, Record of Discussion between Heath and Nixon 'East-West Relations', 2 February 1973 Camp David.
166. TNA/FCO/82/301, Record of a conversation between Home and Rogers, 1 February 1973.
167. TNA/PREM/15/1365, Record of Discussion between Heath and Nixon 'East-West Relations', 2 February 1973 Camp David.
168. TNA/FCO/82/301, Letter from Heath to Trudeau, 15 February 1973.
169. TNA/PREM/15/1804, Brief by the FCO, probably winter 1972–1973.
170. K. Hamilton, 'Britain, France and America's Year of Europe, 1973', in *Diplomacy and Statecraft*, Vol. 17 (2006), pp. 871–895.
171. TNA/PREM/15/1365, Record of Discussion between Heath and Nixon 'Hullabaloo', at 4.00 p.m. Friday, 2 February 1973 Camp David.
172. TNA/FCO/82/301, Letter from Heath to Trudeau, 15 February 1973.
173. TNA/FCO/82/301, Telegram from Home to Tokyo, No. 130, 14 February 1973.
174. TNA/FCO/82/307, Record of a meeting between Home and Kissinger at 3.00 p.m. on Thursday 10 May 1973 at the FCO.
175. TNA/FCO/82/301, Memorandum from H. T. A. Overton analysis of the Heath-Nixon meeting, 12 February 1973.
176. NARA/NSC/Box 942, Memorandum from Kissinger to Nixon, 31 January 1973, secret; and NSC/Box 942 Memorandum from Rogers to Nixon, undated.
177. TNA/FCO/82/301, Extract from Cabinet Meeting, 8 February 1973.
178. Dinan, *Europe*, p. 145.
179. TNA/PREM/15/1555, Record of a conversation between Heath and Pompidou at the Elysée Palace, Morning of Monday, 21 May 1973.
180. Ibid.
181. Yamamoto, 'Détente or Integration', pp. 12–13.
182. Hamilton, 'Britain, France and America's Year', p. 883.
183. TNA/PREM/15/1365, Record of Conversation at the British Embassy, Washington 5 March 1973.
184. TNA/PREM/15/1522, A letter from Graham, FCO, to Roberts, No. 10, 6 September 1971.
185. NARA/NSC/Box 942, Memorandum from Kissinger to Nixon, 31 January 1973, secret.
186. Ibid.

187. The National Security Archive, Washington DC, Kissinger transcripts 786, Memcon, Kissinger and NSC deputies, 7 August 1973.
188. TNA/PREM/15/1936, Extract of a record of a Heath meeting with West German Cabinet 29 May 1973.
189. TNA/PREM/15/1934, A note from Heath to Trend, 10 May 1973.
190. TNA/PREM/15/1934, Memorandum from P. Cradock to Trend, 18 May 1973, seen by Heath 26 May.
191. TNA/PREM/15/1936, Telegram from Cromer 'eyes of the Prime Minister only', No. 2150, 10 July 1973.
192. Bundy, *A Tangled*, pp. 433–436.
193. Cromwell, *The United*, pp. 86–87.
194. Bundy, *A Tangled*, pp. 442–443.
195. Hamilton, 'Britain, France and America's Year', p. 884. For a contrasting opinion, see Bundy, *A Tangled*, p. 436.
196. Cromwell, *The United*, pp. 86–87; Heath, *The Course*, p. 619; and Hill and Lord, 'The Foreign Policy of the Heath Government', p. 301.
197. Bundy, *A Tangled*, pp. 440–441; and Hanhimäki, *The Flawed*, pp. 315–316.
198. TNA/PREM/15/1382, A note from Heath to Bridges, 28 October 1973.
199. Kissinger, *Years*, p. 713.
200. Hanhimäki, *The Flawed*, p. 316.
201. Bundy, *A Tangled*, p. 436.
202. NARA/59, State Department box 2657 Subject Numerical 70–73 Pol UK-US 1-1-73 Secret – EXDIS, to: The Secretary (state), from: EUR George S. Springsteen Acting, October 1973, Possible Pressure Points on the UK, – dissatisfaction with UK as an Ally.
203. TNA/PREM/15/1382, A note from Bridges to Heath, 29 November, seen by Heath 2 December.
204. TNA/PREM/15/1564, Record of a conversation between Heath and Brandt at Chequers, 5.00 p.m. Saturday, 6 October 1973.
205. TNA/PREM/15/1380, Memorandum from C. C. C. Tickell to Mr Wiggin, 'Anglo-American talks on MBFR', 12 October 1973.
206. NARA/59, State Dept Subject Numerical 70–73, Box 2649 Pol 7 UK 2-11-73 Secret Memorandum for Mr Kissinger, 20 September 1973, from: Helmut Sonnenfeldt, subject: Your Meeting with Sir Alec Douglas Home – Year of Europe and defense issues.
207. Ibid.
208. TNA/PREM/15/1380, Memorandum from C. C. C. Tickell to Mr Wiggin, 'Anglo-American talks on MBFR', 12 October 1973.
209. TNA/PREM/15/2093, Letter from Ellliot, FCO, to Bridges, 15 November 1973.
210. TNA/PREM/15/2093, Record of a conversation at Chequers, after luncheon on Friday, 16 November 1973.
211. TNA/FCO/82/307, Note for the Record, Heath's Dinner with American Correspondents on 28 November 1973.
212. TNA/FCO/82/309, Kissinger's Address to the Pilgrim Society, Official Text, The US Embassy London, 13 December 1973.
213. Cromwell, *The United*, pp. 92–93.
214. TNA/FCO/82/309, Brief talks between Home and Kissinger, 12 December 1973.

215. Hamilton, 'Britain, France and America's Year', p. 891.
216. TNA/PREM/15/1564, Letter from Acland, the FCO, to Bridges, 5 October 1973.
217. Cromwell, *The United*, p. 89.
218. *The Times*, 'Without coal, you're dead Mr Nixon tells envoy', 18 January 1974.

Conclusion

1. PREM/15/2089, FCO analysis of the Year of Europe.
2. *The Times*, 'Mr Wilson must realize the "special relationship"' is dead, 12 August 1974, by Louis Heren.

Bibliography

Archival sources

United Kingdom

From the National Archives, Kew, London

Prime Minister's papers (PREM/13, PREM/15)
Cabinet papers (CAB/134, CAB/164)
Foreign and Commonwealth Office (FCO/7, FCO/33, FCO/44, FCO/73, FCO/82)
Defence papers (DEFE/5, DEFE/19)

*Archives, the London School of Economics. From the British Library
of Political and Economic Science (BLPES), London*

LSE\Hetherington, Alastair Hetherington papers
LSE\BOAPAH, British Oral Archive of Political and Administrative History,
    Interviews: The Lord Home, Lord Schakelton, Lord Carr
LSE\Seventies, The Seventies Archive: Interviews: Sir Con O'Neill, Lord Home,
    Harold Wilson, Geoffrey Rippon, Tony Barber

Newpapers and magazines

Press Cuttings at the British Library Newspaper Library at Colindale, and the
Royal Institute of International Affairs:

*The Christian Science Monitor, The Daily Express, The Daily Telegraph, The
Guardian, The Financial Times, The Observer, The New York Times, The New York
Sunday Times Weekly Review, The Times, The Sunday Times*

United States

National Archives, US, NARA, College Park, Maryland

State Department:

Lot File, RG 59 Record relating to the UK 1962–74, State Department
Subject Numeric files 70–73, State Department

Nixon Presidential Materials Project:

Henry A. Kissinger files (HAK)
National Security Council files (NSC)
National Security Decision Memorandums (NSDM)
National Security Study Memoranda (NSSM)

White House Central Files; Whitman papers, Houthakker papers (WHCF)
White House Subject Files, Ziegler papers (here also some from the economic
advisers) WHSF, and WHCF

European Union

The Historical Archives of the European Union
Oral History Project *Voices on Europe* the EUI Archives

Published and printed sources

Cooper, Karen, *I Challenge Ted Heath Pamphlet* (Vaxholm: 1974).
The Declassified Documents Reference System (DDRS, Infotrac by Thomson and
Gale. Internet source).
The National Security Archive, at George Washington University (The Kissinger
Transcripts, Internet Source).
Documents on British Policy Overseas, DBPO, Series III:

– *I Britain and the Soviet Union. 1968–72* (London: HMSO, 1997; Routledge, 1998)
– *II The Conference on Security and Cooperation in Europe, 1972–75* (London:
HMSO, 1997; Routledge, 1998)
– *III Détente in Europe, 1972–76* (London: HMSO, 1997; Frank Cass, 2001)

Government White Paper; *The United Kingdom and the European Communities* (Her
Majesty's Stationary Office, July 1971).
Foreign Relations of the United States, Nixon-Ford Administrations, 1969–1976:

– *Volume I. Foundations of Foreign Policy, 1969–1972*, by Louis J. Smith, David
H. Herschler (eds), David S. Patterson (general ed.) (Washington, DC: United
States Government Printing Office, 2003).
– *Volume III. Foreign Economic Policy, 1969–1973, International Monetary Policy,
1969–1972*, by Bruce F. Duncombe (ed.), David S. Patterson (general ed.)
(Washington, DC: United States Government Printing Office, 2001).

'From EU 6 to EU-25: External Trade Trends with Main Partner Countries', in
External and intra-European Union Trade – Statistical Yearbook, Data 1958–2005
(Eurostat: Office for Official Publications of the European Communities, 2006).
Heath, Edward, *Old World, New Horizons: Britain, Europe, and the Atlantic Alliance*
(Cambridge, Mass.: Harvard University Press, 1970).
Kandiah, Michael D., *The Rise and Fall of the Bretton Woods System*, ICBH Wit-
ness seminar held 30 September 1994, St Peter's College, Oxford, chaired by
Lord Skidelsky, papers by Leslie Presnell and Brian Tew (London: Institute of
Contemporary British History, c2002).
Kaniah, Michael David, ' "The Heath Government" – Witness Seminar in Con-
temporary Record', *The Journal of Contemporary British History*, Vol. 9, No. 1
(Summer, 1995), pp. 188–219.

Nixon, Richard M., *U.S. Foreign Policy for the 1970's: Building for Peace.* Report to Congress (Washington: Government Printing Office, 1972).

Nixon, Richard M., *U.S. Foreign Policy for the 1970's: The Emerging Structure of Peace.* Report to Congress (Washington: Government Printing Office, 1972).

Nixon, Richard M., 'Introduction' by Thomas Helen, *The Presidential Press Conferences* (London: Heyden, 1978).

The Rise of Détente, *Nato the Warsaw Pact and the Rise of Deténte, 1965–1972.* For the International Conference 26–28 September 2002 (Dobbiacco/Toblach. CD-ROM).

Strober, Gerald S., and Hart Strober, Deborah, Interviews. *Nixon: An Oral History of his Presidency* (New York: HarperCollins, 1994).

Symposium, 'The Trade Unions and Fall of the Heath Government', *Contemporary Record*, Vol. 2, No. 1 (Spring, 1988), pp. 36–46.

Working Paper 43, recollections by Sir Christopher Audland and Sir Roy Denman (for Manchester University, History Faculty, 1998–1999, published in 2000).

Memoirs and diaries

Benn, Tony, *Office Without Power: Diaries 1968–1972* (London: Hutchinson, 1988).

Brandon, Henry, *The Retreat of American Power* (London: Bodley head, 1973).

Brandt, Willy, *My Life in Politics* (London: Penguin, 1993).

Burns, Arthur F., *Reflections of an Economic Policy Maker: Speeches and Congressional Statements: 1969–1978* (Washington, DC: AEI, cop., 1978).

Carrington, Peter, *Reflect on Things Past: The Memoirs of Lord Carrington* (London: Collins, 1988).

Castle, Barbara, *The Castle Diaries, 1964–1976* (London: Macmillan, 1990).

Connally, John, with Mickey Herskowitz, *In History's Shadow: An American Odyssey* (New York: Hyperion books, 1993).

Ehrlichman, John, *Witness to Power: The Nixon Years* (New York: Simon and Schuster, 1982).

Garthoff, Raymond L., *A Journey Through the Cold War: A Memoir of Containment and Coexistence* (Washington DC: Brookings Institution Press, 2001).

Haldeman, H. R., *The Haldeman Diaries: Inside the Nixon White House* (New York: G. P. Putman's, 1994).

Haldeman, H. R., *The Ends of Power* (London: Star, 1978).

Healey, Denis, *The Time of My Life* (London: Michael Joseph, 1989).

Heath, Edward, *The Course of My Life: My Autobiography* (London: Hodder & Stoughton, 1998).

Home of the Hirsel, Alec Douglas-Home, *The Way the Wind Blows: An Autobiography by Lord Home* (London: Collins, 1976).

Hurd, Douglas, *An End to Promises – Sketch of a Government 1970–74* (London: Collins, 1979).

Hyland, William G., *Mortal Rivals Superpower Relations from Nixon to Reagan* (New York: Random House, 1987).

Jenkins, Roy, *A Life at the Centre* (London: Macmillan, 1991).

Johnson, Lyndon B., *The Vantage Point: Perspectives of the Presidency, 1963–1969* (London: Weidenfeld & Nicolson, 1971).

Kissinger, Henry, *White House Years* (London: Weidenfeld & Nicolson, 1979).
Kissinger, Henry, *Years of Upheaval* (London: Weidenfeld & Nicolson, 1982).
Maudling, Reginald, *Memoirs* (London: Sidgwick & Jackson, 1978).
Nitze, Paul H., with Smith, Ann M., and Rearden, Steven L., *From Hiroshima to Glasnost: At the Center of Decision* (New York: G. Weidenfeld, 1989).
Nixon, Richard M., *The Memoirs of Richard Nixon* (New York: Grosset & Dunlap, 1978).
Roll, Eric, *Crowded Hours: An Autobiography* (London: Faber and Faber, 1985).
Safire, William, *Before the Fall: An Inside View of the Pre-Watergate White House*, 2nd ed. (Brunswick, NJ: Transaction Publishers, 2005).
Schaetzel, Robert J., *The Unhinged Alliance: America and the European Community* (New York: Harper & Row, 1975).
Shultz, George P., *Turmoil and Triumph: My Years as Secretary of State* (New York: Scribner, 1993).
Whitelaw, William, *The Whitelaw Memoirs* (London: Headline Book Publishing, 1990).
Wilson, Harold, *The Labour Government 1964–1970 – A Personal Record* (London: Weidenfeld & Nicolson, 1971).

Articles and reviews

Boyce, Robert, 'Review of "Using Europe, Abusing the Europeans: Britain and European Integration, 1945–63"', *The American Historical Review*, Vol. 104, No. 4 (October 1999), p. 1379.
Campbell, John, 'Postwar Premiers "Edward Heath"', *Contemporary Record*, Vol. 2, No. 2 (Summer, 1988), pp. 27–28.
Dobson, Alan, 'The Years of Transition: Anglo-American Relations 1961–1967', *Review of International Studies*, Vol. 16 (1990), pp. 239–258.
Ellison, James, 'Defeating the General: Anglo-American Relations, Europé and the NATO Crisis of 1966', *Cold War History*, Vol. 6, No. 1 (February 2006), pp. 85–111.
Ellison, James, 'Separated by the Atlantic: The British and de Gaulle, 1958–1967', *Diplomacy and Statecraft*, Vol. 17 (2006), pp. 853–870.
English, R. and Kenny, M., 'British Decline of the Politics of Declinism', *British Journal of Politics and International Relations*, Vol. 1, No. 2 (June 1999), pp. 252–266.
Hamilton, Keith, 'Britain, France and America's Year of Europe, 1973', *Diplomacy and Statecraft*, Vol. 17 (2006), pp. 871–895.
Heath, Edward, 'Realism in British Foreign Policy', *Foreign Affairs*, Vol. 48, Nos. 1–4 (October [in No. 1] 1969–July 1970), pp. 39–51.
Heath, Edward, 'European Unity over the Next ten Years: From Community to Union', *International Affairs (Royal Institute of International Affairs 1944–)*, Vol. 64, No. 2 (Spring, 1988), pp. 199–207.
Heuser, Beatrice, 'European Strategists and European Identity: The Quest for a European Nuclear Force (1954–1967)', *Journal of European Integration History*, Vol. 1, No. 2 (1995), pp. 199–207.
Holt, Andrew, 'Lord Home and Anglo-American Relations 1961–1963', *Diplomacy and Statecraft*, Vol. 16, No. 4 (December 2005), pp. 699–722.

Kissinger, Henry A., 'Reflections on a Partnership: British and American Attitudes to Post war Foreign Policy', *International Affairs*, Vol. 58, No. 4 (Autumn, 1982), pp. 571–587.

Louis, William Roger, 'Presidential Address: "The Dissolution of the British Empire in the Era of Vietnam"', *The American Historical Review*, Vol. 107, No. 1 (February 2002), pp. 1–25.

Ludlow, N. Piers, 'Book review of "The United Kingdom and the European Community, Volume 1: The Rise and Fall of a National Strategy"', *Cold War History*, Vol. 4, No. 3 (April 2004), pp. 183–185.

Newton, Scott, 'Using Europe, Abusing the Europeans: Britain and European, 1945–1963. Review', *The Journal of Modern History*, Vol. 71, No. 3 (September 1999), pp. 696–698.

Parr, Helen, 'Saving the Community: The French Response to Britain's Second EEC Application in 1967', *Cold War History*, Vol. 6, No. 4 (November 2006), pp. 425–455.

Paul, Kathleen, '"British Subjects" and "British Stock": Labour's Post War Imperialism', *The Journal of British Studies*, Vol. 34, No. 2 (April 1995), pp. 233–276.

Pine, Melissa, 'British Personal Diplomacy and Public Policy: The Soames Affair', *The Journal of European Integration History*, Vol. 10, No. 2 (2004), pp. 59–76.

Pocock, J. G. A., 'History and Sovereignty: The Historiographical Response to Europeanization in Two British Cultures', *Journal of British Studies*, Vol. 31 (October 1992), pp. 358–389.

Reynolds, David, 'A "Special Relationship"? America, Britain and the International Order since the Second World War', *International Affairs (Royal Institute of International Affairs 1944–)*, Vol. 62, No. 1 (Winter, 1985–86), pp. 1–20.

Reynolds, David, 'Rethinking Anglo-American Relations', *International Affairs (Royal Institute of International Affairs 1944–)*, Vol. 65, No. 1 (Winter, 1988–89), pp. 89–111.

Rasmussen, Jorgen, and McCormick, James M., 'British Mass Perceptions of the Anglo-American Special Relationship', *Political Science Quarterly*, Vol. 108, No. 3 (Autumn, 1993), pp. 515–541.

Roy, Rajarshi, 'The Battle for Bretton Woods: America, Britain and the International Financial Crisis of October 1967–March 1968', *Cold War History*, Vol. 2, No. 2 (January 2002), pp. 33–60.

Schenk, Catherine, 'Sterling, International Monetary Reform and Britain's Application to Join the European Economic Community in the 1960s', *Contemporary European History*, Vol. II, No. 3 (2002), pp. 345–369.

Soutou, Georges-Henri, 'Le Président Pompidou et les relations entre les Etats-Unis et l'Europe', *Journal of European Integration History*, Vol. 6, No. 2 (2000), pp. 111–146.

Tomlinson, J., 'Inventing "Decline": The Falling Behind of the British Economy in the Postwar Years', *The Economic History Review*, New Series, Vol. 49, No. 4 (November 1996), pp. 731–757.

Ullman, Richard H., 'The Covert French Connection', *Foreign Policy*, No. 75 (Summer, 1989), pp. 3–33.

Wallace, William, 'Foreign Policy and National Identity in the United Kingdom', *International Affairs (Royal Institute of International Affairs 1944–)*, Vol. 67, No. 1 (January 1991), 65–80.

Vaïsse, Maurice, *Les 'relations speciales' franco-americaines au temps de Richard Nixon et Georges Pompidou* in Relations Internationales, No. 119 (2004).

Yamamoto, Takeshi, 'Détente or Integration? EC Response to Soviet Policy Change Towards the Common Market, 1970–1974', *Cold War History*, Vol. 7, No. 1 (February 2007), pp. 75–94.

Young, John. W., 'Britain and "LBJ's War", 1964–68', *Cold War History*, Vol. 2, No. 3 (April 2002), pp. 84–86.

'Z', 'The Year of Europe', *Foreign Affairs*, Vol. 52 (January 1974), pp. 237–248.

Unpublished thesis and articles

Burr, William, and Wampler, Robert A., ' "With Friends Like These . . .", – Kissinger, the Atlantic Alliance and the Abortive "Year of Europe", 1973–1974' [Draft verion], 22 August 2002, later published in Di Nolfo, E., Nuti, L., and Guderzo, M. (eds), *NATO, the Warsaw Pact and the Rise of Détente, 1965–1972* (Stanford: Stanford University Press, 2006).

Coppolaro, Lucia, 'The United States and EEC Enlargement (1969–1973): Reaffirming the Atlantic Framework', presented at the conference organized by the European Union Liaison Committee of Historians, *Beyond the Customs Union: The European Community's Quest for Completion, Deepening and Enlargement, 1969–1975* at the University of Groningen, 27–29 October 2005.

Hiepel, Caludia, 'Kissinger's "Year of Europe" – A Challenge for the EC and the Franco-German Relationship', presented at the conference organized by the European Union Liaison Committee of Historians, *Beyond the Customs Union: The European Community's Quest for Completion, Deepening and Enlargement, 1969–1975* at the University of Groningen, 27–29 October 2005.

Megens, Ine, 'The Declaration on European Identity of December 1973. The Effect of a Transatlantic Debate and the Result of a Team Spirit Among European Diplomats', presented at the conference organized by the European Union Liaison Committee of Historians, *Beyond the Customs Union: The European Community's Quest for Completion, Deepening and Enlargement, 1969–1975* at the University of Groningen, 27–29 October 2005.

Rossbach, Niklas, Paper to be published [preliminary titles]. 'Britain's Reappraisal of Détente', to be published in Aubourg, V., and Scott-Smith, G. (eds), *Atlantic, Euratlantic, or Europe-America? The Atlantic Community and the European Idea from Kennedy to Nixon* (Paris: Soleb).

Rossbach, Niklas, Paper to be published in an edited volume [preliminary title]. 'Edward Heath's Vision and the Year of Europe' (Brussels: Peter Lang).

Roy, Rajarshi, *The Battle of the Pound: The Political Economy of Anglo-American Relations 1964–1968* (Unpublished thesis, The Department of International History, The London School of Economics and Political Science, November 2000).

Winand, Pascaline, 'Loaded Words and Disputed Meanings: The Year of Europe Speech and its Genesis from an American Perspective', in van der Harst, J. (ed.), *Beyond the Customs Union: The European Community's Quest for Completion, Deepening, and Enlargement, 1969–1975* (Brussels, Paris and Baden-Baden: Bruylant, L.G.D.J and Nomos Verlag, 2007), pp. 297–317.

Yamamoto, Takeshi, 'Uncontrollable Multilateral European Détente: Euro-Canadian resistance to the US/Soviet agreement 1972–73', paper presented

at the First Joint Graduate Student Conference on International History and
European Integration History, in Florence, 4–5 May 2006.

Books and chapters in books

Alderson, Kai, and Hurrell, Andrew (eds), *Hedley Bull on International Society*
(Basingstoke and London: Macmillan, 2000).

Aldcroft, Derek H., and Oliver Michael J., *Exchange Rate Regimes in the Twentieth
Century* (Cheltenham, UK and Northampton, MA: Edward Elgar, 1998).

Aldrich, Robert J., *The Hidden Hand: Britain, America and Secret Cold War Intelligence*
(London: John Murray, 2001).

Aliber, Robert Z., *The New International Money Game*, 6th ed. (Chicago: The
University of Chicago Press, 2002).

Ambrose, Stephen, *Nixon, Vol. I, The Education of a Politician, 1913–1962* (New
York: Simon and Schuster, 1987).

Ambrose, Stephen, *Nixon, Vol. II, The Triumph of a politician 1962–1972* (New York:
Simon & Schuster, 1989).

Ambrose, Stephen, *Nixon, Vol. III, Ruin and Recovery, 1973–1990* (New York: Simon
& Schuster, 1991).

Alford, B. W. E., *British Economic Performance 1945–1975* (Cambridge, New York,
USA: Cambridge University Press, 1995).

Andrianopoulos, Gerry Argyris, *Western Europe in Kissinger's global strategy* (Basingstoke: Macmillan, 1988).

Aron, Raymond, *The Imperial Republic – The United States and the World 1945–1973*
(London: Weidenfeld & Nicolson, 1975)

Ashton, Nigel, *Kennedy, Macmillan and the Cold War – The Irony of Interdependence*
(Basingstoke: Palgrave Macmillan, 2002).

Baker, David, and Seawright, David (eds), *Britain For and Against Europe – British
Politics and the Question of European Integration* (Oxford: Clarendon Press, 1998).

Ball, Stuart, and Seldon, Anthony (eds), *The Heath Government 1970–1974 – A
Reappraisal* (London and New York: Longman, 1996).

Barber, James, and Reed, Bruce (eds) assisted by Gibbs, Richard and Masterton,
Robert, *European Community – Vision and Reality* (London: Croom Helm London
in association with the Open University, 1973).

Bartlett, Christopher J., *The Long Retreat: A Short History of British Defence Policy,
1945–70* (London: Macmillan, 1972).

Bartlett, Christopher J., *'The Special Relationship': A Political History of Anglo-
American Relations since 1945* (Harlow: Longman, 1992).

Barnett, Correlli, *The Audit of War: The Illusion and Reality of Britain as a Great
Nation* (London: Macmillan, 1986).

Baylis, John, *Anglo-American Defence Relations 1939–1984 – the Special Relationship*
(London and Basingstoke: Macmillan, 1984).

Bell, Coral, *The Debatable Alliance – An Essay in Anglo-American Relations*, Issued
under the auspices of the Royal Institute of International Affairs (London, New
York and Toronto: Oxford University Press, 1964).

Bell, Coral, *The Diplomacy of Détente: The Kissinger Era* (London: Martin Robertson,
1977).

Beloff, Max, *The Future of British Foreign Policy* (London: Secker & Warburg,
1969).

Beloff, M. 'The Special Relationship: An Anglo-American Myth', in M. Gilbert (ed.), *A Century of Conflict 1850–1950: Essays for A. J. P. Taylor* (London: Hamsih Hamilton, 1966).

Beloff, Nora, *The General Says No: Britain's Exclusion from Europe* (London: Penguin Books, 1963).

Bell, P. M. H., *France and Britain 1940–1994: The Long Separation* (London and New York: Longman, 1997).

Berlin, Isaiah, *The Proper Study of Mankind: An Anthology of Essays* (London: Chatto & Windus, 1997).

Bernstein, George L., *The Myth of British Decline – The Rise of Britain since 1945* (London: Pimlico, 2004).

Berstein, Serge, and Rioux, Jean-Pierre, *The Pompidou Years, 1969–1974* (Cambridge, UK, New York, NY, USA: Cambridge University Press, 2000).

Bluth, Christoph, 'A West German View', in Davy Richard (ed.), *European Détente: A Reappraisal* (London, SAGE Publication, 1992).

Bluth, Christoph, 'British-German Defence Relations, 1950–80', in Karl Kaiser and John Roper (eds), *British German Defence Co-operation: Partners within the Alliance* (Jane's and London: The Royal Institute of International Affairs, 1988).

Bluth, Christoph, *Britain, Germany and Western Nuclear Strategy*, 2nd ed (Oxford: Clarendon Press, 1998).

Boardman, Robert, and Groom, A. J. R. (eds), *The Management of Britain's External Relations* (London and Basingstoke: Macmillan, 1973).

Booker, Christopher, and North, Richard, *The Great Deception – A Secret History of the European Union* (London and New York: Continuum, 2003).

Boyd, Laslo, V., *Britain's Search for a Role* (Westamead, and Lexington, Mass., US: Saxon House – Lexington Books, 1975).

Bozo, Frédéric, *Two Strategies for Europe: De Gaulle, the United States, and the Atlantic Alliance* (Lanham, Md.: Rowman & Littlefield, 2001).

Bozo, Frédéric, 'The NATO Crisis of 1966–1967: A French Point of View', in Haftendorn *et al.* (eds), *The Strategic.*

Burk, Kathleen, and Stokes, Melvyn (eds), *The United States and the European Alliance since 1945* (Oxford and New York: Berg, 1999).

Bull, Hedley, *The Anarchical Society – A Study of Order in World Politics* (London and Basingstoke, 1977).

Bull, Hedley, and Louis, W. M. Roger, *The 'Special Relationship' – Anglo-American Relations since 1945* (Oxford: Clarendon Press, 1986).

Bundy, Willliam P., *A Tangled Web – The Making of Foreign Policy in the Nixon Presidency* (London and New York: I.B. Tauris, 1998).

Busch, Peter, *All the Way with JFK? – Britain, the US, and the Vietnam War* (Oxford and New York: Oxford University Press, 2003).

Butterfield, Herbert, *The Whig Interpretation of History* (Harmondsworth: Penguin, 1973).

Cairncross, Alec, *Managing the British Economy in the 1960s: A Treasury Perspective* (Basingstoke: Macmillan, 1996).

Cairncross, Alec, 'The Postwar Years 1945–77', in R. Floud and D. McCloskey (eds), *The Economic History of Britain since 1700*. Vol. 2 (Cambridge: Cambridge University Press, 1981).

Cairncross, Alec, 'Economic Policy and Performance', in R. Floud and D. McCloskey (eds), *The Economic History of Britain since 1700, Volume 3: 1939–1992*, 2 Rev. ed. (Cambridge: Cambridge University Press, 1994).

Cairncross, Alec, 'The Heath government and the British economy', in Ball and Selsdon (eds), *The Heath Government*.

Campbell, John, *Edward Heath – A Biography* (London: Jonathan Cape, 1993).

Camps, Miriam, *European Unification in the Sixties, From the Veto to the Crisis* (Oxford: Oxford University Press, 1967).

Catterall, Peter, Conclusion: The Ironies of 'Successful Failure', in Daddow (ed.), *Harold Wilson*.

Childs, David, *Britain since 1945: A Political History* (London: Routledge, 1992).

Clark, Ian, *Nuclear Diplomacy and the Special Relationship: Britain's Deterrent and America, 1957–1962* (Oxford: Oxford University Press, 1994).

Clark, J. C. D., *Our Shadowed Present: Modernism, Postmodernism and History* (London: Atlantic, 2004).

Clarke, Peter, and Trebilcock, Clive (eds), *Understanding Decline: Perceptions and Realities of British Economic Performance* (Cambridge: Cambridge University Press, 1997).

Coopey, R., Fielding, S., and Tiratsoo, N. (eds), *The Wilson Governments, 1964– 1970* (London, New York: Pinter Publishers, 1993).

Coleman, Jonathan, *A 'Special Relationship'?: Harold Wilson, Lyndon B. Johnson and Anglo-American Relations 'At the Summit', 1964–68* (Manchester: Manchester University Press, 2004).

Conze, Eckart, *Die gaullistische Herausforderung – Die deutsch-französischen in der amerikanischen Europapolitik 1958–1963* (München: R. Oldenbourg Verlag, 1995).

Costigliola, Frank, *France and the United States: The Cold Alliance since World War II* (New York: Twayne Publishers, 1992).

Craig, Gordon A., and Loewenheim, Francis L., *The Diplomats 1939–1979* (Princeton, NJ: Princeton University Press, 1994).

Croft, Stuart, *The End of Superpower – British Foreign Office Conceptions of a Changing World, 1945–51* (Aldershot: Dartmouth, 1994).

Cromwell, William C., *The United States and the European Pillar: The Strained Alliance/William C. Cromwell* (Basingstoke: Macmillan, 1992).

Crowley, Monica, *Nixon off the Record: His Candid Commentary on People and Politics* (New York; Random House, 1996).

Crowley, Monica, *Nixon in Winter: The Final Revelations* (London: I.B. Tauris 1998).

Daddow, Oliver J., *Britain and European Integration since 1945 – Historiographical Perspectives on Integration* (Manchester and New York: Manchester University Press, 2004).

Daddow, Oliver J. (ed.), *Harold Wilson and European Integration – Britain's Second Application to Join the EEC* (London; Portland, Or.: Frank Cass, 2003).

Dallek, Robert, *Partners in Power – Nixon and Kissinger* (New York: HarperCollins, 2007).

Danchev, Alex, 'Special Pleading', in Burk, Kathleen and Stoker, Melvyn (eds), *The United States and the European Alliance since 1945* (Oxford, UK; New York, NY: Berg, 1999).

Deighton, Anne (ed.), *Building Postwar Europe, National Decision-makers and European Institutions, 1948–63* (London: Macmillan, 1995)

Deighton, Anne, 'Britain and Three Interlocking Circles', in Varsori, A. (ed.), *Europe, 1945–1990s: The End of an Era?* (London: Macmillan in association with the Mountbatten Centre for International Studies, University of Southampton, 1995).

Deighton, Anne, and Milward, Alan S. (eds), *The European Economic Community, 1957–1963: Widening, Deepening, Acceleration* (Baden-Baden: Nomos, 1999).

Deighton, 'The Labour Party, Public Opinion, and the "Second Try" in 1967', in Daddow (ed.), *Harold Wilson*.

Dell, Edmund, *The Chancellors: A History of the Chancellors of the Exchequer, 1945–90* (London: HarperCollins, 1996).

Dimbleby, David, and Reynolds, David, *An Ocean Apart – The Relationship Between Britain and America in the Twentieth Century* (London: Hodder & Stoughton, 1988).

Dinan, Desmond, *Europe Recast: A History of European Union* (Boulder, London: Lynne Rienner, 2004).

Dinan, D. 'Building Europe: The European Community and the Bonn-Paris-Washington Relationship, 1958–1963', in H. Haftendorn *et al.* (eds), *The Strategic*.

Dobson, Alan P., *The Politics of the Anglo-American Economic Special Relationship* (Brighton: Wheatsheaf Books Ltd, 1988).

Dobson, Alan P., *Anglo-American Relations in the Twentieth Century* (London: Routledge, 1995).

Dockrill, Saki, *Britain's Retreat from East of Suez: The Choice Between Europe and the World?* (Basingstoke, New York: Palgrave Macmillan, 2002).

Duchêne, François, *Jean Monnet: The First Statesman of Interdependence* (New York: Norton, 1994).

Duke, Simon, *The Elusive Quest for European Security: From EDC to CFSP* (London: Macmillan, 2000).

Dumbrell, John, *A Special Relationship – Anglo-American Relations in the Cold War and After* (Basingstoke: Macmillan Press Ltd, 2001).

Dunbabin, J. P. D., *International Relations Since 1945: A History in Two Volumes* (London, New York: Longman, 1994).

Ellison, James, *The United States, Britain and the Transatlantic Crisis, Rising to the Gaullist Challenge, 1963–68* (Basingstoke: Palgrave Macmillan, 2007).

Ellison, James, *Threatening Europe – Britain and the Creation of the European Community, 1955–58*. In association with Institute of Contemporary British History (Basingstoke and London: Macmillan Press Ltd, 2000).

Ellison, James, 'Dealing with the de Gaulle: Anglo-American Relations, NATO and the Second Application', in Daddow (ed.), *Harold Wilson*.

Elman, Colin, and Fendius Elman, Miriam (eds), *Bridges and Boundaries – Historians, Political Scientists and the Study of International Relations* (Cambridge, Mass., and London: The MIT Press, 2001).

Feinstein, C. H., 'The End of Empire and the Golden Age', in Clark and Trebilcock (eds), *Understanding*.

Ferguson, Niall (ed.), *Virtual History: Alternatives and Counterfactuals* (New York: Basic Books, 1999).

Finney, Patrick (ed.), *Palgrave Advances in International History* (Basingstoke: Palgrave, Macmillan, 2005).

Fischer, David Hackett, *Historians' Fallacies: Toward a Logic of Historical Thought* (London: Routledge and K. Paul, 1971).

Frankel, Joseph, *British Foreign Policy 1945–1973* (London, New York and Toronto: For The Royal Institute of International Affairs by Oxford University Press, 1975).

Fry, Geoffrey Kingdon, *The Politics of Decline: An Interpretation of British Politics from the 1940s to the 1970s* (New York: Palgrave Macmillan, 2005).

Gaddis, John Lewis, *The Landscape of History – How Historians Map the Past* (New York and Oxford: Oxford University Press, 2002).

Gardiner, Patrick, *The Philosophy of History* (London and New York: Oxford University Press, 1974).

Garthoff, Raymond L., *Détente and Confrontation: American-Soviet Relations from Nixon to Reagan* (Washington DC: Brookings Institution, 1985).

Gavin, Francis J., *Gold, Dollars and Power: The Politics of International Monetary Relations, 1958–71* (Chapel Hill, London: University of North Carolina Press, 2004).

Giauque, Jeffrey Glenn, *Grand Designs and Visions of Unity: The Atlantic Powers and the Reorganization of Western Europe, 1955–1963* (Chapel Hill: University of North Carolina Press, 2002).

Geddes, Andrew, *The European Union and British Politics* (Basingstoke, New York: Palgrave Macmillan, 2004).

George, Stephen (ed.), *Britain and the European Community – The Politics of Semi-Detachment* (Oxford: Clarendon Press, 1992).

George, Stephen, *An Awkward Partner – Britain in the European Community.* 2nd ed. (Oxford: Oxford University Press, 1996).

Gillingham, John, *European Integration, 1950–2003: Superstate or New Market Economy?* (Cambridge, New York: Cambridge University Press, 2003).

Grant, Wyn, *Economic Policy in Britain* (Basingstoke, New York: Palgrave, 2002).

Greenwood, Sean, *Britain and European Cooperation since 1945* (Oxford: Blackwell, 1992).

Greenwood, Sean, *Britain and the Cold War, 1945–1991* (Basingstoke: Macmillan, 2000).

Grosse, Alfred, *The Western Alliance: European-American Relations since 1945* (New York: Vintage Books, 1982).

Guderzo, Massimiliano, *Interesse nazionale e responsabilità globale: gli Stati Uniti, l'Alleanza atlantica e l'integrazione europea negli anni di Johnson 1963–69* (Florence: Aida, 2000).

Halliday, Fred, *The Making of the Second Cold War* (London: Verso, 1983).

Haftendorn, Helga, Soutou, George-Henri, Szabo, Stephen S., and Wells Jr, Samuel F. (eds), *The Strategic Triangle: France, Germany and the United States in the Shaping of the New Europe* (Washington DC and Baltimore: Woodrow Wilson Center Press and Johns Hopkins University Press, 2006).

Haftendorn, Helga, 'German Ostpolitik in a Multilateral Setting', in Haftendorn *et al.* (eds), *The Strategic.*

Hanhimäki, Jussi, and Westad, Odd Arne (eds), *The Cold War: A History in Documents and Eyewitness Accounts* (Oxford, New York: Oxford University Press, 2003).

Hanhimäki, Jussi, *The Flawed Architect: Henry Kissinger and American Foreign Policy* (Oxford, New York: Oxford University Press, 2004).

Hannay, Sir David (ed.), *Britain's Entry into the European Community – Report by Sir Con O'Neill on the Negotiations of 1970–1972* (London and Portland, Or: Whitehall History Publishing in association with Frank Cass, 2000).

Harbutt, Fraser J., *The Cold War Era* (Malden, Mass.: Blackwell, 2002).

Haslam, Jonathan, *The Soviet Union and the Politics of Nuclear Weapons in Europe, 1969–87 – The Problem of the SS-20* (Basingstoke and London: Macmillan Press Ltd, 1989).

Hathaway, Robert M., *Ambiguous Partnership – Britain and America, 1944–1947* (New York: Columbia University Press, 1981).

Hathaway, Robert M., *Great Britain and the United States: Special Relations since World War II* (Boston: Twayne Publishers, 1990).

Hersh, Seymour M., *The Price of Power: Kissinger in the Nixon White House* (New York: Summit Books, 1983).

Heuser, Beatrice, *Nuclear Mentalities?: Strategies and Belief in Britain, France, and the FRG* (Basingstoke: Macmillan, 1998).

Heuser, Beatrice, *NATO, Britain, France and the FRG: Nuclear Strategies and Forces for Europe, 1949–2000* (London, Macmillan, 1997).

Hennessy, Peter, *The Prime Minister: The Office and Its Holders since 1945* (London: Allen Lane, 2000).

Hill, Christopher, *The Changing Politics of Foreign Policy* (Basingstoke and New York: Palgrave Macmillan, 2003).

Hill, Christopher with Lord, Christopher, 'The Foreign Policy of the Heath Government', in Ball and Seldon (eds), *The Heath Government*.

Hill, Christopher, 'The Historical Background: Past and Present in British Foreign Policy', in Smith, Smith and White (eds), *British Foreign*.

Hirschman, Albert, 'Politics', in Marquand and Seldon (eds), *The Ideas*.

Hollowell, Jonathan (ed.), *Twentieth-Century Anglo-American Relations* (Basingstoke: Palgrave, 2001).

Holmes, Martin, *The Failure of the Heath Government*, 2nd ed. (Basingstoke and London: Palgrave Macmillan, 1997).

Holsti, K. J., *Taming the Sovereigns – Institutional Change in International Politics* (Cambridge: Cambridge University Press, 2004).

Hunt, Michael H., *Lyndon Johnson's War: America's Cold War Crusade in Vietnam, 1945–1968* (New York: Hill and Wang, 1996).

Hutchinson, George, *Edward Heath: A Personal and Political Biography* (Harlow: Longmans, 1970).

James, Harold, *International Monetary Cooperation since Bretton Woods* (Washington, DC: International Monetary Fund; New York: Oxford University Press, 1996).

James, Robert Rhodes, *Ambitions and Realities: British Politics 1964–70* (London: Weidenfeld & Nicolson, 1972).

Iremonger, Lucille, in Mackintosh, John P. (ed.), *British Prime Ministers in the Twentieth Century* (London: Weidenfeld & Nicolson, 1978).

Isaacson, Walter, *Kissinger: A Biography* (London: Faber and Faber, 1992).

Kaiser, Wolfram, and Staerck, Gillian (eds), *British Foreign Policy 1955–64 – Contracting Options* (Basingstoke and London: Macmillan Press Ltd, 2000).

Kaiser, Wolfram, *Using Europe, Abusing the Europeans – Britain and European Integration, 1945–63* (Basingstoke and London: Palgrave – Macmillan in association with Institute of Contemporary British History, 1999).

Keeble, Curtis Sir, *Britain, the Soviet Union and Russia* (Basingstoke: Macmillan, 2000).

Kennedy, Paul, *The Realities behind Diplomacy: Background Influences on British External Policy 1865–1980* (London: Allen & Unwin, 1981).

Kennedy, Paul, *The Rise and Fall of the Great Powers: Economic Change and Military Conflict from 1500 to 2000*, 2nd ed. (London: Unwin Hyman, 1989).

Kissinger, Henry, *The Troubled Partnership: A Re-appraisal of the Atlantic Alliance* (Garden City, NY: Doubleday, 1966).

Kissinger, Henry, *A World Restored* (London: Gollancz, 1973).

Kitzinger, Uwe, *Diplomacy and Persuasion – How Britain Joined the Common Market* (London: Thames and Hudson, 1973).

Krozewski, Gerold, *Money and the End of Empire – British International Economic Policy and the Colonies, 1947–58* (Basingstoke and New York: Palgrave, 2001).

Kunz, Diane, *Butter and Guns: America's Cold War Economic Diplomacy* (New York: The Free Press, 1997).

Lake, David A., *Entangling Relations – American Foreign Policy in Its Century* (Princeton, New Jersey: Princeton University Press, 1999).

Larres, Klaus (ed.) with Meehan, Elizabeth, *Uneasy Allies – British-German Relations and European Integration since 1945* (Oxford and New York: Oxford University Press, 2000).

Litwak, Robert S., *Deténte and the Nixon Doctrine: American Foreign Policy and the Pursuit of Stability, 1969–1976* (Cambridge: Cambridge University Press, 1984).

Logevall, Fredrik, and Preston, Andrew (eds), *Nixon in the World, American Foreign Relations, 1969–1977* (New York: Oxford University Press, 2008).

Lord, Christopher, *British Entry to the European Community under the Heath Government of 1970–4* (Aldershot: Dartmouth, 1993).

Lord with Hill, 'The Foreign Policy of the Heath Government', in Ball and Seldon (eds), *The Heath Government*.

Loth, Wilfried (ed.), *Crises and Compromises: The European Project 1963–1969* (Baden-Baden: Nomos, 2001).

Ludlow, N. Piers, *Dealing with Britain, the Six and the First UK Application to the EEC* (Cambridge: Cambridge University Press, 1997).

Ludlow, N. Piers, *The European Community and the Crises of the 1960s: Negotiating the Gaullist Challenge* (London: Routledge, 2006).

Ludlow, N. Piers, 'A Short-Term Defeat: The Community and the Second British Application to Join the EEC', in Daddow (ed.) *Harold Wilson*.

Lundestad, Geir, *The American 'Empire' and Other Studies of US Foreign Policy in a Comparative Perspective* (Oxford, New York: Oxford University Press; Oslo: Norwegian University Press, 1990).

Lundestad, Geir, *Empire by Integration: The United States and European Integration, 1945–1997* (Oxford, New York: Oxford University Press, 1998).

Lundestad, Geir, *The United States and Western Europe since 1945 – From 'Empire' by Invitation to Transatlantic Drift*, 2nd ed. (Oxford and New York: Oxford University Press, 2003).

Lynch, P., 'The Conservatives and the Wilson Application', in Daddow (ed.), *Harold Wilson*.

Marquand, David, and Seldon, Anthony (eds), *The Ideas That Shaped Post-War Britain* (London: Fontana Press, 1996).

May, Alex (ed.), *Britain, the Commonwealth and Europe – The Commonwealth and Britain's Applications to Join the European Communities* (Basingstoke and New York: Palgrave Macmillan, 2001).

Middlemas, Keith, *Power, Competition and the State – Volume 2: Threats to the Post-war Settlement: Britain, 1961–1974* (Basingstoke and London: Macmillan, 1990).

Meinecke, Friedrich, *Machiavellism: The Doctrine of Raison D'état and Its Place in Modern History* (New Brunswick, NJ: Transaction, 1998).

Milward, Alan, *The European Rescue of the Nation State* (London: Routledge, 2000).

Milward, Alan, *The United Kingdom and the European Community, Volume 1: The Rise and Fall of a National Strategy 1945–1963* (London and Portland, Or: Whitehall History Publishing in association with Frank Cass, 2002).

Milward, Alan, *Politics and Economics in the History of the European Union* (Oxford: Oxford University Press, 2005).

Moravcsik, Andrew, *The Choice for Europe – Social Purpose & State Power from Messina to Maastricht* (London: UCL Press, 1999).

Mommsen, Wolfgang J., 'The Decline of Great Britain: Reality or Optical Distortion?', in O'Brien and Clesse (eds), *Two Hegemonies*.

Morgan, Iwan, *Nixon* (London: Arnold; New York: Oxford University Press, 2002).

Morgan, Robert, *Richard Nixon and the Quest for a New Majority* (Chapel Hill: University of North Carolina University Press, 2004).

Nixon, Richard M., *The Real War* (London: Sidgwick & Jackson, 1980).

Nixon, Richard M., *Six Crises* (New York: Pyramid Books, 1968).

Nixon, Richard M., *No More Vietnams* (New York: Arbor House, 1985).

Northedge, F. S., *Descent From Power – British Foreign Policy 1945–1973* (London: George Allen & Unwin Ltd, 1974).

Oakley, Robin, and Rose, Peter, *The Political Year 1970* (London: Pitman Publishing, 1970).

Oakley, Robin, and Rose, Peter, *The Political Year 1971* (London: Pitman Publishing, 1971).

O'Brien, Karl, and Clesse, Armand (eds), *Two Hegemonies – Britain 1846 and the United States 1941–2001* (Aldershot: Ashgate, 2002).

Orde, Anne, *The Eclipse of Great Britain: The United States and British Imperial Decline 1895–1956* (Basingstoke, Palgrave Macmillan, 1996).

Ovendale, Ritchie, *Anglo-American Relations in the Twentieth Century* (New York: St Martin's Press, 1998).

Palayret, Jean-Marie, Wallace, Helen, and Winand, Pascaline (eds), *Visions, Votes and Vetoes: The Empty Chair Crisis and the Luxembourg Compromise Forty Years On* (Brussels: P.I.E. Peter Lang, 2006).

Parr, Helen, *Britain's Policy Toward the European Community: Harold Wilson and Britain's World Role, 1964–1967* (London: Routledge, 2006).

Philippart, Éric, Winand, Pascaline (eds), *Ever Closer Partnership, Policy-making in US-EU Relations* (New York: P.I.E. Lang, 2001).

Perlstein, Rick, *Nixonland – The Rise of a President and the Fracturing of America* (New York, Scribner, 2008.)

Pierre, Andrew J., *The British Experience with an Independent Strategic Force, 1939–1970* (London: Oxford University Press, 1972).

Pimlott, Ben, *Harold Wilson* (London: HarperCollins, 1992).

Pollack, Mark A., and Shaffer, Gregory C., *Transatlantic Governance in the Global Economy* (Lanham etc: Rowman & Littlefield Publishers Inc, 2001).

Pollard, Sidney, *The Development of the British Economy, Fourth Edition, 1914–1990* (London; New York: E. Arnold, 1992).

Ramsden, John J., 'The Prime Minister and the Making of Foreign Policy', in Ball and Seldon (eds), *The Heath Government*.

Richelson, Jeffrey, T., and Ball, Desmond, *The Ties that Bind – Intelligence Cooperation between the UKUSA Countries – the United Kingdom, the United States of America, Australia, and New Zealand* (Sydney Wellington and London: Unwin Hyman, 1990).

Rosamond, Ben, *Theories of European Integration* (Basingstoke, Hampshire: Macmillan Press; New York: St Martin's Press, 2000).

Rosenberg, Samuel, *American Economic Development* (Basingstoke, Palgrave Macmillan, 2003).

Roth, Andrew, *Heath and the Heathmen* (London: Routledge and K. Paul, 1972)

Sanders, David, *Losing and Empire, Finding a Role – British Foreign Policy since 1945* (Basingstoke and London: Macmillan, 1990).

Singleton, J. and Robertson, Paul L., *Economic Relations between Britain and Australasia, 1945–1970* (Basingstoke, Hampshire; New York: Palgrave, 2002).

Schenk, Catherine R., *Britain and the Sterling Area: From Devaluation to Convertibility in the 1950s* (London, New York: Routledge, LSE, 1994).

Schwartz, Thomas, *Lyndon Johnson and Europe: In the Shadow of Vietnam* (Cambridge: Harvard University Press, 2003).

Seldon, Anthony. 'The Heath Government in History', in Ball and Seldon (eds), *The Heath Government*.

Strange, Susan, *Sterling and British Policy: A Political Study of an International Currency in Decline* (London, New York: Oxford University Press, 1971).

Smith, S., and Smith, M. 'The Analytical Background: Approaches to the Study of British Foreign Policy', in Smith, Smith, and White (eds), *British Foreign*.

Smith, Michael, Smith, Steve, and White, Brian (eds), *British Foreign Policy – Tradition, Change and Transformation* (London: Unwin Hyman, 1988).

Soutou, Georges-Henri, 'President Pompidou, *Ostpolitik*, and the Strategy of Détente', in Haftendorn *et al.* (eds), *The Strategic*.

Summers, Anthony, *The Arrogance of Power: The Secret World of Richard Nixon* (New York: Viking, 2001).

Terriff, Terry, *The Nixon Administration and the Making of US Nuclear Strategy* (Itacha and London: Cornell University Press, 1995).

Thornton, Richard C., *The Nixon Kissinger Years: The Reshaping of American Foreign Policy*, 2nd ed. (St. Paul, Minnesota: Paragon House, 2001).

Thorpe, D. R., *Alec Douglas Home* (London: Sinclair-Stevenson, 1996).

Trachtenberg, Marc, *The Craft of International History: A Guide to Method* (Princeton, NJ: Princeton University Press, 2006).

Trachtenberg, Marc, *A Constructed Peace: The Making of the European Settlement, 1945–1963* (Princeton, NJ: Princeton University Press, 1999).

Tratt, Jacqueline, *The Macmillan Government and Europe, A Study in the Process of Policy Development* (Basingstoke: Macmillan, 1996).

Urwin, Derek W., *The Community of Europe: A History of European Integration since 1945* (London: Longman, 1995).

Young, Hugo, *This Blessed Plot – Britain and Europe from Churchill to Blair* (London and Basingstoke, 1998).

Young, John W., 'The Heath Government and British Entry into the European Community', in Ball and Seldon (eds), *The Heath Government*.

Young, John W., *Britain and European Unity, 1945–1999* (Basingstoke: Macmillan, 2000).

Young, Kenneth, *Sir Alec Douglas-Home* (London: Dent, 1970).

Younger, Kenneth, *Changing Perspectives in British Foreign Policy*, Reprint of 1964 original (Issued under the auspices of the Royal Institute of International Affairs. Westport, Connecticut: Greenwood Press Publishers, 1976).

Wallace, William, *The Foreign Policy Process in Britain* (London: Royal Institute of International Affairs, 1975).

Watt, Donald Cameron, *Succeeding John Bull: America in Britain's Place, 1900–1975: A Study of the Anglo-American Relationship and World Politics in the Context of British and American Foreign-Policy-Making in the Twentieth Century* (Cambridge, New York: Cambridge University Press, 1984).

White, Brian, *Britain, Détente and Changing East-West relations* (London and New York: Routledge, 1992).

Wills, Gary, *Nixon Agonistes: The Crisis of the Self-Made Man*, 1st Mariner ed., original 1969 (New York, Mariner Books, 2002).

Winand, Pascaline, *Eisenhower, Kennedy and the United States of Europe* (New York: St. Martin's Press, 1993).

Woodward, Nicholas, W. C., *The Management of the British Economy, 1945–2001* (Manchester, New York: Manchester University Press, 2004).

Wrigley, Chris, 'Now You See it, Now You Don't: Harold Wilson and Labour's Foreign Policy 1964–70', in Coopey, R., Fielding, S., and Tiratsoo, N. (eds), *The Wilson Governments 1964–1970* (London and New York: Pinter Publishers, 1993).

Index